AT KINGDOM'S EDGE

AT KINGDOM'S EDGE

THE SURINAME STRUGGLES OF JERONIMY CLIFFORD, ENGLISH SUBJECT

JACOB SELWOOD

CORNELL UNIVERSITY PRESS
Ithaca and London

Copyright © 2022 by Cornell University

All rights reserved. Except for brief quotations in a review, this book, or parts thereof, must not be reproduced in any form without permission in writing from the publisher. For information, address Cornell University Press, Sage House, 512 East State Street, Ithaca, New York 14850. Visit our website at cornellpress.cornell.edu.

First published 2022 by Cornell University Press

Library of Congress Cataloging-in-Publication Data

Names: Selwood, Jacob, author.
Title: At kingdom's edge : the Suriname struggles of Jeronimy Clifford, English subject / Jacob Selwood.
Description: Ithaca [New York] : Cornell University Press, 2022. | Includes bibliographical references and index.
Identifiers: LCCN 2021054781 (print) | LCCN 2021054782 (ebook) | ISBN 9781501764219 (hardcover) | ISBN 9781501764233 (pdf) | ISBN 9781501764226 (epub)
Subjects: LCSH: Citizenship—Great Britain—Colonies—History—17th century. | Citizenship—Great Britain—Colonies—History—18th century. | Political rights—Great Britain—Colonies—History—17th century. | Political rights—Great Britain—Colonies—History—18th century. | Suriname—Colonization—History—17th century. | Suriname—Colonization—History—18th century.
Classification: LCC JV1015 .S45 2022 (print) | LCC JV1015 (ebook) | DDC 323.6/0941—dc23/eng/20220206
LC record available at https://lccn.loc.gov/2021054781
LC ebook record available at https://lccn.loc.gov/2021054782

For Rod

Contents

Acknowledgments ix

Note on Spelling, Dates, and Translations xi

Introduction: English Subjecthood at Kingdom's Edge   1

1. Creating an English Suriname (1651–1667)   18

2. Staying English in Dutch Suriname (1667–1687)   42

3. The Glorious Revolution in Suriname (1688–1695)   77

4. Colonial Subjecthood in England and the Netherlands (1696–1737)   97

5. The Many Afterlives of Jeronimy Clifford (1737–1780)   130

Conclusion   162

Notes 169

Bibliography 219

Index 233

Acknowledgments

I could not have completed this book without the help and support of many people. My greatest academic debt lies with those scholars whose generosity helped me to make the leap from studying early modern London to studying colonial Suriname. Alison Games provided thoughtful and detailed feedback on the original manuscript and shared numerous sources. I am grateful to her for her constructive criticism, as I am to the manuscript's other, anonymous reader during the peer review process. Natalie Zemon Davis recommended sources during the early stages of this project and offered insight into maps of Suriname later on. Susan Amussen provided support and gave her thoughts on a conference panel. I am grateful to Suze Zijlstra, Karwan Fatah-Black, and Aviva Ben-Ur for taking the time to meet with me while I was in the Netherlands and for sharing ideas and source recommendations. Eliane Glaser invited me to write a chapter in which I first started thinking about Suriname. Hannah Weiss Muller reviewed an article that became part of this book, and in doing so helped to improve it and recommended essential texts. Dana Rabin helped me to think about the relationship between subjecthood and slavery, while David Worthington shared his insights about Suriname's Scottish connections. Numerous other scholars responded to my various queries about sources, including Laura Leibman, Jonathan Israel, and Robert Batchelor. I also thank the staff of the British and Dutch national archives and the British Library for their in-person assistance, the staff of the Zeeland archives and Surinamese national archives for answering queries from afar, and Karina Salih for searching the grounds of St. Mary Magdalen, Bermondsey, for Jeronimy Clifford's grave (in vain, alas). I am especially thankful to Wim Klooster for helping this book find a home and to Michael McGandy for making it feel welcome once it got there. Thank you, as well, to Clare Jones, Susan P. Specter, Mary Ribesky, and Nicole Balent for helping the book reach its final form.

My friends and colleagues in the Department of History at Georgia State University helped both directly, with their ideas and support, and indirectly, by providing a stimulating environment in which to work. Special thanks go to Jeffrey Young for designing the map of Guiana's rivers and Nick Wilding for reading part of the manuscript, as well as Marni Davis, David Sehat, Harcourt Fuller, Jared Poley, and Michelle Brattain. Thanks go as well to Jessica Berry (of the Department of Philosophy) for reading an early grant application and to Joanna Jury for her work as my research assistant (I'm delighted that you're now my colleague!). I am also grateful to Paula Sorrell for helping to keep the department running smoothly. My many students at Georgia State also deserve my appreciation for persistently nudging me toward greater clarity. A Research Initiation Grant from Georgia State University funded the archival trip in which I discovered Jeronimy Clifford.

Learning to read Dutch was as daunting as it was rewarding. Lauren Ristvet, my friend and former colleague, initially encouraged me to take the leap. A scholar of the ancient world who is proficient in multiple dead languages, she pointed out that it was well within my power to learn a single living one. My colleague Ghulam Nadri provided moral support and checked some of my early attempts at translation. University College, London's distance-learning course in early modern Dutch got me fully up to speed. Thank you to An Castangia for teaching it so well.

Cynthia Herrup deserves a special mention for training me as a historian in the first place and providing ongoing encouragement, advice, and friendship since. She and Judith Bennett also gave me a place to stay in London, as did Cathy and Adrian Stoddart. I am very lucky to have too many friends to name here, without whom I could not have completed this book with my sanity intact (to the extent it still is), especially during a pandemic. However, Wayne and Rhonda Lee, Brett Whalen, Rick Sawyer, Emily Burrill, Lauren Crain, Heather Devlin, Courtney Baker, Randy Trammell, and Lindy Settevendemie all deserve special mention. Thanks go to my family, Roni Powell, Anna Selwood, Piero Jamieson, Hector Jamieson, and Louis Jamieson, for their love and support. Most of all, I thank Ann Claycombe; I am the luckiest person in the world to be able to share my life with you, and my love for you cannot be put into words. Finally, I dedicate this book to the memory of my stepfather, Rod Powell, who was there almost from the very beginning.

Note on Spelling, Dates, and Translations

When quoting from primary sources I have modernized all spelling and punctuation and extended all abbreviations. Unless otherwise noted, dates are as they appear in the original sources, with the exception that the year is taken to begin on January 1. This means that English sources from before 1752 use Old Style, whereas all Dutch sources and English sources from 1752 onward use New Style. Where confusion might arise or the difference in calendar is particularly relevant I have noted which date style is in use. Unless otherwise stated, all translations from Dutch are my own, as are all errors in translation.

AT KINGDOM'S EDGE

Introduction
English Subjecthood at Kingdom's Edge

On 27 August 1728 a man named Jeronimy Clifford wrote to Lord Viscount Townshend, one of the king's principal secretaries of state, to enquire about the fate of a petition "relating to the damages done" to him "by the Dutch at Suriname." Lodging in a bakery next to the Ship Tavern in Charing Cross, the seventy-one year old Clifford complained that he lived "in a starving condition," having "these five months last past . . . not been at one time master of five shillings." His poverty was, he wrote, the result of "the wicked practices of powerful adversaries." He had previously petitioned the Treasury asking for "some subsistence money" but his entreaty had gone unanswered.[1]

This was, on the face of it, a strange request, one fueled perhaps by paranoia or delusions of grandeur. Yet although he now lived in poverty in a bakery, Jeronimy Clifford had once owned one of the largest sugar plantations in Suriname, a South American colony briefly held by England during the previous century. Brought there as a child by his family, Clifford was around ten years old when, in 1667, a fleet from Zeeland seized the territory as part of the Second Anglo-Dutch War. Like many English colonists, his father decided to take a chance under Dutch rule. Yet life remained harsh and in 1675 most members of the English community accepted the Crown's offer of evacuation to Jamaica.[2] Although the Cliffords left, the sale of their plantation fell through, forcing them back to Suriname, where Jeronimy Clifford added to the family's holdings through marriage. In 1696 he finally returned to England, a country he had last seen as a small boy, which was now ruled by a Dutch-born king.

Clifford spent the rest of his life petitioning the English and Dutch governments for compensation for suffering he believed he had sustained during his time in Suriname and for property he had left behind. He had frequently clashed with the colony's governing elite, serving years in prison for what they regarded as his willful insolence and for what he saw as their arbitrary persecution of an English subject. When he left Suriname he had abandoned his family's estate. In England he fell into poverty, spending at least sixteen years in debtors' prison and dying destitute in 1737. In his numerous appeals to English and Dutch officials he repeatedly evoked the 1667 Articles of Capitulation by which England had surrendered the colony. The text, he argued, compelled the Crown to intervene on his behalf and the Dutch to provide redress. For decades he used this and other Anglo-Dutch treaties to underwrite an English subjecthood forged not in England itself but rather far away, on what was then known as the "Wild Coast" of the Guianas.

Jeronimy Clifford provides an example of a colonial inhabitant defining and defending his subjecthood amid shifting sovereignties. He faced a dilemma encountered by many other English people overseas: how to stay English in a profoundly foreign environment. On the face of it, Clifford's status was unambiguous. Baptized in the village of Egham in Surrey in May 1657, he was an English subject by birth in a manner long settled by law.[3] This status remained unaffected wherever in the world he might later move. Yet Clifford's story, as well as the world within which he traveled, shows the extent to which an array of extralegal factors shaped subjecthood, whether in England, its colonies, or territories conquered by its rivals.

People who left England had to sustain their subjecthood in ways both large and small. Colonial governments, in turn, made decisions about whether to recognize people as subjects. When a foreign power conquered an English colony, the subjects there had to choose whether to retain their status, either by leaving or by clinging to it under their new rulers, or whether to let it atrophy by assimilation. All these choices took place in environments that were geographically and demographically very different from England itself. Legal considerations were often the least relevant elements of all. Instead, factors ranging from the disease environment to warfare and the nature of colonial hierarchies shaped who could claim to be an English subject, how they did so, and whether they remained one. Some, like Clifford, might then return to England, or if they had been born overseas, they might travel there for the first time. Their background and experience would, in turn, affect how people in the metropolis perceived them. Who had they been, and who were they now?

This book uses Clifford's case to expose some of the challenges English subjects faced on the imperial periphery, at kingdom's edge. It shows how one man living in a South American colony articulated his subjecthood through two changes in sovereignty, the Dutch conquest of English Suriname and the Glorious Revolution. It then traces how he positioned his status as a colonial subject once he returned to Europe. The book ends by using his posthumous dispute with the Dutch to trace some of the loose ends of seventeenth-century colonial English subjecthood up to the eve of the American revolution. In doing so, it examines some of the long-term implications of England's rivalry with the Netherlands, the memory of which continued to exert an influence decades after a Dutch stadholder became king of England in 1689.

Suriname in the Seventeenth Century

If people in England had heard of Suriname at all, they might, like some in our own time, have done so by reading Aphra Behn's 1688 novel *Oroonoko*; or perhaps they had watched or read Thomas Southerne's play based on her work, which was printed eight years later. Behn's novel was partly set in the colony during the period of English rule, and she was familiar enough with the territory to include its governor, William Byam, as a character. Her narrator describes how the English lived alongside Suriname's indigenous inhabitants "in perfect amity, without daring to command 'em," enslaving instead people who, like its titular character, are "not natives of the place." The text also depicts the region's wildlife in vivid terms, noting the "birds and beasts of wonderful and surprising forms, shapes, and colors."[4] Yet it is unclear whether Behn herself ever set foot in Suriname.[5]

The venture portrayed in *Oroonoko* remained tenuous to the end of the seventeenth century, as the region was colonized by a small number of English, Dutch, and Sephardic Jews, all of whom clung close to the coast. From there they struggled to form a prosperous society by forcing enslaved Africans and—contrary to Behn's assertions—indigenous Americans to work for them. Whether ruled by England, by Zeeland, or, after 1683, by the Society of Suriname, which was a Dutch consortium, colonists faced similar challenges. The region presented a hostile physical environment, with virulent tropical diseases. The colony's governors struggled to establish an ordered society and to keep people from fleeing to more prosperous territories. The success of Suriname as a venture rested on its ability to produce sugar, but that was a labor-intensive process rooted in brutality. The enslaved workers who grew and processed the crop sought their freedom, fighting back through both violent and nonviolent resistance. Because colonists only exercised power close to the sea, many newly arrived Africans escaped to the vast interior, where they established maroon settlements, which were hybrids of the West African societies from which they had originated. Meanwhile, the colony's indigenous population repeatedly attempted to expel the Europeans from their lands.

It was into this world that the Cliffords stepped, sometime between 1663 and 1665.[6] Their new home could not have been more different from Surrey. George Warren's *Impartial Description of Surinam*, which was based on observations made around the same time, describes a land where "warmth and moisture causes a constant verdancy and flourishing of plants."[7] Here the English had established five hundred plantations, "whereof forty or fifty have sugar-works, yielding no small profit to the owners."[8] Life in the colony was, he wrote, best suited to "a mind untaint[ed] with ambition (and that can live according to nature)." For such a person, "no place is more accommodate; whether we regard health, a luxuriant soil, or kind women."[9] With a climate "far more agreeable to age, than youth," Suriname was "healthful enough to temperate sound bodies."[10] It was, however, not without its dangers. Along with chapters dedicated to the colony's flora, fauna, commodities, and settlements, Warren included one on "things there venomous and hurtful" and elsewhere noted the many diseases that awaited new arrivals.[11]

The Cliffords found a land plagued not only by the diseases of which Warren warned but also riven by factional disputes, with conditions deteriorating around the time of their arrival. According to Suriname's governor, William Byam, May 1665 saw the "colony in its meridian, and after this month [it] had its declination and went ever retrogrado." He describes how "a sickness began at our town of Torarica and spread itself in the plantations adjoining [and] swept many away." The outbreak coincided with a visit from the colony's proprietor, Barbados's governor Lord Willoughby of Parham, whose departure was followed by that of two hundred discontented colonists. These events must have substantially weakened the venture, which had an English population of "near 1500 men," mainly Barbadian migrants.[12] Willoughby's reluctance to remain is understandable, and not just because of disease. During the previous year he had been the victim of a failed assassination attempt in Suriname, in which he was attacked by one John Allin during a religious service. The incident was a particularly strong manifestation of the opposition to the proprietor, and to Byam's governance, that was felt by a portion of the English population.[13]

In a 1665 bid to shore up their faltering colony, Suriname's rulers invited Sephardic Jewish sugar planters from the surrounding region to settle there, attracting them with an offer of religious toleration and full English subjecthood. In addition to being able to practice their religion freely, they would also be "considered as English born."[14] Between 100 and 150 Jews chose to move to the colony, joining a small existing population.[15] The community would become vital to the territory, and during the Dutch period grew to form a quarter of all free inhabitants toward the end of the seventeenth century and as much as half one hundred years later.[16]

The attempt to attract Jewish planters failed to save English Suriname, which was captured by the Dutch in 1667. Nonetheless, it helped to create an unusual demographic balance. For eight years, until most English colonists left, Suriname's population was a peculiar mix of English, Dutch, Jewish, African, and indigenous people. While it is hard to determine accurate numbers for this period, by 1674 there were probably as many as three hundred English colonists, around the same number of Dutch colonists, and thousands of enslaved Africans.[17] These identities sometimes overlapped. In 1675 some Jews asserted their English status, demanding evacuation as the king's subjects.[18] Over subsequent years African and Jewish identity also converged, whether in the form of slaves governed by Jewish law, maroon communities whose creole language included elements of Hebrew, or a population of mixed Afro-Sephardic descent that remains to this day.[19]

Zeeland, Suriname's new ruler, struggled to reverse the colony's fortunes. The governor successfully fought to prevent Jewish planters from departing with the English in 1675 on the grounds that this would weaken the colony beyond repair.[20] He also feared abandonment by his fellow Dutch colonists, who were rumored to be seeking refuge in Tobago.[21] The Zeeland States ultimately tried to sell the ailing territory, making various failed attempts to find a buyer. Finally, in 1683, it sold the colony to the West India Company, which partnered with the City of Amsterdam and the van Sommelsdijck family to form the Society of Suriname.[22] The society, in turn, reorganized Suriname's government and enforced greater oversight over its economy. By the eighteenth century the colony was flourishing, with an expanding plantation economy that grew even stronger after the deregulation of the slave trade in 1740.[23]

The meaning and scope of English subjecthood in Suriname changed throughout the second half of the seventeenth century. After trying to make the land their own, English colonists extended the reach of subjecthood when they sought to attract Jewish planters in 1665. Following the fall of the colony in 1667, they tried to form a community of subjects under Dutch rule. After most of the English colonists left for Jamaica in 1675, the parameters of subjecthood then contracted, as Jews who had been left behind abandoned their allegiance to England's king. Jeronimy Clifford was one of just fifteen Englishmen in Suriname by the 1680s, in a colony with a total population of around five thousand.[24] Thus, he was forced to decide what subjecthood now meant in the absence of a community of compatriots.

Subjecthood in a Colonial Context

In legal terms, subjecthood entailed a bond of allegiance with one's monarch, which was most usually acquired at birth. The court decision known as *Calvin's Case* had fully elaborated its implications in 1608 in ways that carried over into a colonial setting. The judges hearing *Calvin v. Smith* sought to determine the status of Scots in England following the accession of James VI of Scotland to England's throne. Did they remain aliens or were they now English subjects? Their ruling concluded that Scots born after James became England's king—the *postnati*—were legally English subjects. However, those born in Scotland before his accession—the *antenati*—remained aliens south of the border. The same logic applied to the English in Scotland. The underlying principle governing this decision entailed that at birth one became a subject in all the territories of one's monarch as they then stood, and not just the jurisdiction where one was born. At this point, as chief justice Sir Edward Coke wrote, one acquired subjecthood by *"ligeanta naturalis, absoluta, pura, et indefinata . . . by nature and birth-right."*[25] This meant that a person born not only in one of the king's three kingdoms but also in any of his colonies was a full English subject everywhere. Jeronimy Clifford, born in Surrey, remained a subject in English Suriname just as a child born there would be considered a full English subject in Surrey.[26]

Aliens could also acquire English subjecthood, although that was relatively rare in the seventeenth century. To become naturalized in England required an act of parliament, a procedure usually reserved for the children of English subjects who had been born overseas (children of merchants or royalist exiles, for example). Immigrants from overseas most commonly availed themselves of a lesser bond of allegiance called denization, which was acquired through the more readily available royal letters patent.[27] Denization also lacked the sacramental requirements of naturalization, making it accessible to non-Anglicans such as the Jews who began to live openly in England starting in the 1650s.[28] However, denization did not provide all the benefits of naturalization. While now under the king's allegiance, a denizen was still an alien by birth and remained unable to inherit land or bequeath property to children born before the date of denization. Denizens also generally paid aliens' customs duties.[29]

The situation was more confusing in England's overseas colonies, particularly during the seventeenth century. Although *Calvin's Case* implied that a person born in an English colony was an English subject, the process of making new subjects and granting denizen status was murkier. In general the mechanism mirrored that in England itself, with colonial legislatures performing naturalization and governors controlling denization. This was, however, not always the case.[30] Moreover, during the seventeenth century a colony's right to naturalize regularly went unrecognized beyond its borders. An alien who was made an English subject by a colonial legislature would routinely still be considered an alien in England itself or even in other colonies. This changed with the Plantation Act of 1740, which recognized colonial naturalization as pertaining in all the king's dominions.[31]

The law, however, only tells part of the story. For example, subjecthood was highly racialized, and indeed, race and subjecthood acted as mutually constituting markers of difference. As racial categories developed to justify the enslavement of Africans and their descendants, they also defined the scope of subjecthood. Subject status, in turn, marked racial boundaries. Although, as James Kettner writes of *Calvin's Case*, "all children born under the king's protection were natural-born subjects in all the dominions," in practice this was not the case for children of the enslaved.[32]

A child born in Barbados in the 1680s to African parents failed to receive the benefits of subjecthood. This was not because England's parliament or courts had limited subject status in colonies to people of non-African descent but because the English on the island regarded the people they called "negroes" as their property. Was it possible for property to possess subjecthood? The authors of the 1688 Barbados slave code seemed to think not when they denied slaves the right to jury trials, contrasting this position with that pertaining to "the subjects of England."[33] While other language from the period is more ambiguous, slaves were subjects only insofar as subjecthood might resemble total subjection.[34]

This situation bore no resemblance to how most English people spoke of subject status by the seventeenth century. While often ill-defined, the benefits of subjecthood generally implied royal protection as well as specific rights, such as rights of inheritance and the ability to petition and receive a jury trial.[35] Slaves lacked recourse to these rights and instead were governed as chattel by codes that aimed to strip them of their personhood. As Susan Amussen has noted, such texts conflated "status with color," identifying "slavery as inherent in bodies, not a product of law and a system of labor."[36] In doing so they rooted subjecthood in whiteness.

Colonial processes were generative of subjecthood as well as destructive, with different kinds of subjecthood created by the exigencies of life on the periphery.[37] People of African descent, while viewed by most white colonists as enslaved by default, sometimes claimed subjecthood through acts of resistance and in doing so affected its meaning. Some maroon communities in eighteenth-century Jamaica signed treaties with the Crown, shaping the resulting subject status performatively with dance and dress during meetings with British officials.[38]

Indigenous people also defined the nature of their subjecthood in a manner that was variously accepted and rejected. During the seventeenth century some in New England articulated a subject status predicated on a direct relationship with the Crown that circumvented colonial governments. Colonial administrations, in turn, claimed authority that denied that circumvention.[39] In Virginia governors acknowledged native people's status as tributary subjects in the face of colonists' frequent objections, even as that recognition remained part of a process of dispossession. Such conjunctions show subjecthood at perhaps its most unstable, being shaped by indigenous politics yet part of an unequal power relationship that allowed for either recognition or negation.[40]

Much about the colonial environment was unanticipated by the law, creating conditions that prompted improvisation under duress. A colonial patent crafted in London could only foresee so many eventualities; or it might contain language so vague as to necessitate innovation. While battling a fatal fever on the coast of South America in the 1660s, the men who governed Suriname tried to save their colony by offering Jews from neighboring Dutch territory full English subjecthood. The resulting 1665 "Grant of Privileges" used expansive language that conferred subject status to all present and future Jewish colonists in a manner that was more inclusive than the rights offered to Jews in England itself.[41] Although Suriname's patent allowed for the creation of new subjects, it was unclear about how this might happen and contained no provisions for according subjecthood to an entire group of people.[42] The grant provides an example of how the colony's disease environment helped determine who became a subject of the king.

Disputes about subject status reflected a range of concerns, from movement and reputation to sibling jealousy. Due to the limited scope of colonial naturalization, a person moving between English colonies might find their subjecthood called into question. This happened in 1682 to Henry Brunett, who, despite having been made a subject in Virginia, found his ship seized by the governor of Nevis. Chief justice Francis North subsequently confirmed that the seizure was legally valid because Brunett's subjecthood only pertained in Virginia itself.[43] Some people who were born in English colonies found their subjecthood questioned when they traveled to England. In May 1699 attorney general Thomas Trevor fielded a query about whether Abraham Mendes, a merchant in London "born of Jewish parents" in Barbados, should pay customs as an alien or as an English subject. Trevor replied, "He is to be taken as one of his Majesty's natural born subjects being born within the king's dominions."⁴⁴

Even those of clear English background were not immune from such challenges. Around the 1650s, Elizabeth Salter, who was born in the English colony of St. Christopher to English parents, had her inheritance challenged by her brother David. Elizabeth's grandfather had granted her a bequest but had denied one to David on the grounds that he was an alien because he had been born in Holland. David sought legal advice from Sir Orlando Bridgeman about whether his sister could inherit "as well as if she had been born in England." Bridgeman concluded that "neither of the children . . . are aliens," a curious decision given David's Dutch birth, although he affirmed the legitimacy of the will. David Salter decided, nevertheless, that a trial might "yet decide the business."⁴⁵

Movement between empires could be particularly fraught, especially when, as in Clifford's case, colonies had also changed hands. While neither the English nor the Dutch ever questioned his English birth, the Dutch States General at one point proclaimed him to have been under its allegiance. Its resolution argued that when he temporarily left Suriname in 1675, he ceased to benefit from the 1667 Articles of Capitulation. Consequently, he had returned as a stranger and should therefore be "owned as a subject of this state."⁴⁶ Meanwhile, the subject status of Dorothy Matson, Clifford's wife, remains hard to determine. Clifford claimed that she was English, while Dutch sources imply that she was Dutch. In her case reputation was the definitive criterion for claims about her subject status, yet that status remains unresolvable.⁴⁷

The extralegal elements that helped to frame the meaning of subjecthood possessed affective qualities that intersected with other kinds of identity. Both Englishness and, by the eighteenth century, Britishness carried contested connotations that depended on context.⁴⁸ Printed texts that discussed Clifford's case after his death situated his struggle with the Dutch within the imperial friction of their own time. One source reconstructed him as a refined, polite, eighteenth-century figure, whom it depicted in contrast to the uncouth Dutch.⁴⁹ Others positioned his imputed suffering at the hands of the Dutch within a broad chronology of their past misdeeds. This stretched back to the 1623 execution of ten English East India Company employees in Amboyna, in modern-day Indonesia, which was termed a "massacre" by English writers and was subsequently enshrined as the paradigmatic example of Dutch cruelty.⁵⁰ As they deployed Clifford's cause for their own purposes, these works contributed to English subjecthood's cultural contours.

Subjecthood, in short, was constructed beyond the law as well as by it, at the margins of empire and at its center, over and against those who were excluded as well as those who benefited from its embrace. It variously expanded and contracted, affected by both colonial placehood and decisions in the metropolis. Although it was a legal category, it also carried cultural and affective elements, converging with national identity while remaining distinct from it. People received different designations with various connotations as they moved around and between empires and as empires moved around them.

This book pays particular attention to what happened to subjecthood during changes of sovereignty. These were common as colonial powers during the seventeenth and eighteenth centuries lost territories to competitors and borders shifted. While some people, like Clifford, lived in colonies that were conquered by imperial rivals, others became subjects of England's king when they came under his dominion. In doing so, they helped to shape the meaning of subjecthood. Groups from Grenada to Bengal made active use of newly acquired subject status in appeals to the Crown and to parliament during the eighteenth century.[51] Yet conquered peoples might also lose subjecthood after they had gained it. In Calcutta the British developed new forms of hierarchical allegiance that differentiated between permanent and temporary subjecthood, with the latter being forfeited when a person left the city.[52] Likewise, Acadians who were expelled from Nova Scotia were left all the more vulnerable for their decades of subjecthood: attacked by the state that had claimed their allegiance, they lacked the protection of any other.[53]

The 1664 English conquest of New Netherland, whereby a substantial population of Dutch colonists fell under English rule, stands with Suriname as among the most significant changes in colonial sovereignty between the English and the Dutch during the seventeenth century.[54] The English takeover of what became New York was, however, just one example in a longer succession of transfers of allegiance in the Hudson and Delaware Valleys. There Dutch, Swedes, Finns, and English encountered each other's claims and became minorities in each other's incipient polities. Throughout, as Mark Thompson notes, "the same conditions that promoted identification with nations and empires also encouraged subjects to forge relationships that bridged or undermined those national and imperial boundaries."[55]

Allegiance and nationality were sometimes conflated and sometimes viewed separately, and they often operated on different trajectories. Thompson argues that in the Delaware Valley, Europeans applied the term *nation* "primarily to identify a people bound together by a common allegiance."[56] Yet while allegiance "could be formally dissolved," nationality remained "sticky," rooted in a sense of peoplehood.[57] By the eighteenth century, national identities that had persisted through multiple allegiances became ethnicities subsumed under British nationhood.[58] In seventeenth-century Suriname, English and Dutch officials had different conceptions of the relationship between allegiance and nationality. The English not only recognized members of the "Hebrew nation" as the king's subjects in 1665, they used that subjecthood as a pretext to attempt to remove them to Jamaica a decade later. The Dutch governor rejected this measure, denying that the colony's Jews were English subjects. They remained behind, shedding any allegiance to the English Crown and fully embracing Dutch rule but persisting as a nation.[59]

The articles and treaties that concluded conflicts formally recognized colonial transfers, and in doing so shaped both allegiance and identity. Leaders of New Netherland's Dutch community conceded the English conquest of their colony in the Articles of Agreement signed with Sir Robert Carr in 1664.[60] Three years later the governor of English Suriname, William Byam, acknowledged Zeeland's victory over his colony by signing articles of capitulation with Admiral Abraham Crijnssen.[61] England and the United Provinces recognized these exchanges of territory, along with others brought about by the Second Anglo-Dutch War, in the 1667 Treaty of Breda.[62] Both sets of articles contained provisions for the behavior and treatment of the newly conquered colonists. The Dutch in New Netherland and the English in Suriname swore loyalty oaths to their conquerors, while being allowed a range of communal rights and privileges. As he pursued restitution throughout his life, Jeronimy Clifford repeatedly evoked the 1667 articles, showing the stock that an inhabitant of a conquered colony might place in such a text.

Taken together, the charters establishing colonies, articles signed in the aftermath of conquest, and treaties recognizing those conquests show the tension between the metropolitan projection of sovereignty and the messiness and mixture of the periphery. Articulations of sovereignty that were projected from the center tended to be expansive in nature. The patent of English Suriname, for example, claimed territory that would extend "by direct lines unto the main ocean called the south sea."[63] Moreover, *Calvin's Case* had framed subjecthood itself as immutable and portable. Yet, as Lauren Benton has argued, "the portability of subjecthood and the delegation of legal authority" in a colonial setting "generated territorial variations."[64] Sovereignty as it actually existed in imperial locations, was contested and uneven, being sent tentatively up rivers, as in Suriname, or extending in tendrils across maritime corridors rather than uniformly filling the blank spaces of maps.[65] It was both delegated to formal officials and claimed, sometimes creatively, by a range of other actors. This "layering of overlapping, semi-sovereign authorities . . . generated a lumpy juridical order, in which legal actors, even rogues . . . engaged in creative legal posturing."[66]

Changes in sovereignty also occurred in the metropolis, with implications for people living in the colonies. The 1689 Glorious Revolution, when the

Dutch stadholder, William of Orange, became king of England, changed the relationship between the Dutch and the English in both North and South America. Dutch colonists in the former New Netherland now had an English king who was a compatriot and, unlike James II, a Protestant. In Suriname, meanwhile, English colonists like Clifford might look to the Dutch stadholder as their sovereign. Although the power of the stadholder there was less direct than that of a king, it nevertheless included broad rhetorical authority. Both Jeronimy Clifford and Suriname's governing elite evoked William III's dual offices and both appealed to the power he held in both countries.

Sources

This book's discussion of subjecthood and sovereignty is centered around Clifford's peculiar story, as reconstructed from archival material from Suriname, England, and the Netherlands. At its heart is a two-volume manuscript written in Clifford's own hand, which he sent to the Earl of Sunderland in 1707 in order to advance his claim for compensation and which is now held by the British Library.[67] This contains not only petitions but also copies of correspondence, accounts, plantation records, legal documents, estate inventories, and sources from colonial Suriname. Jeronimy Clifford is in many respects an unreliable narrator and presents a version of his own life that is both self-serving and, at times, inconsistent. Yet he is nevertheless a reliable source. Clifford's 1707 manuscript contains not only his own narrative and tally of grievances but also reproductions of numerous documents. The original versions of many of these materials, including some of the correspondence from Dutch officials in Suriname, are now lost. Yet those documents that I have been able to corroborate, including some English government correspondence and resolutions from the Dutch States General, demonstrate the accuracy of Clifford's transcriptions and translations. While Clifford presented these papers to government officials to support his case, he also included many documents that contradict his cause, which he then attempted to refute. With the caveat, then, that we will never be able to confirm the accuracy of at least some of his sources, I use the texts he reproduced on the assumption that they are correct copies. Where possible I have cross-referenced those for which versions exist elsewhere, such as records from the Crown, the Dutch government, or the Society of Suriname.

I supplement this central text with a range of other material. State papers relating to the case include petitions, letters, and further supporting documentation that Clifford provided to English government officials as well as those officials' replies. They also contain later correspondence between the Crown and those who took up his case after his death. Dutch government records, particularly the minutes and resolutions of the States General, allow me to trace the response to Clifford's claim by the United Provinces not only during his lifetime but also decades later. I also use other English and Dutch manuscripts to tell the story of Suriname itself, from the period of English rule to its conquest by Zeeland and subsequent existence as a Dutch colony. And because Clifford's case had a long life in print, I am able to use books and pamphlets to chart its changing meanings in the public sphere. Texts produced by Clifford himself show how he appealed to a wider audience as he petitioned English and Dutch officials. Likewise, those texts that were issued by others after his death used his story for their own ends into the second half of the eighteenth century.

The Chapters

The book's first chapter explores the establishment of English Suriname, with particular attention to the meaning and development of English subjecthood in the colony. English colonists, in attempting to make Suriname English, extended the scope of English subjecthood beyond that which pertained in England itself. Subject status expanded outside England at a time when civil war had shaken its foundations in the metropolis. In charting that expansion, the chapter explores the position of the English, Jewish, African, and indigenous populations in Suriname. Chapter 1 provides context for the legal and cultural forms of belonging available to the Clifford family when they arrived in the colony sometime between 1663 and 1665. It pays particular attention to the extension of subject rights to Jews in Suriname via the 1665 "Grant of Privileges" as an example of how the colony's tenuous status and hostile disease environment created the need to bolster the colonial population. The chapter ends on the eve of the 1667 Dutch conquest, an event that changed both the demographic makeup of the colony and the meaning of English subjecthood there.

Chapter 2 uses the example of the Clifford family and the wider colonial population to explore how English colonists preserved their status in the period between the Dutch conquest and the Glorious Revolution. The chapter examines who sought to maintain English subjecthood, who abandoned it, and whose status was contested by the English and Dutch authorities. It begins by examining how the colony's English governors sought to protect English inhabitants through the framing of the 1667 Articles of Capitulation, which defined the rights of English subjects under Dutch rule. The chapter then turns to the evacuation of most of the English colonists in 1675, showing who continued to claim English subjecthood and who ultimately shed it. The Clifford family, along with most of the other English colonists, left the colony for Jamaica. The Crown also tried to remove some of Suriname's Jews on the grounds that the 1665 "Grant of Privileges" had made them English subjects. The Dutch prevented these Jews from leaving, however, and they subsequently abandoned attempts to claim the benefits of English subjecthood.

The second half of the chapter closely follows the Clifford family on its return to Suriname after 1675 and traces Jeronimy Clifford's attempts to secure his status within a territory that was now almost devoid of English subjects. Clifford bolstered his position as an English subject under Dutch rule by asserting his authority as a landowner and slaveholder. In this effort he attempted to secure full legal control over land that he had gained from both his father, Andrew Clifford, and his wife, Dorothy Matson. Here I focus closely on Matson and her marriage to Clifford because land that she brought into the marriage, a plantation called Corcabo, formed the core of Clifford's property claims. English and Dutch norms of marital property had different implications for Clifford's control over the estate. When the colonial authorities disputed his claim that the couple had married in England, questioned Matson's English subjecthood, and asserted Corcabo's Dutch provenance, they undermined Clifford's title to the property. The chapter charts the strategies Clifford used to gain control over the land as well as those that Matson used to protect both her person and the property she had brought into the marriage. It explores the range of options available to them both, including the limitations that gender and the colony's high mortality rate imposed on the choices available to her and how she navigated those constraints. Both Clifford's and Matson's choices variously supported and eroded their positions as English subjects in a Dutch colony (if indeed Matson was English at all).

Andrew Clifford and Dorothy Matson left Suriname in 1685 and 1687, respectively, leaving Jeronimy Clifford in charge of the combined estate. However, the colonial authorities contested his control over the property, evoking its purported Dutch provenance and Clifford's treatment of his wife to prevent him from selling it and leaving the colony. This set up a conflict that came to a head over subsequent years.

Chapter 3 uses Jeronimy Clifford's case to explore the impact of the Glorious Revolution on English subjecthood in Suriname. The accession to power in England of William of Orange had implications not just for England and its colonies but also for English subjects elsewhere, particularly in Dutch territories. It provides a second example of a shift in sovereignty, which serves as a counterpoint to the Dutch conquest. The event shaped Clifford's interactions with Suriname's governors, and the chapter shows how the accession of a Dutch king to England's throne both threatened and bolstered his ability to use his English subjecthood to assert power. The Glorious Revolution began with war between England and the Netherlands, an event that cast Clifford and his fellow English subjects in Suriname as potential enemies. Clifford's refusal to take an oath of loyalty to the Dutch brought him into conflict with the authorities, leading to a brief period of imprisonment. Nonetheless, he still clung closely to his English subjecthood, acting in accordance with the 1667 Articles of Capitulation to defend it.

After the accession to the English throne of William of Orange, Jeronimy Clifford became the subject of a Dutch king who wielded dual power as both monarch and stadholder, a fact noted by Surinamese officials. The rest of the chapter traces Clifford's many conflicts with the colonial authorities, examining what they tell us about English subject status in a Dutch colony after the Glorious Revolution. Disputes between Clifford and Suriname's governors culminated in an unfulfilled death sentence and almost four years of imprisonment. While Clifford's efforts to win freedom frequently referenced his English subjecthood, the colonial authorities invoked William's dual authority as both English king and Dutch stadholder. Clifford ultimately won his freedom after William intervened on his behalf, and he left Suriname for Barbados in 1695 before traveling to England. Yet the implications of his troubled status in the eyes of the Dutch and the fate of his property in Suriname remained unresolved.

Chapter 4 traces Jeronimy Clifford's subsequent fight for restitution as he descended into poverty and, quite possibly, madness. From his arrival in England in 1696 until his death in 1737, Clifford sought compensation for his suffering and the right to remove his property—including its enslaved workers—from Suriname. As he did so the estate itself fell into the hands of others. This chapter explores how he deployed his subjecthood when engaging with the English Crown and its British successor, with parliament, and with the Dutch authorities. It pays particular attention to the ways in which he tried to bolster his subject status in order to convince agents of the Crown to act on his behalf and how the Crown and Dutch authorities responded to those efforts.

Clifford advanced his claim by citing seventeenth-century Anglo-Dutch treaties, and by evoking his birth within England, his marriage, and his own patterns of migration. At the same time he appealed to the broader public by resorting to print. He did so while falling into poverty, which resulted in at least sixteen years in debtors' prison. During this time he not only sought compensation but also employed agents in Suriname to try to regain control of

Corcabo. Clifford's demands for active support from the Crown were sometimes successful and other times spurned. The chapter examines when and why his case gained traction along with the times when it failed to find purchase. It looks at the ways in which he evoked his subject status, how the English (subsequently British) and Dutch authorities supported or undermined it, and what these episodes tell us about metropolitan imperial bureaucracies. As he approached the end of his life, Clifford became convinced that he was due vast riches, a result, he thought, of the Crown having seized Dutch ships on his behalf. However, he died in poverty, without having received restitution. Despite having used his status as a subject to convince the Crown to intercede with the Dutch, his efforts had resulted in failure.

The book's final chapter explores the many afterlives of Clifford's case in the years between his death and the dawn of the revolutionary era. Shortly after he died in 1737, at least two parties revived his claim. One person, who may have been in debtors' prison with Clifford, purported to possess his will and attempted to extort the Society of Suriname. Another group sought to settle Clifford's claim against the society, seeking justice (and profit) on his behalf. The latter party printed a number of pro-Clifford texts, which prompted the issue of other books and pamphlets about the case. The claim's advocates moved the Crown to again intercede with the Dutch, but without achieving satisfaction.

These reverberations of the Clifford case show the uses to which seventeenth-century colonial English subjecthood was being put by the second half of the eighteenth century. Clifford's supporters repeatedly burnished his English credentials in terms of both the legal subjecthood that underwrote his claim and his status as a victim of a historic adversary. While the Dutch were now allies against the French, Clifford's advocates cast them as enemies while portraying Clifford himself as a paragon of English virtue. Printed texts used his case as ammunition in contemporary disputes with the Dutch and evoked friction between the English and the Dutch in eighteenth-century Africa and India as further evidence of the Dutch malice under which Clifford had suffered. At the same time, some efforts to resolve Clifford's claim actively undermined his credentials as a subject, particularly those that evoked his supposed will, which had named French and Hapsburg benefactors.

The last echoes of Clifford's case extend into the 1780s, when Britain and the Netherlands again went to war, this time as a consequence of the American Revolution. Although Jeronimy Clifford's claim disappeared from the historical record without resolution, it had found a variety of proponents in the decades after his death. Not only had these efforts kept alive the memory of a former colony and an old colonial rivalry; they had also spurred the Crown to intercede with an ally by evoking the treaties on which Clifford himself had relied. Those interventions and the case's ongoing salience reveal the loose ends generated by the colonial English subjecthood of the previous century and show how they spawned a conversation that continued past the centennial anniversary of Suriname's conquest by the Dutch.

CHAPTER 1

Creating an English Suriname (1651–1667)

Around 1663 Andrew Clifford, his wife, Alice, and their young son, Jeronimy, settled in the English colony of Suriname, on the northern coast of South America. They originally came from the village of Egham, in Surrey, or at least that is where Jeronimy Clifford was baptized in 1657. They may have moved directly from England to Suriname, although there is some indication that, like many colonists, they migrated by way of Barbados.[1] In 1667, some four years after the family arrived, the territory fell to the Dutch. Once under Dutch dominion, the Cliffords and other English colonists faced the challenge of remaining English in a non-English space. But just how English was Suriname before that time? What did English subjecthood look like when the colony was under English rule? And what sorts of factors shaped its development?

When English people colonized Suriname in the early 1650s they found an environment radically different from England itself. In trying to build an English society in Suriname, colonists faced a range of challenges, from the territory's geography to its flora and fauna, its deadly pathogens, and the competing colonial ventures on its borders. Although they brought their existing notions of belonging with them, their new circumstances shaped their ideas about who could become a subject and what the benefits of subjecthood entailed.

In confronting these challenges, and particularly the high death rate caused by the colony's disease environment, Suriname's governors broadened the contours of English subjecthood far beyond those that pertained in England itself. In an attempt to save the venture from collapse they decided to try to attract Sephardic Jewish planters from neighboring Dutch territory. As part of that effort, in 1665 they offered Jews both religious toleration and full English subjecthood. Although Jews had been allowed to live openly in England since 1656, sacramental restrictions there barred them from naturalization and limited the rights even of those born in the realm. Suriname offered no such limitations; instead, the government offered extensive communal privileges and stipulated that all current and future Jews in the colony would be "considered as English born."[2] Moreover, unlike the norm in England itself or its other colonies, these provisions created new subjects collectively rather than individually. Contrary to its usual attitude toward colonial naturalization elsewhere, the Crown would later recognize the subjecthood conferred to Jews in 1665 as portable, effective not just in Suriname itself but also beyond its borders.

English subjecthood in the Suriname of Jeronimy Clifford's childhood was, then, peculiarly expansive. Its scope contracted after the Dutch conquest in 1667 and the evacuation of most English colonists eight years later. Sephardic Jews shed any claim to subject status, while those settlers in Suriname who claimed to be English subjects did so as members of a tiny community whose origins lay exclusively in the British Isles. By the eighteenth century, when Clifford and others evoked the memory of the short-lived English colony, the inclusive version of subjecthood that had once existed there had been forgotten.

Almost no information has survived about the life of the Clifford family during the period of English rule. Yet English Suriname loomed large throughout Jeronimy Clifford's life and far beyond his death; it was present in his later dealings with Surinamese, English, and Dutch authorities as well as in subsequent retellings of his story. These years provide the declension point for English identity in the colony, a formative period undergirding English colonists' later sense of themselves under Dutch rule that doubtless influenced Clifford's own ideas about subjecthood. However, the identity of later English inhabitants was not the same as the identity of those who had lived under English dominion. As Clifford and others struggled to stay English after the Dutch conquest, they looked back to a period when being under the allegiance of England's king in Suriname meant something very different than in their own time.

The Environment, People, and Pathogens of the Wild Coast

Suriname stretches from the Caribbean coast far into the South American interior, reaching south all the way to the Amazon Basin. Consisting of land that rises from a coastal plain to highlands in the south, even today it remains densely covered by tropical rain forest.[3] The nonindigenous newcomers who seized the land in the sixteenth and seventeenth centuries arrived by sea and made their way into the interior using its waterways, which served as the conduits for their assertions of sovereignty.[4] First arriving in the broad mouth of the river from which the colony took its name, they later established settlements along the smaller tributaries and creeks spiraling out from it. Indeed, for the Europeans, rivers defined the entire region of what they called Guiana, or the Wild Coast, an area encompassing what is today northeastern Venezuela, Guyana, Suriname, French Guiana, and the Brazilian state of Amapá. They named their colonies after the rivers along which they settled, while the riverbanks they failed to populate marked their intercolonial borders (see figure 1).[5]

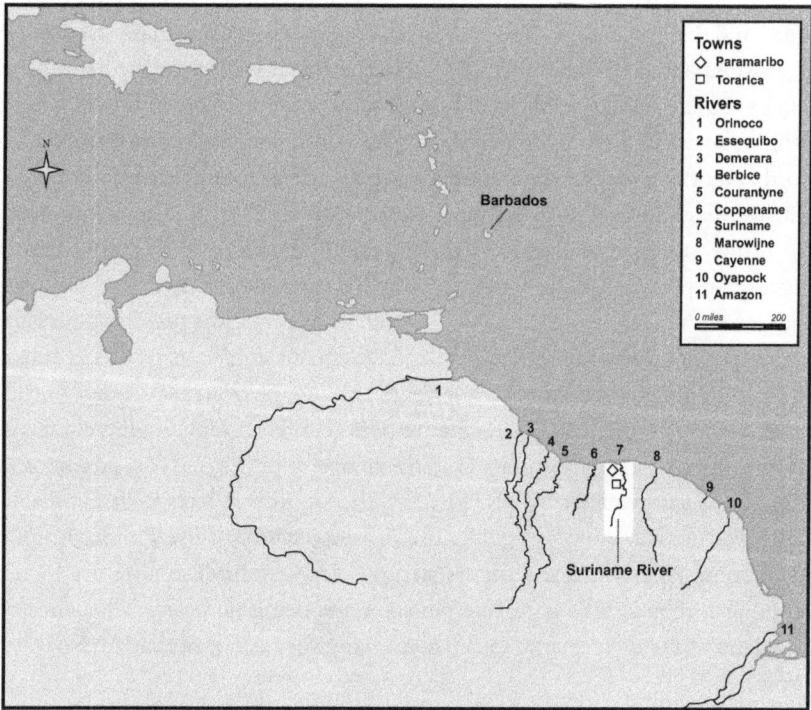

FIGURE 1. Rivers of the Guianas (designed by Jeffrey Young)

The Englishman George Warren began his 1667 *Impartial Description of Surinam*, which was based on three years' observation of an English colony then around fifteen years old, by describing its titular waterway. He wrote that the river's mouth was "barr'd with sand at the entrance," yet "three fathoms deep at high-water" (more during the spring) and a league wide and that it maintained roughly that width for five leagues before gradually narrowing.[6] The river was navigable for thirty leagues (roughly ninety miles). Beyond this point there were "cataracts or falls of water, that descend from ledges of rocks." These formed an impediment to the navigation of the Suriname and other coastal rivers and prevented "the more perfect discovery of that rich continent."[7]

The river teemed with wildlife. As well as "good fish of innumerable kinds," it contained rarer, more striking creatures. These included "the sword-fish, so called from a bone growing at his snout," and "the manatee, who feeds upon bushes by the river side, gives suck like a cow, and eats more like flesh than fish." More dangerous was "the torpedo or num-eel," which, on touching another creature, "strikes such a deadness into all the parts, as for a while renders them wholly useless."[8] The surrounding jungle was similarly full of creatures: the trees teemed with parrots, which were "more common than jackdaws in England," as well as "baboons, quottoes, monkeys, marmosets, cusharees, sloths, and many more."[9] Hare, deer, armadillos, buffaloes and "ant-bears" roamed the ground, along with three kinds of tigers, "black, spotted, and red."[10] Predatory cats were not the only animals that were hazardous to humans. "Snakes, crocodiles, scorpions, bats, ants, mosquitoes, toads, and frogs" were all "in some measure dangerous, troublesome, and unpleasant."[11] However, the land was amply stocked with a bounty of fruit, from oranges, lemons, and limes to plantains and bananas.[12] Warren pointed to the colony's plenitude partly to attract English people to the colony, although he did not sugarcoat its dangers.[13]

The land had been populated by humans for thousands of years. During the early modern period, Europeans described the peoples of the Wild Coast using two broad terms, *Carib* and *Arawak*, both of which obscured a more complex underlying reality.[14] Having assigned their own designations to the local population, Europeans then forged alliances based on those divisions, which in turn fueled real conflicts with real consequences. An imagined "ethnic vendetta" between the Caribs and Arawaks, which had no pre-Columbian past, in turn reified new boundaries.[15] In Suriname, the English came to ally themselves with the people they called Caribs.[16] Warren, for his part, noted the presence of "several nations" and described "the Charibes, or Cannibals" as "more numerous than any of the rest." Echoing common tropes in European accounts of indigenous inhabitants, he pronounced them to be "a people cowardly and treacherous," remarked on the strangeness of their adornments, and imputed lasciviousness to the local women.[17] They were, he wrote, a people devoid of religion aside from "talk of a captain of the skies" and "some knowledge of the devil."[18]

Europeans first began to encroach on Guiana in the sixteenth century. Spanish colonization remained confined to the far west of the region, around the Orinoco River.[19] English activity initially began with raids by privateers who were attracted to Spanish settlements in Trinidad. Sir Walter Raleigh traveled up the Orinoco in 1595 and explored the larger Guiana coast as part of his quixotic attempt to find El Dorado. By the early seventeenth century English and Irish ships were regularly trading with Port of Spain and with Spanish settlements in the lower Orinoco, where Spanish planters illicitly grew tobacco.[20]

Starting in the beginning of the seventeenth century the English had also tried to establish a foothold on the Oyapock River (known at the time as the Wiapoco), which today forms the border between French Guiana and Brazil. While aiming to find gold in the interior, these outposts sustained themselves with cash crops such as tobacco but the settlements petered out by around 1613. Over the next two decades efforts shifted to the Amazon, where English and Dutch planters were growing tobacco by 1616. By 1623 there were perhaps two hundred English and Irish men living on the Amazon Delta. They had been spurred on by the brief existence of the Amazon Company, which was chartered in 1619 but dissolved a year later. English efforts then shifted northward, due in part to Portuguese expansion in the Amazon, although with limited success. The Guiana Company's encampment of around one hundred men on the Oyapock in 1628 lasted only until around 1635.[21]

Meanwhile, the Dutch and the French were also attempting to establish a presence in the region. Dutch efforts were initially most successful to the west, in Essequibo and Berbice (both in modern-day Guyana), which were occupied by the 1630s, shortly after the formation of the Dutch West India Company.[22] France began to encroach on Cayenne (modern-day French Guiana, east of Suriname) by the 1630s, albeit tenuously at first.[23] Some English and Irish men seem to have served the Dutch efforts.[24] There are also hints of an English presence in Suriname itself prior to formal English colonization in the 1650s. Joyce Lorimer suggests that a small number of English "fugitives from the Amazon" settled there in the 1630s and that they remained until the 1650s.[25] Other sources, however, indicate that any earlier presence was soon wiped out. Major John Scott's Restoration-era "Description of Guiana" asserts that three hundred families "employed by the Earl of Warwick" were living there in 1643, only to be "cut of[f] by the natives" two years later.[26]

The disease environment was fundamental to the human experience in Suriname during the sixteenth and seventeenth centuries. The indigenous population—some 750,000 people in the Guianas and Antilles by 1492—was devastated by the virgin soil epidemics brought on by contact with old world pathogens.[27] In turn, the Europeans who carried those pathogens encountered tropical diseases to which they were unaccustomed, some of which were native to the new world and others brought from the old one. George Warren's account shows how one Englishman perceived Suriname's maladies, linking each to social status and moral behavior while viewing indigenous people as a source of contagion rather than its victims. He pointed to the dangers posed by "the fever and ague, the yaws, and the dropsy, called there, the country disease." Fever, which particularly affected recent arrivals, was caused "by bad lodging, and worse diet." Warren blamed yaws on "coition with Indian-women." Dropsy, meanwhile, was due to "that unwholesome flashy kind of nourishment" particularly common to "poor servants," a result of "the hardness of the place, and [the] penury of masters."[28]

The fever to which Warren referred might have been malaria, which was endemic in the Caribbean by the early sixteenth century, or possibly yellow fever, which reached Barbados by the late 1640s, where it killed as much as a seventh of the population. Both diseases came from the old world and thrived in the Caribbean due to the conditions produced by the sugar economy, not least the large-scale transportation of enslaved people. Yellow fever, which in the Americas is genetically almost identical to the variety from West Africa, became endemic in Suriname by the eighteenth century. This aided maroon uprisings, as many people who had escaped enslavement possessed an immunity to the disease that was lacking among recently arrived Europeans as well as the resistance to malaria common among people from West and Central Africa.[29]

The other maladies that Warren mentions are similarly plausible yet hard to confirm. Yaws was present in the Americas before 1492, and the variety found in the Guianas is a close genetic relative of the bacterium that causes venereal syphilis.[30] *Dropsy* is a term still used today for a condition caused by adulterated cooking oil.[31] However, during the early modern period it carried a broader meaning, referring to the accumulation of fluid in the body.[32] Causes ranged from inebriation to the improper generation of blood due to fever, poor diet, or a host of other factors.[33] Other diseases that Warren did not remark on were surely present, perhaps including dengue fever, which may have infected the Scots who attempted to colonize Darien in 1699.[34] However, readers of accounts such as Warren's would do well to heed John McNeill's warning that "retrospective diagnosis is always uncertain."[35]

An English Suriname?

The English finally secured a presence in Suriname in the 1650s. But how English could such an unfamiliar environment be made? As elsewhere around the world, the colonizers of Suriname faced challenges that called for solutions unique to their circumstances. A range of factors shaped the nature of the new society, from the area's geography to the mortality caused by disease and the kinds of crops that it was possible to grow. The decisions made in response to these challenges affected not only the English themselves but also the people who already lived in Suriname, people who had been forcibly brought there to work, and other people from non-English groups who moved there voluntarily. In response to both coercion and choice, English Suriname became something very different than England itself.

Compounding these issues was the fact that Suriname was a Barbadian venture, having been launched by an island that had already become very different from England. During the 1640s and 1650s, as civil war and unrest raged at home, colonists in Barbados began to plant sugar, hoping to emulate its successful cultivation by the Dutch in Brazil and elsewhere. Over subsequent decades the labor-intensive nature of the crop transformed the island, the English Caribbean, and ultimately the Atlantic world. Shifting away from a system of small farmers and indentured workers, Barbados instead came to rely on the labor of enslaved Africans working on large plantations. The elaboration of codes regulating their lives led to the identification of African bodies with unfreedom itself. This codification of enslavement was then copied in Jamaica, which was an English colony from 1655 onward, and later imported to mainland North America through Carolina, which like Suriname was a Barbadian offshoot.[36]

The colonization of Suriname took place under the patronage of Francis Willoughby, Barbados's governor, as part of an expanding "sugar frontier."[37] The transition toward large-scale sugar production and the use of enslaved African workers had enriched the Barbadian gentry while limiting the availability of land for an exploding population. Suriname provided a destination for English Barbadians who had been on the losing side of that consolidation, a place for wealthy planters to expand their holdings, and a potential source of wood and grazing land. It was, as Justin Roberts notes, "the first and most successful Barbadian colony."[38]

The fate of the enterprise was inextricably linked to that of Willoughby himself. Initially a Presbyterian supporter of parliament during the civil war, Willoughby leased the Earl of Carlisle's claim to the West Indies in 1647. He defected to the royalist side and in 1649 Charles II confirmed the lease. Barbados's assembly, which at the time was under the control of a planter-supported royalist faction, approved him as governor a month after his April 1650 arrival in the Caribbean. However, he was unable to strike a balance between the island's different factions and failed to effectively defend it against a parliamentary fleet that arrived in October 1651. Willoughby surrendered during the following January as the fleet's commander, George Ayscue, had offered a settlement acceptable to the planter elite. He left for England two months later. Despite his royalism, the Council of State suggested that letters patent be issued for Suriname in his name, although they seem not to have gained final approval. Willoughby was subsequently imprisoned in 1655 and 1656 for his support of the royalist cause; he was released in September 1657 on condition that he leave for his South American colony. Nonetheless, he remained in England until after the Restoration.[39]

There is some ambiguity about the precise year when English colonists arrived in Suriname and the circumstances under which they did so. John Scott's "Description of Guyana" states that three hundred Barbadian settlers landed under the command of Lieutenant Colonel Anthony Rowse in 1650.[40] Suriname's Restoration grant of proprietorship confirms this year as the date of departure of the first English vessel.[41] Writing to his wife in August 1651, Willoughby referred to the return of a "gentleman" from Guiana with "two Indian kings." Here he stated that he would send "hence a hundred men to take possession," which suggests that colonization did not occur until at least 1651.[42] Willoughby himself traveled to Suriname in 1652 following his expulsion from Barbados. He assumed authority but then sailed for England later that year.[43] Rowse, who was probably part of Willoughby's faction, was also in England in 1652, where he challenged one Richard Holdip for Suriname's governorship, although Holdip appears to have retained his commission from the Council of State. Both Holdip and Rowse then returned to the colony, where they stayed until 1654.[44]

The English population of Suriname grew quickly during the first part of the decade, from 150 in 1652 to over 600 two years later, when the colony began to export timber to Barbados.[45] Willoughby, meanwhile, invested heavily in the venture, providing twenty-six thousand pounds and "300 settlers, food, and provisions," with each colonist receiving at least fifty acres. Single settlers who could not afford the passage received the cost of transportation on condition that they serve Willoughby or become his tenants. He also provided "all the monies, slaves, foodstuffs, stock and tools required to set up the colony for its first eight months."[46]

The period after 1654 to the end of the decade seems to have been one of benign neglect, with Suriname largely ignored by the metropolis. After Holdip's departure Suriname may well have lacked a governor until 1657, when the assembly, which represented the planters, began to choose who would hold the position. Both the governor and the assembly had a one-year term limit, with a council probably appointed by the governor. In 1657 the assembly selected William Byam as governor. An ally of Willoughby who had been banished from Barbados for his royalism, he won successive terms until 1660, when he continued to serve at the pleasure of the king, governing until the time of the Dutch conquest in 1667.[47]

After the Restoration the colony finally received formal letters patent. Issued by the Crown in June 1663, these granted joint proprietorship to Willoughby and Lawrence Hyde, the Earl of Clarendon's second son. The new colony was to be known as "Willoughby Land" and would extend "one English mile . . . beyond the westerly banks of the river Copenam and easterly one mile . . . beyond the river Marawyne." Consisting of forty leagues in breadth, Suriname's territory would continue upriver "and from thence by direct lines unto the main ocean called the south sea."[48] The proprietors, in return, were to reserve thirty thousand acres and a fifth of the gold and silver mined in the colony for the king and pay him two thousand pounds of tobacco annually.[49] (See figures 2, 3, and 4 for maps of Suriname in the 1660s and 1670s.)

The economic strength of the territory came to rest not with gold, silver, or tobacco but rather with sugar. George Warren's *Impartial Description of Surinam* mentions around five hundred plantations at the time of his visit in the 1660s, forty or fifty of which had sugar works "yielding no small profit to the owners."[50] The English had also built a "metropolis" called Torarica "near 20 leagues" upriver from the coast, which consisted of "about one hundred dwelling houses, and a chapel."[51] Contemporary estimates give some indication of the colony's growth. In May 1661 the Committee for Foreign Plantations noted that Suriname had one thousand inhabitants and "yields as good sugar as Barbados."[52] Two and a half years later one Renatus Enys reported a population of five thousand. Also remarking on the quality of the sugar produced, he suggested that the colony would become more profitable "were the planters supplied with negroes, the strength and sinews of this western world."[53] Neither population report notes whether their numbers represented only English colonists or also included Suriname's enslaved workers.[54]

It is impossible to know precisely how many Africans were forced to labor in Suriname during the English period. One source suggests that there were as many as three thousand captive workers in the colony by 1667.[55] The *Trans-Atlantic Slave Trade Database* provides a glimpse of where some enslaved people originated and the suffering they experienced during their passage to the colony. It lists four ships as having arrived in English Suriname with a total of 772 slaves, which is surely an incomplete figure. Other vessels may have

FIGURE 2. *A Discription of the Coleny of Surranam in Guiana Drawne in the Yeare 1667*, London?, 1667 (courtesy of the John Carter Brown Library)

sailed from Barbados, although they do not appear in the accompanying *Intra-American Slave Trade Database*.

The earliest recorded ship, the *Swallow*, began its voyage in November 1663. It was captained by John Wood, who purchased slaves either in the Bight of Biafra or the islands of the Gulf of Guinea. Wood and his men forced 184 slaves on board the ship. In February 1664 the vessel arrived in Suriname, where it stayed for three months. Fifty-four Africans had died during the voyage. The following year the *Happy Adventure* arrived with 243 slaves from Calabar, the survivors of an original group of 300. Of these 61 percent were men, 37 percent were women, and the remainder were children. A year later Captain Peter Butler docked the *William* in Suriname, where 149 enslaved people disembarked.

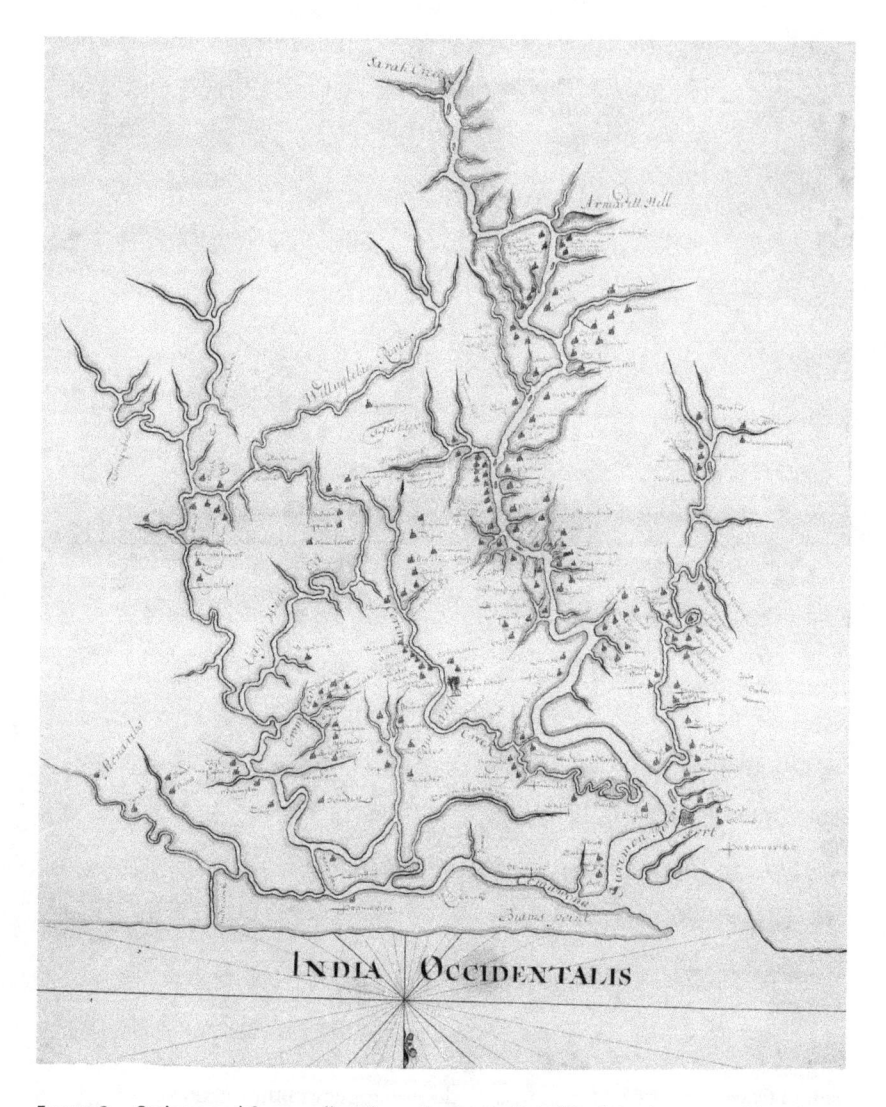

FIGURE 3. *Surinam and Commewijne Rivers*, Amsterdam?, 1667 or later (courtesy of the John Carter Brown Library)

Acquired at New Calabar, they had endured the deaths of 66 of their fellow captives. The *York* arrived in January 1667, shortly before Suriname fell to the Dutch, who captured the vessel sometime after it had delivered its human cargo of 250 people. These were the survivors of an initial 312 slaves purchased in an unspecified African port. The mortality rate for these voyages, then, ranged between 19 and 30 percent.[56]

Missing information and subsequent cultural change make it difficult to determine the ethnicities of the West Africans who made it off of these ships alive

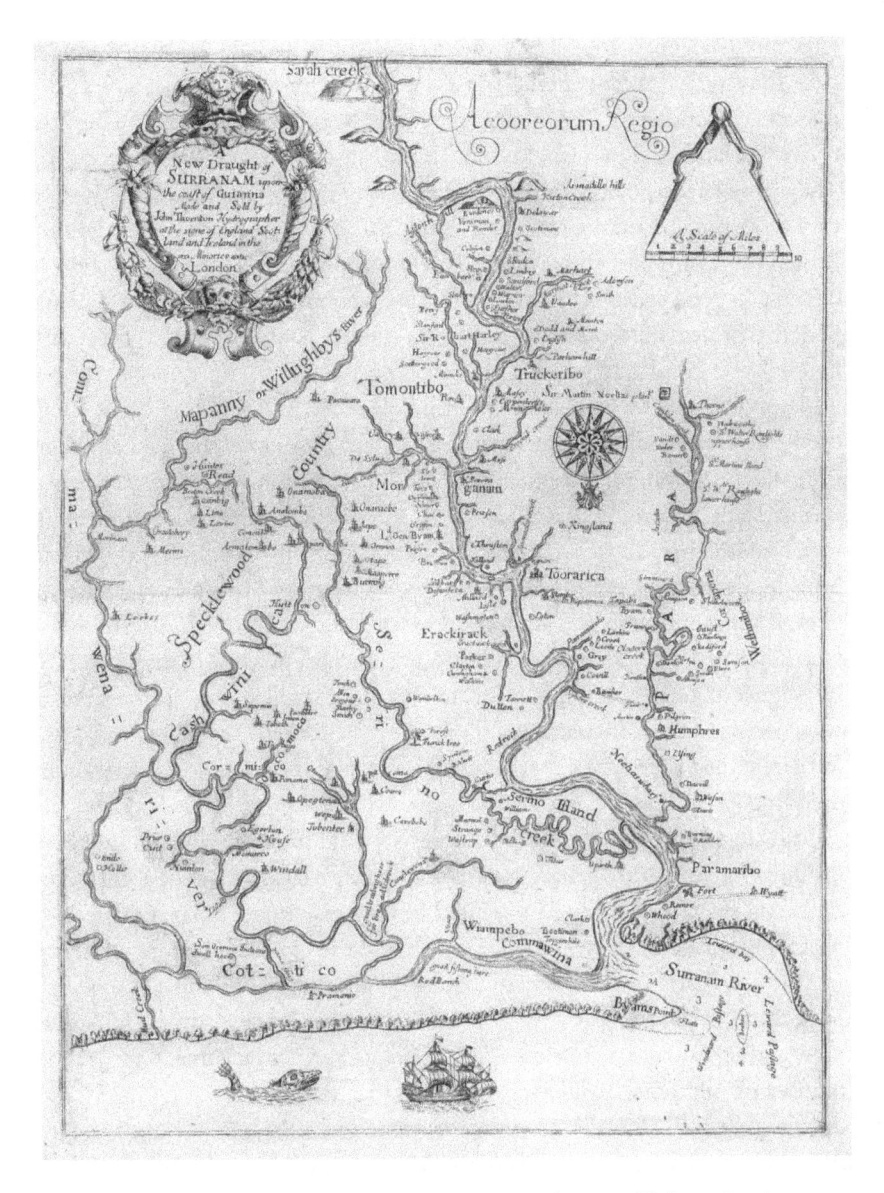

FIGURE 4. John Thornton, *A New Draught of Surranam upon the coast of Guianna*. London, c. 1675 (courtesy of the John Carter Brown Library)

and thus the bonds of allegiance broken by their enslavement. If they were taken somewhere in the Bight of Biafra or Calabar, from the Niger River Delta to the Cross River, they might have been Igbo, Efik, or Kalabari.[57] While some scholars have argued that Igbo identity did not emerge until later, the term does appear in seventeenth-century sources.[58] This includes those relating to

Jeronimy Clifford: a 1685 list of the people whom he held enslaved includes one "Ibbo Will."[59] Some might have escaped to form some of Suriname's first maroon communities, beginning a process of ethnogenesis that gave birth to today's Saramaka, Matawai, Kwinti, Djuka, Paramaka, and Aluku peoples.[60] The creole language now spoken in Suriname, Sranan Tongo, reflects this history as it contains elements of both English and West African Gbe tongues.[61] Enslaved Africans probably worked alongside indigenous people, although it is difficult to get a sense of the number of indigenous slaves during the English period. One account from 1671, four years after the Dutch conquest, suggests a figure of five hundred.[62]

The colony's growth peaked by the middle of the 1660s. In his journal, Governor William Byam reported that in May 1665, "Willoughby Land [was] in its meridian and after this month had its declination and went ever retrogrado." At this point, according to his account, Suriname was defended by almost fifteen hundred men, fewer than half of whom were armed and many of those bearing weapons of poor quality.[63] When Willoughby visited from Barbados around the same time he found the territory under a "contagious sickness" which had "spread itself all over the colony and swept away many people."[64] By August of 1666, according to Byam, sickness had killed over 200 men along with "very many women and children."[65] By the time of the Dutch conquest in March 1667 there were, perhaps, between one thousand and fifteen hundred English settlers left in the colony.[66]

Mortality rates for Suriname's colonists would have been high at the best of times. Statistics other than Byam's numbers are lacking for the English period. However, it is hard to imagine that they experienced a healthier environment than in other tropical colonies. Here the Jamaican picture is telling. In 1730 the island had a white annual mortality rate of around 11 percent.[67] In addition, fertility was low, with around two deaths for every birth in St. Andrew and St. Catharine parishes. Perhaps unlike Suriname, Jamaica had a large number of migrants, as reflected in the fact that among whites, in 1730 St. Andrew parish had 2.35 men for every woman and 4.6 adults for each child.[68] Although similar information is unavailable for English Suriname, the list of English colonists who left in 1675 provides some hints, showing an adult male to female ratio of 1.68:1.00 and two adults for every child.[69] Even accounting for differences with Jamaica, such as fewer migrants or the possibility that colonists to Suriname had previously acquired some immunity to diseases in Barbados, this was a demographically precarious state of affairs.

The epidemic that Byam described afflicted a society that was already weakened by factional discord, which sometimes spilled over into violence. Here the dividing line broadly fell between supporters of Willoughby and his representatives in the colony and those who sought more autonomy. The latter included some members of the council, such as Robert Sanford, who was expelled from the territory for his opposition to the ruling faction. In a subsequent pamphlet, titled *Surinam Justice*, Sanford accused his enemies, particularly Byam, of "an usurped power, and an arbitrary tyrannical way of proceedings, by the force of an army, destroying the birth-right of the subject."[70] John Allin, another opponent of proprietary power, went further, attempting to assassinate Willoughby during a religious service when he visited Suriname in 1664. Willoughby survived, but he drowned at sea two years later. Hostility toward Willoughby and Byam most famously found voice in Aphra Behn's *Orinooko*, although it is doubtful if she ever set foot in the colony.[71]

It was around this time that the Clifford family first arrived in Suriname. Jeronimy Clifford later wrote that they moved there "about the year 1663" after suffering a decline in fortune during the civil war. If so, he would have been around six years old. Perhaps intending to burnish his lineage as a steadfast subject, he described how "Oliver Cromwell['s] party" had "ruined" both his grandfathers "for their loyalty to King Charles the first and King Charles the Second of glorious memory." As a result, his "father and mother were forced to seek their fortunes as many more poor ruined subjects did then on the same account in the West Indies." This suggests that they might first have moved to Barbados, although he may have been using the term "West Indies" to include the South American colony. Both parents were "Protestants brought up in the faith of the Church of England," with his father, Andrew, having been baptized in Ash, in Kent, on 24 May 1623. Clifford provides no details about his mother, Alice, whose name is known only from his own certificate of baptism and the family's appearance on the 1675 list of English subjects leaving the colony. Later evidence suggests that Andrew Clifford worked as a millwright. Perhaps he supplied wood for the sugar plantations, which needed barrels for sugar, or milled specklewood, also known as snakewood, which was an important export. Sources reveal nothing else about the family during the period of English rule.[72]

When the Clifford family landed in Suriname, then, they found a venture that was beginning to flourish yet rested on brittle foundations. Although colonists from Barbados had cleared (or directed their slaves to clear) hundreds of plantations and established scores of sugar works, they remained vulnerable on multiple fronts. As inhabitants of a sugar colony, they had charted a course in which economic prosperity rested on forced labor, which was underwritten by constant brutality. Enslaved people's resistance to that brutality presented a continuous threat to the colony's hierarchy. While attempting to keep their workers in subjection, Suriname's English settlers battled both their own tendencies toward division and tropical diseases, which remained stubbornly indifferent to the fate of their fragile society.

Subjecthood and Belonging in an Unfamiliar Environment

Although it was part of the seventeenth-century English world, being ruled by an English king and populated by English men and women, Suriname's many differences from the metropolis made it difficult to replicate English society. The mixture of unfamiliar geography, an unfavorable disease environment, and a labor system built on an enslaved African workforce produced a setting that bore little resemblance to the Cliffords' home in Surrey. The territory was also surrounded by foreign colonies, which sometimes changed hands violently, as well as indigenous people who were hostile to European invasion. In addition, the population of colonists included people from beyond England. This included a small community of Scots and a substantial number of Portuguese-speaking Sephardic Jews.[73] All these circumstances, from the environmental to the demographic, produced unfamiliar and challenging conditions, which forced colonial authorities to improvise. In doing so, they departed from English norms, including those that defined the parameters of belonging.

The Crown had outlined its desired boundaries for English subjecthood in Suriname in the colony's 1663 patent. In order to encourage English "natives or denizens" to move to the territory, the patent stated that any children they bore there would be legally English. Such offspring were to enjoy the "liberties, franchises and immunities of free denizens of England as fully and amply" as if they had been "abiding and born within any other the dominions of England" or its possessions.[74] Here the terms *native*, *denizen*, and *free denizen*, while used interchangeably, indicate full English subjecthood acquired by birth rather than the more limited status that letters patent of denization conferred to aliens in England.[75] Suriname's grant was thus in keeping with common law and practice: following *Calvin's Case* in 1608, anyone born under the allegiance of the Crown was to be considered a subject in any of the other lands held by that monarch, including the colonies.[76] Such born subjects received the full protection of the king, in contrast to aliens, who paid higher taxes and customs and had limited property rights.[77]

In fact, however, not all people born in Suriname would have received the benefits of English subjecthood. Throughout England's empire the authors of slave codes denied children born into slavery the protections of subject status, a result that came from their being defined as chattel. While no slave code survives for English Suriname, practices there, whether codified or not, probably echoed those of its parent colony, Barbados, whose assembly created its first slave law in 1661. Written at a time when the enslaved population of the island equaled that of the free population, the law, as Susan Amussen notes, "used the word 'slave' only once: instead it referred constantly to 'Negroes.'" Planters in Barbados "assumed that white servants were 'Christians' and British; Negroes were neither, and were by definition slaves."[78]

Africans and their children were therefore not subjects unless it is possible to conceive of a form of subjecthood entirely shorn of rights and protections. Here the language of contemporary sources might be either evasive or direct. A 1664 report to the Privy Council about Barbados's law stated that "Negroes in that island are punishable in a different and more severe manner than other subjects."[79] This suggested that a reduced kind of subject status might be possible. However, Barbados's 1688 slave code was blunt about the antithetical relationship between slavery and subjecthood, as when it denied that jury trials for slaves could "be rightly done as the subjects of England are."[80] Assuming, then, that Suriname's English colonists followed Barbadian practice, the children of Africans would have been born directly into slavery and would certainly have lacked the rights included with English subjecthood. In that sense, as elsewhere in England's empire, they would not have been born as subjects, in contravention of *Calvin's Case*.[81]

Other non-English people could become subjects in Suriname. The Crown clearly intended to attract strangers to the colony, stipulating that they could acquire subjecthood while offering generous provisions for religious dissenters, English or otherwise. The patent encouraged the settlement of those who "will become our subjects and will live under our allegiance." Unlike in England, people who remained aliens were to pay the same customs and duties as the English.[82] Residents of the colony who were prevented by conscience from conforming to the Church of England were to receive "indulgences and dispensations" at the discretion of the colony's governors, provided they remained loyal to the monarch.[83] However, the text made no mention of any specific non-Anglican group, whether dissenting Christians or the Jews who would come to form a substantial portion of the colony's free population.

The language in Suriname's patent that allowed for the incorporation of strangers was not unusual and is present in most other seventeenth-century patents and charters.[84] As early as 1609, Virginia's second charter had referred to "strangers that will become our loving subjects and live under our allegiance."[85] However, strangers were also a potential danger, particularly at a time when the Navigation Acts had elaborated a closed imperial system. Suriname's patent recognized that threat even as it made provisions for non-English colonists, forbidding strangers' vessels from trafficking with the colony without permission, on pain of forfeiture.[86]

The metropolitan authors of the document probably did not envision the settlement of large numbers of free strangers in Suriname. Active recruitment of nonsubjects was rare in England's empire until the end of the seventeenth century, although the idea had begun to gain traction earlier. In 1671 Jamaica's lieutenant-governor Thomas Lynch noted to Lord Arlington, the secretary of state, that Jews and "Hollanders" made "profitable subjects."[87] Responding to anti-Jewish complaints by Port Royal merchants the following year, the Crown recommended that "due encouragement . . . be given to the Jews, the Dutch and other nations to settle and inhabit" the island.[88] However, most of Jamaica's free inhabitants continued to come from the British Isles.[89] North American colonies began actively seeking non-British settlers soon after. William Penn attempted to attract Lutherans to Pennsylvania in the 1680s, and by the following decade Carolina had begun to emulate Maryland's overtures to French migrants.[90] However, such efforts only became standard practice in the eighteenth century, when concerns about population loss in England converged with colonial desires for more inhabitants.[91] Before 1700 it was far more common for colonies to confront the large-scale presence of strangers when territories changed hands, as the English did after conquering New Netherland in 1664. Here they demanded the allegiance of the Dutch, recognizing them as "free denizens" with the same trading rights as the English and confirming their religious liberties.[92]

Although Suriname's patent allowed for the creation of new subjects, it failed to define the mechanism for how this would happen or specify whether they would remain English if they left Suriname.[93] This lack of specificity was common in early colonial grants, where the common references to "strangers" becoming the king's "loving subjects" left unstated the place of admission to subjecthood.[94] In practice the process usually entailed naturalization by colonial assemblies, mirroring the role of England's parliament. Governors, in turn, tended to enact the king's role of granting the more limited status of denizen.[95]

There was, however, a lack of uniformity in how different colonies turned strangers into subjects and inconsistency even within individual territories. In Carolina, the 1665 Articles of Agreement stipulated that it was the role of an assembly to naturalize. The 1669 Fundamental Constitutions, however, allowed for a simpler process that led to the creation of new subjects by individual counties.[96] In Virginia, on the other hand, the House of Burgesses recorded both naturalizations and denizations. Some of these examples adhere to the usual practice in England at the time, whereby new subjects were most commonly the children of English parents and had been born overseas while denizens were immigrants of non-English lineage.[97] This was the case with the Dutchman John Custis, who was "born in the Netherlands of English descent" and was naturalized in 1658.[98] Lambert Grooten, who may have been Dutch and of non-English background, became a denizen the same year.[99] However, Virginia also naturalized aliens of foreign parentage, such as Bertram Servant, a French man, whose record of naturalization was signed by Governor Edmund Andros in 1698.[100]

Colonial naturalization was also usually limited in geographical scope, with naturalized subjects routinely regarded as aliens beyond the colony where they became a subject. In the seventeenth century the Crown often failed to recognize the validity of colonial naturalizations outside the granting territory, with its position ultimately cohering around outright rejection. Only after passage of the 1740 Plantation Act was it clear that fully portable subjecthood could be acquired outside the British Isles.[101] While the grants of some colonies did contain clauses implying "that colonial naturalization had an imperial, and not merely a local, effect," this was not the case with Suriname's patent.[102]

English Suriname was founded at a time when the freedom of some natural-born subjects was contracting. The wars that raged within Britain in the 1640s and 1650s had shaken the conceptual foundations of allegiance, not least by the establishment of a short-lived republic.[103] From this turmoil and its reverberations arose concerns throughout the English Atlantic that the colonies were becoming sites of "lost liberty." Prisoners of war, Irish people resisting English invasion, and some English who had been condemned as rebels or criminals faced transportation and servitude in Barbados, Jamaica, and elsewhere.[104] The Restoration did not end this process. Participants in the 1685 Monmouth Rebellion were shipped in chains to Jamaica, and the number of British convicts sent to the Atlantic colonies between 1718 and 1775 was as high as fifty thousand.[105] While authorities proffered subjecthood to strangers in Suriname and other colonies, they also eroded the freedoms of some natural-born English, Irish, and Scots.

The void in Suriname's patent about both the method of creating new English subjects and the geographical range of their acquired status provided the colony's governors with room to innovate. This leeway, combined with the colony's tenuous circumstances, led to decisions that expanded the boundaries of English subjecthood beyond those that pertained in the king's other territories. By the mid-1660s subjecthood in Suriname had become peculiarly broad in scope, now being conferred collectively rather than individually and also promised to people who were not yet living in the colony.

Broadening the Scope of English Subjecthood: Jewish Settlement and the 1665 "Grant of Privileges"

In 1665, soon after the Cliffords' arrival, Suriname's governors attempted to shore up their ailing venture by inviting Jews from neighboring territories to settle there. Over the previous decade members of the Sephardic diaspora had established an open presence in English territory on both sides of the Atlantic, of which the readmission of Jews to England is the best known. However, this was itself part of a larger process of migration resulting from the expulsion of Jews from Dutch Brazil in 1654 following the Portuguese conquest. This dispersed members of an Amsterdam-oriented community throughout the Caribbean. The recently passed Navigation Acts prevented those who had settled in English colonies from trading directly with their parent community in the Netherlands, so they needed a Jewish presence in London.[106] The resulting overture to the Commonwealth by representatives of the Dutch Jewish community led to Jews living openly in England starting in 1656. This meant that Sephardic merchants in colonies such as Barbados could now trade with Europe without violating English law.[107]

The composition of Suriname's Jewish community came to differ dramatically from that of other English territories. In Jamaica and Barbados most Jews were merchants who settled in urban areas, forming a relatively small population.[108] The governors of both colonies received anti-Jewish complaints, including outright calls for their expulsion.[109] Suriname's Jewish community, on the other hand, ultimately included a large number of planters, who were the recipients of generous privileges. Its population rose as high as two hundred under English rule, probably amounting to 10 percent or more of the colony's free inhabitants. According to one report it came to equal the number of Dutch colonists by 1675.[110]

Some Jews were already living in Suriname when the colonial authorities made their offer. The first clearly documented Jewish settlement occurred shortly after the Restoration, although there are hints of a Jewish presence dating back as far as the 1640s.[111] In 1661 Henry Benjamin de Caseres, Henry de Caseres, and Jacob Fraso successfully petitioned the Crown for the right to settle in Barbados and Suriname.[112] A year later at least one of the three petitioners was living in England's South American territory. Robert Sanford's *Surinam Justice*, printed in 1662, reproduces two depositions that describe events at "the house of Senior [sic] Henrico de Casseres."[113] A further deposition, given by Thomas Duke in November 1661, provides tangential evidence for a

Jewish presence by describing how one Captain Crook stated that "neither Dutch nor Jew should live here."[114] However, the Jewish population remained small in the first half of the decade, probably comprising no more than about thirty people.[115]

The Jewish community only grew to significant numbers from the middle of the 1660s, a result both of flight from conflict in neighboring colonies and direct overtures from the government of Suriname. For the authorities, the attraction of Jewish colonists was a matter of survival at a time when disease posed a serious threat to the viability of their venture. Starting in 1665, around one hundred Jews arrived from Dutch Cayenne, following its capture by the French and subsequent destruction by the English. They may have been joined by about fifty other Jewish settlers fleeing from the Dutch colonies of Essequibo and Pomeroon in western Guyana following an English attack. As they were experienced sugar planters, the new arrivals became central to Suriname's prosperity.[116]

The manner in which Suriname's governors tried to attract Jewish migrants expanded the scope of English subjecthood in the colony. The 1665 "Grant of Privileges by the Governor, Council, and Assembly of Suriname, to the Jews" offered extensive privileges to any members of the "Hebrew nation" who might choose to make a home in the territory. Its provisions far exceeded any rights available to Jews in England itself. While stating the desirability of attracting colonists "of whatsoever country and religion," the grant offered full toleration for the Jewish faith, including the recognition of Jewish law, exemption from serving in the militia on the Sabbath, and a host of other privileges. It also extended full English subjecthood to any present or future Jewish inhabitants.[117]

The grant's authors aimed to encourage settlement by providing as attractive an environment as possible for Suriname's Jews. They began by praising the contributions of the current Jewish population, whose members had "proved themselves useful and beneficial" to the colony. The text then declared that "every person belonging to the Hebrew nation now resident here, or who may hereafter come to reside and trade here . . . shall be considered as English-born." Jews were to have "full liberty" to plant and trade for their own profit as long as they remained loyal subjects of the English king. Their property (real and personal) was secure and they were exempt from most peacetime civic obligations. Equally important were the grant's guarantees of religious freedom. Members of "the Hebrew nation" could practice their religion without fear of harassment, hindering their observances was a punishable offence, and Jewish marriages and wills were declared to be fully legitimate. Jews were exempt from court appearances on holidays and the Sabbath, their courts were recognized, and they were allowed to swear oaths "in conformity with the customs of the Hebrew nation." The community also received land for a synagogue, school, and burial ground.[118]

In offering a series of clearly enumerated religious rights, the grant far surpassed the protections then available to Jews in England. The previous year Charles II had confirmed that Jews could remain in the realm, though only with a pithy statement denying that he had given "any particular order" for their "molesting or disquieting."[119] Until the nineteenth century England's Jews would be subject to restrictions aimed at Christian dissenters, which made them unable to hold office or practice a number of professions. While those born under the king's allegiance were full subjects, the requirement of a sacramental oath barred Jewish immigrants from parliamentary naturalization. Instead, they could only achieve the more limited rights of denization by letters patent, which conferred the ability to purchase land. However, they remained aliens by birth, so were unable to inherit land or bequeath it to children born before their date of denization. Denizens also generally continued to pay aliens' taxes and customs.[120]

The 1665 privileges also provided a degree of communal recognition that was unavailable to Jews in other English colonies, who usually benefited, at best, from a suspension of religious tests.[121] In doing so they drew on existing Dutch precedents, closely mirroring rights extended to Jews by the Dutch West India Company in neighboring Essequibo, which were in turn based on proposals made by Brazilian Sephardic exiles.[122] Such explicit grants of collective toleration were as rare in the wider Dutch world as they were in the English one. As Evan Haefeli has noted, early modern Dutch tolerance usually took the form of "connivance," or the turning of a blind eye, rather than codified statements of protection. Where formal grants of toleration did occur, as in Brazil, they were "always in response to political pressures, especially the exigencies of war."[123] In this sense the rights offered by the English in Suriname echoed Dutch examples in context as well as content, having been framed five months into the Second Anglo-Dutch War in order to attract Jewish planters from Dutch territory.[124]

The grant was also much more generous in the way that it created new subjects than was usually the case in either England or its colonies. It offered to do so collectively, going beyond the usual practice of piecemeal naturalization by declaring an entire class of people to be "considered as English-born."[125] Normally naturalization and denization applied only to specific, named individuals. Some colonies did occasionally naturalize entire groups of aliens by "enrollment," but the grant went further than that, promising full subjecthood even to Jews not yet resident in the territory.[126] Suriname's 1663 patent had made no mention of the possibility of collective naturalization.[127]

Moreover, the grant exceeded the usual temporal and geographical scope of colonial naturalization. It offered to make all future Jewish settlers into subjects, not just those already in the colony. And in asserting that Jews were to be treated as if they were "English-born," it implied that they had gained portable subjecthood, something that colonies were usually unable to confer. English naturalization law "operated retrospectively," deeming "the alien actually to have been born within the protection of the king." Yet strangers naturalized outside England frequently found their subjecthood questioned beyond the granting colony, with authorities seizing their goods on the grounds that they remained aliens according to the Navigation Acts.[128] Those who were literally born under the king's protection, whether in England or its colonies, and those naturalized in England itself were in theory subjects in all of his territories. It was far from clear that the same could be said for aliens who were naturalized in England's overseas possessions during the seventeenth century. However, agents of the Crown *did* recognize the portability of the subjecthood that the 1665 "Grant of Privileges" had conferred to Suriname's Jews. As the next chapter will show, the 1675 evacuation mission attempted to remove them to Jamaica on the grounds that they were English subjects, where, by implication, their status would remain unchanged.

As former residents of Surrey, the members of the Clifford family were probably unaccustomed to having Jewish neighbors, yet shortly after they settled in Suriname, the colony saw the arrival of scores of members of the Sephardic diaspora. The 1665 grant provided for ten acres of land for the newly enlarged Jewish community in Torarica, which was the capital during the English period. It was there that Suriname's Jews built their first synagogue, burial ground, and school.[129] If the Cliffords lived in or near the capital, then, they would probably have encountered Jewish people on a regular basis. What would they have thought of them? That the territory's authorities and, a decade later, the Crown saw Jews as English subjects tells us nothing about the day-to-day views of colonists. But as non-Christians who spoke Portuguese, Dutch, or Hebrew, Suriname's Jews would probably have initially struck the Clifford family as foreign.

Yet the Cliffords had moved to an environment where much was unfamiliar, from the diseases, plants, and animals to the nature of the small society that they now called home. Hailing from a family of ruined royalists, they had sought refuge on South America's Wild Coast, where they were forced to adapt not just to a new climate but also to a new way of life. There they would have seen compatriots forcing people from Africa to work as slaves. Perhaps the practice of chattel slavery also struck them as strange. If so, it was something that Jeronimy Clifford would later get used to and participate in. Would it also have been possible to grow accustomed to unfamiliar forms of inclusion as well as dehumanization and embrace new versions of belonging? If England's experiment in Suriname had lasted longer, would the Clifford family have come to consider their Jewish neighbors to be as English as the English-born?

The legal parameters of English subjecthood in Suriname are clear even if the cultural contours of English identity are difficult to ascertain. The colony's 1663 patent had provided an outline from the perspective of the metropolis, some of which was in boilerplate language similar to the charters of other colonies. This left substantial leeway for people on the ground to innovate. Suriname's unfamiliar environment and the challenges it posed to building and sustaining a viable colony, together with isolation from England itself, meant that its governors had to improvise.

Some of the resulting departures from English norms were common in other colonies too and were perhaps obvious decisions for Suriname's elite to make. This included the denial of the benefits of subjecthood to people of African descent who were born into slavery, which violated the principles spelled out by *Calvin's Case* in 1608. Others, however, were idiosyncratic to Suriname. English colonists there were certainly not alone in facing high disease mortality, which afflicted other colonial ventures as well. However, the demographic makeup of the region was unique. Faced with a collapsing population, Suriname's governors desperately tried to shore up their venture and looked to the surrounding area for answers.

There they found a nearby population of experienced Sephardic Jewish sugar planters who were willing to move due to interimperial conflict. Attracting them required offering generous religious and legal privileges. Here examples were also close at hand, in provisions that the Dutch West India Company had offered to Jews in neighboring Essequibo. The need to attract a group of people meant that the 1665 grant created new subjects en masse. This was far different than the more common individual acts of naturalization offered by most colonial legislatures and the English parliament. Moreover, the vicissitudes of on-the-ground innovation, intentional or otherwise, made the wording of the offer uniquely expansive; it was applicable to all future Jewish colonists and fungible enough to retain force even if the recipients left Suriname.

The result was a peculiarly broad articulation of English subjecthood. While it was the creation of the colony's governor, council, and assembly, many factors had helped to define it. English legal tradition was certainly among these. But it was also the product of the region's diversity, of its colonial rivalries, and of the viruses and bacteria that afflicted those living on the Wild Coast. Subjecthood was shaped by pathogens as well as people.

CHAPTER 2

Staying English in Dutch Suriname (1667–1687)

A few years after the Clifford family arrived in Suriname, the colony fell to the Dutch. Seven vessels under the command of the Zeeland admiral Abraham Crijnssen made landfall in February 1667. The English offered only cursory resistance, surrendering the colony after just a few hours of fighting.[1] According to one report, many English transferred their allegiance to the Dutch after assurances that they could keep their estates and offered to show the victors "every crook and corner of the country, and where the cattle, provision[s] and negroes were."[2] After meeting with the colony's council and assembly, Governor Byam entered into negotiations with Crijnssen to settle the terms of surrender.[3] These were, according to his own narrative, "tedious, we not understanding Dutch well, neither they English, so that all things were twice translated."[4] Ultimately, however, the two sides agreed on articles of capitulation that would dictate the treatment of the English under Dutch rule, which were signed by Crijnssen and Byam on board the ship *Zealand* on 6 March 1667.[5]

Jeronimy Clifford was ten years old at the time.[6] There is no record of the family's experience of the Dutch invasion, but the young Clifford must surely have sensed his parents' fear of what lay ahead. They and their fellow English subjects faced a stark choice. Should they stay in Suriname and make a life under the dominion of England's imperial rival or abandon the colony for English territory elsewhere?

The richer colonists soon fled to Barbados, leaving behind most of the English population, the Clifford family included. The 1667 Articles of Capitulation stipulated that those who remained should swear allegiance to the Zeeland States. However, they had the right to sell their estates and leave the colony at a later date. Over the next few years most of Suriname's English colonists evoked this right, departing in several waves. The English Crown aided them by sending two evacuation missions, in 1671 and 1675. The majority left with the second attempt, traveling to Jamaica. Of the rest all but a handful moved to Antigua in 1680.[7]

This chapter explores how English subjecthood changed in Suriname in the twenty years after the Dutch conquest. The first half examines the period between its capture by Crijnssen's fleet in 1667 and the departure of most of the English settlers in 1675. The remainder of the chapter then uses the case of Jeronimy Clifford to explore what it meant to be an English subject in a Dutch colony that was devoid of a substantial English community.

The 1675 evacuation mission narrowed the scope of English subjecthood in Suriname, shedding the expansiveness of the English period, in which both Jews and Christians had benefited from subject status. Agents of the Crown attempted to remove both English and Jewish colonists. In doing so they echoed the rulers of English Suriname by defining subjecthood to include multiple nationalities while recognizing the portability of the status conferred by the "Grant of Privileges" a decade earlier. The colony's Dutch governor, however, conflated subjecthood and nationality, preventing Jews from leaving by arguing that only the ethnically English, or at best, the British, were English subjects. Although both sides divided Suriname's colonists between the "Dutch, Hebrew, and English nation," they could not agree on which groups were the subjects of England's king.[8] In the end, while most colonists of English nationality left for Jamaica, Suriname's Jews remained behind. They quickly stopped claiming the protections of subjecthood, the parameters of which diminished to include only the small number of remaining English and a handful of Scots.

The Clifford family left Suriname in 1675, only to return: Andrew Clifford a year later and his son Jeronimy in 1684, after time spent working at sea. As one of only fifteen English men remaining, the younger Clifford enacted his status as an English subject in a dramatically new context.[9] While most of Suriname's few English settlers chose to live quietly, Jeronimy Clifford repeatedly clashed with the authorities. The conflicts that were generated as he sought to secure his status as a planter revolved around the origins and control of property derived from his marriage to a woman of ambiguous nationality named Dorothy Matson. Clifford assumed possession over the land that she had brought into their union, a plantation called Corcabo, thus mirroring the English convention of coverture. Matson fought back against his efforts, supported by Dutch law that stipulated joint ownership of marital property. In dealing with the couple's strife, Suriname's governor and council attempted to strike a balance between recognizing the power of a patriarch and protecting one of the colony's largest estates. While Clifford's dispute with his wife ended with him in charge of Corcabo, the authorities placed limits on how he could dispose of it.

The articles of capitulation continued to shape Clifford's behavior as an English subject in a Dutch colony. Although they were written to govern a substantial English community that had now left, Clifford acted in accordance with their provisions, asserting rights as if he were backed by a distant Crown. Even as he sought to consolidate property and power, Clifford maintained that he had the authority to liquidate his assets and leave for English territory. For Clifford the most treasured right that the articles conferred to an English subject was the right to leave with his estate. Thus he bolstered his position as a planter with one eye on the door.

Suriname's English subjects faced an uncertain future after conquest by an imperial foe in 1667. They responded in ways that were dictated by the range of options conferred by the resources at their disposal, as well as by their national, religious, and personal affinities. Clifford's conflicts with the colonial authorities reveal some of what remained of English life once most of his compatriots had left and the colony's Jews had abandoned subject status. Any memories he had of England itself would have been those of a small child, augmented by his experiences as a young man on temporarily leaving Suriname. Yet it was his years growing up as part of a colonial English community that would have formed his initial sense of what it meant to be an English subject. To stay English in Dutch Suriname, he drew on that community's cultural and legal norms, including the articles of capitulation that had governed it as he grew from a child into an adult.

Jeronimy Clifford's position was not unique, even if his story is idiosyncratic. Around the world, the flotsam and jetsam of the seventeenth century's imperial wars had to decide not just where to live but also how to belong. In doing so, they, like Clifford, reached for whatever they could to bind them to distant polities that had receded far beyond the horizon.

Staying English in the Aftermath of Conquest (1667–1675)

English Suriname came to an end as part of the Second Anglo-Dutch War. The conflict, which broke out in 1665, led to a realignment that affected the shape of the two countries' empires into the following century. The Treaty of Breda, which concluded the dispute in 1667, acknowledged the exchange in imperial holdings that had taken place in regions from the Americas to the East Indies. The English recognized the loss of Suriname while the Dutch confirmed England's 1664 conquest of New Netherland. England, in turn, renounced its claim to Cormantine in West Africa and ceded territory in the Banda Islands, in modern-day Indonesia. It also returned St. Eustatius and Saba, which it had previously taken from the Dutch. A war that began thousands of miles away from Suriname upended the lives of the Cliffords, their fellow English subjects in the colony, and many of the territory's enslaved workers.[10] Just as Dutch colonists in New Netherland had to adjust to English rule, so the English in Suriname confronted the new reality of life under Dutch dominion.[11]

Suriname was a valuable prize for an invading power, even as disease had prevented English colonists from exploiting it to its full potential. The venture had already demonstrated its viability as a sugar colony, its interior highlands offered the promise of gold, and the fact of its seizure would project power in the region. It was also vulnerable to invasion, something noted by Governor William Byam in his account of the Dutch conquest. Although Byam had ordered strikes on nearby Dutch territory, by May 1666 he thought the main danger came from France. He wrote that the colony was "not at that time in a condition to offend, nor well to defend itself." He had asked Lord Willoughby, Suriname's proprietor, for supplies, yet none had arrived. The colony would have to see to its own defense. The assembly passed an act ordering "every tenth working negro throughout the colony" to be sent to Paramaribo to build a fort.[12] That August sickness struck, further worsening the situation by killing over two hundred men "and very many women and children." It was, Byam wrote, "a most strange and violent fever, burning within, and yet at the same time, the feet and hands exceeding cold." The outbreak left the colony unable to raise "100 sound men in the whole country to oppose an enemy."[13]

At the beginning of January 1667 Byam, who was now weakened by illness and stricken with gout, inspected the fort at Paramaribo, still fearing a French rather than a Dutch invasion.[14] Although the gates had been built, its walls were less than six feet high in places. He called for volunteers to assemble and prepared the colony for invasion. On 15 February he received news that eight ships had been sighted in the river, vessels that he believed were French.[15]

In fact, however, the ships were Dutch, having departed from Zeeland at the end of December. They anchored on 16 February "about half a league below the fort." Their commander, Admiral Abraham Crijnssen, ordered Byam to surrender the colony, which he refused to do. The Dutch attacked the next day. The English fired their guns for "two or three hours" but were unable to prevent the Dutch from landing.[16] The fort was in no shape to be adequately defended. After consulting with his officers and a member of the council, Byam decided that it was better "to yield on honorable terms . . . then [sic] to oppose to no purpose." He ordered "a flag of truce to be hung out" and offered his terms of surrender to Crijnssen.[17]

The immediate response of the English colonists foreshadowed some of the issues they would later face under Dutch rule, particularly the status of land and the question of ultimate allegiance. In exchange for the laying down of arms and an oath of loyalty to the States, the Dutch promised that the English could "enjoy their estates, and have all privileges." According to Byam, some complied "for gain, others for fear." A number were divided about how to proceed, with some accepting peace and others opting to resist the occupiers. Some soldiers had committed mutiny during the invasion, refusing to fight against the Dutch, and even some members of Suriname's elite viewed resistance as futile. Fearing that further opposition would lead to the destruction of some of the colony's largest plantations, Byam contacted Crijnssen and urged him to avoid action until the two sides had reached an agreement.[18]

After learning that the council and assembly wished to surrender, Byam consented to the drafting of proposals for a settlement with the Dutch.[19] In noting his agreement to do so, he pointed to the need to maintain control over the colony's large enslaved population, for whom the breakdown of order presented an opportunity for resistance or escape. The "insolencies of our negroes," he noted, had led to them "killing our stock, breaking open houses, threatening our women, and some flying into the woods in rebellion." The English were willing to make accommodations with Suriname's conquerors in order to keep those who toiled on their plantations in bondage.[20]

Representatives of the Dutch and the English met in Torarica on 4 March (New Style) to agree on the final contents of the 1667 Articles of Capitulation. The Dutch party consisted of two Zeeland company commanders while Byam was accompanied by three other English men, two of whom were seriously weakened by disease. The Zeelanders balked at a number of the English party's initial suggestions, which they had enumerated in a list of twenty-seven "Proposals to the Enemy." These had pushed for generous rights, including freedom of conscience and "equal privileges with the Dutch" for people of all nations (excluding, presumably, the enslaved).[21] The "first and sharpest dispute" was over the settlers' continued allegiance to the king. They also objected to the English proposition that the proprietor and other absentee landowners retain their estates, asserting that the States demanded their forfeiture. The two sides nevertheless pressed on to "see what we mutually would assent unto."[22]

According to Byam's account the negotiations proceeded with difficulty. Not only were they hampered by the language barrier, but the Dutch were, he wrote, willing to exploit "the distraction and weakness of our condition." Each day the Dutch "would alter something, and propose higher demands." However, the "tottering condition" of the English and their fear of imminent French attack led Byam and his cohorts "to delay no more time, but to hasten a conclusion." The two sides agreed on the final text around midnight on 6 March.[23]

The Dutch had forced the English to concede on the issues of allegiance and the rights of absentee landowners. The second article stipulated that English subjects residing in Suriname swear an oath of loyalty to the Zeeland States. They were also obliged to defend the colony except in the case of an English attack. In that eventuality, the king's subjects should "neither directly nor indirectly assist" an invading English force and should voluntarily submit themselves as prisoners of the governor if he so required.[24] The third article confirmed the estates of "all persons whatsoever, and of what nation soever, whether they be English, Jews etc. that at present do personally inhabit Suriname with their families." However, it also stipulated that Zeeland would confiscate the estates of "all those that do not live in Suriname," even if they had representatives in the colony.[25]

The remainder of the articles largely accorded with the colonists' initial proposals. Current inhabitants had the right to sell their land and leave Suriname with their movable property, including the people whom they held as chattel. They were not to be detained by prior debts, which were to be settled under the supervision of appointed commissioners. Those who were willing to take a chance under Dutch rule could leave with their estates at a later date. They would be permitted to sell their holdings, which the governor should ensure that they could transport "at moderate freight."[26]

The English were to be able to elect their own ministers. Inhabitants of all nations were to "have free liberty of conscience in matters of religion" if doing so was "not inconsistent with the government" and were to have "equal privileges" with the Dutch.[27] While Dutch law held sway, all "acts, laws and declarations" were to be published in both Dutch and English. A colonist had the right to keep arms in order "to keep his negroes in awe" and to defend against "Indians" and "wild beasts." An inventory was to be made of all "the inhabitants, slaves, cattle, coppers etc." in the colony, as well as a "list of the Christian and Hebrew inhabitants . . . in every division." Other articles affirmed the right of colonists to fish, catch turtles, cut specklewood, and trade with indigenous people.[28]

Many of the provisions of the articles mirrored those that were negotiated between the English and the Dutch after the surrender of New Netherland in

1664. These also protected the property of the people submitting to the conquering power. They allowed Dutch colonists to depart with their goods although they limited the right to do so to within six months of the articles going into effect. Colonists were to take an oath of allegiance to the king, and anyone who did so was to be considered a "free denizen" and could trade "as freely as any Englishman" with the king's other dominions. Dutch colonists, like English subjects in Suriname, were also to "enjoy the liberty of their conscience in church discipline as formerly."[29] However, Suriname's articles, unlike those of New Netherland, envisioned a society in which the English and Dutch would "cohabit" as communities living side by side. In doing so they drew on the existing English experience in Suriname, where English and Jews had lived together as subjects, as well, perhaps, on the precedent of the Dutch takeover of territory in Brazil.[30]

From Conquest to Evacuation

The conquest led to the first wave of English departures from Suriname, after a brief period when Henry Willoughby, son of Barbados's governor William (the successor to his brother Francis), retook the colony in October 1667. The Willoughbys had installed a new governor, James Banister. However, the English were forced to hand Suriname back to the Dutch due to the Treaty of Breda's stipulation that England and the United Provinces recognize territories as held on 10/20 May 1667.[31] In February 1668 the Crown ordered its subjects to leave Suriname.[32] After leading the destruction of some of the colony's infrastructure, Willoughby transported the wealthiest English settlers, sixty-seven in all, to Antigua. His party also left with 412 slaves and much valuable property.[33] However, the majority of colonists remained behind, either under duress or simply because they lacked the means to leave.[34]

The Dutch were back in control by April 1668.[35] James Banister, Suriname's final English governor, was among those who stayed and took the oath of allegiance to Zeeland, as required by the articles of capitulation. However, the Willoughbys had instructed him to try to convince the rest of the English to leave. Suspicious that he might be fomenting unrest, Crijnssen sent him to Zeeland as a prisoner that July. Charles II intervened and he was soon freed.[36]

Suriname's new Dutch rulers needed as many English as possible to remain for the same reason that the English had invited Jews to settle in 1665: to ensure the colony's survival. When they invaded in March 1667, Suriname had perhaps between one thousand and fifteen hundred English Christian colonists and two hundred Jews. Of these, Byam reported around five hundred "officers and soldiers," with no more than three hundred in fighting shape.[37] The population fell after the invasion, presumably reflecting the flight of some colonists, down to four hundred male Europeans in October 1667. There were around three thousand slaves in the colony during the same year.[38] A May 1668 Dutch source listed, according to Alison Games, "300 Christian and Jewish children and adults, of whom 69 were men" and 714 enslaved adult males, although she notes that this was probably an undercount.[39] Despite these declining numbers, by April 1670 Governor Philip Julius Lichtenberg reported that Suriname was in good condition, with the majority of English inhabitants remaining. Rumors that "all had affection to go off" were unfounded. None of the respectable English inhabitants were inclined to leave and many remained bound by debt. With God's blessing the colony would soon flourish.[40]

The colony's English subjects, which according to the 1665 "Grant of Privileges" included Jews as well as Christians, were caught between the prospect of life in a Dutch territory and the risks of moving elsewhere. Despite the governor's assessment that most remained tied to Suriname, after only a few years under Dutch rule the majority opted to leave. Their decision to do so was enabled by two evacuation missions, which were organized by the Crown in 1671 and 1675, with most leaving during the second attempt. Neither mission went smoothly. The colonists who tried to leave faced the obstacle not only of their debts but also of disagreements between the English and Dutch over who counted as a subject of the king.[41]

Major James Banister, the former governor, commanded the first attempt to evacuate English subjects, arriving in Suriname on 9 July 1671.[42] Crijnssen's successor as governor, Philip Julius Lichtenberg, had feared his return, even making plans to defend the colony in the event he appeared willing to use force. The English colonists, meanwhile, had been divided about how to proceed, although as time passed most seem to have given up on the prospect of leaving.[43] Yet despite Lichtenberg's fears, Banister did not come to seize the colony. The Crown had already ceded it with the Treaty of Breda, while the Barbadian elite now looked elsewhere, to other islands in the Caribbean and to Carolina. Jamaica now held Charles II's attention and would soon become the home of most of Suriname's remaining English.[44]

Banister's party spent three acrimonious months in the territory, locked in negotiations with its Dutch hosts regarding the settling of English debts. However, the mission failed to secure the release of all but the poorest colonists: Banister reported the evacuation of 105 families and a total of 517 people, with enslaved workers probably constituting a majority.[45] Weighing anchor in early March, the delegation's ships were seen off by most English subjects "of any accompt in the colony, with their wives."⁴⁶ Writing to the king from Jamaica on 8 April 1671, Banister blamed his abandonment of over half the English population on inadequate shipping and the "perverseness of the governor." The Dutch, he suggested, "do well know that that colony is broke if all the English go off."⁴⁷

Included with Banister's letter to the king was a petition from fifty-six of the remaining English colonists asking the Crown to secure their removal.⁴⁸ They presented themselves as the backbone of the colony, the welfare of which "consists in the [Dutch] detaining the intelligent and the industrious planter of whom they have few of their own nation." With many having sold their plantations, the petitioners, expecting evacuation, had run up "extraordinary expenses," becoming "so deeply indebted to the Dutch, that without apparent ruin . . . it was altogether at this time impossible to remove." They asked the Crown to provide two more ships to secure their departure. The colonists would then be able to sell their remaining estates which, with the yield provided by the crops they had planted, would allow them to settle their debts and begin anew in Jamaica.⁴⁹

Not all English inhabitants opted to leave Suriname. Ten colonists with English names signed an 11 March 1671 petition to the Zeeland States proposing measures to improve the state of the colony (along with thirty-five Dutch and Jewish signatories), suggesting that they remained invested in the territory's future. At least two of the English petitioners seem to have hedged their bet: William Cowell and John Venman had also signed the petition to the king requesting transportation to Jamaica.⁵⁰

The proposal of the English planters for evacuation received the endorsement of the Council for Foreign Plantations in August 1671.⁵¹ However, the new attempt did not take place until after the end of the Third Anglo-Dutch War, which broke out in 1672. The conflict, which stemmed from a joint Anglo-French desire to curb the power of the Dutch Republic, proved to be a relative disaster for England, depleting English commercial activity in both Europe and the Americas.⁵² The Treaty of Westminster, which formally ended the war in February 1674, explicitly set the stage for another evacuation of English subjects from Suriname. Recognizing that tensions surrounding the 1667 Articles of Capitulation had "contributed much to the late misunderstanding," its fifth article stipulated that their provisions now be executed "without any manner of tergiversation or equivocation." It was agreed that the king had the right to send a mission to Suriname to enquire into the state of his subjects. After arranging a time for their evacuation, the English could then dispatch vessels to carry them away with "their goods and slaves."⁵³

The End of Expansive English Subjecthood in Suriname

The new mission finally took place in 1675. Like the prior attempt four years earlier, it became mired in contention between the English and the Dutch. Yet this time the sticking point became the scope of English subjecthood. Should the English evacuation effort transport all those who were counted as subjects before the Dutch conquest? If so, the English ships could leave with the colony's Jews, who were English subjects according to the 1665 "Grant of Privileges." Or, as the Dutch maintained, did the king's ships only have a right to transport colonists who were ethnically English, or at least from the British Isles? The episode exposed competing definitions of subjecthood, nationality, and the boundary between the two concepts. In its aftermath, the scope of who counted as an English subject in Suriname narrowed substantially.

The Crown's directions to the English delegation defined in simple terms who was to be transported, referring to evacuees as an undifferentiated body of the king's subjects. In a letter signed on 28 March 1675, Charles II gave authority to three commissioners, Edward Cranfield, Richard Dickenson, and Mark Brent, to secure the removal of his subjects from Suriname. They were to engage in a "full and entire execution" of the 1667 Articles of Capitulation, subsequent articles of 1668, and the 1674 Treaty of Westminster.[54] The previous October the Council of Trade and Plantations had estimated the people to be removed at three hundred English settlers and between eleven hundred and twelve hundred slaves.[55]

Writing to the Zeeland States ahead of the arrival of the English commissioners, Suriname's governor, who was now Pieter Versterre, expressed fears not only that the English might leave but also of the exodus of the Jewish and Dutch nations. He reported the arrival from London of an advance vessel, the *Henry and Sarah*, carrying "an English person named Johan Frost" charged with making a "list of the voluntarily departing English." While many settlers were reluctant to declare their intentions before the arrival of the main delegation, Versterre estimated that out of 120 English (not counting women and children), around 100 would leave, with the others forced to stay only because of the difficulty of selling their estates. The "Jewish nation," meanwhile, planned to send two deputies to Jamaica with the English in order to see what privileges they could negotiate from the colony's governor. And rumors that Holland would take Tobago appeared to offer a possible destination for the Dutch. In short, he wrote, you "would not believe how weak this colony shall be of white inhabitants, when the English nation will have departed."[56]

The language of nationhood present in Versterre's letter, along with the concept of subjecthood, became central to the ensuing Anglo-Dutch negotiations.

By the 1670s Suriname's free inhabitants would probably have recognized each other primarily as members of the English, Dutch, and Hebrew nations while also distinguishing between each other on religious grounds, as Jews and Christians. The term *nation*, as found in the "Grant of Privileges" and 1667 Articles of Capitulation, was long-established in European discourse, having been applied to communities of resident aliens and present in self-identification, including by Jews. Sephardim used it to designate a shared Portuguese background and described themselves as the "Hebrew nation" in their own documents.[57] Versterre also used the term *white*, in contrast to the colony's enslaved Africans and indigenous inhabitants. Unlike in Barbados, the right of Suriname's Jews to hold people as slaves went unquestioned in the late seventeenth century, suggesting that they benefited fully from the protections that "whiteness" conferred.[58] Yet although subjecthood, nationality, religion, and color acted in concert to delineate sameness and difference, for the English and Dutch it was the relationship between subjecthood and nationality that proved to be the most fraught.[59]

The English delegation made landfall at Paramaribo on 4 June 1675. In their initial negotiations, both sides echoed earlier usage by speaking of three nations residing in the colony, the English, Dutch, and Hebrew. According to Cranfield's narrative, Versterre received his party "with civility." By June 10 the governor and the three English commissioners had agreed on a process by which the three nations would settle their debts. In a joint "publication" they ordered that the "Dutch, Hebrew, and English nation[s] . . . draw their accounts . . . which are between themselves, discounting one debt with another as much as possible may be." It also gave notice that the English delegation would remain in the colony for no more than four or five weeks.[60]

In a 9 June letter to the colonists the commissioners promised special incentives for settlement in Jamaica. If the evacuees chose the island as their new home, they would each receive twice the land usually allotted to planters, taking into consideration the number of slaves as well as of free colonists. They would also be provided with aid until they became self-sufficient. The letter instructed the colonists to repair as soon as possible to the ship *America*, where the commissioners would compile a list of their names and the number of their slaves, allowing sufficient time for the settlement of any differences with the Dutch.[61]

According to Cranfield, Suriname's Jews initially raised the idea of leaving with the English mission.[62] He wrote in his report that "the Jews that were inhabitants at the time of the surrender repaired to us and demanded transportation with His Majesty's subjects." The colony's governor immediately opposed the idea. On hearing of the request, Versterre issued an order preventing Jews from departing on the English ships, "telling them his orders from the States was [sic] only to suffer the English to go." The English commissioners, in turn, responded by intervening with the governor on behalf of the Jews, arguing that his attempts to prevent their removal violated the articles of surrender. Because the Jews "had no particular capitulations," the commissioners "presumed they were to have equal benefit of the articles with the English."[63]

Negotiations between the English and the Dutch, according to the commissioners' account, now turned from the settlement of debts to a dispute about the relationship between subjecthood and nationality. The conflict hinged on whether the term *subject* designated only the English nation or was a more general term of allegiance applying to all who fell under the sovereignty of Charles II. In responding to the commissioners' complaint that the Dutch were violating the articles of capitulation, the governor replied that "the fifth article of the late treaty [of Westminster] made mention only of the English removing in his majesty's ships." As evidence for this claim he produced "the articles in Dutch." The English commissioners, in turn, responded by rejecting both the Dutch text and the governor's equation of subjecthood with nationality. Instead they drew on the composite nature of British monarchy, in which allegiance to the Crown transcended individual nationality. Declaring that they refused "to be governed by Dutch translation," they produced "the original in Latin," which "made mention of the word subject . . . which the Jews were to his Majesty before the Articles of Surrender." Moreover, they stated, if the "words subjects [sic] be not allowed to be a general word of comprehension the Scotch and Irish may be detained as reasonably as the Jews." Thus, while Jews were members of the Hebrew nation, they were, like the Irish and the Scots, also full subjects of the Crown, with the same right to evacuation as the English themselves.[64]

Governor Versterre's account of these events, which was sent to Zeeland the following December, presents a picture of English dishonesty and ill-intent, with the commissioners having claimed Suriname's Jews in order to hasten the destruction of the colony. The only echo of the debate about subjecthood and nationality present in the English account is a brief reference to "those of the English nation . . . among which we judged the Scottish and the Irish were also included." The commissioners' claim to Suriname's Jews was a "new pretense," which was made after they had agreed to deal only with English settlers. While their initial aims endangered the colony, the inclusion of Jews would ensure its ruin. These actions were a direct result of royal policy: the king would be satisfied with nothing less than "the delivery of the whole colony." The commissioners' behavior, Versterre wrote, showed the fundamental duplicity of the English: "I judge an honest man very unlucky who must have to deal with that nation."[65]

To the commissioners, Governor Versterre's refusal to allow Jewish subjects to leave brazenly violated the articles of capitulation, a fact also true of his unwillingness to let the English leave with their indigenous servants. According to Cranfield's account, after some "free Indians" (probably local Kalinago or Lokono people) "came voluntarily on board" the English ships, Versterre had demanded their immediate return. Acting at his behest and against the wishes of their countrymen, the commissioners had ordered the ships' masters not to allow their transportation. No indigenous people were to leave the colony on English ships, with the exception of "one free Indian belonging to Mr. Arthur Norris, which the governor gave his consent thereunto."[66] This reluctant order caused "great discontents" among the English. The "masters of the Indians" subsequently demanded that the commissioners "protest against the governor for his injurious detention of them, they having for many years inhabited amongst them as their menial servants." The articles, they asserted, allowed such servants to be removed with their English masters.[67]

Versterre's own account told a different story. He had acted to prevent the removal of the indigenous servants out of concern for the safety of the colony, which was endangered by their people's fears of enslavement by the English. Some of them had approached him on the day the English were due to set sail, expressing concern that the English had persuaded thirty of their number to board their vessels. Yet the English claim that the indigenous servants were members of their families was based solely on the fact that they had occasionally fished or hunted for them. Moreover, their attempt to take them along when they sailed posed a grave danger. While the removal of even a hundred would be "of little harm or benefit" in and of itself, it would provoke a catastrophic response from those who remained. The "Indians" were, he wrote, "a people without reason," who would judge that the Dutch had sold "their friends or children" into slavery. This would, in turn, provoke them to respond with "disasters, murders, fires and robberies."[68] Versterre's fears were well grounded even if his prejudices were not. By 1678 the colony would be at full-scale war with Suriname's indigenous people.[69]

Frustrated by Versterre's actions, the English commissioners responded with a written protest condemning what was, from their perspective, his failure to abide by agreements with the English Crown and the orders of the States General. He had "given a flat denial concerning the removal of the Hebrew nation and free Indians that are domestic and belonging to his Majesty's subjects, having lived for many years in their families." This was despite the fact that, on their part, the commissioners had used "all diligence and earnestness possible" to secure the right of "all that were inhabitants in the time of the surrender" to depart with their estates, "as also the free Indians." The failure to observe the "articles of surrender and treaties of peace" lay entirely on the side of the Dutch, "to the infinite prejudice and hindrance of the Hebrew nation."[70] When the governor responded by suggesting that the two sides sign an "instrument" acknowledging all that they had managed to agree to, the English refused. According to Cranfield, "We thought it not reasonable to sign any stipulations, the Jews being, by the capitulation of surrender, in the same condition as his Majesty's natural born subjects."[71]

The commissioners took their final leave of the governor on 12 August 1675. That day the English colonists unanimously chose Jamaica as their destination, eschewing the king's offer of passage to other English colonies.[72] In a petition presented to Cranfield and his colleagues, they declared that there was no other island "more proper and suitable to our present condition." Their request contained twenty-nine signatures, none with identifiably Jewish names.[73] The English ships *Hercules* and *America* left the mouth of the Suriname River two days later. On 8 September, following "a tedious passage occasioned by calms, currents and contrary winds," the commissioners made landfall in Jamaica, after which they delivered the king's letter "in favor of his subjects" to the colony's governor. Along with the *Hercules* and the *America*, one other vessel, the *Henry and Sarah*, had made the journey, arriving during the previous week. By the end of September all the ships had been unloaded and the mission was complete.[74]

The 1675 mission carried away most of the English colonists, who numbered 250 in total. It also transported almost a thousand enslaved workers. While the ships seem to have sailed with only two Jewish passengers, they managed to carry off a number of indigenous people.[75] One English colonist brought "three free Indians in his sloop," an act that caused the commissioners to fear that the Dutch might seek damages.[76] Others took members of the indigenous population as chattel. While the list of people transported on the *Hercules* and *America* only differentiated between the free and the enslaved, that for the *Henry and Sarah* went further, listing "31 Indians" as well as "120 negroes." As Justin Roberts notes, the vessel's free passengers had fewer slaves per family than those of the other two ships, suggesting that "these apparently less prosperous people may have had a higher proportion of Native slaves."[77]

After 1675 only a small number of people of English ethnicity remained in the colony, and they soon dwindled to a tiny population. In what appears to have been the last attempt to evacuate the Crown's subjects from Suriname, a 1680 mission succeeded in transporting 102 people, "blacks and whites," to Antigua (the exact number of English is unclear).[78] According to one list, the effort left behind 39 English settlers with 212 slaves.[79] However, their numbers rapidly shrank: there were only 15 English men in the colony by 1683–84.[80]

CHAPTER 2

Suriname's Jews, meanwhile, stopped claiming English rights and privileges, a process that for some had likely started after the Dutch conquest. According to Cranfield, the Jews who had initially demanded transportation in 1675 were those who had been "inhabitants at the time of the surrender."[81] Out of a total Jewish population of no more than 250 (roughly equal in number to the colony's Dutch inhabitants), it seems that roughly ten families had asked to be evacuated. If new migrants had joined the settlement since 1667, some members of the community would have had no memory or experience of English rule. Even before 1675 a number of Surinamese Jews might well have begun to throw their lot in with the Dutch.[82]

Some Jews who had been left behind by Cranfield's ships continued to assert subject status for a short time after 1675, holding out hope that they might find a way to English territory. The final list of passengers who were successfully removed to Jamaica was accompanied by the names of ten "persons of the Hebrew nation" who had been prevented from departing by the Dutch. They requested another opportunity to leave with their 322 slaves.[83] In February 1676 the Privy Council received a petition from two of those listed, Aron da Silva and Isaac Perera, complaining that the Dutch continued to prevent the king's Jewish subjects from leaving Suriname. While the council endorsed their removal to Jamaica, there is no clear evidence of their successful departure and no indication that any Jews were evacuated to Antigua in 1680.[84]

Suriname's Jews remained and thrived under Dutch rule. After 1675 the colony's capital moved downriver to Paramaribo while the center of the Jewish community shifted to the village of Jodensavanne. Established in 1685 near the Suriname River, not far from the site of the English capital Torarica, the village consisted of land given by Jewish planter Samuel Nassy, augmented by a gift from the governor. Soon thereafter, one Dutch traveler observed that the settlement was about half the size of Paramaribo, which had about fifty or sixty houses. By the 1690s around 575 Jews lived in Suriname, comprising "one third of the colony's white population." It is probably safe to assume that none claimed English subjecthood, which was a status that no longer made strategic sense for Jewish inhabitants of a Dutch territory.[85]

The 1675 evacuation ended the expansive version of English subjecthood that had existed in Suriname since the issuance of the 1665 "Grant of Privileges." Since the time of the Dutch conquest, colonists had confronted the question of whether it was worth staying. Facing an invading force, some had embraced Dutch rule while others (the wealthiest) fled Suriname. The 1667 Articles of Capitulation had recognized the communal rights of the English nation, although they were silent on whether Jews counted as subjects of the king.

Within a few years the majority of English colonists no longer saw a future under Dutch rule, choosing instead to accept the Crown's offer of transportation. Whether out of affinity or pragmatism, at least ten Jewish families did the same, claiming the protections of subjecthood. The resulting conflict between the English commissioners and Suriname's governor over who could leave exposed the moment at which the scope of subjecthood began to narrow in the colony.

In debating the boundary between subjecthood and nationality, both sides also grappled with Britishness, which the colonial context had thrown into relief. Each party knew that Jews were not the only non-English subjects of England's king. While Cranfield's delegation used the peoples of Britain's three kingdoms as evidence that subjecthood and nationality were separate concepts, Governor Versterre conflated the two, subsuming Scots and Irish into the category of English. If this counts as a British moment in Suriname it was a fleeting one. In the decades after 1675, the colony's tiny English and Scottish population (the number of Irish is unclear) pursued their own interests without communal cohesion. Suriname had become a place where the free population was largely Christian and Jewish and the vast majority of Christians were Dutch.[86]

Staying English after the English Departure: The Case of Jeronimy Clifford

With most of the ethnic English having departed and the colony's Jews abandoning subject status, any remaining English people had to make their way in a radically new context. They now formed a tiny minority among Dutch and Jewish colonists and an enslaved African majority. A 1684 census counted 811 European men, women, and children (579 Christians and 232 Jews) living among 4,137 African slaves and 144 enslaved indigenous people.[87] This count did not differentiate between Dutch and English, presumably because the English no longer formed a significant community. In 1683–1684 there seem to have been just 15 English men in Suriname.[88] The proportion of slaves to settlers had also changed dramatically from the colony's early days, from a near-equal ratio in the period of English rule to a majority of 80 percent enslaved in 1684.[89]

Most English colonists chose to live quietly, leaving few traces. One, however—Jeronimy Clifford—took another course, repeatedly clashing with the colony's government. Unlike the handful of other remaining English, Clifford had left in 1675, only to return to Suriname.[90] The paper trail generated by his obstreperous behavior shows the strategies he used to cling to English status after the departure of most of his compatriots. For Clifford, security as an English subject in Suriname rested in power as a landowner, slaveholder, and patriarch. Yet at all times he maintained the option of leaving for English territory. The articles of capitulation apparently underwrote Clifford's sense of what it meant to stay English in the Dutch colony, not least by continuing to guarantee the right to leave with the fruits of its soil. Suriname's government, meanwhile, responded as if the agreement were redundant, given that most of the English had left. In later years, when they framed their respective narratives of these years of conflict, both Clifford and the Dutch authorities would state these positions explicitly.[91]

The list of English subjects who left Suriname for Jamaica with the 1675 evacuation mission includes an entry for Andrew Clifford, who was traveling with his wife, Alice, and his eighteen year-old son, Jeronimy.[92] Unlike most of their fellow colonists, the family left without enslaved workers. The 250 departing English colonists took 981 slaves with them, accompanying 69 out of the 108 individuals or families on the passenger list, in numbers ranging from 1 or 2 to as many as 80.[93] If control over enslaved labor was a measure of wealth, then the Cliffords were among the poorest of the English evacuees.

The Clifford family, however, seems not to have lived in poverty. Rather, their condition on leaving was the result of a sale gone wrong. Andrew Clifford had sold his estate to a man named Roland Simpson but had sailed from Suriname with Simpson still owing him £240.[94] Simpson was a thorn in the side of a number of colonists and of the English evacuation delegation as well. Commissioner Edward Cranfield named him as the reason why a number of planters had been unable to leave, accusing him of having "enriched himself during the late wars by deserting the English interest."[95] In a June 1676 letter he stated that the Cliffords were "now miserable in Jamaica" due to Simpson's failure to pay the £240 he owed. Two other planters, William Pringall and Henry MacKintosh, complained that they had been forced to remain in Suriname due to a contract made with Simpson.[96] The Cliffords, it seems, had been lucky to make it out of the colony despite Simpson's machinations.

Andrew Clifford left Suriname with a bill of exchange from Simpson for his plantation, which was redeemable in London. The transaction fell through, however, forcing his return to Suriname. According to his son Jeronimy, writing later, the bill was to be drawn on "one John Limbrey, then gentleman to the Earl of Mu[l]grave, now Duke of Buckingham," who resided in London. However, after sailing from Jamaica to England they found that Limbrey "would neither accept nor pay the said bill of exchange." The elder Clifford returned to Suriname in 1676 in order to resolve the matter.[97] The younger Clifford followed a few years later, resettling in the colony early in the next decade.

Jeronimy Clifford later wrote that the failed sale was due to a conspiracy between Suriname's governor and Roland Simpson. His father was the colony's "principal millwright and wheelwright," essential skills that compelled the governor to force his return. At the governor's request, Simpson had sent word to John Limbrey in London, instructing him to refuse to accept the bill of exchange that he had given Andrew Clifford for his estate. This made the elder Clifford return to the colony to either compel Simpson to pay the bill or "have his plantation restored him," efforts that Suriname's government frustrated until 1684.[98] Whatever his actual involvement, Limbrey may have been a former planter in Suriname: a 1667 map of the colony includes the name "Limbry" in the southern reaches of settlement.[99]

The circumstances of the Cliffords' departure and subsequent return had long-lasting implications for the security of their property and their rights as English subjects in the colony. Regardless of whether Jeronimy Clifford's claim of a conspiracy was true, the fact that they had left with the 1675 evacuees only to return raised troubling questions about their position. According to the 1667 Articles of Capitulation, any English colonist remaining after the Dutch conquest had the "power to sell his estate." The governor was to ensure "that he be transported [out of the colony] at moderate freight," along with his property.[100] But what about the status of returning English colonists? Were they still covered by the articles or did they arrive as new immigrants, fully bound by the mercantilist restrictions of Suriname's charter?[101]

These questions lie at the core both of Clifford's friction with the colonial authorities and with his long-running dispute with the Dutch after he returned to England in 1696. From then until his death in 1737, he pressed for restitution for his tribulations with the colony's government and for property that he had to leave behind. Most of what we know about Clifford's life in Suriname comes from sources generated by these later efforts. These include copies of documents from his time in the colony as well as texts authored later, both by Clifford himself and by his Dutch adversaries. Together they tell a story that, while partial, shows the tensions that resulted from Clifford's adamant assertions of his ongoing rights as an English subject.

Clifford had no doubt that the articles still applied to him and his father even though they had left in 1675. Over subsequent years he repeatedly argued that the 1667 agreement had given him the right to sell his estate and leave with his movable goods at any point in the future. He insisted that although he and his father had made several voyages to Europe, they had never abandoned the colony, where they had continuously maintained property. As he wrote in 1701, this meant that their departure could "be no argument to bar us from the benefit of the Articles of Capitulation." Both father and son had "liberty to go out and come into Suriname, as long as we live."[102] Responding to his later efforts for compensation, the Dutch States General disputed this interpretation. Although Clifford was "a born Englishman," the fact that he and his father had left with the other English settlers meant that they had fulfilled the contents of the 1667 capitulation.[103] As a result, on his return to Suriname he should "be considered alike with all strangers that established themselves in Suriname and consequently owned as a subject of this state." As far as the Dutch were concerned, he had none of the special rights conferred on English colonists at the time of Suriname's conquest by Crijnssen's fleet.[104]

Clifford's Marriage to Dorothy Matson and Corcabo's Disputed Origins

This disagreement about Clifford's status following his return is further complicated by contrasting accounts of his time away, his marriage, and the provenance of his plantation, Corcabo. Clifford gained the bulk of his estate through his marriage to a woman named Dorothy Matson. His account of their relationship diverges from that of the States General about the location of their wedding, the origins of her property, and indeed her own presumed nationality. These differences either bolster or undermine Clifford's own status as a landowner in Suriname.

The story is as much Dorothy Matson's as it is Clifford's. In order to claim his place as a planter in the colony, Clifford asserted control over land that she had brought into the marriage, acting as if he had rights akin to those conferred by English coverture. His efforts clashed with Dutch marital law, which stipulated joint ownership. Matson fought to maintain control over the property. The ensuing conflict entangled the couple with Suriname's authorities, leading to restrictions on the estate. Regardless of whether Matson was English or Dutch—her nationality remains unclear—her resistance to Clifford's efforts eroded his own expansive assertions of the rights of an English subject in a Dutch colony.

Clifford first met Matson on board a ship. As he later told the story, before returning to Suriname his father had apprenticed him to a surgeon, in whose service he had made several voyages at sea, "both of men of war and merchantmen." However, "his master coming to fail before his time was fully expired," he decided to join his father in Suriname. He was subsequently employed as a surgeon aboard the ship of one Samuel Lodge, which sailed for Guinea "and from thence to Suriname with negro slaves." On arriving in the colony in 1682, he found that his father had returned to England to retrieve papers related to the disputed bill of exchange. Clifford then crossed the Atlantic once more, on a vessel called the *Antigua Merchant*, bound for Amsterdam. On board he met a couple, Dorothy Matson and Charles Meersman. After Meersman died during the voyage, Clifford "courted his widow," marrying her in London.[105] The States General's account differs in some minor details. Here Samuel Lodge was "an interloper," on whose ship Clifford first returned to Suriname. After Lodge decided to settle in the colony, Clifford found another position as a ship's surgeon on a vessel bound for Zeeland. He met Matson en route and won her hand, marrying her in Zeeland after the ship made landfall rather than in London.[106]

The *Trans-Atlantic Slave Trade Database* loosely corroborates some aspects of Clifford's account. It lists Samuel Lodge as the captain of the Royal Africa Company ship the *Wellcome*, which arrived in Barbados in May 1681 with a human cargo of 162, the survivors of 227 people who had been forced onboard at Calabar. In 1683 a ship called the *Welvaren* docked in Suriname; it was co-captained by one Samuel Engelsman (Englishman), who may have been the same person. It had arrived from Texel, after stopping at the Bight of Benin to take on 467 enslaved Africans, 73 of whom died during the passage. While the database does not list Clifford's Amsterdam-bound voyage, an English ship called the *Antigua Merchant* was active around the same time, disembarking 195 slaves, the survivors of a group of 243, in Antigua in 1677.[107]

The States General was wrong, at least, about where the couple married. The wedding took place, as Clifford himself claimed, on 2 August 1683 (Old Style) "at the little or Trinity Minories in London . . . not in the province of Zeeland," as the States had falsely declared.[108] This is confirmed by the parish's register, which contains a 2 August 1683 entry for "Jeronimy Cliffard bachelor and Dorothie Masman widow both of St. Mary Whitechapel, married by Mr. Weston."[109] Other details, however, are harder to untangle, and the marriage record itself only corroborates the location of the couple's wedding, especially as neither Clifford or Matson seem to have spent much time in Whitechapel. The listing of Matson's name as "Masman" could be a corruption of "Meersman," the surname of Clifford's predecessor as her husband. However, in most other sources she appears as "Matson" or "Madson" and not as "Dorothy Clifford." This might reflect the Dutch practice of women retaining their original last names after marriage, with "Matson" being her maiden name. If so, this may provide circumstantial evidence that she was, in fact, Dutch. Matson also seems to have had a sister in Suriname who was married to a Dutch man named Thomas Baroen, although no sources appear to list her name or place of origin.[110]

In Clifford's telling, Matson was unequivocally English, with property in Suriname that also originated from a subject of the English king. She had been born in Teckell, in Yorkshire (possibly modern-day Tickhill), and had traveled to Suriname in 1665. Two years later she married an Irishman, Manus Clark, who was "then the sole owner of the plantation named Corcabo." When he died he "gave her all he had[,] ... particularly the aforesaid plantation, with all the slaves, cattle, and other appurtenances thereunto belonging," except for one enslaved man, who received manumission.[111] In 1668 she then married one Roland Corbitt, an English subject, who was born in Yorkshire "of an English father and a Brabant mother." Their union made him "entitled to the plantation named Corcabo." The following year Corbitt partnered with Pieter Versterre, the former governor of Suriname, "for the [half] of the said plantation," although he remained in "whole management of the same." With Versterre's assistance the plantation grew to "about one hundred slaves." He then dissolved the partnership, "for which purpose he made one other plantation named Mattappy." Corbitt died in 1675, and the following year Matson married one Abraham Schoors, a Zeeland surgeon who worked as a director on another estate. Schoors, by his marriage to Matson, was now "entitled to the half of both the plantations named Corcabo and Mattappy." He bequeathed his land to her on his death, which occurred in 1681.[112]

Until this point, according to Clifford, Matson was simply a conduit for the passage of property between her various husbands. With her next marriage, however, she took active measures to protect her estate. Before she and the Zeeland-born Charles Meersman married in 1682 they signed a prenuptial contract stipulating that "he should have no power over her estate." This agreement allowed Meersman to make use of half of her land's "profit or interest" while they were married. However, Matson was "acquitted from paying any debts" contracted by her new husband "either before or after marriage." As a result, Clifford wrote, "It appears that Meersman never was in the least entitled to either of the plantations named Corcabo and Mattappy, nor to any part of his wife's estate." Matson's fourth husband died within a year of the wedding. Their prenuptial agreement meant that when Clifford married her in London in 1683, she was "in possession of her own estate," although "not by virtue of her husband Meersman['s] will."[113] According to Clifford, she then signed a very different prenuptial contract with him, in which she gave him "the full power of her whole estate" with the exception of some money "for her own disposal." This meant that he had "full power either to sell or transport" what was now his own plantation, "with or without his wife's consent."[114]

The account of the States General tells a very different story, in which Matson's property was of Dutch origin, as she herself may have been, and in which Clifford lacked sole title to Corcabo. Matson's former husband, Charles

Meersman, had been born a subject of the United Provinces, and her two previous husbands, Abraham Schoors and Roland Corbitt, were also Dutch. She had gained her estate partly through her marriage to Corbitt and partly in a partnership the couple had had with Hendrina van Hardenbergh, Pieter Versterre's widow. By the time Clifford returned to Suriname with Matson, Van Hardenbergh had married one Harman van Haagen, who, "having no liking to the said Clifford nor his manner of living," dissolved the partnership. The two parties drew lots and Clifford became owner of Corcabo "in the name of his wife," while Mattappy went to Van Haagen (the Society of Suriname's records corroborate this transaction).[115] The narrative of the States General makes no mention of Manus Clark, the Irishman who, in Clifford's version, was the original source of the plantation. The report also refers to Corcabo as "the possession of a subject of this state," perhaps implying that Matson was herself Dutch, if not by origin then at least by virtue of her many Dutch marriages.[116] It makes no mention of a prenuptial contract between Clifford and Matson.

Both Dutch and Surinamese laws regarding marital property suggest that if this account were true then Clifford might only have had joint title to the plantation. According to laws laid out in the colony in 1669, in the absence of a prenuptial contract goods were to be jointly held. In the event of death, a couple "may with testament, jointly or separately, dispose of their respective goods at will." If one or both parties died intestate, "his or her goods [were to] fall to the nearest friends and heirs of the dying."[117] This broadly accorded with laws in the United Provinces, which also stipulated the common ownership of marital goods. However, property, while jointly owned, was subject to varying degrees of male control. In Holland men had the right to "both the management and the disposal of the common estate." In practice this approached something like the English legal norm of coverture: "a husband . . . could sell both his wife's movable and immovable property," even without her permission, while she lost the right to dispose of her estate. However, in other Dutch provinces the male right to sell marital property only applied to the wife's movable goods. Throughout the Netherlands, as in Suriname, all these arrangements could be modified by prenuptial agreements.[118]

Clifford, however, presented himself as having lawfully acquired clear title to his own plantation, which he had gained by marrying an English woman. She, in turn, had originally inherited the land by virtue of her marriage to an Irish subject, and her ownership had been unaffected by her various future marriages. However, according to the States General he had no independent claim to Corcabo, which he held only "in the name of his wife," whom he had married in Zeeland, "under the government of their High and Mighties." She had, in turn, gained title to the land from one of her three previous husbands, who were all Dutch, and through partnership with the widow of a former governor of the colony. The plantation therefore "did not belong to . . . Clifford as his own right but as the right of his aforesaid wife. . . . And by consequence as the possession of a subject of this state." In short, he "had no estate of his own."[119]

Dorothy Matson lies at the center of both these accounts. Her contested status underscores the central role that widows played in the transmission of property within a patriarchal system, often between multiple husbands. It is unclear why her husbands died but her frequent remarriages probably reflect the high mortality rate caused by Suriname's hostile disease environment. Clifford was either her fourth or fifth husband, and by his account she remarried within a year of each man's death. In his version of the story each husband before Meersman gained full ownership of her property. Her prenuptial contract with Meersman then gave her sole title to the estate, whereupon another contract with Clifford ceded it entirely to him. Here Clifford asserts something resembling the English legal norm of coverture, at least for part of the story. The claims of the States General rested on the more egalitarian Dutch marital property rules, in which husbands and wives held estates in common even if in practice men exercised substantial control. While we may never know which account is accurate, Clifford's version is strikingly self-serving in its contradictions.

Matson's role as conduit for Corcabo might have been a function of either power or vulnerability. On the one hand she seems like a classic example of the "widowarchy" that was identified by Edmund Morgan in colonial Virginia. In a colony with high mortality, a gender imbalance, and greater female longevity, widows exerted power as desirable spouses by consolidating and extending property through multiple marriages.[120] The same situation pertained in Dutch colonies, including those far from the Americas. Widows in Batavia, for example, also consolidated wealth between marriages, generally remarrying soon after their husbands' deaths, which reflected a free population with more men than women.[121] And Suriname certainly had a gender imbalance: the 1684 census counted 467 white men to 185 white women (Jews and Christians), a ratio of over 2.5 men for every woman.[122] Yet while Morgan interpreted the short time between remarriage as a sign of female agency, it could also exemplify its absence. Cultural and legal norms must have made remarriage the only feasible choice for some women.[123]

Although Dorothy Matson had the option of remaining a widow, it is unclear how viable that path would have been for her. If we believe the account of the States General, Hendrina van Hardenbergh, the widow of former governor Pieter Versterre, tried to go it alone, managing her own property by entering into partnership with Matson and her then-husband Roland Corbitt. However, Van Hardenbergh, like Matson herself, soon found a new husband. It is difficult to generalize from these two examples, and the balance between vulnerability and agency in their case is hard to divine. But whether by choice, circumstance, or a combination of both, Dorothy Matson remarried in short order. And when she entered into a union with Jeronimy Clifford, she found a husband who was intent on gaining full control over her property.[124]

Suriname's administration changed around the time of Jeronimy Clifford's return to the colony, leading to the creation of institutions with which he repeatedly clashed. Zeeland had assumed responsibility for governing the territory after seizing it from the English in 1667. However, the Dutch province was eager to offload its new acquisition. It made repeated attempts to sell it, first to Stadholder William III in 1675 and then, when that effort failed, to Holland, the admiralty of Amsterdam, and to various private individuals.[125] A sale finally took place early in 1683, when Zeeland sold Suriname to the West India Company.[126] The company was unable to come up with the 260,000 guilders due for the sale and therefore sought partners for the venture. This ultimately led to the participation of the city of Amsterdam and Cornelis van Aerssen van Sommelsdijck, the scion of a wealthy Dutch family. Together the three parties formed the Society of Suriname in May 1683. The society was to govern the colony in place of the West India Company, with Van Sommelsdijck serving as governor.[127] From this point on, as G. W. van der Meiden notes, Suriname would have "the character of a proprietary colony."[128]

The sale led to an overhaul of Suriname's governance, resulting in greater oversight from the Netherlands and the establishment of new administrative bodies in the colony itself. Suriname's new charter stipulated that the governor exercised supreme authority, assisted by a "Council of Polity." This body consisted of ten of the colony's "most distinguished, wisest, and moderate" settlers serving lifelong positions, whom the governor chose from a list drawn up by all free colonists (presumably this was limited to male adults). Convened by the governor, the council met to discuss important matters, and it also exercised jurisdiction over criminal cases. A separate judicial council oversaw civil cases, also in conjunction with the governor. This was composed of six counselors who were chosen for two-year terms, this time from a list drawn up by the Council of Polity. Meanwhile, the West India Company was to see to the colony's defense.[129] Over the course of more than a decade, both the governor and the council would find their moderation, if not their wisdom, tested by repeated encounters with Clifford.

Clifford's Establishment as a Planter

Following his return to Suriname, Jeronimy Clifford moved to expand control over his family's land. He did this by establishing new legal relationships with his father and his wife, both of whom left the colony a short time later. At the same time, he also made arrangements for his own permanent departure by buying land in Jamaica. These transactions provide a detailed snapshot of Corcabo in the mid-1680s while showing the shifting property relations between family members. And in the case of Dorothy Matson they do much more, suggesting that for Clifford, control over land involved control over his wife, which he attained through physical force.

The choices made by the members of the Clifford family reveal some of their priorities. In buying land in Jamaica and aiming to move his estate there Jeronimy Clifford asserted rights akin to those possessed by the English who had left in 1675, which were underwritten by the 1667 Articles of Capitulation. Although he was consolidating his Surinamese estate, his ultimate goal was to move to English territory. Andrew Clifford's choice to leave also reflects an ongoing affinity for England, showing that perhaps he had only returned to resolve the disputed sale of his land. Dorothy Matson's choices, as we will see, were perhaps most complex of all, and they do little to shed light on her ambiguous nationality. Stepping out from under her domineering husband, she asserted control over the property she had brought into the marriage, and in doing so seemingly resisted both his English affinities and his patriarchal control. Yet the episode ended with her, too, moving to England, leaving Jeronimy Clifford in nominal control of Corcabo, although, due to her efforts, he was unable to dispose of the estate as he pleased.

Once Andrew Clifford had resolved the disputed bill of exchange with Roland Simpson he was free to leave for England.[130] Before his 1685 departure, Andrew Clifford gave his son full power of attorney over his estate. The nature of the elder Clifford's property is unclear. While Simpson had owed him £240 in 1675, no sources provide the name of a plantation, the Clifford name is absent from early colonial maps, and a 1680 source lists him without slaves.[131] After receiving power of attorney, Jeronimy Clifford then transferred a third of his own estate over to his father. This meant, in effect, that the younger Clifford owned less property than before but controlled more: he now owned two thirds of Corcabo, compared to his father's newly transferred third, but he controlled it all along with any land owned by Clifford senior. He was now legally in charge of the family's entire estate, with the power to "manage, sell, and transport his [father's] interest in the plantation." Taken together, the Clifford holdings in Suriname were, according to one 1701 pamphlet, "very considerable[,] . . . raising about one sixteenth part of all the sugars produced in that colony."[132]

Clifford's sale of land to his father took place on advantageous terms that seem designed to protect him from a colonial government that he viewed as hostile to his own interests. The transfer took place on 21 April 1685, ten months after the younger Clifford assumed power of attorney over his father's affairs. Meanwhile, the latter formalized his last will and testament.[133] The deed of sale valued the plantation at 580,372 pounds of sugar, making a third worth 193,457 pounds. Although Andrew Clifford would now own a third of his son's estate, the deed placed significant limitations on how he could dispose of the property. He was forbidden from selling or transporting his share of Corcabo without the consent of his son. Moreover, after his death the land was to revert back to its original owner, along with "all its appurtenances and dependents." Meanwhile, Jeronimy Clifford was to continue managing the ceded third of the plantation, including paying a salary to its directors. For this he was to receive 5,000 pounds of sugar a year from his father. This agreement was to remain in effect as long as both Cliffords were alive. Both men signed the deed in the presence of Marcus Broen, secretary of the province of Suriname Rivers, along with two witnesses.[134]

The deed of sale provides a detailed glimpse of the state of Corcabo at the time of the transfer. According to a survey the plantation was composed of 2,388 acres. The enslaved population included fifty-four "good working negro slaves," valued at 4,000 pounds of sugar each, together with one "cripple[d] negro woman" (worth 1,000 pounds of sugar), twenty-six "boys and girls children" (1,200 pounds each), one "Indian girl" (1,000 pounds), and one "Indian man" and two indigenous women (worth, collectively, 8,000 pounds). This meant that a total of eighty-five people were enslaved on Corcabo, whose lives were valued by the Cliffords as the equivalent of 257,200 pounds of sugar. The Cliffords valued their livestock in the same general range as the people who worked their land. The nine working horses were, in fact, each worth more than the able-bodied slaves, at 5,000 pounds of sugar each. Two young horses were worth 3,000 pounds each, four working oxen were worth 3,000 pounds each, and two young bulls were valued at 2,500 pounds each. The plantation's seven cows were assessed at 2,800 pounds each, with twelve calves worth 1,000 pounds each. The deed's inventory also listed Corcabo's other assets, from its mill and mill house to punts, canoes, stills, weapons, and assorted tools.[135]

With the transfer complete and his son now authorized to run his affairs, Andrew Clifford returned to England in 1685.[136] At the same time, Jeronimy Clifford was also making plans for his own departure. That year he bought land in Jamaica, on which he intended to settle.[137] Clifford also states that around the same time he received a "deed of gift" from "Mr. Oliver Hampson and Elizabeth his wife . . . for 480 acres of land in St. Elizabeth's Parish in Jamaica." The property, which had originally been "granted by patent" to Elizabeth's father, one Francis Watson, bordered the estates of former English commissioners Marcus Brandt and James Banister.[138] It is unclear why the Hampsons would have given him this land. However, the names of both Oliver Hampson and Francis Watson appear on the list of the evacuees who left Suriname in 1675.[139] The gift might, then, have been an attempt by the family of one successful evacuee to aid another in settling in Jamaica.[140]

Clifford's full autonomy as a planter also required a new legal relationship with his wife. In 1686 the couple voided their prenuptial contract, an event that the revocation agreement framed as a mutual decision. The following year Dorothy Matson left Suriname for England, never to return. Before departing she gave Clifford full power of attorney, allowing him to dispose of her property as he saw fit. But why void the prenuptial contract if, as Clifford had maintained, it already gave him full control of Corcabo? And why would Matson give Clifford power of attorney if such an act were redundant?

Behind these events lies a complex story, one in which Clifford and Matson competed for control of their marital property and in doing so appealed to law, national status, and gender roles in different ways. Clifford marshaled his power as a patriarch, shaped by English norms of coverture that led him to assume that he should have title over the property that Matson had brought into the marriage. This, he asserted, made him free to liquidate the estate and move to Jamaica. Matson, in turn, alleged that he had threatened her, beaten her, and aimed to reduce her to poverty, all in an attempt to usurp land that rightfully belonged to her. She fought back against his efforts to control Corcabo by petitioning the colonial authorities and asking them to dissolve the marriage. In doing so she charged that Clifford, as an English subject, had behaved as if the laws of the colony did not apply to him.

However, as a woman in a patriarchal society, Matson had limited options. Although Dutch marital law was more egalitarian than its English counterpart, women in the United Provinces also navigated societal inequalities and were hemmed in by cultural norms that regulated female speech and action.[141] In Suriname, as in the Netherlands, social order was at a premium, perhaps made more vital in a society with an enslaved majority, high mortality, and the many other challenges of colonial life. Matson's ability to challenge her husband ultimately depended on the authority of the colony's male governors, who were mindful of their role as custodians of stability. In responding to the couple's discord they walked a fine line between backing a patriarch and addressing charges that an English subject improperly sought to liquidate a substantial estate.

The couple had signed their prenuptial contract in Zeeland, eight days before they were married in London.[142] Clifford provides accounts of its contents that conflict with a later copy of the document. Writing in 1703, he characterized the contract as giving him "full power" over Matson's entire property, aside from a cash amount "reserved for her own disposal." It thus gave him the ability "either to sell or transport all what the government of Suriname calls his wife's estate."[143] Clifford's index entry to the agreement in his own papers summarizes it in broadly the same terms. Here he lists it as a "contract of marriage made between me and my wife wherein she reserves out of her goods only £400 sterling at her disposal and all the rest of her effects she gives over to my disposal."[144]

Yet the actual text of the prenuptial contract suggests common ownership. Sworn before witnesses and a notary public in Middelburg, it stipulated that the couple's goods be joined "for their common use between them except four hundred pounds sterling of the bride's money." This was to be reserved "for her own use to do with it what she pleases," including "the interests and profits of the same." The groom agreed never to revoke this agreement without his bride's consent. In the event of the dissolution of the marriage, she was to have the benefit both of that money and of "half of the goods and effects which are brought into commonality by them." Moreover, her four hundred pound reserve was immune from any debts contracted "before or after marriage by the said bridegroom."[145]

The agreement broadly follows norms of Dutch marital property, in which a couple's goods are jointly held, although of course this does not make them immune from male attempts at full control. However, the document is silent about Clifford's right to dispose of the marital property. It was signed in Zeeland, but it is, perhaps, telling that in his later response to the States General he rooted his "full power either to sell or transport" the property not only in the contract itself but also in "the laws of Holland."[146] This was the province where a husband had the right to sell not only his wife's movable goods, as was the case elsewhere in the United Provinces, but also her immovable property.[147] Although Clifford may have been using "Holland" as a metonym for the entire Netherlands, it may also be that he referenced the province because its laws conferred husbands with powers most closely resembling English coverture.

The subsequent annulment of the prenuptial contract also suggests that it undermined Clifford's full claim to Corcabo. On 18 July 1686 the couple appeared at the home of Hendrick van Schandell, scrivener, "in Commawina River on the plantation Penourabo," in order to revoke their agreement. In the presence of Van Schandell and two witnesses they declared their initial contract "null and void out of singular love and affections which they have for each other." It was, they announced, "both their wills and pleasure" that their prior agreement and "any part thereof shall not be observed nor fulfilled in law or otherwise." Rather, it was to "be as if the said marriage contract had never been made."[148] The revocation did not stipulate what the legal relationship between the two now became.

Dorothy Matson's Side of the Story

While the wording of the annulment indicates mutual consent, or even love, Dorothy Matson told a very different story early the following year, in which Clifford had used violence to compel her agreement. According to her account the contract's revocation was part of his larger efforts to gain full control over her estate, which he intended to transport to Jamaica. In a petition to Governor van Sommelsdijck she detailed her husband's "tyranny," alleging that he had beaten her, had threatened to kill her, and had committed infidelity.[149] Her initial hopes that the two would live together "in an easy and Christian-like manner" had been dashed.[150] She asked the governor to appoint two commissioners to hear her case and allow the dissolution of their marriage.[151]

Matson began her complaint by calling attention to Clifford's attempts to erode her property. Since the couple had settled in Suriname he had, she wrote, "on all occasions endeavored to convey my whole estate from hence to England, or to some of the English islands."[152] He had bought land in Jamaica, paying for it with her own assets, something which she disapproved of because she "should not choose to fall into an English colony." In the three years since they had been married he had transported between twenty-four and twenty-five thousand guilders to England, having "squandered away great part of it with whores and in extravagant debauchery." Matson also noted that without informing her he had "made over one third part of the Corcabo plantation" ahead of moving to Jamaica, presumably a reference to the transfer of property to his father.[153]

Clifford had, she wrote, "forcibly compelled" her "to violate and infringe certain conditions in a marriage contract." She had complied only "to sooth his tyranny in some measure." That tyranny was "daily enforced by ill usage, blows, and even with threats of murdering me if I did not acquiesce to his will in every respect." This could be confirmed by their servants, who were "as well Christians as slaves."[154] Matson accused her husband of open infidelity as well as violence. "Not content with pursuing his wild debaucheries in England," Clifford had threatened to "send for one of his mistresses here in order to insult me with her in my presence." He had subsequently acted on this threat, bringing to Corcabo a woman who had arrived "in the last English ship" and lodging her in a nearby house.[155]

Having usurped Matson's property, Clifford then took measures that would reduce her to poverty. He had given his father "115 ounces [of] plate" that belonged to her. Ahead of his planned move to Jamaica he had taken "50 or 60 hogsheads of sugar in goods for his outset" and borrowed several hundred guilders, which she would have to pay back after he left. He aimed, she wrote, to ruin her estate and plunge her into "everlasting misery."[156]

Dorothy Matson asked the governor to appoint two commissioners to whom she could state her case and requested that he annul her "unfortunate marriage." It was, she wrote, "impossible . . . to cohabit with such a tyrant any longer." She needed the commissioners because she was "totally ignorant and incapable in every respect" of defending herself in court. Matson emphasized that Clifford believed he could "do with his wife here just as he pleases" because he was "an Englishman and he is not subject to the laws and customs of this country." She also asked "that the abovementioned whore may be arrested and kept in safe custody" while proceedings were underway between her and her husband.[157] The governor concurred on 3 February 1687 and ordered the appointment of Bastian Thyssen and Gorert de Bruyn to investigate her allegations. He also ordered the arrest of "a certain woman named Mary Regland," the woman whom Matson had accused of being Clifford's mistress.[158] The authorities later identified her as "Maria Tanner, widow of John Reglens," a man whom they had previously banished from Suriname.[159]

The two commissioners, who were both members of the Councils of Polity and Justice, issued their findings in the matter four days later. They had traveled to Corcabo to interview Clifford and Matson to enquire into "the differences betwixt them." After presenting Matson with her own petition, they asked her if she understood its contents and stood by its assertions.[160] She answered that she did, "excepting that she was not beat in the time the marriage articles were dissolved, though she has often been beat before and since that time." Clifford had, moreover, sworn "with bitter imprecations and oaths . . . that if it was not then annulled she should have no peace with him."[161]

Jeronimy Clifford rejected his wife's accusations. He denied sending "money or goods" to England or its islands, having only "taken there just what he wanted." The plot of land in Jamaica had been given to him as a present by Oliver Hampson, for which he had given ten gold pieces in return. The charge that he had sent off twenty-four or twenty-five thousand guilders "in money or sugar" was false.[162] Clifford claimed to have annulled the grant of a third of his plantation to his father, although he had given him "an obligation."[163] Also, he had merely loaned his father plate and had since asked for it back. Moreover, the sugar and borrowed money that Matson had accused him of using for his departure had largely been directed toward the plantation's use, a fact he could demonstrate from the estate's accounts.[164]

Clifford denied that he had been unfaithful or that he had forced his wife to alter the terms of their marriage, which he wished to continue. Her charge that he had squandered money on "whores and debauchery" was untrue, he asserted. He acknowledged bringing Mary Regland to Corcabo on his boat after her recent arrival from Barbados, but due to "his wife's uneasiness" he had then taken her to the house of his brother-in-law, "Mr. Baroen."[165] Moreover, he had only aimed to "assist her with his advice and service," especially given that "she is his kinswoman." In an attempt to "avoid further uneasiness" he then had his slaves transport her to the fort in his boat. He denied ever having lived with her or even knowing where she had lodged in London, acknowledging only that "since her first coming to her lodgings [she] had been but once with him."[166] The breaking of his marriage contract had not taken place "by force or threats" and he would not agree to an annulment.[167] He also denied that he had ever stated that his status as an Englishman meant "he was not subject to the laws and customs of this country." Rather, he affirmed that he was "willing to submit himself" to the laws "as he ought to do."[168]

Corcabo Sequestered

Two months later Dorothy Matson retracted her allegations against Clifford, disavowing them in a 10 April 1687 letter to the governor and the Council of Polity and Justice. She claimed she had been "misled and drawn away by the ill advice of some persons who were the cause of that misunderstanding between her and her husband." Since then she had "been better informed and finds things otherways" and was "very sorry that she has complained of and against her husband to his excellency." The couple had, she said, reconciled that February "in the presence of Mr. Abraham van Vredenburgh," a member of the council. Since then they had "lived peacefully with each other." She stated that she "doth annul and make void a certain contract" that the couple had made in Van Vredenburgh's presence, revoking its contents and "all other proceedings commenced between her and her husband." Matson was, she stated, "very well satisfied and contented with her husband" and asked the governor and the council "to stop and void all proceedings made hitherto" between herself and Clifford.[169]

The authorities were faced with a dilemma. If they believed Matson's initial charges, they could protect the integrity of one of the colony's largest plantations; yet they could only do so by undermining a patriarch's authority over his wife. On the other hand, if they believed Clifford's side of the story, they then endorsed the erosion of the estate by an English subject who was apparently attempting to move its effects out of the colony.

The court (as the council referred to itself) responded by both rebuking Matson and taking measures to prevent Clifford from disposing of the couple's common property. After considering her retraction "and having further well examined her," it declared "her to be a weak and silly woman who has suffered herself to be misled and drawn away by her husband and others." At the same time, Clifford had "to the prejudice of his wife endeavored to carry her goods out of this colony," something "which the court would willingly prevent." To do so it named three commissioners to make an inventory of Corcabo, including the two men who had investigated Matson's initial complaint.[170]

The authorities professed to act in the interests of the couple's marital harmony while punishing Matson for her willfulness. The council ordered that the two "shall not transport nor diminish nor make away their estate." However, as long as Clifford and Matson would "live and correspond well together," they might make use of "the interest and produce of their plantation." It would then "leave them to the free disposal of their goods according to the law and custom of the land." This order was for Matson's own benefit, as the council was acting "for the preservation" of her "goods and willing her much joy with the reconciliation of her and her husband." However, it also condemned her for "the present and future costs" of the matter, fining her five thousand pounds of sugar to be used "towards building a new council house in Suriname." It did this because of her "forwardness and ill-nature" and "for an example to all other ill-natured women," as well as for the trouble she had caused.[171] The order was signed by Governor van Sommelsdijcke himself.

Dorothy Matson moved to England two months later, where, according to Clifford, she intended to remain for the rest of her life. According to one eighteenth-century text she died in London in 1708 "without issue."[172] Before leaving Suriname she appointed her husband as "her true and lawful attorney." The June 1687 agreement authorized him "to manage her goods," as well as Corcabo and all of its "negroes, horses, cattle, and other movables." It also gave Clifford the power to sell the plantation, to settle any debts that she owed or that were owed to her, and to transport its slaves and livestock "to any other place or island." He was empowered to prosecute any recalcitrant debtors and, as her attorney, was not obliged "at any time hereafter to give any account of his administration or direction to anybody whatsoever."[173] Clifford later emphasized that this agreement had been made "only to show to the court [that] my wife's inclination was to have me sell and remove my estate to Jamaica to inhabit under the English government." He already had full power to sell or transport "what estate I had with my wife in marriage as if it had been mine before marriage," a right derived from both their union "and the statutes and laws of Holland." Suriname's government was, he claimed, "very sensible" of this fact, even though it held his estate in arrest for years afterward.[174]

Clifford himself had no doubts about the meaning of these events. Suriname's government sought to prevent him from liquidating his estate and moving to Jamaica. Moreover, this was his estate alone, not land held in common with his wife (aside from the third that he had transferred to his father, which he still controlled and would one day inherit). As he later wrote, when trustees named by the court inventoried Corcabo in May 1687 as part of the sequestration, they violated both the 1667 Articles of Capitulation and the 1674 Anglo-Dutch treaty of peace. Furthermore, this arrest on his estate was just the beginning of "many vexations," all of which aimed to prevent him from "obtaining liberty" by moving to English territory.[175]

The episode had played out amid tensions between Clifford and Matson's wider family, which he also interpreted as a sign that the authorities favored her and were persecuting him. On the same day that Matson recanted her allegations, her brother-in-law Thomas Baroen won a legal victory against Clifford. Only Clifford's side of the story seems to have survived, as described in two ways in a later compendium of grievances. One version lists a "sentence ... upon a frivolous complaint" by Baroen, which led to Clifford being fined 11,500 pounds of sugar.[176] The other states that the same day saw a sentence against him in favor of the fiscal (who exercised prosecution powers in the colony) and Baroen, "who owed the proprietors of Suriname for two slaves which he could not pay for." The governor received payment for the enslaved workers by means of a fine levied against Clifford, damages that he later listed at 18,328 pounds of sugar.[177]

There are no clues as to why these fines carry the same dates as Matson's retraction. Was Thomas Baroen, her sister's Dutch husband, involved in a larger feud with Clifford, perhaps out of loyalty or to keep Corcabo in the family and out of his hands? He appears to have been much less wealthy than Clifford: the 1684 census lists him as owning just one slave and paying the Society of Suriname 150 pounds a year in sugar, compared to Clifford's fifty-three slaves and 4,610 pounds.[178] Why, then, would Matson retract her allegations on the same day that Baroen won a victory? Or did Clifford, writing much later, merely record a date that was otherwise loaded with significance? Clifford certainly thought that the authorities took Baroen's side because they also favored Matson: he recorded their annulment three months later of a debt that Baroen owed him, stating that they did so "by reason he was married to my wife's sister."[179] However, Baroen himself was missing in action when Matson complained to the governor about her husband and seems not to have played a direct role in the episode.

Dorothy Matson struggled to retain her estate in the face of what we would today call domestic abuse and ultimately capitulated to her husband's will. Appealing to the governor was one of her few available options when confronted by a husband who was intent on ignoring Dutch norms of common marital property. Briefly stepping out from under Clifford's authority, she alleged mistreatment and asked for commissioners to hear her case. Yet her subsequent retraction disavowed not only her initial complaint but also her own agency, blaming others for what was now described as a "misunderstanding between her and her husband."[180] The governor and the council had stepped in to defend her interests, but only because she was "a weak and silly woman," who was deserving of punishment as much as protection.[181] She was caught between a domineering husband, the competing property norms of two countries, and the powerful men who ran the colony in which she resided. It must have taken significant courage to complain about Clifford's mistreatment; yet the only rhetorical space she could inhabit was one that emphasized female weakness.

By the summer of 1687 Jeronimy Clifford had consolidated his position as a planter in Suriname, having asserted control over both his father's property and the estate that Dorothy Matson had brought into their marriage. It was, however, a pyrrhic victory. Alone in the colony after both had sailed for England, he was left in charge of Corcabo. Yet due to the authorities' restrictions, he was unable to dispose of the plantation and move its effects and enslaved workers to Jamaica.

The context in which he now acted was radically different from both the English Suriname he had known as a small child and the Dutch colony where he had lived until the age of eighteen. He had spent his early years in a territory that was under the sovereignty of his own king, with fellow subjects who included both English Christians and Sephardic Jews. After the Dutch conquest in 1667, he and his family had continued to live among a substantial community of the king's subjects, Christians and Jews alike. The articles of capitulation that were signed between the English and Dutch at the time of conquest conferred them with communal rights that included freedom of religion and the ability to leave the colony with their estates.

Although the articles spoke of the English, Dutch, and Jewish nations, they failed to explicitly state that Jews were subjects of England's king. That ambiguity signaled the contested status of Suriname's Jews during the Crown's 1675 evacuation mission. The subsequent departure of most ethnic English and the prevention of Jews from leaving narrowed the scope of English subjecthood in the colony. From that point on, to be a subject of England's king in Suriname was to be a member of the English nation or else part of the small community of Scots who also owed him allegiance. By the time Jeronimy Clifford returned to Suriname in the 1680s, all but a few of the remaining English settlers had sailed for Antigua.

Clifford's conflicts with the authorities over his marital property provide a glimpse into how he framed his identity in this new environment. He clung closely to his own status as English, both when consolidating his property and in trying to remove it to Jamaica. The English practice of coverture shaped his assumption that he owned the land that Dorothy Matson had brought to their marriage. His assertion of the right to sell that land and to take what (and who) he could to an English colony accorded with the 1667 Articles of Capitulation, a connection that he later made repeatedly. Moreover, at least according to Matson, Clifford saw himself as immune from Suriname's laws because he was English. Whether or not this assertion was true, he continued to operate as if he were part of a significant community governed by treaty rights that were backed by the power of the Crown.

Yet the nature of royal power was changing. Within a few short years the Dutch stadholder would become Jeronimy Clifford's king, in events that became known as the Glorious Revolution. His friction with the colonial authorities continued into this new era. Now, however, Suriname's governor and council could evoke the name of the monarch to whom he owed his loyalty.

CHAPTER 3

The Glorious Revolution in Suriname (1688–1695)

In November 1688 a Dutch fleet under the command of William III, Prince of Orange, invaded England. Invited by a section of the elite to check the perceived absolutism of the Catholic king James II, William would become king of England, reigning jointly with his wife Mary, James's daughter. These events, which were later dubbed the "Glorious Revolution," served as a pivot point in Anglo-Dutch relations. England's bitter rival, an adversary in three wars since the middle of the seventeenth century, became its close partner. The two countries now shared the same ruler, with William both reigning as king of England and serving as stadholder of the United Provinces.[1]

In Suriname both colonial administrators and colonists confronted a shift in sovereignty that was very different than the Dutch conquest of 1667. The seizure of Suriname that year by Crijnssen's fleet had forced the English colonists to choose whether to leave or try to remain English under Dutch rule. The 1675 evacuation had then led to the departure of most ethnically English settlers and the shedding of subjecthood by the colony's Jews. Now the Glorious Revolution raised the issue of what it meant to be an English subject in a Dutch colony after a Dutch prince had become England's king. During the initial period of conflict, Suriname's authorities had to decide whether they could trust the small number of remaining English, while the English, in turn, weighed their own loyalties. William's subsequent victory then altered the ways in which both those governing the colony and members of its English minority might evoke the distant authority of a man who served as both king and stadholder.

Jeronimy Clifford's many conflicts with Suriname's government threw these issues into stark relief. The governor jailed him for refusing to swear allegiance to the Dutch before news arrived that William had prevailed, an event Clifford later framed as a violation of the 1667 Articles of Capitulation. Although that agreement had defined relations between Suriname's English subjects and their Dutch rulers up to 1675, the authorities now seemed to view it as redundant and Clifford as falling entirely under their jurisdiction. After the threat of war subsided, the colony's governor and council proved willing to summon not just their stadholder's Dutch authority but also his status as English monarch. In 1691 they sentenced Clifford to a lengthy term in prison following a dispute with a Scottish planter, evoking William's position as king when they did so. Clifford, in turn, eventually won his freedom by asking his monarch to intercede with the States General, benefiting from the influence he exerted in the United Provinces.

The Glorious Revolution offered English colonists in Suriname both promise and peril, raising the question of multiple allegiance in new ways. Subjects of England's king could, perhaps, find comfort in the fact that he now held nominal sway in a territory that a foe had conquered two decades earlier. Yet Clifford's example shows that when friction occurred, the benefits of English subjecthood could be thin indeed. It was little wonder, then, that after years in a Paramaribo prison he would try to avail himself of his sovereign's role as the Dutch stadholder.

The Glorious Revolution in an American Colonial Context

The Dutch attack against England in 1688 raised the possibility of wider conflict in the two countries' colonies. After William's victory England then joined the Netherlands in an anti-French alliance.[2] Both phases had implications for the status of colonists living in conquered territories. During the initial war between England and the United Provinces, the Dutch in New York and the English in Suriname became potential enemies of their respective colonies' governments. Following the conflict's conclusion, both populations then lived under a king-stadholder who, while deriving very different powers from his English and Dutch offices, projected authority in both empires. The two previously conquered populations once again fell under bonds of allegiance derived from their countries of origin, not just that of the dominions where they now lived. At the same time, colonial governments gained a new reserve of symbolic power on which they might draw.

News of the Dutch invasion of England traveled slowly to the Americas. William had landed in Torbay on 5 November 1688 and formally declared his victory over James II on 12 January 1689. On February 19 the Privy Council ordered the proclamation of the new monarchy.[3] Barbados was the first English colony to learn of these events, with initial rumors arriving by the middle of November 1688 and the proclamation of William and Mary occurring by May. Roughly the same time frame prevailed in England's other sugar-producing islands.[4] From there news spread to North America. Maryland received news of a possible Dutch invasion of England by January 1689, probably from Barbados.[5] Virginia proclaimed its loyalty to William and Mary by late April, Pennsylvania by November, and Carolina not until the following year.[6]

William's accession carried particular significance in New York due to its previous status as a Dutch colony and its substantial remaining Dutch population. The stadholder's anti-French and anti-Catholic credentials predisposed Calvinists of all nationalities to support him, although Dutch inhabitants were perhaps the most ardent.[7] News of William's landing first reached the colony by February 1689.[8] By the end of May a militia revolt was under way in New York City, led by Jacob Leisler, a German-born former officer in the Dutch West India Company.[9] Participants vented their frustrations at the marginalization of the Dutch that had taken place under English rule, with artisans taking members of their community's elite to task for their close ties with the English.[10] The uprising's antipopish fervor and the fear of French attack in turn made targets of the small number of French Catholics.[11]

Dutch colonists had sworn an oath of allegiance to the king and his government after the English conquest of New Netherland in 1664.[12] However, for participants in Leisler's rebellion, this bond of loyalty was undercut by suspicions that James II was a popish tyrant or, at the least, was under the sway of Jesuits and evil counselors.[13] After William's victory, the Dutch in New York became subjects of a Dutch-born king. In the long term, however, this failed to stem the forces of cultural erosion. By the eighteenth century assimilation had begun to dissolve many of the distinctive features of Dutch culture in the colony.[14]

For the Netherlands and the wider Dutch colonial world, the events of the Glorious Revolution were but one part of the larger Nine Years' War, a conflict in 1688–1697 that renewed hostility with France. Dutch colonial officials did not have to worry about a change of regime in the metropolis, thus avoiding the anxieties about the transfer of allegiance that plagued their English counterparts.[15] However, during the initial phase before James II's defeat, English colonists, where present, became possible allies of an invading English force. Once it was clear that William's invasion of England had succeeded, French colonists remained a potential internal threat.

The outbreak of war in 1688 raised the issue of how to treat colonists who might be loyal to an enemy. In Suriname these were part of recent experience, having arisen during the Franco-Dutch War of 1672–1678, of which the 1672–1674 Third Anglo-Dutch War was a part.[16] Although French and English had then been potential wartime allies of the enemy, in practice, suspicions had been muted. In 1672 authorities had confined the English to their plantations and their leaders to Fort Zeelandia, but the community seems largely to have escaped serious fears that it might aid an invasion.[17] After the signing of a peace agreement with England in 1674 and the departure of most English settlers a year later, only the remaining French were a potentially disloyal European minority. Yet despite the threat posed by France in neighboring Cayenne, which the Dutch seized briefly in 1676, Suriname's French settlers appear not to have inspired much fear. Only a small number of French speakers lived in the colony, most probably Walloon Protestants descended from migrants to the Dutch Republic.[18] The authorities took active measures against them only after reports of imminent French invasion reached Suriname in 1677, whereupon they ordered French permanent residents to be handcuffed and others to be confined to the fort. The invasion failed to take place, although fears of French attack continued until news of the September 1678 Franco-Dutch peace reached the colony.[19]

During the Glorious Revolution, England was an adversary of the Dutch Republic only during the short time before William prevailed against James. However, if Jeronimy Clifford's account is to be believed, authorities in Suriname took measures to ensure English loyalty, such as imprisoning him until he agreed to take an oath of allegiance to the Dutch.[20] France was of longer-term concern, although it failed to take Suriname, where, as in 1677, the authorities took the precaution of imprisoning some French colonists. However, French troops burned plantations in Berbice, to the west, and attempted to ransom twenty thousand guilders from Zeeland to prevent further destruction. Suriname's governor released the French prisoners in exchange for the voiding of payment for Berbice's protection.[21]

William III's dual offices of king and stadholder differed vastly in scope and power. Yet while he was certainly no monarch in the Dutch Republic, his successful invasion of England indicated the degree to which the strength and authority of the stadholder had expanded under his tenure. During the early seventeenth century, the office, which was chosen by the individual provinces, had had authority in political and judicial matters but not military affairs.[22] Although it then accrued more power, it was abolished in 1650.[23] Over the resulting twenty-two-year period without a stadholder, republicans and Orangists wrestled with the ultimate locus of sovereignty, the former locating it with the states of each province and the latter with the municipalities. The young prince of Orange, meanwhile, served on the Council of State and, by February 1672, held the military positions of captain and admiral-general.[24] The stadholderless period came to an end later that year after invasion by France and its allies shook Dutch politics to its core. Orangists capitalized on popular anti-French sentiment and the perception that the States General was responsible for the national catastrophe of the so-called *Rampjaar* (year of disaster). By July Zeeland and Holland had made William stadholder.[25]

Although the United Provinces remained a republic, the speed and thoroughness with which William consolidated his power led to accusations of monarchical behavior and intentions. Assertions that he aspired to ultimate sovereignty were prevalent enough that the States General forbade voicing of that viewpoint.[26] By the time that a ruinous trade war with France erupted in the second half of the 1680s William had further strengthened his position, making a previously unthinkable response feasible: the curbing of French power by an invasion of England, turning an enemy nation into an ally by deposing James II.[27] William's subsequent accession as king of England only increased concerns about his monarchical tendencies at home, misgivings that were seized on by French propaganda asserting that he desired a Dutch throne. Meanwhile, some supporters in the Dutch Republic readily observed similarities between his position as a limited monarch in England and his role as stadholder.[28]

William now exerted both real and symbolic authority not just in England and the United Provinces but also in the colonies of both nations around the world. While the de jure and de facto powers of king and stadholder continued to differ, they bound both English and Dutch to him. In New York, Dutch colonists could look on William as a recognizably Dutch symbol of authority, not just as their English sovereign; and in Suriname, he was both the stadholder of the Dutch inhabitants and king to the small number of English colonists. The colony remained governed by the Society of Suriname, making his authority there indirect at best. Yet colonial officials readily evoked his title as stadholder to underwrite their actions, and when dealing with Jeronimy Clifford, they also summoned his title as king.

Being English in Suriname during the Glorious Revolution

By the eve of the Glorious Revolution, Clifford's main concern was finding a way to leave Suriname, which involved selling Corcabo and transporting its movable property to English territory. This included the people whom he forced to work its land and claimed as chattel. However, in the wake of his wife's complaint the previous year he lacked full control over the estate. In 1685 he had transferred a third of the property to his father, Andrew, who left for England that year. The wording of the transaction allowed the younger Clifford to determine the fate of the portion, ownership of which would revert back to him at his father's death.[29] Two years later Dorothy Matson had complained to the authorities, alleging that the transaction was part of an attempt by her husband to seize her land and remove its effects to Jamaica. She had also accused Clifford of committing adultery, assaulting her, and threatening to kill her.[30] However, within months she retracted all allegations, gave Clifford her power of attorney, and left for England, never to return. Before she left, the authorities responded by declaring her to be "a weak and silly woman," fining her, and placing Corcabo under sequestration.[31]

Alone in Suriname as 1688 dawned, Jeronimy Clifford was ostensibly in charge of the estate, although he was unable to sell it and leave the colony. Instead he focused on using its profits to fight his case. On 6 April he "took freight for fifty hogsheads of sugar in the ship of one Captain Reneyer Weyman." He planned to use this to fund the "necessary expense in Europe" that would come from lodging complaints with both the king of England and the States General and from seeking permission to remove his property to Jamaica. The governor of Suriname, he later claimed, learned of his plan and ordered Captain Weyman not to carry his goods. Forced to seek a different way to transport his sugar, Clifford "slipped [them] in another ship without opportunity of insurance." The vessel sank during its voyage to Holland, causing him a loss that he later claimed amounted to 26,456 pounds of sugar.[32]

With his uninsured shipment of sugar at the bottom of the sea, Clifford tried another method of funding an appeal in Europe. In July 1688 he made a contract with Samuel Lodge to rent out his plantation for four years. This was presumably the same Samuel Lodge on whose ship Clifford had worked as a surgeon and who had, according to the States General, subsequently settled in Suriname.[33] The agreement provides a glimpse of business dealings between members of the colony's tiny remaining English community and how the region's high mortality might cause those dealings to go awry. In return for the use of Corcabo, which then contained "79 slaves, 14 horses, 41 head of cattle, and 89 acres of sugar canes," Lodge would pay Clifford 127,600 pounds of sugar each year, "clear of all taxes, costs and charges whatsoever." Once the four years were over he would return the plantation "in the same condition it was in when he received it, and with the same number of slaves, horses, cattle, and acres of sugar canes, etc."[34] This arrangement would allow Clifford to "go to Europe to get an order from the States General for liberty to remove his slaves and effects to Jamaica."[35] However, the plan fell apart when Lodge died after only five months renting the plantation, leaving Clifford worse off. Even in this short time Corcabo had, Clifford later claimed, suffered "great damages."[36] Lodge's executors returned the estate to him, although this took place "without any satisfaction" for the harm the episode had caused, which he subsequently tallied at 39,404 pounds of sugar.[37]

While Clifford was trying to raise money, Suriname's governor was busy undermining his title to land that he had bought in Jamaica—or at least this is what Clifford alleged. In September 1688 "one Bonetta Aries a reputed Spaniard" prosecuted Clifford over title to a tract on the island, repeating previous legal action taken in July 1687.[38] Aries, Clifford claimed, had "pretended himself heir" to property that Clifford had legitimately acquired there.[39] Despite his protests "that land in Jamaica was only triable in Jamaica and by the English laws," the authorities ordered that Clifford be imprisoned and fined.[40] Although Clifford identifies Aries as Spanish, he might have been a converso: the 1684 census counts one Benito Aries among Suriname's Christian colonists while also listing Isaac Aries among its Jews.[41] The authorities would later allege that the land in question was the same parcel that Clifford claimed to have been given by Oliver Hampson, one of the English settlers who had left Suriname in 1675.[42]

By the end of 1688 Clifford's attempts to fund a challenge to Corcabo's sequestration had come to naught, the result, at least by his account, of both bad luck and the continued machinations of the authorities. He remained intent on exercising the right to transport his property to an English colony, as guaranteed by the 1667 Articles of Capitulation. Yet as contentious as things were as the year drew to a close, they would only become more so as the ripples of the Glorious Revolution reached Suriname.

The conflict that erupted between England and the United Provinces during the early phase of the revolution called renewed attention to Clifford's status as an English subject in a Dutch colony. The first inklings of trouble occurred when, by his own account, the governor held him responsible for the actions of another Englishman. At some point in 1688 "one Captain Woodbury," on hearing "rumors of a war," had sailed from Suriname without paying his creditors. The governor ordered the arrest of ninety hogsheads of Clifford's sugar "for no other reason, than because Mr. Clifford was Woodbury's countryman."[43] However, the governor may, in fact, have had other motives. Woodbury's ship, the *Bristol Merchant*, had arrived from New England with cargo that included goods belonging to Clifford and there is evidence that Clifford himself was either the sole or joint owner of the vessel.[44]

By the following year the war had forced the issue of English subjects' possible dual loyalties to the fore. On 20 April 1689 the governor ordered Clifford's arrest for, as he later wrote, refusing "to take an oath of fidelity" to the Dutch "to fight against my own nation." This demand was, he claimed, "right contrary to the oath which is stipulated in the articles of capitulation made upon the surrender of Suriname in 1667."[45] Although William of Orange had prevailed by this point, Suriname's governor had ordered the oath "before the news of the Revolution in England arrived at Suriname." Clifford refused to comply, "saving of his allegiance to the government of England," and the Surinamese authorities "imprisoned him, and would take no bail for him." They also forced him to bring back to shore thirty slaves whom he was preparing to send to Barbados. When he protested his detention, the governor and the council "fined him 30,000 weight of sugar and sentenced him to beg pardon of them upon his knees."[46] His incarceration seems to have lasted for three and a half months.[47] He was finally released after being forced to take the oath "by an order of their court," without which he would have "continued in prison, and rotted there."[48]

The loyalty oath contained in the 1667 Articles of Capitulation had required English colonists to defend Suriname against external enemies. However, in the case of an English attack, they were merely obliged to "keep . . . quiet and neither directly nor indirectly assist" England's forces, willingly submitting to imprisonment if the governor requested.[49] Suriname's authorities had followed its stipulations in 1672, during the last period of warfare between England and the United Provinces, ordering most English settlers to stay on their estates and imprisoning the community's leaders.[50] Why, then, would it choose to violate the articles by forcing Clifford to take sides against England?

In 1689, unlike during the last Anglo-Dutch war, Suriname lacked a substantial English community as most English subjects had left for Jamaica with Cranfield's mission. The colony's government might well have asked Clifford to fight against his native country simply because it no longer saw the 1667 treaty as applicable. Alternatively, the skittishness that news of war could cause, particularly given the slow speed at which information traveled, might have led Suriname's rulers to evade the letter of the treaty in the name of security. The remaining English settlers, although few in number, remained potential allies of forces opposing William. While there is no evidence that Clifford himself harbored Jacobite tendencies, the governor of the nearby Leeward Islands, Nathaniel Johnson, repudiated the new king, a position that led to his resignation.[51]

The initial outbreak of the Glorious Revolution might also have exposed the ambiguity of Clifford's status rather than simply his potential disloyalty as an English subject. The States General later took the position that Clifford's abortive 1675 abandonment of Suriname had effaced his English subjecthood and placed him firmly under its jurisdiction. A 1700 resolution stated that while he was "a born Englishman," he should "be considered alike with all strangers that established themselves in Suriname and consequently owned as a subject of this state."[52] If the colony's government had held the same view eleven years earlier, Clifford's overt identification as an English subject would have been a problem, and one rendered much more acute during a time of Anglo-Dutch war.

Given Clifford's tumultuous behavior, it is difficult to discern the boundary between issues of belonging and issues relating to the enforcement of order. Was he as blameless as his tally of injustice suggests or did he merit censure simply because he was a persistent thorn in the side of Suriname's governors? Was he unfairly persecuted for being English when Captain Woodbury left without paying his debts or rightly held accountable for a maritime venture in which he held a stake? Did the colony's governors improperly fine and humiliate him for protesting imprisonment or fairly chastise him for pushing back against their authority? Whatever the underlying truth, these actions established a pattern that would continue long after the stadholder of the United Provinces became England's king and Jeronimy Clifford's sovereign.

Conflict with the Colonial Authorities under a King-Stadholder

In September 1691 Clifford began another prison term, this time for three years and eight months. The catalyst for his imprisonment was his conduct during a dispute with a Scottish planter, Henry MacKintosh, over a claim to the ownership of an enslaved worker. His incarceration was, however, also a rebuke by the authorities for the sum total of his behavior since his return to Suriname. Clifford later framed his loss of freedom as a continuation of his previous arbitrary punishment, one more episode in a series of violations of his rights as an English subject. Yet England and the Netherlands now shared a king-stadholder. Clifford's sentence, as well as the manner in which he ultimately gained his freedom, shows how the Glorious Revolution changed the ways in which both a colonist and Suriname's governing elite might evoke the authority of a distant ruler. During Clifford's sentencing, the fiscal and the court pointed to the fact that they acted in the name of Clifford's English king. Clifford, however, gained his eventual release by using the power of that king's status as Dutch stadholder in his favor, successfully appealing to William III to intervene with the States General on his behalf. In Suriname, the dual offices of William of Orange cut both ways.

MacKintosh, Clifford's adversary in the dispute, was a member of a small Scottish community in Suriname with roots that stretched back to 1667. As David Worthington's research has shown, his presence provides "evidence of a north Highland-led slave-owner circle" in the colony by 1674, the earliest year when his presence is evident. By 1680 he "was the third largest plantation owner from the Stuart kingdoms there" as measured by the number of people kept enslaved.[53] Working "within a Dutch imperial framework," he acted independently of Edinburgh and London.[54] This, as well as the wider trade in sugar between Suriname and the Highlands of which he was a part, suggests an adeptness at moving within the interstices of empire in the years before Anglo-Scottish union. Allan MacInnes has suggested a further significance, arguing that MacKintosh's conflict with Clifford was part of a larger effort by "the Scottish planting elite in Suriname . . . to expropriate disaffected English planters."[55] However, the episode appears to be an isolated incident rather than part of any wider friction between English and Scots settlers in the colony.

In July 1691 MacKintosh petitioned Suriname's governor and council, complaining that Clifford had sought to annul the sale to him of "a certain negro man named Caesar for the sum of six thousand pounds of sugar." He alleged that Clifford, concluding that he could get more money for Caesar elsewhere, had had all the sugar from MacKintosh's boiling house impounded. The produce was, Clifford had argued, owed to the heirs of Samuel Lodge, whose estate he now administered. With his sugar having been seized, MacKintosh was unable to pay Clifford, who used this as a pretext to back out of the sale. In response, MacKintosh asked the authorities to order its release and force Clifford to "deliver over the aforesaid negro . . . according to the price and conditions he has sold him for."[56]

The authorities took a dim view of Clifford's actions. After reading MacKintosh's petition, the Court of Polity removed the hold on his sugar and ordered Clifford to immediately deliver Caesar and abide by the original terms of the sale.[57] Clifford, however, dragged his heels. The governor, declaring that the "obstinate" Clifford had refused to "fulfill the sentence in court pronounced against him," issued an ultimatum. On 1 September he ordered the fiscal to tell him "this last time" to immediately hand Caesar over. If he delayed in doing so, Clifford was to be brought "into the foreport of . . . the fort here upon his own cost" and must remain under arrest at his own expense until he held up his end of the bargain.[58]

Responding to the fiscal, Clifford replied that he had acted in good faith and that the whole affair was a case of mistaken identity. He declared that he had never resisted the sentence against him, which he was "ready to fulfill punctually . . . without any manner of design or fraud." In fact, he had delivered Caesar to MacKintosh's house within days of being ordered to do so. MacKintosh, however, had "refused to receive him, saying that he had bought one other negro man of the same name of Caesar which formerly belonged to Captain Lodge." The dispute, then, was not "about fulfilling of the sentence" but rather "which of those two negroes being both of one name . . . is sold and bought." If MacKintosh could prove that he had bought the man previously held enslaved by Lodge, then Clifford would hand him over. Rather than enforcing the existing sentence, "which doth not distinguish which negro is bought or sold," the governor and council should decide "which of the two negro men shall be delivered." Clifford stood ready to follow their orders, "as it is the duty of all good inhabitants."[59]

Within a week Clifford was a prisoner in Fort Zeelandia. He petitioned for release on 6 September 1691, reiterating that he had tried to meet all his obligations. After MacKintosh's complaint that past July, he had in fact delivered the Caesar who was tied to Lodge's heirs. He did this "under a protest only to fulfill the governor's orders," so that he could return to running his plantation and his "merchandising trade." After taking the enslaved man to MacKintosh's plantation, he had directed the *schout* (the Dutch equivalent of a bailiff) "to receive the full quantity of 6,000 pounds of sugar in payment for him." Failing that, the *schout* was to return Caesar to Clifford for nonpayment and to serve MacKintosh with a warrant to appear before the court. The burden would then be on MacKintosh to prove that Clifford had, in fact, sold him Lodge's former slave. This exchange seems to have fallen through, however, which resulted in another complaint from MacKintosh and Clifford's subsequent confinement to the fort.[60]

In asking for his freedom, Clifford evoked his own dual status as someone who owed fidelity both to Suriname's Dutch authorities and to England's king. Emphasizing that he had "taken his oath of allegiance to this government" in accordance with Suriname's charter and the court's directions, he asked for a hearing and discharge from arrest. In doing so he requested that he "be treated as a burger and free inhabitant of this colony and also as a born subject of the king of Great Britain." MacKintosh, meanwhile, should pay him "the cost of this suit" together with "reparation for the damages and affronts" that he "had sustained through this dispute."[61]

Clifford had defended his position by pointing to the fact that his allegiances were both local and British. Yet the king who claimed his loyalty and whose protection he evoked was now Dutch. He did not raise this point overtly, but perhaps he did not need to. Suriname's authorities would have been aware that Clifford's king was also their stadholder. Clifford also explicitly referred to his monarch as king of Great Britain, not just of England. While this might have been simply a matter of convention, it might also have been a deliberate strategy to emphasize that William III's local authority extended to Scots like MacKintosh as well as to English colonists like himself. In either case, the Court of Polity was unmoved. It declared Clifford's petition "to be frivolous and very full of lies" and its author as seeking "nothing but trouble and malice and disputes." It referred the matter to the fiscal, who was "to bring in his action against the petitioner."[62]

The next day Clifford announced a different strategy, doubling down on Dutch dominion by informing the governor and the council that he would go over their heads to their superiors in the United Provinces. He would take his case to "the Lords High Council in Holland," who he was confident would rule in his favor. The authorities in Suriname might very well force him to turn over the enslaved Caesar, whom MacKintosh desired to possess. However, MacKintosh should then provide assurance that he would return him if Clifford's appeal succeeded. Moreover, he should also be willing to "pay all the costs, damages, and interests . . . according to the sentence which may come to be pronounced against him MacKintosh in Holland."[63]

The court responded by summoning Clifford to the council chamber, where it asked him three times if he stood by the contents of his complaint. On hearing that he did, it ordered that he remain in detention. It then instructed the fiscal "to make up and bring in his action against the said Clifford for his insolence."[64]

The provisional fiscal was Bastian Thyssen, one of the commissioners whom the governor had appointed to hear the case that Dorothy Matson, Clifford's wife, had brought against her husband in 1687.[65] He issued his charges against Clifford in January 1692, making it clear that the disagreement with Henry MacKintosh was simply the most recent example in a long litany of bad behavior. In fact, since returning to Suriname in 1684 Clifford had "caused a great deal of disturbance in the colony." Moreover, he had acquired land in Jamaica not as a gift or honest purchase from Oliver Hampson but rather by deceiving its rightful owner, Benito Aries.[66] Repeating Matson's 1687 allegations, the fiscal charged that Clifford had attempted to remove his wife's property from Suriname and had "profusely squandered away a great deal of money with whores and other debaucheries." Matson had alleged that Clifford had brought a woman named Mary Regland to the colony and kept her as a mistress. Clifford had, Thyssen wrote, mistreated the couple with whom he had lodged her after they objected to "misbehavior, which they could not avoid seeing." The authorities had since banished Regland.[67]

The fiscal affirmed Matson's initial account of her marriage. She had suffered Clifford's "abuse, blows" and threats "to murder her," which were intended "to compel [her] to annul her marriage settlement and contracts." She had since departed the colony for England, having "tired of such a life." Clifford's violence extended to other women: when one Margaret Mills had testified to his poor behavior, including his conduct in England, he had had his slaves "drag her along like a brute beast." He had also abused his brother-in-law, Thomas Baroen, "turning him out of his house, and behaving to him in an insolent manner," which had forced the governor and the council to intervene in order to prevent "such acts and outrages."[68]

The Glorious Revolution had made Clifford's disloyalty clear. Despite the sequestration that had followed Dorothy Matson's 1687 complaint, he had continued to try to remove the estate from Suriname, including by an attempt to send slaves to Barbados. According to the fiscal, Clifford indeed had a stake in Captain Woodbury's ship the *Bristol Merchant*, which he had jointly bought toward the end of 1688.[69] When news of war with England reached Suriname, Clifford had helped Woodbury flee.[70] Unable to "keep himself easy" during a time of impending conflict, Clifford had himself tried to leave for Barbados "under pretense of following Woodbury's ship." However, his attempt to gain the council's permission to depart failed because he "was greatly to be suspected in such perilous times" as he had "no good will to this country and the Dutch nation." This was evidenced by his refusal "to take the oaths as all burghers are obliged to do."[71]

Clifford's "frivolous and fraudulent" actions against Henry MacKintosh were, then, part of an extensive catalog of misdeeds. He had since ignored the sentences against him, written "seditious petitions," and threatened the colony's authorities. The fiscal ended by noting that he was bringing his action against Clifford in order to prevent "further disturbances and irregularities," which "may be expected."[72]

Thyssen was unsparing in his final summation and sentencing recommendation, which he announced on 9 January 1692. This was, he declared, a case that "cannot be pardoned without a great punishment," for "it is no small matter to endeavor to delude and lead astray the judges." Clifford had penned petitions which were "filled with lies" and "full of threatening words." He had "irreverently and disdainfully slight[ed] the council[,] . . . which is a crime that lends to the destruction of this government." And government "cannot subsist without respect and authority."[73]

The fiscal explicitly evoked the fact that the authority of Clifford's king, as stadholder, held sway in Suriname. Clifford had "cast away all respect and reverence which he owed to the governor," whose commission represented both "their High and Mighties the States General of the United Provinces and his majesty of Great Britain their stadholder." He had "accused the governor publicly of doing him injustice" in the presence not only of the "whole council" but of "all the common people." He had "then also spoken several other ill-natured foul and trifling words" which, along with his accusations against the governor, showed that "he is a mutinous person and a disturber of the common peace." He concluded by declaring that Jeronimy Clifford should be "brought to the place of execution . . . there to be punished with a cord that . . . death followeth." His estate was to be confiscated for Thyssen's own use.[74]

In examining the fiscal's case against Clifford, the criminal court opted for mercy; and just as Thyssen had evoked the dual role of William III as stadholder and British king in proposing the execution of an English subject, the court did the same in its act of mitigation. While acknowledging that the fiscal's demands "are rightly grounded," it declared itself "more inclined to clemency than to the outmost rigor of justice." Acting "in the name of . . . the States General of the United Provinces, . . . his present majesty of Great Britain their stadholder," and the directors of the Society of Suriname, the court commuted Clifford's death sentence. Rather than being strangled with a cord, he should spend seven years imprisoned in Fort Sommelsdijck and pay a fine of 150,000 pounds of sugar. Of this, 60,000 pounds would go to the provisional fiscal, 50,000 to the colony's Treasury, and 4,000 to the building of "a new prison or house of correction," as well as to other costs. The order was signed by the governor, Johan van Scharphuizen.[75]

Jeronimy Clifford remained in prison until May 1695, a time he would later describe as "near four years in great misery and cruelty."[76] It was also a period of sustained activity on his part. On 10 December 1691, two months after his initial arrest and a month before he was sentenced, he sold another third of Corcabo to his father, presumably in an attempt to further protect his holdings.[77] Andrew Clifford sent his notarized approval of the sale from London the following summer even though he had granted his son power of attorney before leaving for England in 1685.[78] During his time in Fort Sommelsdijck Clifford also purchased a vessel and pursued his release. Meanwhile, according to his own account, the colonial authorities tried to frustrate his attempts to manage his affairs.

The inventory that accompanied the 1691 deed of sale shows how Corcabo had changed since the time of the first transfer from son to father in April 1685.[79] It describes the plantation as consisting of 1,500 acres, substantially less than the 2,388 acres named in the 1685 transaction although roughly the same as listed in another account of its earlier size.[80] Ninety-eight enslaved people now worked its land, up from the eighty-five listed in the previous deed. This included thirty-nine men, thirty women, seven "great boys," six "great girls," and sixteen other children. The inventory included the slaves' ascribed names, including one man called Caesar. While some of the other names were similarly classical (for example "Great Hector" and "Little Hector"), some hint at geographical origins, whether true or imputed, including "Jan Congo," "Ibbo Will," and "Angola Mingo." With the exception of two indigenous people, all enslaved workers were Africans or of African descent. Of these, the inventory valued men at forty-five hundred pounds of sugar each and women at thirty-six hundred pounds. It also listed two runaway men, valued at two thousand pounds each, and one runaway woman, listed at fifteen hundred pounds.[81] Clearly, resistance reduced a person's value.

The terms of the transaction echoed those of the 1685 transfer. The total value of Corcabo was listed as 857,467 pounds of sugar, with the third of the property now being transferred worth 285,820 pounds. This was in contrast with the third transferred six years earlier, which had been worth 193,457 pounds, the entire plantation having then been valued at 580,372 pounds. The elder Clifford was once again forbidden from selling the property without his son's consent, and on his death it was, like with the first third, to revert back to the younger Clifford's ownership. The latter was to continue to manage the estate, for which he was to receive 5,000 pounds of sugar from his father's share each year.[82] All this meant that, in strictly legal terms, Jeronimy Clifford now owned just a third of Corcabo, although in practice he claimed control over the entire property.

During his time in prison Clifford took measures either to export the plantation's produce or to ship some if its effects to English territory. Shortly after being sentenced in January 1692 he purchased a boat, the *Bruyn Fish*, "an English built prize ketch retaken from the French," which he made "ready to sail to Barbados." The governor thwarted these efforts, however, causing the vessel to be "cut from her anchors and driven to sea and lost with part of her loading." Clifford claimed that the resulting damages amounted to 125,675 pounds of sugar.[83]

Meanwhile Clifford continued to incur further penalties from Suriname's government. On 6 March 1692 he incurred a fine of 9,000 pounds of sugar for an overseer's violation of the arrest on produce due for Captain Woodbury's debts. He tallied the resulting damages at 14,332 pounds.[84] Two months later the court seized seven hogsheads that should have been "marked by the cure master."[85] More fines and sentences were levied during the following year, although his papers list no cause: 43,182 pounds of sugar on 24 January 1693 and a further 9,032 pounds on 17 September.[86] He also claimed that while he was in prison the authorities had interfered with his obligations as executor of the estate of Francis Bruninge, with whom, according to the fiscal, he had jointly owned Woodbury's ship. Bruninge had died in 1692 while himself administering two other plantations. Being deprived of the 8 percent commission for his management of the three estates had, Clifford claimed, cost him 300,000 pounds of sugar.[87]

In Clifford's telling the Society of Suriname had known of his plight from the beginning, informed both by the authorities and his own efforts to gain his release. In January 1692 the fiscal had sent it a "packet" of papers concerning his case. According to "several captains of ships" this "came safe to their hands in Amsterdam." In April 1693 he wrote a "letter of complaint" to the society, providing "a full account of the unjust dealing and violence of their governors" against his "person and goods." He also claimed that the society had learned of the details of his case "by the relation of several skippers and others from Suriname," whom it had examined "both before and after" receiving his letter. Yet it had done nothing to secure his release.[88]

Freed by the King-Stadholder

When Clifford finally won his freedom in May 1695 it came as a consequence of William III's dual status as king of England and stadholder of the United Provinces. A 1701 pamphlet, probably written by Clifford himself, suggests that he had used "relations in England" to appeal to the king, who in turn interceded with the States General.[89] Elsewhere Clifford asserted that a number of luminaries had spurred the king to action. In a December 1696 petition to the States General he wrote that "the governors of Barbados, Jamaica, and New York" had presented his case to the king. The secretary of war had then appealed on his behalf to Grand Pensionary Heinsius.[90]

The States General issued its order for Clifford's release on 16 October 1694, directing the governor to let him "depart from Suriname with his effects unmolested, without further detaining him." Its resolution relates the contents of his successful petition to the king. Clifford, "a natural born subject of his said majesty," described how he had bought land in Jamaica "with an intent to transport himself and his personal estate thither." The governor had not only prevented him from leaving the colony but had also "endeavored to ruin him" by "denying him the liberty to sell his estate," imprisoning him, and confiscating some of his property. In this version two former governors of Barbados, Edwyn Stede and James Kendall, had attempted to intercede with Suriname's governor but to no avail. Clifford was denied any appeal, bail, or access to the necessary papers to fight his case. He asked the king to intercede with the States so that he might both gain his liberty and permission to "obtain leave to return with his goods."[91]

The order from the States General took several months to reach Suriname. According to Clifford it only reached the colony because he had "paid 57,687 pounds of sugar to the governor of Barbados for a privateer sloop" to carry them.[92] Governor Johan van Scharphuizen finally ordered his release on 4 May 1695, directing the fiscal to "let him depart from hence with his effects without detaining him any longer."[93] Clifford had, at least, left his mark on his place of imprisonment. While incarcerated he had been "forced to build two houses in the Fort Sommelsdijck for himself to live in." Although the governor had ordered one of them to be "broken down," the other was "left standing in that fort when he was enlarged."[94]

Clifford wasted no time in making arrangements to leave Suriname, ensuring, at least according to his own account, that he made an orderly and honorable departure. On 26 May he asked the secretary of the colony "to acquaint all people of my going from thence, with my slaves and goods," as "custom and law" required six weeks before departure. By this means, he later wrote, "I summoned all persons, that had anything to pretend of me, or my father's plantation I left there, to receive satisfaction of me, which they did."[95]

Before leaving the colony Clifford demanded restitution for his years of imprisonment in Fort Sommelsdijck and what he perceived as the persecution that had preceded them. On 5 August 1695 he asked Suriname's secretary to deliver to the governor a "book of accounts" concerning his "pretension against the colony" and its proprietors. The governor and council should pay him "4,728,418 pounds of sugar" in damages; if they refused, they were to let him know how much they would be willing to offer.[96] Rather than responding to his claim, the council requested a Dutch translation of his accounts.[97] This was, Clifford later wrote, "a plain denial of them to repair my damages." The council's members knew English and were in no need of a translation. This was also true of the governor, "who doth not only speak but also writes and reads English as well as most born Englishmen."[98] On 2 October Clifford responded with a petition which "the governor would not receive nor answer." Finally, on 10 October he protested against the governor's refusal to hear his complaint. There is no evidence that he received a reply.[99]

Clifford left Suriname for good three days later and sailed for Barbados, where he remained until the following March. He then embarked for Europe, traveling first to England and then to the Netherlands, where he began a lifelong pursuit of his claim for damages.[100] He appointed one Francis Le Brun to run Corcabo in his absence, giving him authority to export its sugar.[101] In a twist linking the plantation's fate to a central figure in Clifford's life, Le Brun later married Sarah Lodge, the daughter of Captain Samuel Lodge, and by 1703 she and a subsequent husband had seized possession of the land.[102]

Jeronimy Clifford had been unable to sell Corcabo or remove its effects and enslaved workers because the authorities had sequestered the two thirds of the estate that he had sold to his father. This was a result of Dorothy Matson's 1687 complaint to the governor about her husband's sale of the first third, which had taken place two years earlier.[103] In response the governor and council had ordered the couple not to "transport nor diminish nor make away their estate" and had appointed commissioners to inventory its assets. If they were to "live and correspond well together" they might benefit from the plantation's "interest and produce" and ultimately be left to the "free disposal of their goods." However, this did not happen. Matson soon departed for England, never again to set foot in Suriname.[104] The authorities apparently then viewed the second sale, which took place in 1691, much as it had the first, as part of an illegitimate ruse to remove property from the colony. A 1701 pamphlet, probably printed by Clifford himself, describes the ultimate consequences of the restrictions placed on the estate. Clifford succeeded in transporting "the little remainder of his third part of the stock of the plantation to Barbados, leaving his father's two thirds of the plantation with its stock in Suriname." The estate was, the pamphlet reported, "ruined, and no sugar comes from it."[105]

The Glorious Revolution ended four decades of intermittent Anglo-Dutch warfare, which involved conflicts that had caused colonies to change hands in both the Americas and around the world. As New Netherland became New York, Dutch colonists found themselves living in English territory, while in Suriname an English population fell under the dominion of the United Provinces. Each group had tried to accommodate itself to new rulers, swearing oaths of loyalty and making peace with life under a former enemy. The events of 1688–1690 upended those accommodations while reframing the allegiance owed by both conquered colonial minorities and the authorities that governed them. In New York, a sizable Dutch community saw in the new Dutch king the possibility of Calvinist salvation from Catholic rule.[106] In Suriname, an experiment in Anglo-Dutch "cohabitation" had ended in 1675 with the departure of most English colonists, apparently rendering the articles of capitulation redundant in the eyes of the colony's government.[107] Did the accession of a Dutch stadholder to England's throne offer the remaining English colonists new protections in their stead or did it mean that the king of England now acted in the Dutch interest?

Issues of loyalty and allegiance again became paramount. The initial period of conflict, like the century's earlier Anglo-Dutch wars, cast English colonists as a potential threat. Jeronimy Clifford complained of treatment that, he later argued, violated the 1667 articles, a sign that the authorities were still concerned about the English while having, perhaps, a freer hand with which to prevent dissent. Once it was clear that William had prevailed, the dynamic shifted in a way that afforded both Clifford and the colonial government new avenues by which to summon higher authority. Clifford evoked his status as the subject of an English monarch to the governor and council, while they, in turn, readily deployed William's position as both king and stadholder against him. The circumstances of Clifford's release from prison then show the authority of the king-stadholder at work in ways beyond rhetoric. Clifford petitioned his king as an English subject, possibly with the help of former English colonial governors. William then intervened with the States General, over which he exerted influence as stadholder, and in turn the States General sent instructions to Suriname's governor to free him.

In the years surrounding the Glorious Revolution, multiple allegiances in Suriname were both problematic and the source of opportunity. Clifford faced competing claims to his loyalty, stemming from his birth, the colony of his residence, the state governing that colony, and the new king-stadholder, who commanded authority both there and in his native land. After his return to Suriname in 1684 the colony's government apparently viewed him as no longer deserving of the protections of the 1667 articles. Instead, the government now asserted, he owed allegiance, as the fiscal claimed, "as all burghers are obliged to do."[108] Later the States General took this position further, asserting that he should be "considered alike with all strangers" and "owned as a subject of this state."[109] During the short period of Anglo-Dutch war in 1688, Clifford became a potential ally of the enemy; and starting in 1690 his status as an English subject meant that he owed the colony's rulers more fidelity, not less, as they could now act in the name of his king, their stadholder. Clifford, meanwhile, presented his status during these years as clear and unchanging: he was simply an English subject who continued to deserve the protections the articles afforded. Even so, he too might benefit from William's accession to the English throne, as the authority of his king now held sway in the halls of the States General.

While multiple and shifting loyalties were nothing new, having been features of life in Europe, the Americas, and elsewhere for centuries, imperialism brought new complexities and asymmetries of power. When Europeans seized land around the world, they enslaved, displaced, or demanded submission from indigenous inhabitants while settling conquered territories with both their own populations and other people whom they brought to work for them. Some of those colonies then changed hands, forcing authorities to decide when the different groups who fell under their jurisdiction could be trusted and when they were a threat. Colonial populations living through these transfers of power, in turn, had to choose whether to obey new rulers, resist, play both sides, or flee. The decision was not always a clear one, and it was shaped by which group one belonged to and whether one was free or enslaved. Some had far more options than others.

Jeronimy Clifford confronted these questions from a position of profound privilege and entitlement. He had tried to navigate dual shifts in sovereignty: the aftermath of a colonial conquest and the accession of the prince of that conquering power as king of his native land. While choosing to remain consistently and vocally English, even he had tried to benefit from the promises afforded by multiplicity. However, he did so with only partial success, succeeding in securing release from prison and the right to leave the colony but leaving valuable land and assets behind. Meanwhile, the people he had kept enslaved on Corcabo faced a very different range of choices. Clifford's failure spared them from being uprooted to Jamaica or Barbados, a passage they would have made not because they were English subjects but rather because an English subject claimed them as his property. Instead, they continued to toil on the sequestered estate while possibly engaging in acts of daily resistance or embracing the hope offered by revolt or marronage.

After 1695 Clifford traveled from Suriname to the centers of colonial power in England and the Netherlands. From that time until his death in 1737 he fought for compensation and control of the estate that he had left behind in South America. His efforts (the subject of the next chapter) show what happened when one man took an English subjecthood forged in a distant colonial periphery back to the metropolis and brought it to bear against two powerful imperial bureaucracies.

CHAPTER 4

Colonial Subjecthood in England and the Netherlands (1696–1737)

Jeronimy Clifford left Suriname determined to appeal his case, seeking compensation for his suffering along with the freedom to remove Corcabo's goods and enslaved workers from the colony. Although the plantation technically belonged to his father, Clifford had power of attorney and was heir to the sequestered estate. His first destination was Barbados, from where he wrote to his attorney and manager Francis Le Brun in December 1695 and sent him twenty-five hundred guilders to be used to run the plantation.[1] From Barbados Clifford then set sail for Europe, aiming to petition the West India Company, the Society of Suriname, and the States General. He was in England by the end of July 1696, when the government issued him with a pass to travel to Holland accompanied by "his servant maid Elizabeth Cranwell, and Michael, a negro boy."[2] By October he had reached Amsterdam, where he presented Suriname's proprietors with an "insinuation" for damages.[3]

Clifford's efforts in the Netherlands proved unsuccessful, and by the following decade he had turned his attention to English officials, beginning a lengthy barrage of petitions and correspondence that sought the help of Crown and parliament in interceding with the Dutch. He also made his case in print, publishing pamphlets highlighting his past suffering and the merits of his quest for damages. Initially sympathetic to his plight, the Crown deployed its envoys to make his case to the Dutch. Meanwhile Corcabo itself fell into ruin, seized by the heirs of the now deceased Le Brun.

As Clifford pursued his case, his personal fortunes declined. By 1704 he was confined to debtors' prison, where he remained for at least sixteen years. During his incarceration he continued to bombard the government with letters and petitions, which now included desperate requests for financial support. As he sank further into poverty, he became increasingly convinced of both the justice and the value of his claim. Meanwhile, the Crown's support turned to indifference. By 1727 Clifford was free, living at a bakery next to a tavern in Charing Cross. In his final years Clifford came to believe that vast riches from Dutch ships seized on his behalf awaited him in the Treasury. He died a decade later, having failed to collect the immense wealth he imagined he was owed.

Who was Jeronimy Clifford to officials in London and the Hague, the metropolitan centers of the English and Dutch empires? He claimed to be a wronged English subject who deserved compensation, but what rights did he really have and what underwrote them? This chapter explores what happened when Clifford brought his colonial grievances to Europe. It traces how he articulated his status and the merits of his case and how English and Dutch officials decided how to classify him and judge the worthiness of his claim.

Although he would never receive the compensation he thought was his due, Clifford found a hearing in the English halls of power and gained a degree of support from the Crown. What progress he made came not just because the king's subjects were not supposed to suffer abroad at the hands of foreigners but also because he could claim the protection of Anglo-Dutch treaties. He used these advantages both to underwrite his English subjecthood and to make his case for compensation, successfully moving his government to action.

Clifford's status as a colonial English subject had originated in his birth in English territory. In his case this had taken place in England itself, although the children of English colonists were also subjects (a condition denied in practice to those of enslaved Africans, who inherited their parents' unfree condition). After the Dutch conquered Suriname, a number of accords had underwritten the benefits of English subjecthood. These included the 1667 Articles of Capitulation, which were signed after a Zeeland fleet took the colony, and the 1674 Treaty of Westminster, which had ended the Third Anglo-Dutch War.[4] Clifford asserted that the protections these agreements afforded remained in effect decades after the conquest of Suriname, the departure of most English subjects from the colony, and his own return to Europe. His argument was persuasive enough to move agents of the Crown to diplomatic intervention and even the consideration of reprisals against the Dutch.

Other, more ambiguous, factors also defined Clifford's status, particularly in the eyes of the States General. His own appeals and the resulting English diplomatic intervention failed to achieve resolution partly because officials in the Hague disputed the applicability of Anglo-Dutch treaties to his case. But they also went further, calling into question his right to claim the protections of English subjecthood. For Dutch officials, Clifford's reputation, his patterns of movement, and the provenance of his property nullified his rights under treaties like the articles of capitulation. They also limited the jurisdiction to which he could appeal. While he remained a de jure English subject, he was, they argued, also a de facto subject of the United Provinces and thus had no right to his sovereign's backing. Clifford's nationality was both more fungible and more contested than birth, law, or treaty would suggest.

These negotiations took place in the world created by the Glorious Revolution; yet that world was changing. The dual imperial cultures with which Clifford contended were those of two allies who had become embroiled together by the early eighteenth century in the War of the Spanish Succession. This alliance limited possible conflict over his claim. At the same time, Clifford's attempts at compensation never fully benefited from Anglo-Dutch cooperation. William's status as stadholder had helped free him from prison in Paramaribo, but it failed to resolve his case. The king-stadholder's successor, Queen Anne, held no Dutch office. Instead Anglo-Dutch comity took the form of corruption, or so Clifford argued, accusing one English envoy of colluding with officials in the Hague to defraud him.

Despite a Hogarthian descent into poverty, Clifford's sense of boundless entitlement remained unbowed. Petitioning from debtors' prison, he continued to position himself as an English victim of Dutch predations. His incarceration was, he argued, part of his wider persecution and thus a result of plotting by his adversaries, and his suffering was comparable to the most famous colonial English victims of Dutch malfeasance. Even through ruin, Clifford used agents in Suriname to try to regain Corcabo, but his efforts ultimately failed. While losing his own freedom, he remained intent on controlling his former estate and exerting authority over the people who were forced to work its land. Although his reach far exceeded his grasp, he pursued the profits of their labor to his death.

Colonial Subjecthood Backed by Treaty

Clifford arrived in Europe intent on seeking redress, which he pursued first in the United Provinces and then in England. The Glorious Revolution now defined the relationship between both countries, which had become close allies. He had returned having spent most of his life thousands of miles from England, much of it in a territory under non-English rule. In order to gain traction for his case, he needed to articulate to authorities in both countries why he deserved compensation. This hinged not just on his past treatment but also on his status as an English subject. In a colonial setting, through conflict and transfers of sovereignty, this had been sustained not just by inertia or force of will but also by written agreements between sovereign states. As a result, when pursuing his claim Clifford repeatedly evoked Anglo-Dutch treaties, relying especially on the protections conferred by the articles of capitulation signed in Suriname in 1667. Such agreements allowed him not only to bolster his case for compensation in two metropolitan centers of power but also to burnish his own credentials as an English subject after a lifetime spent overseas.

To make his case in the United Provinces, where he had arrived by the autumn of 1696, Clifford had to contend with the institutions of Dutch colonial rule. He began with the Society of Suriname. His papers provide differing accounts of its response though they all suggest that his efforts went nowhere. In one version the society's directors responded to his request for 224,718 guilders and 5 stuivers in compensation by stating that they were "not concerned in this affair."[5] In another version the society made an initial offer of 60,000 guilders before ordering "their governors . . . to ruin Mr. Clifford's interest in Suriname" and their intermediaries to target his land in Barbados.[6] That December he redirected his efforts to the States General, using the king's envoy Edward Villiers, the future Earl of Jersey, to deliver his claim.[7] Along with his petition he included a lengthy "memorial" of the damages he had suffered from 1685 to 1695, totaling 4,494,365 pounds of sugar in value.[8] The States General considered his case and on 16 February 1697 concluded that it "doth not concern the Society of Suriname," against which Clifford had no legitimate grievance. The States advised instead that he should prosecute "all such persons as he concludes hath damaged him . . . in the ordinary courts of justice where he shall think fit."[9]

In Clifford's telling, Jersey, whose position as envoy had so thoroughly enmeshed him with local officials that he was willing to swindle one of the king's subjects, conspired with the Dutch to defraud him. As he later recounted, on 10 February 1697 he had tried to enlist Jersey's help by offering part of his total claim against the Dutch of 243,625 guilders. Of this amount, 100,000 would go either to the English king or the States General "to contribute towards maintaining the war against France." Jersey would get 20,000 guilders for his own use. Clifford would then receive 80,000 guilders in cash and 40,000 more "in negro slaves," and the remaining 3,625 would be left "to an abatement."[10]

Things did not go as planned, however. In 1699 Clifford learned that Jersey had taken the 80,000 guilders in order "to pay his debts in Holland" after his appointment as envoy had ended. The king had, Clifford speculated, received 100,000 "for his own private or public use." This left him with just 40,000 guilders, which were currently "in the hands of the Society of Suriname at Amsterdam." The amount was suspiciously identical to the amount for which George Clifford, one of the society's directors (and no relation) then proposed to settle the case, and which Clifford had rejected as too low.[11]

Clifford's side of the story, which is the only surviving account, paints a picture of an English representative willing to serve Dutch interests in exchange for money. Jersey had, according to Clifford, colluded with the Society of Suriname so that his "person and estate may have been sold to the Dutch." His namesake in the society had paid off both the Crown and Jersey while leaving only a small sum for compensation. The full truth of the matter was yet to be known. However, Clifford was adamant that he "never gave any power" to Jersey "nor to anybody else" to receive such large sums on his behalf or to bargain away his rightful settlement.[12]

The Earl of Jersey did at least prove useful in confirming Clifford's conviction that his case was backed by treaties signed between the English and the Dutch. On the behest of the secretary of state, the envoy had commissioned "two Dutch advocates of the first reputation" to look into the case. In September 1697 they concluded that Clifford had indeed been "highly wronged, injured and damaged." His claim was supported by the 1674 "treaty of commerce" between England and Holland. This required the States General to redress the complaint of any "British subject" who alleged "unjust sentences pronounced by their governors beyond [the] sea."[13] Perhaps spurred on by this assessment, in January 1698 Clifford wrote to the Council of Trade and Plantations asking for a copy of the surrender agreement that was signed when the Dutch had conquered Suriname in 1667. "This dispute," he wrote, "depends on the articles of capitulation."[14]

Having failed in the Netherlands, Clifford and his father turned to parliament, which confirmed that their case was underwritten by international treaty and bolstered by William III's dual position as king-stadholder. The Commons read their appeal in April 1698 and referred it to committee.[15] The resulting report sided overwhelmingly in their favor. It noted that the court in Suriname that had sentenced Clifford to prison had acted "in the name of the States General, His Majesty of Great Britain, as their stadholder, and of the directors, patrons, and lords of the said colony." Clifford's case "seems to be a public and national concern," and "the denial of reparations is contrary to the twelfth article of the [1674] treaty marine between England and Holland," which stipulated that "right ought to be done for any unjust sentences, in three months." The committee concluded that both Cliffords "have been greatly injured at Suriname." The House, it asserted, should ask the king for justice and restitution in their case.[16]

In the end the committee failed to make its report to the Commons. Instead it urged the Cliffords to petition the Crown, having received assurances that they would obtain satisfaction. Writing in 1701, Clifford charged that this was due to intervention by the Earl of Jersey, who acted in concert with "the then Dutch Ambassador."[17]

Clifford soon received explicit endorsement from the Crown, which confirmed that his case, which was backed by treaty, merited intercession with the Dutch. As England's allies they should offer rapid redress. On 2 September 1698 Sir Joseph Williamson, the ambassador to the Hague, penned a "memorial" to the States General in support of Clifford and his father, asking that they be allowed to remove their estate from Suriname in accordance with the 1667 articles. They should also receive amends for "the great losses and damages which they allege they have since suffered" by imprisonment and fines. Williamson noted that nothing was more important to the Anglo-Dutch alliance than "to have speedy and full justice administered . . . where their subjects may pretend matters of complaint one against another."[18]

The States General's 30 December 1698 response denied that the articles of capitulation applied to the Cliffords while affirming that they might remove their goods from Suriname in the same manner as other strangers. Jeronimy Clifford had gained the bulk of his plantation through marriage to the "widow of one Maasman" and had previously held only a small amount of land in Suriname. He was no longer covered by the 1667 peace with England and must be considered the subject of a competing state. However, this meant that the fifteenth article of the charter of the Society of Suriname permitted him, as it did all other foreign subjects, to transport goods from the colony without a passport or other special permission. Although such permission was superfluous, the States was still willing to grant it anyway, permitting the removal of his and his father's effects, as long as they paid all outstanding debts. The Cliffords nevertheless remained bound by the other provisions of the colony's charter. Of these the resolution mentioned article 4 (stipulating payment of duties), article 12 (requiring the use of ships sailing from the Netherlands), and article 11 (forbidding impinging on the trading territory of the West India Company, particularly Africa's coast).[19]

The States General had not provided for any compensation. In December 1699 it again reiterated that Clifford was free to transport his effects from Suriname but must seek damages elsewhere and referred him to its previous resolutions, which had directed him to the ordinary courts.[20] Clifford persisted and sought access to papers related to his case, which the States allowed on

16 December.[21] Despite having been referred elsewhere, he then asked the States for 250,000 guilders in compensation, a request that it rejected.[22]

Clifford had hit a dead end in the Netherlands and was beginning to try the patience of officials in London. He had petitioned secretary of state James Vernon in March 1699, subsequently following up in person. In a letter to Ambassador Williamson, Vernon wrote that "the Suriname Clifford came hither this morning and would have me believe that he offered to submit his cause to trial before the ordinary judges." He wanted to know which court he should bring his case to, "which he could get no directions in." Vernon disapproved of Clifford "pretending to put an interpretation upon the W[est] India Company's charter contrary to the meaning the States understood it in." Clifford had asked Vernon to speak to the Dutch ambassador, which Vernon refused to do "but by the king's order."[23]

Finding no success in either the Hague or London, Clifford took to print for the first time, publishing pamphlets in 1699 in both English and Dutch. Printed appeals to a broader public soon became one of his central strategies as his petitions to authorities in both the Netherlands and England hit repeated dead ends. Ten surviving pamphlets advocated Clifford's case during his lifetime, printed in 1699, 1701, 1704, 1711, 1714 and 1720, with another undated text appearing by 1718. Six of these pamphlets bear Clifford's name while the rest, although anonymous, are so close in content and tone to these six that it is safe to presume his authorship.[24] He seems, however, to have aimed his two 1699 pamphlets at a narrow, official audience. His manuscripts mention an "English printed case to the House of Commons" and a "printed account current in Dutch . . . delivered to the States General and to the proprietors of Suriname," both created that year.[25] Elsewhere, he wrote that it had cost him four guilders and fourteen stuivers to produce "my case in Dutch which I printed and delivered over to the States General, the States of Holland, the proprietors of Suriname, and to all the magistrates in the Hague."[26]

The two texts differ markedly from each other. The three-page English-language *Case of Andrew and Jeronimy Clifford* addressed parliament after it had abandoned their cause due to purported Dutch interference. Its preamble asserts that the committee's report on the Cliffords' case never made it to the House because "the Dutch ambassador, by his agents, interposed, and promised satisfaction." The committee then advised the Cliffords "to desist prosecuting their petition any farther" and instead to ask the king to intercede with the States General. Unlike a later version of the story, which was printed in 1701, it makes no overt mention of the role of the Earl of Jersey. The narrative concludes by describing how Williamson's memorial had failed to achieve redress and appealing to the House to resume its advocacy of the case.[27]

Clifford's Dutch-language pamphlet consists largely of a meticulous accounting of his grievances, with damages totaling 389,618 guilders and 2 stuivers.[28] It includes seven pages of itemized suffering, from various civil and criminal sentences in Suriname to claims for damages and expenses incurred while seeking redress. Reiterating his recent attempts to receive compensation, including the enlistment of aid from parliament and Ambassador Williamson, it describes parliament's report as delivered to the king rather than stalled by collusion between Jersey and the Dutch ambassador. Holding the States General responsible for settling the case, Clifford concludes by asking for a passport so that he and his father may transport their goods out of Suriname and for satisfaction for the "loss, damage, and disadvantage" that they had suffered.[29] The States, he writes, must "by special resolution pronounce a sentence to . . . [his] benefit, and at the cost of the West India Company or the Society of Suriname, without further delay."[30]

Clifford had gained support for his case from both parliament and Crown, the latter sending its ambassador to intercede with the States General on his behalf. He had appealed to officials in both the United Provinces and England by pointing to Anglo-Dutch treaties that, he argued, stipulated speedy redress. The 1667 Articles of Capitulation, as well as later treaties that were signed in 1674, called on the Dutch to allow him to remove his property from Suriname and provide compensation for his suffering. Clifford used these agreements to remind Crown officials that colonial English subjecthood entailed active protection from wrongs perpetrated by imperial rivals. Although he had spent most of his life in distant South America in a colony that had been Dutch for three decades, his subject status and the treaties that underwrote it demanded their backing. At the same time, other factors worked against him. The States General refused to recognize that the articles of capitulation were applicable or that he had any claim against the Society of Suriname. English officials lost interest, while the Anglo-Dutch alliance did nothing to hasten resolution. Williamson had suggested that a speedy settlement would show comity between the two nations at work. Yet the only partnership that Clifford could discern was collusion between Jersey, the Dutch ambassador, and the Society of Suriname. His case became stalled by corruption and bureaucratic inertia.

Colonial Subjecthood Defined by Reputation and Migration

The States General's rejection of Clifford's claim rested on assertions about his reputation that called into question his right to the benefits of English subjecthood. It argued that his prior patterns of movement, the nature of his marriage, and the provenance of his property negated his case. Clifford was a stranger like any other in Suriname, devoid of the special status conferred on English subjects by the articles of capitulation. Indeed, the States General claimed that he fell under its jurisdiction and was, at least in this sense, a de facto Dutch subject. Like others he might use ships that sailed from the Netherlands to remove his property from Suriname but did not deserve compensation. To assert that the Crown had purview in the matter was to contest the sovereignty of the United Provinces. Clifford responded in print with his own claims about the implications of mobility, arguing that frequent commerce between Suriname and English colonies supported his right to use English ships to remove his estate's assets. His own movements, meanwhile, had done nothing to negate the benefits that the articles accorded to natural-born English subjects. Both arguments show the importance of perception, particularly with regard to movement, in defining the implications of colonial status. Depending on the interpretation of his past Clifford might either merit his government's protection or fall entirely within the orbit of the Dutch.[31]

The States elaborated its position in reply to a further English intervention on Clifford's behalf, made in 1700 by Alexander Stanhope, Jersey's successor as envoy to the Hague. Stanhope framed his memorial as both a defense of the rights of English subjects under the 1667 Articles of Capitulation, which remained undiluted by time under Dutch dominion, and an attempt to avoid Anglo-Dutch tension. He asked the States to press the Society of Suriname for compensation for the Cliffords and provide the means by which they might remove their effects from the colony. According to Stanhope, they had been "unjustly oppressed by the governor and council of Suriname" and the younger Clifford had "particularly suffered in his person and estate." However, as "a subject of his Majesty," he "ought not to be deprived of the benefit of the capitulation of Suriname, how long so ever a stay he has made in that colony." He remained covered by the rights conferred to English subjects in 1667, having never made "any engagements . . . to forfeit his birth-right." Swift action by the States General would, Stanhope suggested, "prevent all that might give any ill understanding between the subjects of the one and the other nation."[32]

The States General responded the following December, denying Clifford's right to appeal to the English Crown on grounds that he was a Dutch subject by reputation, with property and mobility that placed him firmly under its jurisdiction. Its overall position hinged on three points: that the case was "an object of justice" and could not be determined politically; that it did not concern either the West India Company or the Society of Suriname; and that Clifford had no grounds to ask for the intercession or protection of the English king.[33] Moreover, his claim for damages was based on "loss of imaginary gain," having been spuriously enlarged to the point of exorbitance. He had, in fact, "never had a penny of his own" and had instead gained all his land in Suriname from his wife; moreover, he had subsequently diminished her estate through "disorderly expenses."[34]

While Jeronimy Clifford claimed to own property in Suriname, in fact he "had no estate of his own."[35] His title to Corcabo was derived entirely from his wife, Dorothy Matson, whom he had met on a vessel bound for Zeeland following a brief return to the colony. Her husband had died at sea and Clifford had married her after the ship made landfall. The couple then returned to Suriname, where he took Corcabo "in the name of his wife."[36] Matson had herself gained the plantation through an earlier marriage, and all her previous husbands were Dutch.[37] The States' wording strongly implied that she was Dutch too, referring to her as "an inhabitant of this state" and to Clifford's claim to Corcabo "as proceeding from a subject of this state" (although this might refer to one of her husbands).[38] Taken together, this meant that Clifford had no right to evacuate his property by virtue of the 1667 Articles of Capitulation, which "could not be applicable the less."[39]

Clifford, in fact, was himself "reputed for a subject" of the States General. Although he was "a born Englishman," he and his father had departed with the evacuation of other English settlers after the colony's conquest by the Dutch. When they returned to Suriname, they did so without the protection of the articles of capitulation.[40] Rather than being treated as an Englishman, Clifford should therefore be "considered alike with all strangers that established themselves in Suriname and consequently owned as a subject of this state."[41] The same was true of his father, who, having returned to the colony "as all strangers did come," had "as little reason as his aforesaid son" to "desire the protection or intercession of His Majesty of Great Britain in this affair."[42]

The States General claimed sole jurisdiction over all strangers in its territory, whether in its colonies or the metropolis, and any appeal to a foreign monarch posed a direct challenge to its sovereignty. In rejecting Clifford's entreaty to the English king it was merely following such rules "as were owned and observed in all politic kingdoms and states." To go against these rules "would occasion very much confusion and in effect deprive the domestical sovereign and judge of all respect and jurisdiction." An Englishman like Clifford who was married and established "under the government of the States" should not be able to "claim the authority of the king of England." The same was true of all strangers in the United Provinces, including "all the French, Spaniards, Italians, [and] Germans that reside here who are very numerous." Allowing foreigners "to claim the protection of their original sovereign" was "against the laws of nations." These stipulated that judges in a given country act "without any difference of nations," and without appealing to the monarch under which an injured party was born.[43]

Clifford's pattern of mobility had made him a stranger to Suriname and a de facto Dutch subject, placing him under the States' jurisdiction with no legitimate right to appeal to his original sovereign. While the 1667 Articles of Capitulation had established particular rights for the king's subjects, the Cliffords had left with the 1675 evacuation of the English, which had concluded the treaty. Thus, it was now no longer relevant to their case. Having "roved here and there for several years," Jeronimy Clifford had then returned to inhabit a plantation that was of Dutch provenance. The good news was that, while not covered by the articles, he and his father were, like other migrants, free to remove their effects from Suriname. Passes to do so were unnecessary, although, in accordance with its previous resolutions, the States was willing to provide them. It also reiterated that while Suriname's charter allowed the removal of property, it required the use of ships sailing from the United Provinces, payment of duties, and avoidance of the West India Company's trading territory.[44] The issue of damages, however, remained "an object of justice," which did not concern the Society of Suriname, the West India Company, or the States General itself.[45]

In a pamphlet printed the following March, Clifford countered the States' assertion that mobility and time had limited the applicability of treaties or his right to the protection of the king.[46] As "a born subject of England" he remained covered by the 1667 Articles of Capitulation and the 1674 Treaty of Peace between England and the United Provinces. The States' contention that he and his father had forfeited their right to appeal to the Crown due to their "several voyages" from Suriname was "absolutely overthrown."[47] The 1667 articles provided them with the "liberty to go out and come into Suriname, as long as we live, without lessening the benefit" it accorded. Similarly, the 1674 treaty allowed English colonists to "depart with their goods and slaves" not just in one instant, such as the Crown's evacuation missions, but in perpetuity.[48] The king, Clifford maintained, "has owned us for his own subjects, who have not forfeited our birthright of England, our native place." This was evident in the monarch's role in freeing him from imprisonment and by the subsequent deployment of the Crown's representatives on Clifford's behalf. Moreover, even if he and his father were erroneously considered "as Dutch men," the charters of the West India Company and the Society of Suriname still stipulated "a more serious consideration" of his "sufferings."[49]

The States had used a mischaracterization of Suriname's charter to justify restricting how he and his father, as strangers under its jurisdiction, might remove their property. The resolution had cited the charter to assert that the Cliffords must use ships sailing from the Netherlands, pay the duties accorded to Dutch shipping, and avoid areas of Africa where the West India Company traded.[50] Yet according to Clifford, the charter only stipulated these constraints for "shipping trading for Suriname" or exporting its produce. There were, however, no limitations on vessels moving the "goods or slaves" of planters, who might "buy or hire all such ships, as we shall think convenient for the use of our transportation."[51]

Clifford also noted that the States' position conveniently ignored its own toleration of interimperial trade. English ships regularly came and went from Suriname, arriving from "New England, New York, Virginia, Carolina, Barbados, and other places belonging to his Majesty of England," selling "provisions and horses" and loading "timber and molasses for Barbados, and other places." Why, then, was he "not permitted to go thither with English vessels, from England or Barbados, as other English, and as their charter allows of?"[52]

In stating his own position about the movement of people and property Clifford had identified a central tension between Suriname's regional and metropolitan trade. The Society of Suriname's 1682 charter articulated a mercantilist vision in an attempt to curb the high volume of trade with non-Dutch areas (particularly Barbados) that had existed since before Zeeland had seized the territory from England. Article 12 stated that the colony's "trade and navigation ... shall only take place directly from this country [the Republic]. Fruits, wares and produce are not allowed to go anywhere else than to this country. The same goes for the provisions needed by the said colony. They can only come from this country, and from nowhere else."[53] Clifford's criticism of the States' use of this text was correct, albeit pedantically so: the article did not explicitly mention planters' personal goods or the enslaved workers whom they regarded as their property. However, his larger point about the high volume of trade with English colonies was the more salient one. The Society of Suriname was never able to curb its colony's reliance on commerce beyond the Dutch system. In 1704 it gave up trying altogether, joining the West India Company, which had "generally allowed interimperial intercolonial shipping from its other Caribbean domains, especially from Curaçao."[54]

Recognizing the jurisdictional implications of reputation, Clifford also pushed back against the States' characterization of his marriage and the provenance of his estate. He denied that he had married "a Dutch woman of Zeeland" and so "must be governed as a Dutch man." His wife was "an English woman, born in Yorkshire, in England, so no Dutch woman." Besides, goods gained since Suriname's conquest, "either by marrying with an English woman, or by our planting and merchandizing," must be treated in the same manner as those acquired before.⁵⁵ Clifford was English, as was his wife, and he and his father remained covered by treaties that England had signed with the United Provinces. Yet the States, he wrote, sought nothing less than "to strip us of our birth-right of English men, to prevent our complaint in England, and his Majesty from protecting us."⁵⁶

The States General had used Clifford's reputation to erode his English subjecthood. Although never questioning his English birth, it had declared that his marriage, his patterns of movement, and decades in a Dutch colony had rendered him a stranger with no special treaty rights. In fact, he was to be considered a Dutch subject, at least by implication. The States' argument was a jurisdictional one and ambiguously framed. Although it seemed not to deny Clifford's ongoing de jure English subjecthood, it pronounced that status legally meaningless as far as his case was concerned. This nullification had occurred "from the time after his return with his wife to Suriname," after which point he was considered "as a subject of this state" ("als een onderdaan van [deze] staat").⁵⁷ This was a statement about sovereignty, which made no claim on Clifford's identity. However, like all strangers in the United Provinces, he fell under the States' laws and no others. Countering with a robust defense of an English subjecthood unaffected by his years under Dutch dominion, Clifford rejected the States' contentions. Neither conquest, movement, reputation, nor marriage could weaken rights that were accorded by birth or guaranteed by treaty and that merited the ongoing intervention of the Crown. Turbulent as they were, the wind and waves of colonial life left no mark on the protections that his status as an English subject conferred.

Contending with Metropolitan Imperial Culture during the War of the Spanish Succession

Over subsequent years agents of the Crown gave Clifford's case limited support, neither fully backing nor entirely dismissing it. Although moved to act by seventeenth-century treaties that continued to exert force, the men reading his petitions were part of a metropolitan culture that was increasingly distant from the world that had produced those agreements. Another English envoy intervened with the States General on Clifford's behalf, one official entertained the possibility of reprisals against the Dutch, and the Privy Council commissioned a report about his case. Yet at a time when England and the United Provinces were allies in the War of the Spanish Succession, actions that might jeopardize relations with the Dutch were never a serious option. A product of a colonial environment in which Anglo-Dutch enmity was paramount,

CHAPTER 4

Clifford sought resolution even as the terrain created by the Glorious Revolution began to shift under his feet. With the death of William III and the accession of Queen Anne in 1702, his monarch was no longer stadholder of the United Provinces, a dual status that had always carried mixed implications. Torn between faith and fury, he remained convinced of the justice of his cause and increasingly frustrated at its lack of resolution.

Clifford sought further help from parliament in 1701, the same year the king urged the Commons to support the Dutch Republic. The House read his petition that April and referred it to committee. A later source states that "no report was made" and blamed the lack of action on "the circumstances of the times."[58] That May the king sent a message to the Commons about the perilous state of the United Provinces, asking that it be "sensible of those immediate dangers to which they stand exposed." It was, he wrote, "most evident, that the safety of England, as well as the very being of Holland, does very much depend on your resolution in this matter."[59] The House passed a motion to "effectually assist" the king "to support his allies in maintaining the liberties of Europe" and resolving to "immediately provide succors for the States General."[60]

Turning to the Crown, Clifford requested copies of papers that supported his claim that the 1667 articles had conferred him with perpetual rights. Petitioning the Committee for Trade and Plantations, he asked for lists of the Christians living in Suriname at the time of the Dutch conquest and the English settlers who had left with Banister and Cranfield. He also requested "a copy of the protest that Mr. Crandfield [sic] made against the Dutch government of Suriname at his departing thence in 1675."[61] The committee ordered that "copies be accordingly given him."[62] The list of passengers leaving with Cranfield had included the Cliffords.[63] The commissioner's protest had voiced frustrations about the governor's refusal to allow the evacuation of Jews who had lived in the colony before the conquest, whose English subjecthood the Dutch disputed. It had also asserted that the recent Anglo-Dutch peace treaty allowed for the removal of Suriname's English settlers, along with their estates, in ships that "should at any time be sent, without exception or hinderance whatsoever."[64]

These documents would have provided evidence that Clifford and his family were living in Suriname at the time of the Dutch conquest and had left eight years later. Cranfield's protest, moreover, supported an expansive view of the evacuation of English subjects, both in terms of who should be included (Christians and Jews) and when they might leave with their property ("at any time"). While Clifford was probably indifferent to the fate of Suriname's Jews, he was deeply invested in the assertion that his right to remove his estate from the colony lacked an expiration date.

In 1702 the Crown responded to further petitions from Clifford by supporting both another intervention with the States General and the option of reprisals if the Dutch refused to act. Clifford had asked for "an empty ship or two to sail from England or Barbados to Suriname."[65] In a report issued that May, Sir John Cooke, the queen's advocate, recommended royal intercession. Citing article 5 of the 1674 Anglo-Dutch peace treaty, he suggested that the queen write to the States requesting that it order Suriname's governor to let Clifford "transport his goods and slaves" from the colony. This should take place "in such ships, and to such places as her majesty shall direct." If the States failed to give him "speedy and effectual relief" while recognizing the facts contained in his petitions, "letters of reprisal" would be the queen's only legal recourse "on behalf of her injured subject."[66] The Council of Trade and Plantations, agreeing that Clifford had suffered great hardship, recommended that the queen's envoy in the Hague take the case to the States General.[67]

Cooke had evoked a treaty from the previous century to argue that Clifford, as a wronged English subject, merited not just the backing of the Crown but also its endorsement of force on his behalf. Although letters of reprisal remained hypothetical, he had put them on the table during a time when England and the United Provinces were allies in a continental war. Were they a serious option or just a rhetorical flourish? Unlike her predecessor William III, who had served as both king and stadholder, Queen Anne held no Dutch office. Had Cooke raised the possibility of reprisals out of recognition that she now lacked leverage in the United Provinces? Or had he done so simply because violence should answer the violation of a treaty? Years later, Clifford would assert that the reprisals Cooke proposed had actually taken place, resulting in vast sums awaiting him in England's Treasury from thirteen seized Dutch ships.[68] There is, however, no evidence that this was anything other than fantasy.

Clifford's attempts to resolve his case through patronage had received mixed signals, ranging from Jersey's imputed embezzlement to Cooke's expansive backing. As a result, he careened between optimism and pessimism. By October 1702 he was convinced that he would soon find relief. In a petition to the queen he wrote that he had "always found the States-General well inclined to do me justice." In fact, in 1698 a member of the States had told him "that if his late Majesty did but espouse my case heartily, they would restore my estate in 14 days' time." It was the Earl of Jersey who had impeded progress, taking Clifford's money and currying the favor of both English and Dutch officials.[69] Where Jersey had failed him, Stanhope might be trusted. Clifford had granted the envoy power of attorney the previous July, asking that he settle his case for fifteen thousand pounds, sell his plantation for five thousand pounds, and sell his other interests in Suriname and the Netherlands for twenty-five hundred pounds. He now asked for a settlement of at least forty thousand pounds, using Stanhope or another agent of the Crown to sell to the Dutch "all I have in Holland and Suriname at a moderate price." He preferred to cut his losses rather than "live any longer in Suriname, or damage that colony by removing my estate from thence."[70]

When progress stalled Clifford lashed out at the Crown, accusing it of betrayal. In a May 1703 petition to Secretary Charles Hedges he wrote that his "own nation refuses to do him justice, but inclines for to abandon him." Indeed, it wished "to force him to leave England, his native place, and to return again to Suriname, to inhabit there, without obtaining satisfaction for his excessive wrongs, which are not denied by any of the Dutch nation." He proposed a settlement of ten thousand pounds and "an annuity or an office" worth five thousand pounds. He would then be willing to "acquit them of his whole pretention," selling "his estate in Suriname to the Dutch at a moderate price, to make both nations easy."[71]

Receiving no answer from Hedges, Clifford unleashed his fury against Jersey. In a letter that July he noted the use of "strategems . . . to keep me out of my right, by encouraging people to imprison me, to stop my effects, and to give me no credit, and also to way-lay me, and to trap me in my words within this city . . . all done to weary me out, and to deprive me and my family of my own; which I question not but your lordship may have some knowledge of." He was, however, willing to move past this attempt to ruin him as long as he received satisfaction. He asked that Jersey either pay him 120,000 guilders plus interest from 1697 or provide him with the £10,000 and the £5,000 equivalent that he had asked for in his petition to Hedges. He would then sell his property in Holland and Suriname. Jersey did not reply, however.[72]

The Crown had not, in fact, abandoned his cause, Stanhope having presented another memorial to the States General on his behalf on 22 June 1703. This largely reiterated the points he had made in 1700. Clifford was due 389,618 guilders in damages, need not seek justice in the ordinary courts, and should be allowed to remove his estate in accordance with the fifth article of the 1674 treaty of peace.[73] According to the 1766 publication *The Dutch Displayed*, Stanhope's request went nowhere, having "made no farther impression than what had been produced from such as were presented before."[74] Clifford, meanwhile, continued to press his case, writing to English officials and again taking to print.[75] In a petition read in council on 10 February 1704, he wrote that he had been reduced "to the utmost extremity," asked for more action on his behalf, and forwarded numerous supporting documents.[76]

The council responded that day by ordering a report into Clifford's case, which was the last major act of government support for his cause during his lifetime. It empowered the commissioners for trade and plantations to ask "some able merchants" to examine his claim and to conclude how much was due him in compensation.[77] At the end of the month Clifford provided the names of three merchants who were "willing and ready" to do so: "Samuel Shippard in Bishopsgate Street . . . Jacob Oosterland in Fanchurch Street . . . [and] John Gardner secretary to the new East India Comp[any]."[78] Satisfied with his suggestions, on 2 March the board wrote to the three men to pass on the relevant papers.[79]

By seeking resolution in the administrative heart of England's empire, Clifford had attained enough access to government officials to secure another envoy's intercession, the consideration of reprisals, and the commissioning of a report. This was despite the fact that England and the United Provinces were allies in a continental war and his monarch was no longer a Dutch stadholder. Or were agents of the Crown merely paying lip service to his cause? The Anglo-Dutch treaties of the previous century exerted sufficient influence to move them to act to defend an aggrieved subject with a plausible story of injustice. Yet Clifford's account of the Earl of Jersey's actions shows what could happen when patronage went awry, describing an envoy willing to use a supplicant's assets to escape debts accrued while serving overseas. This range of responses, taken together, suggests a metropolitan imperial culture that was at once both receptive and opportunistic. A supplicant like Clifford was both deserving of support and easy prey. Insofar as his claim had merit, it was also a source of potential enrichment. Regardless of whether Jersey had really colluded with Dutch interests, Clifford perceived himself to be the victim of "strategems" that might cause him to lose his freedom. Paranoid or not, those fears proved to be justified.

A Colonial Subject in London's Debtors' Prison

The next month Clifford was arrested and sent to debtors' prison, where he remained for at least sixteen years.[80] He blamed his incarceration on those who were trying to derail his claim and strongly suspected the involvement of the three merchants charged with investigating its merits. Fallen into poverty and ruin, he continued to petition the Crown for relief. Although confined for debt in London rather than imprisoned by an imperial rival in Amboyna or Paramaribo, he cast himself as among the most notorious English victims of Dutch misdeeds overseas. Even in the metropolis he remained a persecuted colonial subject. This was despite the fact that the Anglo-Dutch alliance proved no obstacle to official sympathy for his cause. The merchants, as it turned out, issued a report that strongly backed his claim for compensation and was endorsed by royal officials. Refusing to be satisfied, Clifford rejected their suggested remuneration as insultingly low. The Crown took no further action on his behalf, at least while he remained alive.

Clifford explained his plight in a May 1704 letter to the Council of Trade and Plantations. He had met with Shepherd, Gardner, and Oosterland at Skinners' Hall on three occasions in March, where together they had examined his various papers. After adjourning until 6 April, Gardner had suggested to Clifford that they "remove their meeting from Skinners' Hall [to] a coffee house." Suspecting a plan to detain him, Clifford resisted the change of venue. However, when he went to Skinners' Hall to meet Gardner he was confronted by "one Robert Caruthers a Scotchman that I owed but £1–8–2 to and [with] whom I never had any further dealing." There two sergeants arrested him "in a £200 sterling action . . . under false pretension of a £100 debt." A writ of habeas corpus was issued on 8 April "for want of bail," his friends in London having been "persuaded or deterred" from coming to his aid. All this, Clifford wrote, was done "purposely by my adversaries to compel me to compose or sell this pretention which I have against them according to their pleasure."[81]

The three merchants charged with investigating his claim had, Clifford feared, played a role in his detention. He suspected that they had "some knowledge" of his arrest "and that they side with my adversaries to endeavor to persuade and force me to take my case out of her Majesty's hand." Gardner had assured him that his imprisonment would not delay the examination of his case, yet progress had since stalled, and Clifford's subsequent enquiries had only resulted in "delays and excuses." He asked the lords commissioners to hasten the report so that he might pay his debts and support not only himself but also his family "that at present is in want."[82]

Clifford had found himself in the Fleet, which, along with the Marshalsea and King's (or Queen's) Bench prisons, confined London's debtors (see figure 5). The Fleet had served this role since at least as early as the fourteenth century and would continue to do so until its abolition in 1842.[83] There, as in the wider world, money talked. The prison was divided between the crowded cells of the "common side" and the more expensive (and salubrious) "master's side."[84] Commitment fees varied by status and condition. According to the 1729 Table of Fees, the poorest on the common side paid nothing while the warden charged those who were denied the benefit of the poor box 13s. 4d. Prisoners on the master's side paid £1 6s. 8d. The latter also paid rent of 2s. 6d. per week for a room with their own bed (including bedding and sheets). If they either shared a bed or provided their own bedding they could pay half that, and they could lodge at the bargain rate of 7 ½ d. a week if they did both.[85] The prison's war-

FIGURE 5. William Hogarth, *A Rake's Progress*, plate 7, 1735 (courtesy of the Metropolitan Museum of Art)

dens also exacted money for everything from access to a minister (2s. by 1727) to a fee when discharged from the prison (this was 7s. 4d. by 1729).[86]

Over subsequent years Clifford complained of the Fleet's miserable conditions, although it is unclear whether he lodged in the common side or the master's side. Prisoners could also pay for day release, although this was expensive and required the company of a keeper.[87] More usually, they might pay for the right to live outside the prison itself though still within the "rules" of the Fleet, in an area close by that was inside the warden's jurisdiction. This ran, as Roger Lee Brown notes, "along the Fleet ditch southwards to Ludgate hill," east to Cock alley, "north along both sides of the Old Bailey to Fleet lane, and down both sides of that lane" back to the prison. Aside from Ludgate hill this was an impoverished area, crowded with lowly residences and slaughter houses, although those within its bounds would have been able to entertain themselves within its many taverns and gaming houses.[88] By 1747–1748, 145 of the prison's 364 debtors lived within the rules.[89] To do so prisoners had to provide security against possible attempts to escape and pay an annual fee based on a percentage of their debts. This varied and in Clifford's time could be negotiated with the warden in exchange for a gift. One 1729 report suggests that the combined cost of residing within the rules, factoring in both fees and gifts, came to an average of around four pounds per prisoner, presumably for a year. However, complaints suggest that the warden often levied additional charges.[90]

Throughout his years of confinement Clifford not only bombarded government officials with petitions but also arranged to have pamphlets printed. How he accomplished this remains a mystery; he clearly had some money at his disposal. By June 1713 he was living, according to one of his letters, "within the Rules of the Fleet," next to a coffee house in the Old Bailey.[91] Was he supported not just by successful entreaties for relief but also by friends? How did he afford paper and ink let alone the cost of printing pamphlets? And how did he eventually pay to live beyond the prison itself?

In the year following his April 1704 imprisonment, Clifford pushed the merchants to complete their report, enquiring about its progress from the Fleet. By November he had, on their advice, "moderated and brought down" his "just pretention as low as possible."[92] In January 1705 he wrote to Shepherd asking for news, which would "prevent my troubling [Her] Majesty with any more petitions." Clifford suggested settling for "£30,000 sterling in money, or £20,000 sterling in money with a civil office equivalent to £10,000 sterling more" although, he warned, "this is my lowest and last proposal."[93] On 23 February he wrote from the Fleet that Shepherd, Gardner, and Oosterland had visited him, inspecting his accounts. They had since written a draft of their report, with Shepherd and Gardner agreeing to meet two days later at Skinners' Hall "to finish the same." However, the merchants had since ignored his enquiries about its status.[94] On 20 April he sent additional papers relating to his case to the commissioners of trade and plantations and asked that there be no further delays.[95]

Even from the Fleet Clifford positioned himself as among the most famous English victims of Dutch predations around the world, a wronged colonial subject whose suffering cried out for justice. On 30 April he wrote to the commissioners to remind them of the larger stakes. The "damage" afflicted on him in Suriname was "like unto those injuries done to Major Banister in that colony and to the English at Amboyna in the East Indies." James Banister, governor after the English briefly retook Suriname in October 1667, remained once the Dutch regained control, after which he was arrested for fomenting unrest, sent to Zeeland, and then freed at Charles II's behest. The 1623 Amboyna massacre was of an older pedigree, having resonated for almost a century as the paradigmatic example of Dutch malice toward the English. Clifford cast his travails as yet another manifestation of the antipathy that had motivated Dutch behavior in both cases. Moreover, although England and the United Provinces had since become allies against France, Suriname's inhabitants had failed to pull their weight. The colonists, he wrote, "are rich and are und[er] few or no taxes," having "contributed nothing towards the charge of the late or this present wa[r] against the common enemy to all mankind." Thus, both Dutch cruelty and Surinamese indolence underscored the need for a just settlement.[96]

While languishing in debtors' prison, Clifford had fallen into dire poverty. He concluded the same letter by reminding the commissioners of his "present great want." Without sustenance, he wrote, "both myself and my poor wife who I am not able to support must in few days certainly perish or come to the charge of the parish." He was, in short, "in a deplorable condition without clothes, money or credit."[97] He also petitioned the queen directly, seeking money to sustain himself until his claim was resolved. Without aid, he wrote, he "must certainly perish in a gaol for want of bread."[98] On 3 May 1705 the Queen-in-Council recommended that the lord high treasurer provide "some allowance towards his subsistence whilst the said difference is depending." The council also urged the lords commissioners of trade and plantations to expedite the report into Clifford's affairs.[99]

On 10 May 1705 Samuel Shepherd and John Gardner finally issued their report, which concluded strongly in Clifford's favor. (Oosterland, it seems, had disappeared from the picture.) The two were "humbly of the opinion that the several sentences" against him "were unjust" and that he should receive compensation from either "their high and mightinesses the States General of the United Provinces, or the West India Company of Holland, or [the] Society of Suriname."[100] The nine-page report tallied the amount due Clifford for his specific sufferings, mostly in pounds of sugar, with some amounts in guilders and the final sum converted to pounds sterling. This included his 1692 dispute with Henry MacKintosh "about the sale of a negro slave," which had precipitated his most lengthy incarceration. The merchants noted "that the government of Suriname carried the prosecution against Mr. Clifford to such a height that the fiscal prosecuted him for his life." Although it was commuted, the resulting seven-year prison sentence and fines were worth 150,000 pounds in damages. He was also due 12,666 pounds for "costs of execution &c." and an additional 6,000 pounds for "the said negro slave" being taken from him "and given to Henry MacKintosh" while he was in prison."[101]

When all was said and done, the Dutch owed Jeronimy Clifford a grand total of £13,514 11 s. and 8 d.[102] The total "fines and costs" due to Clifford had amounted to 428,778 pounds of sugar. He was also owed twelve years' interest on this sum at 10 percent per year, totaling an additional 514,533 pounds.

The report had also factored in compensation for wrongs ranging from stolen sugar to "the damage he sustained in his plantation affairs by his absence near four years."[103] In addition, it included payment for the costs Clifford had incurred fighting his incarceration. The merchants had not, however, considered "the confinement of Mr. Clifford's person, the loss of his reputation, and many other consequential damages that attended his sufferings." For these they had "not presumed to make any estimation," preferring to "refer it to the wisdom and judgment" of the lords commissioners, "who are proper judges of an affair of this nature." Shepherd and Gardner concluded their report by stating that Clifford had "been barbarously treated and highly abused and wronged."[104]

Although the merchants had provided a ringing endorsement of Clifford's claim against the Dutch, he was unhappy with their conclusions. Writing from the Fleet on 12 May 1705 he told the commissioners that he had, in fact, been "very much wronged" and suggested they compare the report with a tally he had made on 31 October.[105] For good measure he included a four-page "abstract of his whole accounts."[106] Casting himself "wholly at her Majesty's feet," he waited to hear her offer.[107] On 23 May he wrote to the board asking for further subsistence money and correcting an error in his previous letter.[108]

The lords of trade and plantations, on the other hand, endorsed the report. Noting that the merchants had reduced Clifford's initial demand of £35,000 to £13,514 11 s. 8 d., they stated that they thought its articles were "clearly and fairly stated." Because Clifford's case deserved the queen's "grace and favor for the more speedy recovery of his debts," they recommended that she once again intercede with the States General on his behalf.[109] The Privy Council approved their recommendation on 9 July 1705, ordering Secretary Harley to "lay the same before her Majesty at a convenient time for her . . . further pleasure therein."[110]

Despite having the council's backing, Shepherd and Gardner's report seems not to have led to an additional royal appeal to the States General. Instead, like countless reports written since, it faded into obscurity without effect. When Clifford wrote to Secretary William Popple on 4 June 1705 asking for a copy he was told that he should send someone to the office himself, "for we have at present no hands to spare to do it."[111] No resulting English intervention with the Dutch appears in the States General's records. Later printed accounts of Clifford's plight also fail to mention subsequent action. The 1766 publication *The Dutch Displayed* simply states that after the "lords of trade made their report thereon to her majesty. . . . Mr. Clifford's case was then absolutely considered as a matter of state; and he made constant applications in Holland for redress, to the time of his death, which happened in 1737."[112]

Poverty and Entitlement: Regaining Corcabo from London

Even while descending into poverty in London, Clifford was attempting to regain control of Corcabo, employing agents in Suriname to act on his behalf. On leaving the colony in 1695 he had appointed Francis Le Brun, his attorney, to manage the sequestered estate in his absence.[113] Clifford later alleged that Le Brun's wife Sarah Lodge (the daughter of Captain Samuel Lodge, on whose ship he had worked) had seized control of the plantation with her new husband, Gabriel Delasalie.[114] Two intermediaries, William Mills and Thomas Caruthers, initiated legal action in the colony on Clifford's behalf in order to regain possession of the estate. Caruthers describes these faltering efforts in three letters, which Clifford included in papers sent to the Board of Trade and Plantations in April 1705. They paint a vivid picture of the dilapidated state of Corcabo by the early eighteenth century, along with the frustrations experienced by the parties acting for its distant claimant.[115]

The plantation had fallen into ruin in Clifford's absence. In his first letter, dated 19 June 1703, Caruthers describes it as "in a very indifferent condition," with "the mill house and boiling house . . . ready to fall." The land was incapable of growing much sugar, although "in two or three years" it would be able to produce "four or five hundred pounds per annum." The estate's enslaved workers remained. There were, he wrote, currently "sixty-two slaves young and old, many children and three old women and one man that cannot go to the fields," along with "old Rebecca which you made free." These included "forty the best slaves in Suriname [who] can go to the field every day."[116]

Caruthers's attempt to retake the estate had been complicated by both his employer's circumstances and his own ill health. His letters to Clifford had gone unanswered and he had had "great difficulty in obtaining possession of your plantation by reason of the 10,000 guilders you have arrested in Holland." Meanwhile, conditions in Suriname had taken their toll on him, leading to "four weeks in an extraordinary sickness." Although he was now able to walk again, he had been "several times given over for dead." Clifford's other intermediary, "poor Mr. Mills," had fallen sick "at the same time" and died "in five days of a violent fever."[117]

The now deceased William Mills had had some success in representing Clifford's interests. In April 1703 he had petitioned the governor and the Court of Polity, asking that they order Sarah Lodge, Francis Le Brun's widow, to deliver Corcabo over to him.[118] The court had concurred, issuing a provisional order to that effect.[119] Caruthers now sought to complete his work. On 10 July 1703 he succeeded in getting consent from the Court of Polity to take over the plantation's management.[120] This was, however, only a temporary victory as the legal tide would turn against him early in the next year.

By the following January, Caruthers was embroiled in a dispute with Gabriel Delasalie, Sarah Lodge's current husband. The colony's clerk had issued a summons to Delasalie on Caruthers's behalf, ordering him to turn over "copies of all the accounts, books, quittances, and other papers" relating to Corcabo's administration. Delasalie had responded that he would provide the accounts if Caruthers was willing to "adjust and balance the same," a process that would, presumably, gain him money. Caruthers had protested that he lacked the power to do so and only had authority to receive the papers and convey them to Clifford. On 12 January 1704 Delasalie petitioned the Court of Polity, demanding that it compel Caruthers to show authorization from Clifford to adjust Corcabo's accounts. He was ready to make a settlement, turning over the plantation's books in the process, though only if Caruthers was able to fully settle on Clifford's behalf.[121]

Caruthers wrote to Clifford from Corcabo on 20 January 1704 lamenting the situation.[122] While he had access to the plantation itself, thanks to Delasalie's intransigence he could not procure the papers vital to its management. He had tried to bring Clifford's "affairs here to a happy conclusion" but had told Delasalie he could not settle the plantation's accounts "without the advice and knowledge of my [master]."[123] And there the matter lay. Delasalie refused to turn his papers over for examination, "saying that one account of 80,000 lb sugar was not so lightly given over, and that he must have end of all disputes with Mr. Clifford." This, Caruthers suggested to Clifford, revealed "upon what foot he stands."[124] The ongoing legal dispute made it difficult to manage the plantation. However, Caruthers wrote that he had planted a new crop of sugar cane and would let Clifford know in his next letter whether he would be able to ship any of the plantation's produce.[125]

Writing from Corcabo on 30 March 1704—just over a week before Clifford's confinement to the Fleet—Caruthers reported that he had made no further progress. Since his last letter in January "there has nothing been acted, being obliged by the sentence of the court to desist in proceedings till I receive a new procuration in Dutch." He hoped that Clifford had received his previous reports, and waited "impatiently" for a reply. He was, he wrote, "much troubled at your long silence, not having received a line from you since my departure from Amsterdam. . . . I know not whence the defect is, nor can I believe you have omitted writing."[126] Until he heard from Clifford all was at a standstill: "I can act no more in your affairs at court, till I have a new procuration from you, nor can I send you any more sugar till I have your advice."[127]

Caruthers's account is supported by a 28 January 1704 letter to Clifford from one Gideon De Bourse, which Clifford also included in papers he forwarded to the Crown. De Bourse had aided William Mills, translating documents into Dutch for him. He too recounted the fruitless struggle to obtain Clifford's papers from Delasalie, describing the Court of Polity's reluctance to secure their release. Even if Caruthers did not have a sufficient procuration to settle accounts with Delasalie, he should, De Bourse argued, still have access to the papers. He himself was willing to serve Clifford. However, because he was a member of Suriname's Council of Justice, he could not act as his solicitor. Signing off, De Bourse wished Clifford well in his future endeavors.[128]

Despite the efforts of Mills and Caruthers, Clifford's attempt to regain control of Corcabo had faltered. That he had even tried shows the extent of his own sense of entitlement. As he fell into poverty in London, Clifford still thought it natural that he might continue to manage land on the other side of the world. This included exerting indirect power over the scores of enslaved people working on his former estate. How he attempted this remains a mystery. Caruthers complained of Clifford's lack of communication but presumably received at least an initial payment at some point. How did Clifford afford to do this? And why choose agents from the British Isles to manage affairs in a Dutch colony? Was there a link between Thomas Caruthers and Clifford's imputed creditor Robert Caruthers, the Scotsman whose action had confined him to the Fleet? If the latter acted in the name of the former, then Clifford lost his freedom not because of a Dutch conspiracy but rather because he clung to the position of plantation owner and slaveholder.

It is doubtful that Thomas Caruthers held on to the estate for long, given the absence of letters from his master and his inability to procure Delasalie's accounts. Maybe Clifford's replies had gone astray or his descent into poverty had distracted him from the efforts of his representatives in Suriname. Perhaps the pursuit of compensation from the Dutch had simply eclipsed the attempt to regain control of his land, even as Mills and Caruthers worked on his behalf thousands of miles away. Clifford was certainly willing to use Caruthers's letters as evidence to bolster his claim, sending them to the board with other papers and claiming damages of 174,885 pounds of sugar from Sarah Lodge.[129] But while he pursued his case for recompense, Corcabo itself fell into ruin, sliding further out of reach.

"I Am Vastly Rich, Nay Vastly Rich": A Colonial Subject's Delusions of Wealth

Clifford remained imprisoned for debt until as late as 1720, a period during which he continued to pursue his case in both petition and print. By the final years of his incarceration he believed that vast riches awaited him in the British Treasury from bonds posted by the Dutch after officials had seized thirteen of their ships on his behalf. This was, presumably, inspired by Sir John Cooke's 1702 allusion to possible letters of reprisal.[130] If he could just get the appropriate government officials to act, he could win his freedom, escape poverty, and take his rightful place as a wealthy man. While probably delusional, the assumptions underlying Clifford's claims of wealth are revealing. The force of his colonial English subjecthood, underwritten by treaties from the previous century, had, he thought, finally moved the Crown to act against the Dutch. And despite his earlier experience of fraud at the hands of the Earl of Jersey, he remained the subject of a monarch whose servants protected his interests. No one had embezzled the money that had resulted from the ships' seizure, which was waiting for him to claim as compensation for his years of suffering.

During the preceding years in debtors' prison Clifford had launched numerous enquiries about his case, all of which hit dead ends. By August 1705 he was again asking the queen to intervene with the States General. In the same petition he asked that the Court of Holland in the Hague determine a suit he had brought against "the heir of one Lodge in Suriname" in 1698 "for a considerable sum of money due to me."[131] Later that year he wrote from the Fleet suggesting a settlement of £110,000 in damages.[132] By March 1706 he was petitioning Robert Harley, noting in his papers that he had "not had any answer."[133] Within a year Harley had asked how much he demanded. Clifford responded that he was willing to accept 120,000 guilders (plus interest), taking payment in "lands, exchequer notes, bank bills &c. or otherwise," as the queen would see fit.[134] Replying via his chief clerk, Harley stated that he would write to the queen's minister in Holland.[135] However, he seems not to have acted further.

By 1707 Clifford had been told by "a gentleman at court" that the queen had placed the matter in the hands of the Earl of Sunderland. Consequently, he forwarded Sunderland a trove of papers related to his case, stating that his "whole pretension of damages shall be discharged" if he could only be paid the amount he had asked of Harley. For ten thousand pounds more, he wrote, "I will either sell or abandon all my plantation, monies and effects in Holland and Suriname and will give such discharges and transfers as shall be required of me." Clifford suggested that the money paid to him "remain in the treasury for the service of my Queen and country during this present war," so long as he be paid interest at 5 percent per annum every six months.[136]

These papers contain the last mention of Dorothy Matson. On 17 April 1707 she signed a "general procuration and deed," once again giving her husband power of attorney (as she had done in Suriname in 1687). Clifford had, perhaps, had the document drawn up in anticipation of a final settlement of his claim. Matson authorized her husband to "sell and remove out of Suriname to any of the English islands, or to dispose of in that colony either by a private or by a public sale the plantation called Corcabo." She described the estate as "invested in us both" by marriage, with Clifford having full power to dispose of it "to any persons either in England, Holland, Suriname, or elsewhere as he shall think fit." As her attorney, Clifford was free to act on her behalf, without obligation "to give any account of his proceedings and administration . . . to anybody in the world, no not to myself." The document is followed by an attestation from Sir Thomas Rawlinson, made the next day, that Matson had acted "with her own free will . . . without any compulsion from her husband." An alderman and former lord mayor, Rawlinson lived in the Old Bailey, close to the Fleet.[137]

Sunderland seems not to have proceeded with the case. In March 1711, after four more years in debtors' prison, Clifford once again wrote to the Council of Trade and Plantations. He now asked for forty thousand pounds in compensation, again offering to provide any amount awarded to him for the use of the Crown during the current war with France as long as he was paid interest.[138] In February 1712 he wrote to the Earl of Dartmouth, raising the possibility that the Dutch had already paid the amount due to him to either the Earl of Jersey or the late king. If this were true, then "the government of England may become my debtor." He would be willing to take "an equivalent for my said debt in the South Sea Company" or be paid in ready money. If it was still owed by the Dutch, he would accept whatever amount the queen recommended.[139]

The site of Clifford's detention changed the following year. In a June 1713 letter to Secretary Popple he had written that he was "still confined within the Rules of the Fleet," noting on the bottom of the page, "I lodge in the Old Bailey next door to Johns Coffee house."[140] By December that year, however, he wrote to him from "Queen's Bench rules," where he lived next to another coffee house in Mint Street, Southwark.[141] An accompanying letter to the board explained his new location. The new warden of the Fleet, Mr. Huggins, had denied Clifford a day's liberty to attend to his affairs. As a result, he had removed himself "by a habeas corpus from the Fleet to the rules of the Queen's Bench."[142] His December letter included another large trove of documents and a request to proceed without a solicitor. His own, one Mr. Atkinson, had declined to continue Clifford's case against the Society of Suriname due to Clifford's "want of money."[143]

By 1714 the Council of Trade and Plantations had finally lost all patience with Clifford. He wrote to Popple three times that year before receiving a reply.[144] Responding that April, Popple informed him that "their lordships command me to acquaint you that they have already done all they can in that affair."[145] Rather than giving up, Clifford again took his cause to the wider public. The next month he printed *The Case of Jeronimy Clifford, Merchant and Planter of Surinam*, which again tallied the damages due to him and told the story of his thwarted efforts for recompense. He framed this as "a short abridgment" of a text previously printed in March 1711, which was delivered that year to the Privy Council and the Dutch envoy and in 1713 to parliament.[146] The 1714 pamphlet concludes with an appeal that "this honorable house ... take this very hard case into their most serious consideration," asking that "he may now at last be effectually relieved."[147]

Clifford became convinced that successful reprisals had been made on his behalf against Dutch ships and that huge sums of wealth awaited him in the Treasury. He just needed to convince the right officials to release the money to him. He petitioned George I three times in 1717 and once more the following January.[148] In February 1718 he wrote to Lord Stanhope, to whom, he believed, the king had referred his petitions. "It hath been intimated," he wrote, that on Queen Anne's orders, "thirteen large Dutch ships laden with 10,000 hogsheads of Suriname sugars bound for Amsterdam" had been seized in the Isle of Wight in 1710. The ships had not been allowed to continue their voyage until "sufficient security was given ... to satisfy me my demands for the damages done me by the governor and Company of Suriname." Over the last two years he had learned from "several creditable people" who had knowledge of his case "that I am vastly rich, nay vastly rich (although it be unknown to myself)." They had told him that he should "apply to the lords of the treasury" to learn how much money there was "in the exchequer and plantation office upon this score."[149] He asked that Stanhope not "obstruct his Majesty's doing me full justice in this matter." Enclosing his accounts, he requested payment in "tallies or other national stock ... for the principal money and the interest due thereupon."[150]

Petitioning the Treasury for resolution later that year, Clifford endorsed text penned by a scribe with a shaky signature.[151] He was now sixty-one years old and had been fighting for compensation for more than two decades. A tally of the petitions read notes the result of his enquiries: the page for 13 August 1718 states simply "Jeronimy Clifford . . . rejected."[152]

Clifford made a handful of final attempts to settle his case throughout the next decade, none of which received any traction from government officials. In May 1720 he again resorted to print, producing a twelve-page pamphlet listing the "costs, damages and interests" that he had incurred in Suriname from 1685 to 1695 "and since to the 10th of May 1717." The text also rehearsed his many futile attempts to receive compensation.[153] He was still confined as a debtor at the time of printing, stating in the pamphlet that he had been "imprisoned in the Rules of the Fleet and King's Bench prisons, ever since April, 1704."[154]

The potential fortune awaiting Clifford came not only from Dutch vessels seized on his behalf but also from Surinamese gold, or so he intimated to the Lords of the Treasury sometime after 1720. Drawing on a 1713 letter from a friend in Holland, he suggested that the detained ships had been freed after having given "bonds to answer my demands of the colony of Suriname." He also quoted from a letter from Thomas Caruthers, whom Clifford described as the "now deceased . . . late director of my plantation," who was apparently still in contact, and perhaps his employment, until very recently. Writing in March 1718, Caruthers had reported that "a gold miner has made proof of a new found mine and found good gold but little." Clifford was optimistic about the chance of finding further riches. He suggested that "although the vein of the mine they are upon doth not produce much gold," once the mine was further excavated, "the ore may yield more gold than they expect." The rest of the document's pages are missing.[155] Was Clifford suggesting that the Treasury help him mine for gold in Suriname, augmenting the wealth from the bonds the Dutch had posted for their thirteen ships' release, which he believed lay somewhere in its coffers? Or was he simply underscoring the colony's wealth and thus the merits of his claim there?

Although impoverished, Clifford had come to believe that he was a rich man because, he thought, a seventeenth-century treaty had compelled the Crown to defend one of its aggrieved subjects. The queen had, he asserted, ordered "her lord high admiral" to act "pursuant to the 23rd article of peace made with Holland in the year 1667" to detain Dutch ships.[156] This article of the Treaty of Breda allowed for the confiscation of property to satisfy an injured party.[157] The seizure was, he presumed, the result of "an order in Council made in my favor the 9th of July 1705."[158] In fact, on that day the Privy Council had simply endorsed the merchants' report about the merits of his case, recommending only that this be conveyed to the queen "for her majesty's further pleasure therein."[159] Nevertheless, Clifford clearly thought he was on the verge of imminent wealth. If he could get his hands on the money (including interest) his ordeal would finally be over.

Clifford was probably free from debtors' prison by July 1727. That month he petitioned the lords of the Treasury, asking for "some subsistence money" and stating that he was now living "at a bakers next door to the Ship Tavern at Charing Cross." He included instructions on how to disburse the vast fortune that he believed awaited him. For twenty years, he wrote, he "had neither father nor mother, brother nor sister, wife nor child living to leave what God has been pleased to give me in this world." (This suggests that Dorothy Matson had died soon after giving Clifford her power of attorney in April 1707.) Owing to this lack of close heirs, he was providing the Lords of the Treasury with a list of more distant relatives. In 1718 a "near relation" had given him "an account of the names of 106 relations . . . then living in Kent," all of whom were descendants of "two brothers and one sister my late father Mr. Andrew Clifford had." Without justice from the king in his case against the Dutch he feared that his "whole estate will sink into the hands of foreigners," to the detriment of his "said poor relations." However, with the help of the Lords of the Treasury he would be able to "feed the hungry and clothe the needy and to send the rich empty away." Once his case was settled, he asked that half of any amount due to him immediately be given to his impoverished relatives and that they receive the rest of his fortune on the day he died.[160] He included extensive documentation in support of his case, which he had also sent to the Privy Council. Many of the pages are endorsed with Clifford's frail signature. He was now aged seventy.[161]

The last surviving papers directly attributable to Clifford date from 1728. In a 27 August letter to Lord Townshend, who had previously promised to bring his case to the king, he complained that "these five months last past I have not been at one time master of five shillings." He was "kept in a starving condition at my lodgings next door to the Ship Tavern at Charing Cross." This was the result of "the wicked practices of powerful adversaries," which prevented him from meeting Townshend personally at Hampton Court.[162]

In another petition to Townshend, also written that month, Clifford again laid out his case and claimed that vast riches were available to him if only officials would act on his behalf. He complained that on 7 January of that year Sir Robert Walpole had advised him "to let drop my complaint against the Dutch and to trouble myself no further about it." This, Clifford wrote, was impossible for him to do. He had been informed that "great sums of money" had been "paid into the exchequer or treasury" for him on the late queen's orders. Allowing for 6 percent interest, this "may now amount to above

£100,000 sterling." This money "hath or will be sunk and divided amongst some covetous people here," who desire him "to return back again to Suriname without . . . obtaining relief herein." Meanwhile, the colony's proprietors in Amsterdam had stolen the produce of his plantation.[163]

Returning to Suriname was not an option. Its government, knowing that the Crown had abandoned him would, he wrote, "not treat me and my estate there better than they did formerly while I was an inhabitant in that colony." Indeed, its members would likely act "out of revenge for my complaining against them here . . . [and] again by their arbitrary power without any cause prosecute" his life and confiscate his estate.[164] With Clifford suffering persecution thousands of miles away, his heirs in Kent would then "never be one penny the better for what I have in this world."[165] He asked that Townshend present the petitions and accounts he had enclosed to the king so that he might find relief.[166]

One of the documents that Clifford included suggests, remarkably, that he was still attempting to manage Corcabo while living in poverty in London as late as the 1720s. A 19 September 1727 letter from Clifford to one John Bout, who appeared to be acting on his behalf in Suriname, both contained instructions about selling the plantation and indicated ongoing involvement in its management. Replying to a recent letter Bout had sent from Suriname, Clifford stated he would be willing to sell Corcabo for "ten thousand pounds sterling" to "the widow of the late Mr. William Pedy." Failing this, he would sell the estate either to her brother, who was currently in Holland, or to one of her contacts in Amsterdam. If they were unable to pay in full he would consider credit "at four per cent interest." Clifford also mentioned that he had an attorney in Suriname, one Abraham Vereul. In a 28 June letter Vereul had informed him that his "new mill house and new boiling house are entirely finished" and that he would ship sugars to him by the end of July.[167] Clifford himself was, however, skeptical that this was possible without the permission of "the governor and Council of Polity." However, they "had made themselves masters of my plantation by detaining the same" and had caused it "to be arrested by Gabriel de Lasalie without any cause since the year 1696."[168]

Is it possible that Clifford was actively managing a plantation in far-off Suriname from a bakery in Charing Cross, using an agent and an attorney to try to secure its sale while also improving its mill and boiling houses? Or were Bout and Vereul merely leading him on, deceiving an impoverished old man who had once been one of Suriname's richest planters? Had Clifford descended into fantasy? He was clearly tortured by the thought of tens of thousands of pounds, maybe as much as one hundred thousand pounds, held for him in the Treasury or the exchequer. This money lay just out of reach, on the verge of falling into the hands of his enemies. Did he, then, simply imagine he still had a hand in the running or selling of his estate, which he hadn't seen for over thirty years?

Now an old man, Clifford seemed to fear that his destiny might yet lie in Suriname, with "covetous people" causing him to again become an ill-treated English subject in a Dutch colony.[169] Yet even after all this time, Corcabo's virtues remained clear in his mind. The plantation, he wrote, "can make more sugar in one year with . . . 100 slaves than other plantations above mine can do in two years with the same number." It was, according to the Dutch, "the flower of that colony for fruitfulness of the earth, finest of air and healthfulness of man and beast."[170] And it remained, as it had for decades, beyond his grasp.

Jeronimy Clifford died in 1737.[171] A map of Suriname produced that year by the cartographer Alexander de Laveaux lists Corcabo as owned by one Charles Godefroy.[172] He left the world, according to a later text, "without making any will and without obtaining any satisfaction from the Society of Suriname." He had "sunk to rest, under the pressure of such a train of misfortunes as seldom happen to the lot of man, in the eighty-first year of his age."[173] For four decades he had fought his case, petitioning both English and Dutch officials for restitution and the right to remove his estate from Suriname. In doing so he contended with the bureaucracies of two imperial centers. Officials from each had to decide how to interpret the merits of his case, which depended in part on who Clifford himself claimed to be.

He presented himself in relatively simple terms, as an English subject by birth and the resident of a former English colony, whom the Dutch had cruelly persecuted. A number of Anglo-Dutch treaties protected English subjects whose rights had been violated, from the 1667 Articles of Capitulation to the 1674 Treaty of Westminster. These treaties obliged the Crown to intercede in the event that the Dutch denied redress. Clifford's colonial English subjecthood, which was grounded in birth and had been violated by an imperial rival, required active defense by his sovereign's government.

English officials largely concurred in theory, even as their measure of support varied in practice. A succession of functionaries agreed that Clifford's case had merit and warranted the intercession of English envoys with the Dutch government. At the same time, a number of practical concerns limited how far the Crown was willing to go on his behalf. The English and the Dutch were allies in a continental war, making any intervention other than diplomats' "memorials" unlikely. At least one official raised the possibility of further action in the form of reprisals, but despite Clifford's later conviction that these had taken place they appear to have remained hypothetical. Agents of the Crown were responsive to Clifford's entreaties but only to a point, after which they made it clear that he was trying their patience. The Anglo-Dutch alliance seemed to work more against Clifford than for him, limiting the scope of royal action or, if his account of Jersey's corruption is accurate, providing opportunities for collusion against his interests.

The Dutch questioned not just the merits of Clifford's case but also his right to appeal to his own sovereign, and in doing so undermined the protections conferred by his English subjecthood. Indeed, they went further, questioning his de facto status as an English subject. Although he was born in England, his marriage and patterns of mobility meant that Anglo-Dutch treaties were inapplicable to his case. He and his father had left Suriname in 1675, thus nullifying the application of the articles of capitulation. Clifford's estate, Corcabo, was of Dutch provenance, having been derived from marriage to a woman who was either Dutch herself or had acquired it from a previous Dutch husband. When Clifford returned to Suriname he did so as a stranger, under the sovereignty of the Dutch Republic. As a result, he had no right to appeal to the Crown and no valid right to compensation.

As he fell into poverty and ultimately lost his freedom Clifford employed a variety of strategies, from petition and print to the employment—albeit, perhaps, without pay—of agents in Suriname itself. While none of these efforts succeeded, his sense of the value of his claim took an inverse trajectory to that of his own condition. The poorer he became, the wealthier he thought he was.

The possibility that his case might yield riches continued long after Clifford's death. The words describing his fate as sinking under a "train of misfortunes" were written in 1763, in a book produced by a group claiming to be his "legal representatives."[174] Others asserted that they had found his will and that he had, bizarrely, named as his executors "the Company of the Mississippi in France and in case of their refusal or negligence the Emperor of the Romans."[175] His death, in short, was far from the end of the story. Jeronimy Clifford's claim to Corcabo and dispute with the Dutch would have a posthumous life that lasted to the eve of the American Revolution.

Chapter 5

The Many Afterlives of Jeronimy Clifford (1737–1780)

Toward the end of 1738 a man named Mandel wrote to the secretary of the Society of Suriname. He claimed to possess a copy of Jeronimy Clifford's will and to have access to documents that supported his claim, which was worth over half a million pounds. Over the next few months Mandel attempted to extort the society, suggesting he could make the case disappear in exchange for the more modest payment of ten thousand pounds. The society struggled to make sense of Mandel's story and the supposed will, which had, rather oddly, named both the French Mississippi Company and the Holy Roman Emperor as Clifford's heirs. The Dutch envoy to England, who was tasked with looking into the matter, concluded that Mandel and a party of cohorts had been in debtors' prison with Clifford, where they had come into possession of some of his papers. The will was either a fake or the product of a madman and should not be taken seriously.[1]

Two decades later another group took up Clifford's cause, claiming to act as the "assignees" of his estate and asking that the Crown intercede with the Dutch. Its efforts were successful, resulting in a 1762 memorial to the States General from British envoy Sir Joseph Yorke, which was the first government intervention with the States on Clifford's behalf since 1703.[2] Around the same time printed texts appeared that placed Clifford's story within a larger pattern of Dutch malfeasance reaching back to the Amboyna massacre of 1623, some of which was probably part of the same campaign. This party denied that it was connected to Mandel's earlier efforts or that Clifford had ever produced a will. As in earlier years, the Society of Suriname and the States General responded by denying that Clifford's cause had merits. Nor was this the end of the story. One more claimant pursued the matter into the 1770s and possibly beyond, taking it into the revolutionary era.[3]

Like *Jarndyce v. Jarndyce*, the seemingly endless legal dispute in Charles Dickens' *Bleak House*, Clifford's case lasted for decades, stretching not just from the time he left Suriname in 1695 to his death in 1737 but past the centennial of Zeeland's conquest of the colony. In remaining alive for so long, Clifford's claim perpetuated invented memories of English Suriname and of Anglo-Dutch rivalry. England and the British state that replaced it in 1707 were no longer opponents of the Netherlands. Yet Clifford's advocates continued to cast the Dutch as villains, prolonging old enmities and, with them, the memory of England's seventeenth-century empire. Their efforts spawned printed discussions of the vices and virtues of the Dutch that engaged not just with national stereotypes, but also with the relative merits of the United Provinces' Orange and republican factions. These discussions reframed Clifford's case for a new era, placing it not just in the context of past Dutch misdeeds against the English but also that of contemporary Dutch actions in colonial settings ranging from West Africa to Bengal. At least one retelling remade Jeronimy Clifford for the age of Enlightenment, endowing him with the eighteenth-century English virtues of refinement and politeness and rendering him very different from the troublesome, uncouth Clifford we find in Dutch sources.[4]

By the 1760s Britain's empire encompassed territory from the North American interior to the Indian subcontinent. It was both stronger and more expansive than its English counterpart had been a century earlier. When the Cliffords had first settled in Suriname, the transition toward greater central control of the colonies had only just begun, as had the prosperity that would grow from the labor of enslaved Africans. Britain was now ruled by its third Hanoverian monarch, the result of a Protestant succession rooted in the Glorious Revolution, when a Dutch stadholder had become king of England. Since then the role of the United Provinces in Britain's conflicts with France had shifted, from military ally during the wars of the Spanish and Austrian successions to neutral party in the Seven Years' War. The 1780s would see a fourth Anglo-Dutch war, very different from its predecessors, which resulted from the United Provinces' willingness to trade with the new republic that had been formed by Britain's rebellious American colonies.[5]

Jeronimy Clifford's claim found support throughout the eighteenth century, from Mandel and his cohort of debtors to his estate's supposed "assignees" and, ultimately, the Crown itself. His supporters pursued the case because they thought there was money to be made, either by extorting the Society of Suriname or by reaching a settlement. In doing so, they seized on a loose end from an earlier phase of empire. Even someone like the once-impoverished Mandel could try to play imperial powerbroker. The Crown, meanwhile, remained sufficiently persuaded of the merits of the case and its obligations under the previous century's Anglo-Dutch treaties to again intercede with the Dutch government.

The many afterlives of Jeronimy Clifford expose some of the vernacular contours of English subjecthood in the eighteenth century. The various posthumous evocations of Clifford tell the story of a colonial subject from a number of metropolitan angles. In disloyally proffering a Surinamese fortune to the French and Hapsburgs, one version confounded observers, who noted that this treated his prior allegiance as disposable, to the benefit of a current adversary. Another rendition of Clifford provided a paradigmatic example of wronged subjects everywhere, showing how seventeenth-century treaties still compelled the Crown to defend one of its own even decades after his death. Other depictions demonstrated archetypes of virtue and stoicism at the hands of the Netherlands, linking contemporary colonial defeats with a long history of Dutch anti-English antipathy that went all the way back to Amboyna. These examples, in turn, raised doubts about the Glorious Revolution, which was imputed to have served Dutch interests over those of England, perhaps to the point of tarnishing the subsequent bond between subject and monarch.

Hostility toward the Dutch was, to be sure, a niche prejudice by the 1760s, when France served as Great Britain's prime enemy; but it was nevertheless more than just an artifact of a previous century's colonial rivalry. Drawing on recognizable tropes of Dutch cruelty, Clifford's proponents repeated the story of a persecuted English man in a conquered colony, using it as a bridge between older examples like Amboyna and their own time.[6] As they did they demonstrated the continued resonance of a colonial English subjecthood that, while rooted in a time before the Glorious Revolution, helped to explain contemporary events and demanded action in the present. Although it was a residual language from an earlier phase of empire, like Clifford's story it refused to remain in the past, instead exerting an ongoing salience a hundred years after Suriname's loss to the Dutch.

A Disloyal Clifford's Will: Subjecthood Effaced

In 1737, the year of Jeronimy Clifford's death, the Berlin-born cartographer Alexander de Lavaux produced the definitive eighteenth-century map of Su-

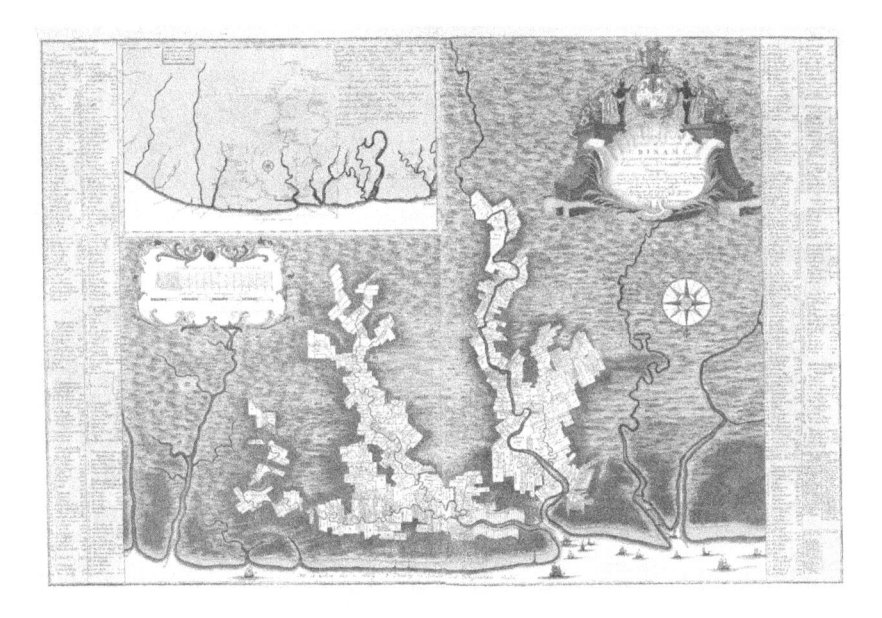

FIGURE 6. Alexander de Lavaux, *Algemeene kaart van de Colonie of Provintie van Suriname*, Amsterdam, 1737–57 (courtesy of the Rijksmusem)

riname (see figure 6). Six years earlier the society had decided that it needed a new map of the colony in order to take into account changes in property lines and to address the continuing flight of enslaved workers. Lavaux's map depicted a thriving territory of over four hundred plantations, listing the location and size of each, along with the names of their owners.[7] It portrayed Corcabo as a nine hundred acre plot owned by one Charles Godefroy, which bordered a straight stretch of the Commewijne River.[8] The conclusion of Lavaux's work was, however, followed by his precipitous decline in fortune. In 1741, after falling out of favor with Suriname's governor, he fled to Saint Eustatius on a British ship, traveling from there to Saint Christopher. As a military officer he was now guilty of desertion, and at the request of the Dutch the British returned him to Suriname. He was imprisoned in Fort Zeelandia, the same site as Jeronimy Clifford's initial incarceration in 1691, and remained confined there until 1744, when the authorities commuted his sentence and banished him from the colony.[9]

Lavaux's connection to Clifford went beyond sharing the same prison in Paramaribo. The cartographer had, it seemed, had a chance encounter that resulted in Clifford's exposure as a less than loyal English subject. In late October 1738 a man named Mandel wrote to Secretary Van Meel of the Society of Suriname, describing a conversation he had had after crossing paths with

Lavaux in London.[10] After Lavaux had mentioned that he was on the way to Suriname, Mandel "remembered and communicated to him an affair . . . of importance" to the society, namely, Jeronimy Clifford's "vast claim." Clearly struck by its significance, Lavaux asked Mandel for a "short explicative memorial" that he could pass on to his employers. However, as Lavaux was about to leave for Suriname, Mandel decided to contact the society himself. He believed that he was, as he wrote to Van Meel, "the only person that can serve you, I mean the Company, in it."[11]

Mandel's service amounted to a shakedown. Clifford's claim was "a large sum indeed," totaling six hundred thousand pounds, and had "made a great deal of noise" during his lifetime. He had, Mandel wrote, "died about fifteen months ago filled with resentments from the justice of his cause," having "left a last will, [a] copy of which lies before me, with the documents relative to it." After naming a number of small beneficiaries, Clifford had "appointed the Mississippi Company in France his universal executors and in case of their refusal or neglect the Emperor of the Romans." His will named "a fund out of which they might indemnify themselves." Mandel, meanwhile, had "the means to stifle an affair . . . which at some time or another may in my opinion prove troublesome to your company." He knew "where this testament is and the original pieces that justify it." Moreover, he wrote, "I also know the means how to get it into my power, which is enough said for the present."[12]

The society strained to reconcile Clifford's supposed choice of beneficiaries with his lifelong professions of loyal English subjecthood. According to a later report by the company, its board had suggested two possibilities. On the one hand, the will might have "been an extravagance of the deceased." Clifford had "always boasted that he was a subject of the Crown of England and assumed that honorable appellation in all his memorials and remonstrances." The contents of the will contradicted this patriotism, naming "as his sole and only heirs a foreign people not favored by the English." Alternatively, the document might be "an imposture forged by this Mr. Mandel and his associates in order to intimidate . . . the Society and thereby to draw from them a large sum of money." The society instructed Van Meel to engage further with Mandel in order to learn the truth of the matter and to "demand of him a copy of this odd testament."[13]

The following month Mandel wrote back to Van Meel with more details about how he might be of service to the society and informing him that a copy of Clifford's will was on its way.[14] While the original testament was not in his possession, he was able to "influence the person who has it," with whom he had "some credit." It underwrote a claim that was no "phantasm or trifle," but rather a matter that had invited the attention of the Crown, having remained unresolved during Clifford's lifetime only because of the unfavorable situation in Europe.[15] Luckily Mandel had "found a method to have it and it is now a copying." Although it was "too bulky" to send with the present letter, he assured Van Meel that "in my next you'll certainly receive it." The original will and all supporting documents were "laid up within a strong box" over which, Mandel wrote, "I can make myself master by means of a reasonable composition." However, because it was in the possession of "persons of distinction" a "small matter" would not suffice.[16] Mandel ended by asking Van Meel to send him a ticket in the Hague lottery, for which he would provide reimbursement, a possible reference to the Dutch national lottery established by the States General in 1726. In a postscript he wrote that he had his "own house in Suffolk Street, Charing Cross," the same part of London where Clifford had lived before his death.[17]

Mandel sent the copy of Clifford's will three days later.[18] Thanks to his efforts, the society could now "get clear of a load which sooner or later will become very troublesome." It was in its interest "to make an accommodation," which would free it from the affair and provide it with "all the lands and effects of the deceased who has no blood relations." His services were a bargain, as the value of Clifford's estate was far greater "than all that will be insisted on for accommodating." He would acquire the original will and the strong box of supporting papers. There would then be "no vestige of this affair left remaining, so that the whole of it may be erased and scratched out of the memories of men."[19] After urging the society to move quickly, Mandel repeated his request for a ticket in the Hague lottery. He closed with an exhortation to Van Meel: "Now is your time to make rich."[20]

The contents of the will were indeed confounding. Dated 4 October 1730, it began by naming a number of annuities, starting with eighty pounds a year to Mary Bowlings, Clifford's "present servant maid . . . aged about 40 years." Her mother, Johanna Whitepin of Hackney, was to receive twenty pounds a year. Other annuities followed in similar amounts, including one to "Mary Randsom, being a crippled woman, who keeps a tallow chandlers shop at the house of Richard Wallis by Charing Cross."[21] The will contained a provision that contrasted with Clifford's own attempts to control his wife's property.[22] It stipulated that the husbands of Bowlings, Whitepin, Randsom and other female beneficiaries "shall not be permitted . . . to receive any of their aforesaid life rents, without a special order of their respective wives."[23] The testament also provided one hundred pounds for his mourning and bequeathed two thousand pounds "unto Mr. Chammorell the present secretary or resident of the King of France at the Court of Great Britain." And it made arrangements for Clifford's burial, stipulating that he be laid to rest in Stepney with his "late wife and father," with fifty pounds provided for the parish's poor. "About eleven or twelve hundred pounds" was allocated to pay his debts.[24]

Jeronimy Clifford had apparently become a Francophile late in his life, using his claim against the Dutch, England's former enemy, to benefit Britain's eighteenth-century adversary. He asked that "Mr. Chammorel or any other minister of state from his most Christian Majesty the King of France here in England" administer the will's provisions "in the absence of my heirs and executors."[25] His testament named "the worshipful gentlemen the owners of the Mississippi Company at Paris," along with "their heirs and successors forever," as recipients of the bulk of his "very considerable inheritance." This included all the "lands, houses, slaves, horses, cattle, money, goods, effects, and outstanding debts . . . from the government of Suriname and others." It also encompassed all his "live and dead stock," whether "in England, Holland, Suriname, Barbados, Jamaica, or any other place in the world." The Mississippi Company's directors were also to serve as his executors. The king, meanwhile, was to grant them "letters of reprisal in due form and time," as well as "a sufficient number of ships, and men," so that they might pursue his claim.[26]

Perhaps wisely, Clifford made contingency plans in case the Mississippi Company refused to accept his bequest or failed to fulfill the requirements of his will within eighteen months of his death. In that eventuality "His Majesty King Charles, the present Emperor of Germany" should serve as his heir and executor.[27] Of course, the Holy Roman Emperor, unlike the French, might not be able to "take Suriname by way of reprisal" due to "want of ships." Therefore Clifford suggested another way for the emperor to recover his debt, which was worth around six hundred thousand pounds. The Hapsburg ruler could use the "five hundred thousand pieces of eight" paid "annually to the States General of the United Provinces, for support of their troops, in their barrier towns in the Spanish Netherlands." In this way he could "without the least trouble, clearly set off and be paid the aforesaid debt due to me, from the colony of Suriname."[28]

The society took its time to make sense of the will. Mandel still had not received a reply by December 1738, when he again wrote to Van Meel, in a tone that had changed from solicitous to impatient. He had sent the copy of Clifford's testament "with a great deal of difficulty and at a great expense" and supposed that his efforts "at least merited thanks." In the absence of a response he had "hitherto lulled asleep the persons concerned," who had given him fifteen more days to learn the society's wishes and who "do not think proper to explain their mind."[29] Meanwhile, he had resolved to "no further meddle in it on any consideration whatever," having only become involved in the matter at "the request of Sieur Delavaux," the cartographer. While he did not regret having done so, he anticipated that the society would only appreciate his actions when it was "too late . . . to be of any further use." He again concluded by mentioning Van Meel's failure to send him a ticket in the Hague lottery, a request he had not supposed "would have been in the least disagreeable."[30]

In March 1739 the society sent a copy of the will to the Dutch envoy in London, one Mr. Hop, and charged him with bringing the episode to a close. Writing back with his assessment the following month, Hop concluded that it had been "drawn up by a man that was quite out of his senses" and had made "very frivolous" claims against the society. The matter, "under the direction of Captain Mandel," seemed to involve the "playing of pranks." Hop promised to speak to Mandel to "see what there is to be done with him." Although the will had no merit, it was, he wrote, "better to be masters of these papers in order to hinder all foul practice as much as possible."[31]

Hop met with Mandel later in April. Although he was convinced of the frivolity of the will, he asked Mandel what his employers proposed. After conferring with them Mandel reported back that they wished to settle the case for £10,000. This was, he said, the same sum that the society had offered Clifford seven years earlier "for a full discharge of all pretensions" and that Clifford had rejected "with scoff." However, Mandel's employers would be "very contented" with that amount. It was "very little and reasonable" given that the claim itself was worth £577,000 and that they would have to pay around £5,000 in "legacies and other debts" from the settlement. Time was, however, of the essence, and Hop must provide the society's answer within two weeks.[32]

Refusing to be pressed, Hop demanded that Mandel either reveal whom he worked for or demonstrate his "lawful authority." Yet Mandel remained evasive, saying only that he represented "persons of honor and character and that he acted by their orders." The two men parted with Mandel feeling "much dissatisfied." Offering his assessment, Hop wrote that he knew nothing of the society's alleged offer to settle with Clifford for ten thousand pounds, on which Mandel's party based its claim.[33]

In a May 1739 letter Hop recommended that the society pay Mandel off with a small sum despite the supposed testament's lack of merit. However, this action was not to be taken lightly, for disposing of a will was "in itself a dirty action." It would also be difficult to do, as there were "several copies of the said will." The original was "in the hands of one Mr. Browne," who Hop thought was its real author. Mandel, meanwhile, was in no position to guarantee "against any future claims or demands." He, Browne, and "one Mr. Every" were "persons of a very bad character" who intended to "pluck something from the Society" and then pass the will on to the Mississippi Company, its principal beneficiary. Hop had concluded that the three men had been "with Clifford in prison for debt, and by that means they became masters of the papers, and got knowledge of this affair."³⁴

Hop confirmed that the society had never offered to settle with Clifford for an amount equal to the sum that Mandel's party now demanded. He had enquired with one Mr. Furley, who had supposedly made the offer on the society's behalf, an assertion that Furley denied. Rather, he had sometimes given Clifford subsistence money "on behalf of Mr. Bout, merchant at Rotterdam." Furley had repeatedly asked Clifford if he would be willing to sell his plantation to Bout. Clifford had responded "in an extravagant way," stating that he would accept £150,000 "and such like mad stuff, when at the same time the man was immerged in misery and poverty."³⁵

In short, Clifford had become a stranger to reason during his later years, vastly inflating his claims against the Society of Suriname. While he was in debtors' prison three unsavory characters had learned of his case, believing that it had some merit. Either Clifford had written a bizarre last testament, bequeathing the fictitious wealth due to him to French and Hapsburg beneficiaries, or one of his fellow inmates had concocted a false will based on his papers. Now their representative, Mandel, was attempting to extort the society, selling Clifford's supposed will and supporting papers so it might be rid of the claim.

The society took Hop's advice. It gave Mandel "a present of twenty guineas" to "keep him in good humor" and decided to end all further contact. Writing back on 30 June 1739, Mandel expressed his gratitude, "offering his services hereafter."³⁶ He tried his luck one last time eight years later, writing to Van Meel in November 1747 to inform him that he had "not lost sight of the affair," and in fact had new information. Clifford's relations were, he wrote, "on the point of addressing the French legatees, the Mississippi or India Companies, supported by their king," in order to execute the will. Luckily Mandel was once again available to serve the society, having "some influence on the same footing as formerly proposed." He asked Van Meel if he might "now accept of the offer I then made," urging him to "make a speedy determination."³⁷ The society was having none of it. According to a later report it was "convinced of Mr. Mandel's villainy and that of his associates," noting that his claim that Clifford had living relatives contradicted one of his earlier letters. It decided not to write back and "therewith all the other negotiations were ended."³⁸

The posthumous Clifford that Mandel presented was, as the society noted, either disloyal, a madman, or a work of fiction. If the will was genuine, then Jeronimy Clifford had abandoned his fidelity to the British Crown, choosing instead to benefit its current nemesis, France, with compensation from the Netherlands, the previous century's adversary. Failing that, his fortune was to go to the Holy Roman Emperor, another foreign power. It is unclear why Clifford would have made these choices, given his lifelong professions of loyal subjecthood. Perhaps they were a manifestation of the same grandiosity that had led him to believe that vast wealth awaited him from Dutch ships seized on his behalf. If so, then he must have ended his years so disillusioned with his claim's lack of traction that he was finally willing to turn against his own country and embrace rival powers instead. It is a measure of Clifford's consistent zeal as a subject that such a decision appears plausible only as an act of insanity.

If Mandel and his cohorts had forged the will, then they had certainly captured Clifford's tone, even if their choice of beneficiaries ran counter to his allegiance. This suggests that they may have known Clifford well and may indeed have been in debtors' prison with him.[39] At the very least they must have had detailed knowledge of his case, either through his printed pamphlets or, as they claimed, from his papers. If so, then men of little means—although, like Clifford, of possible prior wealth—thought they could manipulate the proprietors of a distant Dutch colony.

Whether a product of imagination or unreason, this was just one of Jeronimy Clifford's many afterlives. Rather than fading away, his case would grow in importance over subsequent decades, once again becoming a matter of state, an affair pursued not just by debtors and scammers but also by envoys and ministers. In doing so, it would shed light not only on the legacy of a lost colony and an old imperial rivalry but also on the meanings and uses of colonial English subjecthood in the second half of the eighteenth century.

A Loyal Clifford as a Posthumous Matter of State

Shortly after Mandel's last letter to the society, a new party emerged that purported to represent Clifford's claim. This group, which was active through the 1750s and 1760s, argued that the Anglo-Dutch treaties of the seventeenth century continued to compel the defense of the rights of colonial subjects. The 1667 Articles of Capitulation and the 1674 Treaty of Westminster made Clifford's claim a matter of state. As an English subject he was due redress, without which those treaties ceased to carry meaning or force. This argument persuaded Crown officials to act on Clifford's behalf, prompting a memorial from Britain's ambassador to the Hague, Sir Joseph Yorke, to the States General. The States responded to Yorke by asserting, as it had decades before, that the case was a matter of law rather than of state. Clifford's advocates had no standing to evoke the Crown's intercession because Anglo-Dutch treaties were inapplicable to his case. If he had been wronged it was as an individual, not as an English subject, and his advocates must seek redress in the ordinary courts. The case thus drew a contrast between collective and individual rights. Either Jeronimy Clifford stood for all English subjects, meaning his claim was backed by treaty and impelled royal intercession, or the claim held no broader meaning.

Clifford's case first reappeared in June 1748, when the British government received a request for a copy of a 1705 report into the affair, along with other related papers. This came from one Mr. Brown, who claimed in a letter to the board of trade to be the "agent for Henry Brown, Esquire, executor and administrator to Jeronimy Clifford, late of the island of Suriname." Although unaware that Suriname was not, in fact, an island, the purported representative of Clifford's estate intended to pursue his claim against the Dutch and the board ordered "copies of the said papers to be prepared and delivered to him."[40] Were either of these two Browns the man of the same last name who Hop had claimed was in league with Mandel? If so, the group had changed strategies and now was presenting itself as the executor of Clifford's will.

Soon afterward another, more tenacious party began to actively pursue Clifford's claim. This group evoked seventeenth-century treaties to argue that the Dutch had violated Clifford's rights as a subject, successfully moving the Crown to act on his behalf for the first time in half a century. It denied that he had made a will, and disavowed all connection to Mandel.[41] The party petitioned the king in 1759, having first begun its efforts with a memorial to the Prince of Orange nine years earlier, which had been thwarted by its recipient's death.[42] According to a 1761 report by the attorney general, its members referred to themselves as the "assignees of the estate and effects of Jeronimy Clifford, heretofore residing at Suriname, in South America, merchant and planter, and late of London, deceased." The petition had nine signatories, the first of whom, George Lookup, would later serve as the spokesperson for the group in correspondence with the Society of Suriname.[43]

The petitioners evoked Clifford's English-born subjecthood and the treaties that, they argued, required the Crown to act, recounting his repeated attempts to receive restitution and his government's abortive interventions with the Dutch. They noted that Clifford "from time to time, during all his life renewed his applications, as well in England as in Holland for redress until the year 1737 when he died."[44] Now, as his lawful representatives, they were "entitled to the same relief which he ought to have had in his life time." Meanwhile, the governor and council of Suriname had come into the possession of his plantation, "which has produced one sixteenth part of all the sugars made in that colony." Yet Clifford had, through the course of his life, only received "1,249 hogsheads of sugar and no more."[45] As a man of English birth, Clifford was a subject of the Crown at the time of Suriname's loss to the Dutch. This made him "entitled to all the benefits arising from the . . . Articles of Capitulation, and also as an Englishman to the treaties of 1667 and 1674."[46] As Clifford's representatives, the petitioners asked the king to "interpose" with the States General so that they might receive "satisfaction . . . for all the losses and damages" he had suffered, which amounted to a "considerable sum."[47]

The 1759 petition prompted a full-scale revival of Clifford's case, which included intervention by the British government and a renewed response by the Dutch. The claim first found favor with attorney general Charles Pratt, who wrote a December 1761 report into the matter, which was directed to the Earl of Bute. After examining supporting documents, he stated that he was convinced that "the substance of the . . . petition was well founded." The case was, however, "rather a matter of state than of law."[48] Satisfaction should be sought with the States General, "according to the treaties of 1667 and 1674."[49] Following Pratt's report, Bute sent the case to the Privy Council, a committee of which concluded that Clifford "had been greatly injured by the governor and council of Suriname" and recommended that the king "order his minister at the Hague to represent the case" to the States General. George III concurred on 12 April 1762.[50]

The Crown formally acted that July, when ambassador Joseph Yorke presented a memorial to the States General demanding that Lookup's group receive the compensation that Anglo-Dutch treaties stipulated were due to a wronged subject. Yorke emphasized that Clifford had "suffered the most cruel persecutions, and the most harsh and unparalleled treatment" while in Suriname. His subsequent claim for compensation was "proved by the most authentic vouchers, and supported by the decisive opinions of the most eminent civilians." This had led both William III and Queen Anne "to demand of their High Mightinesses the justice due to this unfortunate subject of Great Britain." Clifford's "representatives and assignees" had revived the prosecution of the case, but to no effect, leading Yorke to intervene on the king's behest. The king had instructed him to emphasize "how unjust it would be to refuse satisfaction to persons whose right was so well founded." A denial of Clifford's claim would constitute "a violation of the capitulation of Suriname, and of the treaties of peace which happily subsist between the two nations." The "affair had been depending near a century"; however, the king "was too much persuaded of the equity of their High Mightinesses to entertain a moment's doubt of their readiness" to bring the case "to a speedy determination, without further delay."[51]

The States General sent a copy of Yorke's memorial to the directors of the Society of Suriname, asking for their advice in the matter.[52] In October 1762 they responded with a lengthy report, which both dismissed the merits of Clifford's case and offered a scathing critique of his posthumous representatives.[53] Echoing the position that the States had taken in response to earlier English interventions, the directors questioned Clifford's title to Corcabo and the applicability of treaties signed between England and the United Provinces. Clifford and his father had left with the other English evacuees following Suriname's conquest, thus completing the terms of the articles of capitulation.[54] Upon returning to the colony, he had acquired Corcabo only by virtue of a marriage that had taken place in Zeeland, to a woman whose title to the estate came from a previous Dutch husband.[55] Clifford's conflict with Suriname's government and his subsequent incarceration were the result of his bad character and poor behavior, including the terrible way in which he had treated his wife.[56] As a result, neither "he nor his effects could be comprised in the treaties of peace concluded with the Crown of England [in] 1667."[57]

The report then recounted Clifford's various attempts to elicit the help of English officials, who ultimately saw through his attempt to frame his case as a matter of state. After his release from prison in Suriname and return to Europe, Clifford had relentlessly pestered both the English and the Dutch. The States General had declared that his case against the Society of Suriname had no merit and that he should instead pursue the matter in "the ordinary courts of law."[58] Refusing to take no for an answer, Clifford had then convinced a series of English envoys to press his cause. Ambassador Villiers had ultimately "conformed himself to the Society's sentiments" and "never more meddled in this disagreeable affair." However, Clifford's "obstinacy in refusing to have recourse to law . . . increased daily."[59] In 1698 he had convinced Ambassador Williamson to present a memorial, although it was never entered into the States' registers.[60] Clifford later employed Ambassador Stanhope to do the same. However, when Stanhope learned the full details of the case he concluded "that Clifford was in the wrong in refusing to submit to the judge ordinary . . . and meddled no more in this affair."[61]

Faced with repeated rejections, Clifford had eventually abandoned his own case, which a dubious party of questionable loyalty to the Crown had now revived. After Clifford had "let his cause lie dormant," the society had gone "for more than one third of a century without ever hearing this affair mentioned directly or indirectly." The English government must have convinced Clifford "of the unjustice of his cause."[62] The case's recent reemergence was due to the efforts of Mandel's party, which the directors clearly conflated with the group now pressing Clifford's claim. Echoing Hop's 1739 assessment, they noted the baffling contents of Clifford's supposed will, which appeared to have been written by someone who had lost the use "of his right senses." Why, they asked, would "a born Englishman . . . pass by his own nation and appoint for his heirs a nation that has no relation with his," one with which there "reigns a perpetual jealousy"? Clifford was a "zealous Englishman who in all his memorials and remonstrances loudly boasts of his birthright and always calls himself a born subject of Great Britain. " Yet he had appealed not to his own king for recourse but rather to "a foreign prince," and had done so "at a time . . . when the same two nations are engaged in a bloody and expensive war." Moreover, the same was true of the men who had revived Clifford's claim. They too had "made a demand for and in the name of the enemies of their native country." If indeed they "are Englishmen they are surely most severely punishable."[63]

The society's directors advised the States General to stick to its previous resolutions that Clifford's case lacked merit, emphasizing that it was not a matter of state. Ambassador Yorke should inform the king of "the true situation of this affair." They were confident that he would agree with the States' prior resolutions "and chastise according to their deserts the persons interested and representors," who had sought his aid and had "attempted to surprise his piety."[64] The States General agreed, sending Yorke a copy of the society's report so that he might "see the true state of this affair from its origin till the present time."[65] It reiterated that Clifford's case was "the object of ordinary justice" rather than "a state affair." Objecting to the Crown's intervention, it argued that neither Clifford nor his posthumous advocates "were justly entitled to his Britannic Majesty's protection in this case or had any right to demand his intercession."[66] The States expected the king to "not only dismiss the parties herein interested, and their representatives; but also [to] declare his resentment at their indecent conduct in this matter." Moreover, he should "annul the extravagant testament on which they found their claim," declaring that "neither the persons pretending to be thereby entitled or their representatives may make a bad use thereof in other nations."[67]

Lookup's party pushed Clifford's case in print as well as petition, affirming to a wider public that England's seventeenth-century treaties demanded that a deceased subject receive redress. The group appears to be behind two texts. The first, the 1760 *The Conduct of the Dutch, Relating to Their Breach of Treaties with England*, was an initial salvo, appearing shortly after the circle had solicited the Crown's help. The year after the States General rebuffed Yorke's memorial, in 1763, the party produced another work, *The Case and Replication of the Legal Representatives of Jeronimy Clifford*.[68]

While the two texts are anonymous, their contents evince a connection to Lookup and his associates. Over more than two hundred pages *The Conduct of the Dutch* relates the "unparalleled injuries and cruelties" suffered by Jeronimy

Clifford, together with the "present state of this affair." Interspersed within his story, along with verbatim excerpts from petitions and official papers, are interludes on the "state of public affairs," which place the case within the context of wider Anglo-Dutch relations. Taken together, these ingredients attempt to demonstrate "the treachery and injustice of the Dutch, towards the English."[69] *The Case and Replication* runs to almost five hundred pages and provides a direct response to the Society of Suriname's 1762 report to the States General, which it reproduces in translation.[70] Some sentences directly copy passages from *The Conduct of the Dutch*. Elsewhere the book echoes its predecessor in the way it recounts the story of Clifford's tribulations and subsequent quest for restitution and the efforts of his posthumous advocates.[71] It explicitly disavows all connection between the self-declared assignees of Clifford's estate and Mandel's group, denying the existence of a will.[72]

Both works emphasize that the previous century's Anglo-Dutch treaties demand the robust defense of a wronged subject. *The Conduct of the Dutch* equated a resolution of Clifford's case with justice for Britain as a nation. This provided a chance for the Dutch to atone for past misdeeds. It was a small irony, but a suitable one, that the Anglo-Dutch treaty of 1674 provided justification for his compensation. The agreement had, to this point, disproportionately benefited the United Provinces while doing nothing to help "poor England."[73] Moreover, the fact that so many decades had passed since Clifford had suffered at Dutch hands only underscored the need for haste, giving "stronger inducement for national justice, and proper satisfaction."[74] The validity of his claim was "not to be the less regarded on account of the distance of time."[75] The Dutch should restore his property and compensate for the wrongs they had inflicted. In this manner "the memory of an unhappy gentleman may yet be revived, his sufferings known to his countrymen, and justice done to his representatives."[76]

The authors of *The Case and Replication* emphasized that in denying Clifford justice the Dutch had violated their treaties with England and that the same treaties now demanded action backed by force. The society's assertion that the Cliffords had abandoned Suriname after its conquest and thus were no longer covered by the 1667 Articles of Capitulation was baseless. Rather, it was the Dutch themselves who "broke the capitulation of Suriname soon after it was made." The 1674 peace treaty had then allowed for the departure of the colony's remaining English subjects, "as also for the security of those who were inclined to stay."[77] Meanwhile, Jeronimy Clifford's "effects were never withdrawn from Suriname, where they now remain, together with his plantation, which was arrested in 1684, and confiscated in 1692."[78] The authors suggested that the Crown should settle Clifford's claim by granting his legal representatives letters of reprisal against the Dutch. This echoed the position taken by advocate-general Sir John Cooke in 1702.[79] Clifford himself had pursued this avenue, although with no luck. He had instead died intestate in a state of "indigence and distress." However, "as the claim is still fully existing, reprisals will still lie against those who committed the offence."[80] Success was now a possibility, as the Crown had been "fully convinced of the justice of this claim" and of the legitimacy of those now pressing Clifford's case.[81]

Clifford's representatives had resorted to print with the hope that public awareness might further his cause. Yet the party was no closer to achieving a settlement. George Lookup, the group's spokesperson, resumed his efforts in 1768, after the Dutch envoy signaled that they should take their appeal directly to the Society of Suriname.[82] As he did so he continued to assert that Clifford's English subjecthood, which was underwritten by seventeenth-century treaties, demanded royal intervention. Lookup made it clear that this continued to include the use of force and that he believed British reprisals against the Dutch were possible.[83]

Writing to the society's secretary, Van Meel, in June 1768, Lookup demanded a final settlement. Claiming to speak for those "representing the late Jeronimy Clifford," he explained that the "concerned" had had a "general meeting." They had agreed to deal directly with the society provided it empowered either Van Meel or someone of equivalent status to resolve the case. That way, he wrote, "This affair which makes so much noise, and has been too long in suspense, may be adjusted without any delay."[84] Van Meel replied on 27 July, denying knowledge of Lookup's group. While "not unacquainted with the pretentions of the so named heirs of Jeronimy Clifford," the States General's 1763 response to Yorke's memorial had offered the final word in the matter. The case, he wrote, "must be debated in justice," and he was confident that the society would prevail in any court action. If Lookup took the matter further, it should be with its directors and not with him.[85] The company's directors, in turn, stated in an August 1768 letter that they could not proceed further because Lookup was "an unknown to us." While they could consider the matter further if he made his "quality known" to them, they too pointed to the States General's existing resolutions, stating that they "must be called upon in law."[86] Replying to the directors, Lookup insisted that Clifford's claim was "a matter of state" rather than "an object of ordinary justice" and that his group "expected a ready compliance."[87]

In further correspondence Lookup emphasized his party's legitimate credentials, which were grounded in law and recognized by the Crown. His group's "title to represent Mr. Clifford universally is indisputable." The archbishop of Canterbury's prerogative court had granted his party "letters of administration" and the King-in-Council had recognized its right to act on

Clifford's behalf. He and his colleagues had nothing to do with the "sham will" in the society's possession and rather "derive[d] their right, immediately from the common law of this land."[88]

The directors were unconvinced, refusing to have "any manner of treaty" with Lookup or his party until they could confirm their identity.[89] And they remained unpersuaded after Lookup forwarded further documentation about the "quality" of his "appointers."[90] In late November Lookup replied with documents that, he claimed, showed that the Privy Council and "gentlemen of the first rank in the profession of the law" supported Clifford's claim. His letter, he wrote, was accompanied by a report by the current Lord High Chancellor to the council, which it had approved. Lookup reminded the directors that Clifford's tribulations were "a matter of national concern, or in other words a matter of state, meriting the attention . . . of our natural sovereign, and the care of his ministers."[91]

The exchange eventually ended in a deadlock, with Lookup insinuating that the British government might resolve the case with reprisals against the Dutch. The directors' final letter, written on 7 March 1769, had contained no concessions.[92] Ending the correspondence later that month, Lookup replied by accusing them of acting as "sole judges" in their "own cause" rather than "doing justice, for all the barbarous inhumanities, perpetrated on Mr. Clifford." Their answers had been "merely evasive" and intended to "perplex the affair." He informed them that he had "laid the whole correspondence" before the king's "principal secretary of state for the northern department" and predicted that with the British government once more involved, "justice will at last take place, notwithstanding your efforts to prevent it." He ended by reminding them that an order "relative to letters of reprisal" had been made on 4 November 1763.[93] This referenced the Privy Council's response to a petition from Richard Kilsha, one of Lookup's cohorts, in which a request for reprisal had been referred to committee, although with unclear results.[94]

Having failed to reach a settlement with the Society of Suriname, Clifford's representatives again appealed to the Crown, emphasizing their own legitimacy as English subjects and their right to redress. In July 1769 they sent Sir Joseph Yorke a detailed reply to the society's 1762 report. Noting that the matter "ought to have been decided near a century ago," they accused the society of attempting to "darken and perplex the present dispute under a cloud of words."[95] Their reply sought to affirm their credentials and distinguish them from Mandel, "a cheat and imposture" who had presented a will that was "a downright forgery."[96] Clifford had, in fact, never "made a will in favor of foreigners" or even "any will at all." Unlike Mandel, they had a legitimate right to pursue his case. They were "all natural born Englishmen, who claim under a legal course of administration, granted them in the prerogative court of Canterbury," acting "not, as legatees or creditors, but as administrators and assignees."[97] This had been acknowledged "by their own sovereign, as appears from his royal interposition in their behalf."[98] The society's directors should know that letters of reprisal would be granted "in favor of Mr. Clifford's legal representatives, if their just demands are not immediately satisfied."[99]

There is no indication that the Crown ever endorsed reprisals against the Dutch. George Lookup's group seems to have made its final effort in November 1770, when the Board of Trade and Plantations read "a memorial of Joseph Cortissos of London, Notary Publick." Cortissos had acted as translator for papers that the party had sent to the Crown in 1763, including the society's report that had identified its efforts with those of Mandel. He now presented himself as "agent to the lawful representatives of Jeronimy Clifford, late of Suriname, merchant, deceased" and asked for "copies of certain papers" related to the case. The board concurred, ordering the papers to be delivered to him.[100] The group appears to have taken no further action.

Unlike the baffling, disloyal claimant presented by Mandel, the Jeronimy Clifford advanced by George Lookup's party had remained a steadfast English subject until his dying day. His subjecthood was grounded not just in birth as an Englishman but also in the protections afforded by international treaties, particularly the 1667 Articles of Capitulation and the 1674 Treaty of Westminster. These treaties stipulated Clifford's right to redress from the Dutch who had so wronged him, supported by the direct intervention of the Crown. Echoing the strategies pursued by Clifford himself, this argument was persuasive enough that the British government chose to advance the case for the first time in decades.

For Lookup's group, Clifford had been wronged not as a discrete individual but rather in his specific capacity as an English subject, making the case a matter of state with implications for their own time. In mistreating him and failing to provide compensation, the Dutch had abrogated treaties that had been signed to protect the rights of all who fell under the king's protection in his former colony. If the Crown failed to defend Clifford, then those treaties became meaningless, as would others signed to protect colonial subjects' rights. In this sense, the case's lack of resolution did not simply leave untied a loose end from the previous century; it also threatened subjects in the present. This made the affair urgent enough to merit reprisals by the Crown against the Dutch.

The States General and the Society of Suriname, meanwhile, stuck to the position that Jeronimy Clifford's claim lacked larger significance. If he had been wronged—and it was far from clear that he had been—it was only as an individual and any attempt at recourse belonged in the ordinary law courts. Yet this attempt to contain the case failed to prevent further efforts to impute it with broader meaning. Reverberating in print through the 1760s, Clifford's story provided a framework for the discussion of past Anglo-Dutch relations, contemporary colonial friction between the two powers, and the merits and implications of the Glorious Revolution.

Affective Subjecthood in Anti-Dutch Polemic

Depictions of Jeronimy Clifford proliferated along with evocations of his case. The works produced by Lookup's group were part of a larger printed debate about the attributes of the Dutch that mixed old grievances with contemporary concerns, using Clifford's case for a variety of eighteenth-century ends. His proponents grounded their defense of English subjecthood in affective arguments and not just appeals to international treaty, thus tugging on their readers' heartstrings. They did so both by conjuring the positive virtues inherent in being English and dolefully recounting the wrongs that their countrymen had suffered abroad at the hands of their foes. This entailed the creation of new versions of Clifford, which exemplified the eighteenth-century virtues of refinement and politeness while stolidly enduring Dutch cruelties that continued into the present age.

Clifford's qualities were apparently such that he was still remembered in Suriname by the middle of the eighteenth century. In 1755 one Edward Ephraim Cooke had traveled to the Dutch colony from Nova Scotia, where he had lived since 1749. He had been trading with Suriname for the past five years. Now he spent three months there, during which time he got to know most of its more prominent colonists. Cooke was particularly interested in the territory's English past. He learned from a number of Dutch settlers "that some descendants of the old English inhabitants were then remaining in the colony." The same men told him "that it was a great pity that the descendants, or representatives, of one Mr. Clifford, an Englishman, did not come over to Suriname, and claim his property." His plantation, it was widely acknowledged, had once been the "finest . . . in that province." They and the colony's other "principal inhabitants" were surprised that no one had traveled from England to take possession of it, as the estate was "the undoubted right and property of him or his representatives."[101]

Cooke's account comes from an affidavit supposedly signed in London on 16 September 1760, which is reproduced in *The Conduct of the Dutch, Relating to Their Breach of Treaties with England*. This and the other text associated with Lookup's party, *The Case and Replication of the Legal Representatives of Jeronimy Clifford*, depicted a virtuous Clifford whose memory had been slandered by the Dutch. Any tales of Clifford's poor behavior during his time in Suriname were motivated by Dutch jealousy of his English refinement. The society had, for example, alleged that one Herman van Haagen had dissolved a partnership with Clifford in 1684 out of dislike for his "person, and his manner of living."[102] According to the authors of *The Case and Replication*, such opprobrium was to be "expected from a Dutch colonist in partnership with such an Englishman." Clifford was "tall, genteel, handsome, and graceful" and thus able "to captivate the affections of more Dutch ladies than one." His "manner of living" was "not in the boorish Dutch taste, but in good English politeness and hospitality," and his table was "frequently and generally honored by the best women of fashion in the colony." Whether they were "gay, or, perhaps, wicked women" was something that "Mr. Clifford could not help."[103]

This refined, sociable Clifford stood in marked contrast to the churlish, troublesome man described in the Society of Suriname's 1762 report to the States General. According to the society, Clifford had behaved in "a morose, rebellious, surly, and shocking manner." He had also "spent and dissipated his wife's effects in the company of wicked women," having "despised and abused ... [her] in a shameful manner both by words and actions," even "threatening her life." This "compelled her to break and annul their contract of marriage." Clifford's bad conduct had led to his condemnation as "a mutinous fellow and a disturber of the public repose." The provisional fiscal had then sentenced him to death, a punishment that Suriname's criminal court had commuted to seven years' imprisonment.[104]

The Case and Replication, however, described this picture as riddled with falsehoods. The Cliffords' marriage, in particular, had been the subject of an all-out assault by the Dutch authorities. They had tried to undermine the couple's affection for each other, "depriving a woman of that generous and tender regard due to a man, whom either love or gratitude had made dear to her." In doing so "they took every opportunity of filling her nuptial pillow with tormenting thorns."[105] They had even fabricated a petition by Matson against her husband, making up a story of abuse that "was entirely false, and calculated only to cover the most iniquitous transactions against Mr. Clifford."[106]

The Dutch, the text asserted, had sought to negate Clifford's English subjecthood while denying him the privileges due to one of their own. The governor had jailed him for his refusal "to take any oath [to the United Provinces], without a reservation of his allegiance to the Crown of England."[107] He did eventually swear an oath that made him "a naturalized Dutchman," although he remained "an Englishman by birth." This meant that he still "retained his allegiance to his Britannic Majesty, and was therefore also a subject of the British state." The Dutch, however, had undermined his status on both counts, refusing him "the privileges of a naturalized Dutchman, and those of a British born subject."[108] Unbothered by Clifford's apparent dual loyalty, the authors of *The Case and Replication* were, however, vexed by the Dutch attempt to negate his position as an English subject.

Although it was a legal status rooted in allegiance to the monarch, English subjecthood remained intertwined with the larger, more amorphous virtues that accompanied Englishness. According to both *The Case and Replication* and *The Conduct of the Dutch* Jeronimy Clifford clearly evinced these characteristics. Not only had he been "tall, genteel, handsome, and graceful."[109] He had also lived his life as a loving husband, who treated his wife, the source of his estate, with nothing short of tenderness. As a born Englishman he carried a natural affection for his sovereign, an affinity that, along with the bonds of allegiance, his proponents drew on to marshal Britain's backing. Yet the Dutch had slandered his good name, undermined his marriage, and called into question both the legal and affective qualities of his English identity.

By the middle of the eighteenth century the Anglo-Dutch alliance that had been established by the Glorious Revolution had begun to fray. Ongoing competition for colonial resources led to conflict between Britain and the Netherlands in locales from India to West Africa. At the same time, the United Provinces proved to be an unreliable ally against France, instead adopting a neutral stance in the Seven Years' War.[110] Clifford's proponents in print placed his treatment into a larger pattern of Dutch behavior both around the contemporary world and in the past. His experience was, after all, just one example of the difficulties faced by English subjects overseas, not least in the face of persistent Dutch malice.[111]

Texts from the 1760s advocating Clifford's case stressed parallels between his experience and the 1623 Amboyna massacre, when the Dutch had executed ten English employees of the East India Company in what is now Indonesia. In doing so they relied on their readers' familiarity with an incident that, as Alison Games notes, served as a "cultural touchstone."[112] Reiterated in print for well over a century, the story had long provided "a metaphor for universal cruelty committed by a wider array of people." However, it retained the specific cruelty of the Dutch as its central element.[113] Mid-eighteenth-century writers would have assumed that their readers "were familiar with the episode not only in general but also in its particular details," using it to convey "the continued complexity and urgency of Anglo-Dutch relations."[114] Amboyna provided a way for Clifford's advocates to position his suffering in relation to both the past and the present.

In contextualizing Clifford's story, such works posited a version of subjecthood defined by suffering that explained how a United Provinces long in decline could gain victories against an expanding British empire. Seen in the cumulative light of earlier events in Suriname and the Indonesian "Spice Islands," Anglo-Dutch friction in the mid-eighteenth century was yet another manifestation of innate Dutch hostility toward the English. Fueled by anti-English animosity that transcended space and time, the Dutch continued to add to their earlier record of treaty violations and persecution. English subjects around the world were first and foremost victims of the Dutch.

The Amboyna massacre, while lamentable, at least provided an example for which the Dutch had been forced to atone. As noted in *The Conduct of the Dutch*, Oliver Cromwell had compelled the nation to pay three hundred thousand pounds for its crimes. And "the Dutch cruelty exercised on the unhappy sufferers at Amboyna, was very like their treatment to Mr. Clifford at Suriname." It stood to reason that "where the case is similar to a known precedent, the redress ought to be the same."[115] It was not, the authors wrote, necessary to elaborate on the "many other striking occasions, down from the massacre of Amboyna to the late attempt at Calcutta" (referring to a 1759 Anglo-Dutch clash in Bengal). Each told a similar story, and what mattered most was restitution.[116]

Another work, the 1766 *Dutch Displayed*, did find cause for elaboration. This placed Clifford's case within a larger recitation "of the barbarities, rapines and injustices, committed by the subjects of Holland upon those of England, since the commencement of the Dutch republic to the present times."[117] Although about half the text focuses on Clifford's tribulations and attempts by his posthumous representatives to resolve his claim, it positions them as elements of a much larger story. A frontispiece image of the "torments inflicted by the Dutch on the English in Amboyna" underscores that this work is about much more than Clifford. The picture depicted the Dutch torturing an English victim, using an eighteenth-century version of an image that had circulated in various iterations since 1624.[118]

The book opens with a reminder of Dutch ingratitude: "Every quarter of the globe witnesses their barbarity to England" even though it is England that secured their independence from Spain.[119] This is followed by a detailed discussion of Amboyna, "in which we see the most striking specimen of the cruelty inherent in Dutch dispositions."[120] Tales of Dutch piracy and warfare with the

English then precede a treatment of Suriname and Clifford, which was followed by examples of contemporary Dutch misdeeds around the world.[121]

In Africa Dutch malice threatened to displace the English while at the same time generating acts of courage and loyalty that both effaced ethnic difference and created subjects from affection. The Netherlands' "constitutional enmity to England" made victims out of the English in Africa.[122] (The work itself generally favors "English" rather than "British" as a descriptor.) The Dutch, meanwhile, were guilty of "inhumanities of which we could never justly accuse our more natural rivals the French."[123] The story of a 1750 attack on the English at Dixcove, in modern-day Ghana, includes an account by a French captain, who has "the humanity of a British born subject."[124] Here the English are reduced to weakness, and by "nefarious means the whole of the windward part of the gold coast . . . has fallen into the hands of the Dutch."[125] Africans who fight with the Dutch are "savages," while the text casts the people conquered by them as virtuous victims, the Dutch having infringed on "the natural rights of the inhabitants, our allies."[126] Meanwhile, the "headman" in Atchuma "has always acknowledged himself an English subject . . . and declares he will quit his country for ever rather than submit to so despotic a people as the Dutch."[127] The extension of English power in Africa, meanwhile, is predictably unproblematic, with the English enslavement of Africans remaining unmentioned.

Events in India show that the Dutch had inherited the inclinations of their ancestors even as they were haunted by their past transgressions. *The Dutch Displayed* describes a 1759 Dutch attack on the English during which the Nawab of Bengal allied with the Dutch East India Company to oust the company's British counterpart. Although the English prevailed, the Dutch had attempted to cut "the throats of our countrymen in that part of India."[128] The Dutch plan to displace the English serves, for the author, as "indelible proof" that "as a nation, [they] inherit every vice with which their ancestors have often been so justly reproached by ours."[129] After relating the course of the battle and the subsequent English triumph, the text describes the Dutch fear of massacre by their victors, which stems from their own history and inclinations. Such an idea "could never enter into the breast of an Englishman."[130] However, the Dutch "probably recollected the various massacres they had committed upon the English," their "conscious guilt" leading them to fear being "offered up [as] victims at the altar of that revenge."[131] Tortured by both their prior misdeeds and present predilections, the Dutch are unable to fathom English mercy.

The Dutch Displayed ends with a reference to Clifford, placing the resolution of his claim in the context of wider resistance to the Dutch depredations it had described. The author urges the reader to reconsider "unduly cherishing a nation which, without intermission, watches for our ruin, and for a total eradication of our commerce." Before calling for justice for Clifford's representatives, the text defends the right of the English to settle in Java and urges restoration of the king of Bantam, "who survives under our protection in Bengal." It then urges Britain to "declare the treaty in 1674 of no force" and, if necessary, to "revoke all the treaties we have made with the Dutch," as they have failed to show "reciprocal faith."[132] It was, in short, time to push back against "our false friends of the Netherlands" and to "receive that satisfaction which is due by the laws of God and man."[133]

The use of Clifford's case as an example of Dutch cruelty reached its apex in a series of letters to the *Public Advertiser* printed in 1767. These letters not only connected the Amboyna massacre to Clifford's own treatment but also argued that both examples merited a restitution that, if denied, justified the expulsion of the Dutch from both Suriname and the Spice Islands. Signed by "Gabriel Touverson" in a pseudonymous nod to Gabriel Towerson, one of the Englishmen the Dutch had executed in Amboyna in 1623, the letters drew a direct line from the massacre to Clifford. As the pseudonymous author declared in the April 29 letter, "Amboyna and Suriname join their voices together."[134]

Touverson depicted the Dutch as innately inclined toward cruelty. He bolstered his own observations with excerpts from two 1624 texts, the *True Declaration*, a translated Dutch East India Company account of the events in Amboyna, and the English company's rejoinder, *An Answer unto the Dutch Pamphlet*.[135] The Dutch in Amboyna had subjected the English to "torments unknown to the inquisition itself."[136] Moreover, as a nation they made "no scruple of committing such barbarities in cold blood, which the English are wont to shudder at, even when they are intoxicated with liquor."[137]

The Dutch persecution of Jeronimy Clifford in Suriname was a manifestation of the same qualities that had directed their actions in Amboyna. His case was not just one of property seizure or failure to receive compensation but also one of cruelty and physical suffering. Having endured "numberless persecutions," Clifford "was condemned to be whipped to death, for no other crime but presuming to claim the rights of an Englishman . . . by virtue of the capitulation and subsequent treaties." Suriname's governor and council were "of the very same stamp with those of Amboyna," expressing piety before perpetrating brutality.[138] And although Clifford had lived through both his Surinamese and English incarcerations, in Touverson's narrative he had died "broken-hearted in a prison" after a life that "was a continued martyrdom, in vainly suing for justice." Meanwhile, "the impious robbers and their adherents and protectors [had] rioted in the spoils of his noble fortune."[139] There was, however, hope that rightness would prevail. The Dutch, Touverson wrote, "may soon find to their cost, that, as the blood of my name's sake . . . still cries to heaven for vengeance, so *Jeronimy Clifford, being dead, yet speaketh.*"[140]

The Crown had now taken up Clifford's case, finally offering the hope of restitution. Indeed, the Dutch might come to regret not having reached a settlement during his lifetime. "How many thousand pounds might the Dutch have saved," Touverson wondered, "had they done Mr. Clifford immediate justice when he demanded it[?]" Now what had once been a "private injury" had become "a public concern, and an affair of state."[141]

Just as Clifford had the right to compensation, so Britain retained a claim to both Amboyna and Suriname, from which the Dutch should be ousted if they fail to settle past wrongs. During the 1620s the Dutch had illegally expelled the East India Company "from the Spice Islands." Yet the British retained "as much right to our share" of them "as we have to the whole colony of Suriname, which was ceded to the Dutch on certain conditions." Those conditions had been "most infamously broken," and the Dutch were now "mere usurpers and robbers." In consequence, "the honor of the whole nation, requires, that they should be dispossessed, if they refuse any longer giving immediate satisfaction."[142]

A century after Abraham Crijnssen's Zeeland fleet had conquered Suriname, the pseudonymous Gabriel Touverson imagined a reversal of the English capitulation. Whether it was realistic to expect the Crown to recapture Suriname or oust the Dutch from Amboyna was beside the point. Both Jeronimy Clifford and Touverson's original namesake had borne the brunt of Dutch cruelty, two of countless English people overseas whose status as subjects merited justice.

The Dutch antipathy toward the English seen in Amboyna and Suriname continued into the present time, a fact demonstrated by attacks on the king's subjects as they benignly conducted their affairs from Africa to Bengal. Texts like *The Dutch Displayed* bore witness to an animosity that showed no sign of abating even after a century and a half. In doing so they defined the overseas English by their experience of suffering, depicting them as virtuous victims even during a time of British imperial expansion. This paradox of ongoing victimhood was made worse by the fact that England and the United Provinces were supposed to be partners in the fight against France. The accession of a Dutch prince to England's throne in 1689 had heralded this now shaky alliance. How, then, to situate the reign of William III within this story of implacable Dutch hostility without appearing to be disloyal to a former king of England?

English Subjects of a Foreign King: The Glorious Revolution in Eighteenth-Century Anti-Dutch Polemic

Positing the Dutch as England's enemy raised uncomfortable questions about the Glorious Revolution and, by extension, the nature of subjecthood under contractarian monarchy. If the Dutch were England's foes, had the events of 1688 really been a Dutch invasion? Even if, in Lockean terms, this had constituted a legitimately contractarian episode, it still remained problematic. James II's absolutist impulses may well have rendered him a tyrant, dissolving his kingship in a way that justified inviting William of Orange to invade. But what, then, were the implications for subjects of the newly minted William III if the Dutch character innately inclined toward the persecution of the English? Perhaps perfidy lay not with the Dutch as a whole, or with the House of Orange, but instead with the republican faction that had historically opposed it? Even so, could the English ever truly be loyal subjects of a foreign-born monarch, especially if subjecthood was inextricably bound to the more amorphous, affective elements of Englishness?[143]

The Conduct of the Dutch, one of the texts apparently associated with George Lookup's party, explicitly condemned William III for advancing the Netherlands' interests over those of his newly acquired kingdoms. The Anglo-Dutch alliance had led Clifford to hope for swift redress on leaving Suriname.[144] Yet there were plenty of signs that the new king was willing to overlook his subjects' concerns. William had betrayed the Scots, whose venture in Darien, "in the neighborhood of Suriname," had collapsed because "it was found advisable at court to make a sacrifice of that colony."[145] The Dutch, who were "jealous of this Scotch settlement," had concluded that "it might be prejudicial to their interest from Curaçao to the Spanish main." William had thus acted in his capacity as stadholder rather "than his being king of Scotland." Only parliament offered a counterweight against this Dutch influence, through the Commons' ability to "exert a true English spirit."[146]

Hostile both to William and to the wider House of Orange, the book offered explicit sympathy for the Dutch anti-Orange faction. The decline of the United Provinces as a power had mirrored the eclipse of the republic and the rise in influence of the stadholder. The text describes the republican Jan de Witt, who was killed with his brother in 1672 by an Orangist mob, as a "great man" and concludes that now "the republic is . . . far from being the same [as] it was in their time, and is not worthy [of] the name of a maritime power."[147]

While its anti-Orange sentiments led *The Conduct of the Dutch* to compliment de Witt, the text ultimately cast aspersions on the Dutch as a whole, whose behavior as allies had demonstrated bad faith. The supposed bond between England and the Netherlands was ultimately a sham. Although the two countries were formally united against France, "the English always bore the greatest burthen . . . and the Dutch lightened their burthen by degrees."[148] Clifford's case exposed the hollowness of the alliance. While "it is in the interest of Holland to live in perfect harmony with England," his treatment had sown discord. Dutch "rank and reputation" relied on "an exact performance of solemn treaties"; yet in his case, "it is plain they have violated their engagements with England."[149]

The Dutch Displayed, on the other hand, evaded possible disloyalty to William of Orange by placing the blame for Dutch depredations at the feet of the republican faction. This was true even in the case of current Dutch acts against the English around the world. The leader of the 1759 attack on the English in Axim, in modern-day Ghana, was "a descendant from a family famous for their adherence to the De Wit[t] faction." This means that he is "an enemy to the partisans of the family of Orange, from whom we never received an injury."[150] Explaining further, the text noted that the "ancient republicans, descended from the supporters of the De Wit[t]s, are now our enemies in Holland." Dutch mistreatment of the English overseas is "by their influence."[151] Toward the end of the work the author emphasizes that he or she "would not be understood to accuse all the Dutch of those crimes, breaches of faith, and violences . . . mentioned." Rather, "they are all to be placed to the account of the Anti-Orange faction, which has always been too powerful in Holland."[152]

Yet the text also resorted to broader anti-Dutch sentiment. When the Dutch stadholder was king of England, its author wrote, "we were almost perpetually embarrassed with continental wars on Holland's account."[153] While the English and Dutch had fought together as allies in Europe, the behavior of the Dutch had been "execrable," with England's supposed ally prone to "treachery."[154] Dutch actions in Europe, as in other parts of the world, reveal the "dissimulation, cruelty and avarice" of the entire nation, not just of the republican faction.[155] In this light, the author's denial that the text charges "the Dutch in general as a people with the black roll of inhumanities here rehearsed" is unpersuasive.[156]

The 1767 *Dutch Modesty Exposed to English View* took a similar tack, ostensibly praising the House of Orange while falling into a wider condemnation of the Dutch as a whole. The work answered a pro-Dutch text that had appeared the year before, *A Short and Modest Reply to a Book Intituled the Dutch Displayed*, which was written in the voice of a recent resident of the Netherlands who was, presumably, English.[157] This text had accused England of failing to appreciate William of Orange, who had "been the means of establishing the constitution on the principles of liberty and freedom."[158] Elsewhere the work had nodded toward republican egalitarianism, noting the "equality of condition" that "prevails in the Republic of Holland," together with the absence of "overgrown nobles."[159] Clifford's sufferings had been the fault of the English Crown, which had failed to see to the welfare of one of its subjects.[160]

In answering this attempt to vindicate the Netherlands *Dutch Modesty* defended "the innocence of the illustrious family of Orange" and denied that it attacked the Dutch more generally. The residents of "Vaderland are not to be reproached" with the "inhumanities" against the English that its author describes. Rather, "the party really guilty . . . is, the rampant foes of that illustrious house, [who are] too often, too numerous in the provincial and general assemblies of the States."[161] Yet like *The Dutch Displayed*, the work also depicts cruelty toward the English as a national rather than a purely factional trait. Dutch behavior in Africa reveals "their unchecked . . . barbarities towards every person that passes under an English denomination, and unluckily comes within the power of their fort-masters."[162] (There is no mention of either side's treatment of Africans.) Indeed, Dutch behavior "from the ancientest to the latest times" shows "a continued malevolence," and "an irremitting implacable malice at their honest neighbors of England."[163]

This wider hostility ultimately implicated the House of Orange too. Clifford's sufferings, according to *Dutch Modesty*, demonstrated not only direct Dutch animosity but also the fact that the English government had fallen under Dutch influence. On the one hand, the Dutch remained responsible for "the crimes of their forefathers at Suriname." The States General had "committed a manifest injustice towards a subject of England, and all the world knows that the States of Holland never die."[164] Yet the English government at the time was also to blame, having failed to act after assessing the damages due to him.[165] This disregard was due to Dutch influence. The Crown should have "demanded Mr. Clifford and his effects by a ship of war" in 1694, "but could this be expected while Dutch councils bore so much great sway at St. James's?" Clifford had been a victim of "the then negligence of the Dutchified court of London."[166]

An appendix dedicated to Clifford's case also calls attention to Dutch influence after the Glorious Revolution. Here the author denies that the English could have sent ships to aid him. A 1674 Anglo-Dutch treaty stipulated that this depended on the States General's providing passports, something it had refused to do.[167] At the same time, the author blames Clifford's failure to receive justice on "a Dutchman being then our king."[168] The lack of resolution since the death of William III was harder to explain. Inaction by Queen Anne's government was "to the disgrace of my country." Clifford's case remained unresolved even at the time of writing, and "[w]hat retards it our ministers only can tell."[169] The affair should serve as a warning, "for whenever injustice becomes a measure of government, nobody knows where it will end."[170]

Eighty years after the Glorious Revolution, the accession of William of Orange to the throne continued to place anti-Dutch polemicists in an uneasy position. It was difficult to contain complaints about the United Provinces to the country's Orangist or republican factions. Yet decrying an earlier Dutch presence at court and condemning the king-stadholder had troubling ramifications for the present. The authors who advocated for Clifford's case were subjects of Great Britain's third Hanoverian king, George III, who had acceded to the throne in 1760. His grandfather, Hanover's elector, had become king by virtue of the 1701 Act of Settlement, which had stipulated that only a Protestant could rule.[171] The origins of the Protestant succession, which departed from the hereditary principles that had pertained for centuries, rested in the moment when a faction of England's elite had invited a Dutch prince to invade. Had subjects' true affection for their monarch survived this contractarian break?

None of the pro-Clifford texts of the 1760s showed signs of overt Jacobitism; yet the questions they raised about the Glorious Revolution had implications for the legitimacy of the Hanoverians, whose right to rule remained underwritten by the logic of 1688.[172] During that year England had either chosen a foreign king or been invaded by one. If William's Dutchness rather than his foreignness were the problem, then the Hanoverians escaped untinged. But what if the affective elements of English subjecthood made any choice of a foreign-born king problematic?[173]

It is likely that Clifford's case was so long-lived that it continued into the Fourth Anglo-Dutch War of 1780–1784, which was a consequence of the American Revolution, reemerging in the decade after George Lookup's party abandoned its efforts.[174] Sometime after 1774, but probably by 1780, one James Laman petitioned the Earl of Hillsborough, secretary of state, claiming to act as a "creditor of the late Jeronimy Clifford, planter of the island of Suriname." Laman stated that he had a copy of Clifford's "last will and testament," details of which echo the copy possessed by Mandel. He asked "the prerogative court of the Archbishop of Canterbury for letters of administration" in order to settle the case.[175]

Laman had made sure that the parties named in Clifford's will no longer claimed its contents. He had, he wrote, "first duly applied to the French king as properly invested with the matters of the Mississippi Company," which Clifford had named as heir to his plantations. The French government had told him that the king of France "could not interfere therein" because the Mississippi Company had ceased to exist before Clifford's death. Laman had then "applied to her imperial majesty Maria Theresa Queen of Hungary and Bohemia." Clifford had named her father "the Emperor Charles" as heir "in case the Mississippi Company refused to accept of his said bequest." After he had informed the queen that she could "take administration" of Clifford's property, "her minister Count De Belgioso" had told Laman that "she would not take any concern or intermeddle in the business."[176]

Having done his due diligence with the French and the Hapsburgs, Laman then applied to the prerogative court of the archbishop of Canterbury. On 7 June 1774 judge George Hay had refused his request for "letters of administration" for the will, arguing that doing so "might bring on a Dutch war." Instead he advised Laman "to go and settle it with the Dutch." Laman then appealed to the High Court of Delegates, which also warned him that proceeding with the case might lead to "rupture with the Dutch," not least because the claim exceeded a million pounds. Although it had noted that there was "no legal objection" to the will's validity, the court had refused to grant him administration due to "political reasons of state."[177]

Laman concluded his petition by asking the Crown to again take up Clifford's claim and alluding to a new Anglo-Dutch conflict. Any obstacles to its pursuit had now been "removed by the present rupture between the Crown of Great Britain and the States of Holland." He patriotically offered to "make over his interest to his Majesty" so that the Crown could pursue it "as a matter of state as it ever has been" or by "some other legal means." And if the king were to decline his offer, Laman would, of course, be glad to "be admitted to the letters of administration prayed for."[178]

If the "present rupture" to which Laman alluded was the 1780–1784 Fourth Anglo-Dutch War, then Clifford's story had lasted long enough to see the Dutch change from enemies to allies and back to enemies again.[179] Two decades later English troops would return to Suriname. Britain seized the colony on the eve of the Napoleonic wars, occupying it in 1799–1802 and 1804–1816.[180] By the time forces from England again found themselves on the Wild Coast Jeronimy Clifford's case seems finally to have died.

Jeronimy Clifford had many afterlives. The first posthumous Clifford, the alleged author of Mandel's will, was both generous and disloyal, making bequests to assorted London characters while reserving the bulk of his wealth for French and Hapsburg beneficiaries. These are choices so confounding that he seems most plausible as either fabricated or deranged. The version of Clifford advanced by George Lookup's group, on the other hand, was an English subject of impeccable fidelity. Backed by the force of the previous century's Anglo-Dutch treaties, his case both deserved and had received renewed royal intervention. Yet texts associated with Lookup's party depict a Jeronimy Clifford markedly at odds with that of earlier years, one who was graceful, refined, and polite, indeed a paragon of Enlightenment virtues. This, in turn, complemented a version of Clifford that was present in many of his proponents' depictions, an innocent victim of the Dutch who forms a link in a chain of persecution stretching from the Amboyna massacre of 1623 to contemporary predations in India and Africa.

Jeronimy Clifford's posthumous lives reveal more than just reimaginings of the man himself, showing some of the characteristics of vernacular English subjecthood by the mid-eighteenth century. Clifford's case brought the messiness of the periphery back to the metropolis in the form of old disputes, ambiguous identities, and juxtapositions with former enemies. As in England itself, subjecthood overseas involved far more than simply legal status. Slippery qualities such as loyalty, affection, and reputation also defined its parameters.

A century-old conflict between two empires that were no longer at war continued to shape the meaning of English subjecthood. Clifford's advocates successfully moved the Crown to again intercede with the Dutch by evoking the 1667 Articles of Capitulation and the 1674 Treaty of Westminster. These treaties made Jeronimy Clifford far more than an individual victim of unique circumstances. In their presentation he became a representative for all subjects wronged by the Dutch. His case demanded restitution and, failing that, maybe even military action, a result of a bond with his sovereign that compelled a response decades after his death.

Affective elements, both positive and negative, intertwined accounts of colonial subjecthood with the more amorphous qualities of Englishness. The graceful, Enlightenment Clifford merited defense as a subject precisely because of his refined English manners, in contrast to the boorish, cruel Dutch. At the same time, accounts of the Dutch persecution of English subjects from Amboyna, Suriname, Africa, and Bengal attempted to move readers to sympathy and, perhaps, to action. That a burgeoning British empire could suffer defeats at the hands of a depleted former enemy might make some sense if it had been caused by a century and a half of relentless hatred.

It was the English, not the British, who appear as victims in these anti-Dutch sources, even though they were written long after the 1707 Act of Union. That union had occurred in part because of English desires to cement the Protestant succession throughout Great Britain. While not espousing Jacobitism, Clifford's posthumous advocates remained uneasy about the Glorious Revolution seven decades after it had occurred. For some, William III had advanced the interests of the United Provinces at England's expense. And if the Dutch were England's implacable foes, could English subjects ever be loyal to a Dutch king or could a Dutch king ever be the true protector of the realm? More troubling still for a Georgian audience, did English subjects require a monarch of English birth or lineage?

The British readers who encountered Jeronimy Clifford's claim in print benefited from the fruits of an empire that was very different from England's more tenuous holdings of a century earlier. Clifford's case vanished from view just as this first British empire was unraveling, when the loss of thirteen North American colonies began to shift the imperial center of gravity eastward. Britain would, of course, continue to maintain territory in the Americas. Adding to its Canadian and Caribbean possessions, in 1796 its forces captured Berbice, Essequibo, and Demerara from the Dutch. Situated to the immediate west of Suriname, these regions were unified in 1831 and renamed British Guiana, an arrangement that continued until Guyanese independence in 1966.[181] It is, perhaps, ironic that when Britain took Suriname as part of the same confluence of events it held onto it for little more than fifteen years, just as England had in the seventeenth century.

Conclusion

In 1608 the judges who heard *Calvin's Case* had wrestled with some of the implications of the accession of a non-English king. In doing so they clarified the legal terms of subjecthood and responded to some of the difficult questions raised by transnational allegiance. The bond between subject and monarch was something formed at the moment of birth in one of the king's territories, making Scots born after 1603 the king's English as well as his Scottish subjects.[1] The ruling took place when England barely had an empire, a year after the establishment of Jamestown. But it implied that all people born on land under the king's dominion were his subjects, wherever in the world those territories might be. In practice, however, factors that were far more fungible—and much more capricious—played a role in determining who received the benefits of English subjecthood.

Much had changed between the reign of James I and the time when the Clifford case disappeared from view. The growth of an empire, along with events from the civil war and regicide to the Glorious Revolution, Protestant succession, and Act of Union, had shifted the ground on which subjecthood stood. Unlike England in 1608, Britain in the 1770s held territory that spanned the globe. People were born under George III's dominion not just in England, Scotland, and Ireland but also in India, Barbados, and Virginia. Others became subjects when new land came under British rule.[2] But not all people born in British colonies benefited from the protections of subjecthood. By 1775 British ships had transported well over two million enslaved Africans across the Atlantic.[3] Despite the implications of Calvin's Case, the children of those who survived the passage were not accorded the blessings of birthright subjecthood.

In 1772 another court case, *Somerset v. Stewart*, attempted to resolve some of the domestic implications of what was by then the long-established British practice of enslaving people. That year James Somerset, a West African man held as a slave on a ship set to depart for Jamaica, sued for a writ of habeas corpus.[4] A Scottish merchant named Charles Stewart had brought Somerset to England from Virginia. Somerset escaped Stewart's clutches only to be recaptured, after which Stewart planned to sell him in the Caribbean. His subsequent legal action, which was brought about with the help of abolitionists, was successful, and the ruling, written by Lord Chief Justice Mansfield, allowed him to go free. Although some contemporaries and later scholars viewed *Somerset's Case* as a definitive pronouncement against slavery in Britain, it only prohibited the removal of slaves from the country.[5] People remained enslaved in England into the nineteenth century, although in the wake of the case many were forced to sign apprenticeship contracts, allowing both work without pay and involuntary transportation back to slave colonies.[6]

When juxtaposed, *Calvin's Case* and *Somerset's Case* show how slavery shaped subjecthood. *Calvin v. Smith* implied that anyone born under the king's allegiance was a subject in all his dominions. *Somerset v. Stewart* shows that this had never functionally been the case, at least since the adoption of chattel slavery, not because it made an explicit statement about English subjecthood but rather because it did not. Somerset's own subject status was not at issue. As someone born beyond the king's dominion in Africa, he was not a subject by birth and he would not have been naturalized.[7] Rather, as Dana Rabin has noted, Mansfield's decision "highlighted the contradictions between the ideology of equality before the law . . . and the reality of bodies bought and sold."[8] His ruling defined colonies "as foreign countries," regions "so different and distinct that the range of their law did not extend to England and vice versa."[9] Yet people not just in England but throughout its empire took subjecthood to confer certain rights, which they readily contrasted with the condition of slavery. These ranged from inheritance and trial by jury to the treaty-backed royal protection to which Clifford appealed throughout his life. *Somerset's Case*, in denying that colonies could negate the benefits of subjecthood in England, acknowledged that they might annihilate them elsewhere.[10]

This was far from the first English court to grapple with the reality of colonial slavery and the enslaved people who were subsequently brought to England. Two centuries of inconsistent legal decisions had preceded *Somerset*. As early as 1569, before the English enslaved widely, one ruling had maintained that

CONCLUSION

"England was too pure an air for slaves to breathe in." In 1677 the ruling in *Butts v. Penny* stated that slavery was allowed in England, a decision that was echoed in 1694 by *Gelly v. Cleve*. In 1701 Chief Justice Sir John Holt ruled that "as soon as a negro comes into England, he becomes free," while a colleague concluded that "the laws of England take no notice of a negro."[11] Meanwhile, slaveholders ignored unfavorable pronouncements, thus ensuring that slaves were present in England throughout the seventeenth and eighteenth centuries.[12]

As *Somerset's Case* shows, these tensions between colonial and metropolitan subjecthood remained unresolved even by the 1770s. Although *Calvin v. Smith* had defined subjecthood expansively in 1608, within a century some English colonies were denying its rights to the majority of people within their jurisdictions.[13] In *Somerset v. Stewart*, Justice Mansfield had made a valiant effort to square the circle but the dissonance remained. It would persist for at least as long as slavery itself and would find new life in the limitations and hypocrisies of citizenship in the republic that was born soon thereafter from thirteen of Britain's North American colonies.

Jeronimy Clifford lived his life midway between these two landmark cases, and his own subjecthood reflects the contradictions that they illuminate. As an active participant in the same processes that enslaved James Somerset, he claimed subjects' rights that included the authority to possess the people who had worked his land and receive compensation for their value. Along with the entitlement of a slaveholder, many other, related colonial factors also affected the tenor of his subjecthood. These factors ranged from disease and demographics to the shifts in sovereignty brought about by conquest and dynastic change. Together these elements formed the world in which Clifford spent his first four decades and in which he defined his identity. The second four decades, during which he deployed his colonial subjecthood in England and the Netherlands, testify to the permeability between empire and metropolis that Mansfield's ruling sought to keep at bay.

Clifford's family had brought him to Suriname when he was just a small boy, soon after its foundation by English Barbadians, when the venture already mirrored its parent colony's recent transition to a slave society. Around the same time Suriname's governors extended subjecthood to any members of the "Hebrew nation" who moved there as part of a bid to save an ailing venture that had been weakened by contagion. Clifford's youth was in the years after the 1667 Dutch conquest, when the Articles of Capitulation of that year defined the rights of the English community of which he was a part. The 1675 departure of most of Suriname's English settlers then narrowed the scope of subjecthood in the colony. After being prevented from leaving, Jewish colonists abandoned their allegiance to England's king. When Clifford returned

CONCLUSION

following his own abortive departure, he did so to a colony where being an English subject meant being part of a tiny minority, all with origins in the British Isles. Rather than assimilating, he clung closely to his subject status and to rights grounded in articles of capitulation written to govern a population that was now absent. Throughout his many conflicts with the colony's ruling elite, he positioned his subjecthood as simultaneously immutable and under assault.

Although convinced that he was a beleaguered victim of the Dutch, Clifford exerted the power of both a slaveholder and a patriarch. By 1685 he kept eighty-five people enslaved on Corcabo, the plantation he had recently gained through marriage. And he asserted the right to move them to an English colony not because they were English subjects but rather because he viewed them as an English subject's property. Suriname's laws stipulated joint ownership of marital assets, yet Clifford exerted claims to the total control of Corcabo that accorded with English coverture. His apparent use of physical violence as well as his verbal threats forced his wife, Dorothy Matson, to abandon her title to the estate and leave for England. Yet because of her initial objections to his behavior, the colony's government sequestered the two-thirds of Corcabo that Clifford had transferred to his father. The fact that he was never able to remove the property or its people to English territory would become, in his mind, a major infringement of the 1667 Articles of Capitulation and his rights as a subject.

In 1689 colonial Suriname experienced a second shift in sovereignty when a Dutch prince became England's king. Clifford felt the ripples of this distant event and claimed that during the initial period of Anglo-Dutch conflict the territory's governor had persecuted him because he was English. The Glorious Revolution broadened the scope of rhetorical authority available both to Clifford and to Suriname's government. The fiscal evoked the stadholder's position as the English sovereign when he recommended that Clifford be sentenced to death for disorderly behavior in 1692. The criminal court did the same when it commuted the sentence to imprisonment. And Clifford, in turn, appealed to his king, their stadholder, to intercede with the States General, winning his freedom in 1695.

Returning to Europe the following year, Clifford pursued compensation in both London and the Hague. From then until his death in 1737 he tried to convince two imperial bureaucracies that his case had merit and the authorities in Suriname had violated his rights as an English subject. Falling into poverty and, ultimately, years of imprisonment for debt, Clifford evoked the treaties that he saw as underwriting his subjecthood to move the Crown to act on his behalf. It obliged on multiple occasions, sending its envoys to interpose with the States General and commissioning a report into his cause. Yet at a time of

CONCLUSION

Anglo-Dutch comity its actions only went so far, almost certainly short of the reprisals against Dutch ships that Clifford, in his later years, believed had made him a rich man. And the States General refused to be moved, regarding his claim as spurious, calling into question his right to appeal to the Crown, and claiming that he was under its jurisdiction. Meanwhile, despite impoverishment, Clifford used representatives in Suriname to try to regain control over Corcabo's land and laborers. Penury in London was no hindrance to slaveholding, at least in his mind.

There were many posthumous Cliffords, generated both by people trying to gain the supposed wealth of his claim and by texts with anti-Dutch axes to grind. These provide a sense of what colonial English subjecthood meant by the second half of the eighteenth century. While it was an anachronism after the Act of Union, it was a vital one, which was amenable to contemporary uses. The most confounding Clifford, that found in his supposed will, was a man who was oddly disloyal, willing to cede his claim to France and the Holy Roman Empire. One group of claimants proffered a version in both petition and print that more closely accorded with the words of Clifford himself, as wronged by a foreign adversary and supported by treaties that demanded action. Yet they also bent him into a shape that conformed to eighteenth-century polite culture. Others used Clifford to express a language of martyred colonial English subjecthood rooted in anti-Dutch discourse, with his experience used as evidence of a Dutch antipathy that stretched back to the 1623 Amboyna massacre. This provided a vocabulary for understanding their own times, and particularly how the English, the motive force of burgeoning British power, continued to suffer around the world at the hands of the Dutch. In doing so some texts expressed unease about the legacy of the Glorious Revolution, which, while falling short of overt Jacobitism, questioned the legitimacy of allegiance to a Dutch king. This had troubling implications for the British subjecthood of their own time and its fidelity to a Hanoverian monarch.

When Jeronimy Clifford returned to England he brought with him not only his own sense of what it meant to be an English subject but also an enslaved person who was presumably denied all of subjecthood's protections. The 1696 pass that the Crown granted to him for travel to Holland listed one of his companions as Michael, a "negro boy."[14] While it is possible that Michael was free, it is likely that Clifford claimed him as property, perhaps having purchased him in Barbados, where he first stopped after leaving Suriname. Only one source mentions Michael and his ultimate fate is unknown.

More central to the course of Clifford's life was the man whom he knew as Caesar, and over whose possession he and Henry MacKintosh had clashed in

CONCLUSION

1691. The dispute about Caesar's sale was the catalyst for Clifford's arrest, the fiscal's actions against him, and his imprisonment for over three years, which formed the core of his narrative of persecution by the Dutch. Sources are almost as silent about Caesar as they are about Michael. The name that he himself used is predictably absent, while that given to him by his captors was common enough to allow Clifford to claim that the dispute was a result of mistaken identity.

Perhaps the man whom Clifford and MacKintosh fought over had been born in English Suriname, which is a possibility if he was in his mid-twenties or older at the time of the dispute. If so he was an English subject according to the strict wording of *Calvin's Case*, although he was denied the benefits of that status in practice. Or maybe he had been born Igbo, Efik, or Kalabari in West Africa and had crossed the Atlantic in chains on a ship on which he would have witnessed the deaths of scores of his fellow captives. Either way, his unfree state was the antithesis of the English subjecthood that Clifford had gained at birth and that he evoked throughout his life. That subjecthood remained, in Clifford's eyes (as Edward Coke wrote in 1608), *"absoluta, pura, et indefinata,"* even as life in Suriname shaped the rights that it conferred and the rights it denied to others.[15]

Notes

Introduction

1. NA UK, CO 278/1, page unnumbered. The letter appears on the first leaf of CO 278/1. Pagination begins on the following leaf. Clifford mentions in a July 1727 letter that his lodging next to the Ship Tavern was a bakery (NA UK, T1/259, no. 35, fol. 153v).

2. For the capitulation treaty, see "Articles Concluded." For life for the English under Dutch rule and the 1675 evacuation, see Games, "Cohabitation, Suriname-Style" (which includes some discussion of Clifford); Selwood, "Left Behind"; Zijlstra, "Anglo-Dutch Suriname."

3. For Clifford's baptism, see the record for Jeronemy Cleford, Baptism, 24 May 1657, Egham, St. John, Surrey, EG/1/2, *Anglican Parish Registers*, Surrey History Centre, accessed via *Ancestry Library*.

4. Behn, *Oroonoko, or, The Royal Slave*, 3–4. For a modern edition, see Behn, *Oroonoko*. For Thomas Southerne's play see Southerne, *Oroonoko*. See Rich, "Heroic Tragedy in Southerne's Oroonoko," for a critical analysis.

5. Barber, "Power in the English Caribbean," 207n84. Carolyn Arena argues that Behn's work was influenced by real conflicts in Suriname involving African and indigenous slaves during both the English and Dutch periods. See Arena, "Aphra Behn's *Oroonoko*."

6. Clifford provides contradictory dates for the year when he and his father first moved to Suriname, listing the date, variously, as "about the year 1663" (BL, Add. MSS, 61644C, fol. 62r) and as 1665 (Clifford, *Jeronimy Clifford's Answer*, 4; the pamphlet can be found in BL, Add. MSS, 61644C, fols. 45r–46v).

7. Warren, *Impartial Description of Surinam*, 27. Warren describes his observations as "a present of three years collection" (A2r).

8. Warren, *Impartial Description of Surinam*, 17.

9. Warren, *Impartial Description of Surinam*, A2r.

10. Warren, *Impartial Description of Surinam*, 4.

11. Warren, *Impartial Description of Surinam*, 20–22, 4–5.

12. William Byam, "Narrative of the state of Guiana and Surinam 1665–1667," BL, Sloane MSS 3662, fol. 27r. A slightly less detailed version, from Bodleian Library, Ashmolean MSS 842, fols. 109–22, is printed as Byam, "Exact Narrative." There it lists the population as "upwards of 1000 men" (199). As Alison Games notes, more Barbadians settled in Suriname during the English period than settled in Carolina later in the century ("Cohabitation, Suriname-Style," 202n9).

13. Barber, "Power in the English Caribbean," 207–10. Barber suggests that Aphra Behn's *Oroonoko* was a "black/white inversion" of Allin's attack (*Disputatious Caribbean*, 122). See also Sanford, *Surinam Justice*; Games, "Cohabitation, Suriname-Style," 202–3.

14. "Grant of Privileges."

15. Rens, "Analysis of Annals," 36.

16. Vink, *Creole Jews*, 28.

17. Games, "Cohabitation, Suriname-Style," 216. I discuss population figures in more detail in chapters 1 and 2.

18. See Selwood, "Left Behind," and chapter 2.

19. See Davis, "Regaining Jerusalem," esp. 31; Vink, *Creole Jews*, esp. chap. 8; Ben-Ur, *Jewish Autonomy*.

20. For an English account of this episode, see NA UK, CO 278/3, 151–52. The Dutch governor's version can be found in Pieter Versterre, letter, 16 December 1675, ZA, 2035-271. Both are discussed in Selwood, "Left Behind," 594–95. A transcription of ZA, 2035-271, and a large portion of the other manuscripts in the Zeeland Archives under inventory number 2035, including most that are cited in this book, can be found at http://files.archieven.nl/239/f/GIDS102/2035-transcripties.pdf. This material, along with digital images of the manuscripts, is accessible via the Zeeland Archives under "Gids 3: Ingekomen stukken betreffende Suriname en omliggende kwartieren, 1667–1683," https://www.zeeuwsarchief.nl/onderzoek-het-zelf/archief/?mizig=210&miadt=239&micode=GIDS102&miview=inv2. I am grateful to Alison Games for bringing this source to my attention.

21. Pieter Versterre, letter, 8 May 1675, ZA, 2035-257, discussed in Selwood, "Left Behind," 592–93.

22. Van der Meiden, *Betwist bestuur*, 33, 40–41.

23. Fatah-Black, *White Lies and Black Markets*, 5–9.

24. Games, "Cohabitation, Suriname-Style," 237. See 237n99 for the total population. There was also a small circle of Highland Scots in Suriname by the mid-1680s, whose presence dated back at least to 1667 (Worthington, "Sugar, Slave-Owning, Suriname," esp. 4–6).

25. *Calvin v. Smith*, in Wood et al., eds., *English Reports*, 77:383. As Coke wrote, "There is but one head of both [kingdoms], and the *postnati* and us joined in ligeance to that one head" (77:394).

26. For the ramifications of *Calvin's Case* in England's colonies, see Kettner, *Development of American Citizenship*, 65. Hannah Weiss Muller provides a comprehensive discussion of the case and its colonial implications, particularly for the eighteenth century, in chap. 1 of *Subjects and Sovereign*.

27. Page, ed., *Letters of Denization*, i–ii; Ross, "Naturalisation of Jews in England," 60.

28. Ross, "Naturalisation of Jews in England," 62.

29. Page, *Letters of Denization*, i; Ross, "Naturalisation of Jews in England," 60. After 1700, natural-born subjects were allowed to inherit from alien ancestors, which served to reduce some of the disabilities of denization (Ross, 60). Statute 22 Henry VIII c. 8 stipulated that denizens must pay the same rate as nondenizen aliens for customs and duties, excepting Hanseatic merchants (*Statutes of the Realm*, 3:325–26).

30. Kettner, *Development of American Citizenship*, 83.

31. Kettner, *Development of American Citizenship*, 79–80, 94–96 (for the scope of colonial naturalization), 74–75 (for the 1740 Plantation Act). I discuss methods and examples of colonial naturalization further in chapter 1.

32. Kettner, *Development of American Citizenship*, 65.

33. "An Act for the Governing of Negroes," 160.

34. For more ambiguous language, see, for example, "Report of Mr. Sergeant Baldwin re. Laws of Barbados," CO 29/3, 6, quoted in Amussen, *Caribbean Exchanges*, 133.

35. The point about the lack of definition comes from Hannah Weiss Muller (*Subjects and Sovereign*, 46–47), who locates such positive rights as ascendant in the eighteenth century, in contrast with "an older language of privilege" (47). Carla Gardena Pestana notes the prevalence of a rhetoric of rights throughout the English Atlantic during the mid-seventeenth century, which was tied to subjecthood and, during the Interregnum, "shared Englishness" (*English Atlantic*, 166). By the 1630s an English ruling had affirmed that the inheritance rights of both natural-born and naturalized subjects were safe even from the royal prerogative (Kettner, *Development of American Citizenship*, 38–39).

36. Amussen, *Caribbean Exchanges*, 134. Amussen identifies this usage in Barbados as early as 1661.

37. See Hannah Weiss Muller's *Subjects and Sovereign* for this dynamic during the middle and later eighteenth century.

38. Wilson, "Performance of Freedom," 47, 73. For examples of treaties, see 58, 65, 85.

39. See Pulsipher, *Subjects unto the Same King*.

40. See Ruediger, "Neither Utterly to Reject Them." Ruediger argues that tributary subjects often stood "on the divide between subject and alien . . . treated as whichever the English preferred at any given moment" (25). Mark Thompson notes that by the eighteenth century, subjecthood was largely denied to indigenous people and people of African descent (*Contest for the Delaware Valley*, 214–15).

41. See "Grant of Privileges." At the time, Jewish immigrants to England were unable to become full English subjects due to sacramental restrictions (Ross, "Naturalisation of Jews," 62).

42. For Suriname's 1663 patent, see Hartsinck, *Beschryving van Guiana*, 522–58. See 533–34 for language on the creation of new subjects. I am grateful to Natalie Zemon Davis for pointing me to this source. The patent is summarized in *Calendar of State Papers Colonial, America and West Indies*, vol. 5 (1661–68), 6 May 1663 (no. 451).

43. Kettner, *Development of American Citizenship*, 94.

44. BL, Add. 30218 (*Revenue Opinions, 1673–1707*), fol. 235r. Even Jews born in England proper had their subjecthood questioned. See, for example, fols. 206v, 235r–v.

45. "Legal Case Regarding Inheritance of David Salter's Heirs ca. 1650–1660s?," Folger Shakespeare Library, call no. X.d.564. I am grateful to Alison Games for sending me this source.

46. BL, Add. MSS, 61644C, fols. 41r–v (quotation on fol. 41v). See also chapter 4.

47. I discuss Matson extensively in chapter 2.

48. There is a large body of literature on both Englishness and Britishness. For early modern Englishness constructed via travel writing, see Suranyi, *Genius of the English*

Nation. The classic study of Britishness in the eighteenth century remains Colley, *Britons*. For some of the affective qualities of colonialism, see Ruediger, "Tributary Subjects." I discuss affective aspects of subjecthood in chapter 5.

49. *Case and Replication*, 266.

50. See, for example, *Public Advertiser*, 20 July 1767, issue 10199 (letter 26). For a detailed examination of Amboyna and its meanings, see Games, *Inventing the English Massacre*. I am grateful to Alison Games for sharing sources from the *Public Advertiser*.

51. Muller, *Bonds of Belonging*, 211–13.

52. Muller, *Bonds of Belonging*, 206.

53. Thompson, *Contest for the Delaware Valley*, 214.

54. See chap. 10 of Haefeli, *New Netherland*.

55. Thompson, *Contest for the Delaware Valley*, 10. Thompson's book provides a comprehensive treatment of the relations between these groups in the seventeenth-century Delaware valley.

56. Thompson, *Contest for the Delaware Valley*, 5.

57. Thompson, *Contest for the Delaware Valley*, 6. Here Thompson uses the term *national affiliations* as well as Benedict Anderson's *nation-ness* (on the latter, see Anderson, *Imagined Communities*, 4). Throughout this work I use the word *nationality* in a broad sense to encompass the qualities of imputed or self-identified national affiliation.

58. Thompson, *Contest for the Delaware Valley*, 13.

59. See also Selwood, "Left Behind."

60. See "Articles of Agreement."

61. See "Articles Concluded."

62. Treaty of Breda, in Chalmers, *Collection of Treaties*, 1:133–61. For a comparative discussion of the New Netherland and Suriname articles, see chapter 2 and Games, "Cohabitation, Suriname-Style," 208–9.

63. Hartsinck, *Beschryving van Guiana*, 527.

64. Benton, *Search for Sovereignty*, 3.

65. Benton, *Search for Sovereignty*, 2. Benton examines sovereignty in relation to rivers and oceans in chaps. 2 and 3, respectively.

66. Benton, *Search for Sovereignty*, 290.

67. "Papers submitted to Sunderland," BL, Add. MSS, 61644 B–C. The papers include an accompanying letter from Clifford to Sunderland, dated 18 July 1707 (BL, Add. MSS, 61644C, fols. 96r–v).

1. Creating an English Suriname (1651–1667)

1. Clifford provides contradictory dates for the year when he and his father first moved to Suriname, although in two places he lists the date as "about the year 1663" (BL, Add. MSS, 61644B, fol. 3v, and BL, Add. MSS, 61644C, fol. 62r). He names the year as 1665 in Clifford, *Jeronimy Clifford's Answer*, 4 (the pamphlet can be found in BL, Add. MSS, 61644C, fols. 45r–46v). Clifford states that the family moved to the "West Indies" in BL, Add. MSS, 61644B, fol. 3v. Elsewhere he states that the family "went from England to Suriname" (BL, Add. MSS, 61644C, fol. 62r). He may well be using the term "West Indies" to include Suriname. For Clifford's baptism, see the record for Jeronemy Cleford, Baptism, 24 May 1657, Egham, St. John, Surrey, EG/1/2, *Anglican*

Parish Registers, Surrey History Centre, accessed via *Ancestry Library*. The baptism record only lists the name of Jeronimy's father. However, we know from later sources that his mother was called Alice (*Calendar of State Papers Colonial, America and West Indies*, vol. 9 (1675–1676 and Addenda 1574–1674), 22 September 1675 [no. 675, vii]). That the name "Alice" refers to Andrew Clifford's wife is verified by NA UK, CO 278/3, 102.

This chapter includes some material first published in Jacob Selwood, "Left Behind: Subjecthood, Nationality, and the Status of Jews after the Loss of English Surinam," *Journal of British Studies* 54, no. 3 (July 2015): 578–601, https://doi.org/10.1017/jbr.2015.59 (© 2015 Cambridge University Press, reprinted with permission), which was initially developed in Selwood, "Present at the Creation," 198–203.

2. "Grant of Privileges."

3. For a comprehensive overview of Suriname's geography, see Ouboter and Jairam, *Fauna of Suriname*, 3–10.

4. Here Suriname's rivers provide an example of the "corridors of control" identified by Lauren Benton as central to "imagining and enlarging empire" (*Search for Sovereignty*, 2).

5. This point is also noted by Fatah-Black in *White Lies and Black Markets*, 21.

6. Warren, *Impartial Description of Surinam*, 1. Warren describes his observations as "a present of three years collection" (A2r).

7. Warren, *Impartial Description of Surinam*, 2–3.

8. Warren, *Impartial Description of Surinam*, 2.

9. Warren, *Impartial Description of Surinam*, 9, 11.

10. Warren, *Impartial Description of Surinam*, 10–11, 12.

11. Warren, *Impartial Description of Surinam*, 20.

12. Warren, *Impartial Description of Surinam*, 15.

13. This point is noted by Alison Games in relation to Warren's description of disease ("Cohabitation, Suriname-Style," 203).

14. For an overview of the indigenous population of the Guianas during the pre-Columbian period see Hyles, *Guiana and the Shadows of Empire*, 11–15. Hyles notes that the term *Arawak* has historically referred to the Tainos and *Carib* to the Kalinagos, both of whom originate from the river valleys of the Guianas (11). The people termed Arawak also included the Lokono in Trinidad, Orinoco, and the coast of Guyana (Whitehead, "Carib Ethnic Soldiering," 361). The terms *Carib* and *Arawak* remain in use today to refer to linguistic groups. Whitehead notes that *Carib* should appropriately denote "the Karinya of mainland South America" but not "the so-called Island Carib [who] are actually Arawakan speakers" (379n8).

15. Whitehead, "Carib Ethnic Soldiering," 360.

16. Games, "Cohabitation, Suriname-Style," 202. Whitehead, however, suggests the opposite, noting Dutch and English alliances with the Arawak "to the economic and military detriment of the local Carib" (365).

17. Warren, *Impartial Description of Surinam*, 23–24. For an analysis of imputations of treachery in North America, which did not always carry negative connotations, see Kupperman, "English Perceptions of Treachery."

18. Warren, *Impartial Description of Surinam*, 26.

19. Hyles, *Guiana and the Shadows of Empire*, 17.

20. Lorimer, "Failure of the English Guiana Ventures," 3–4.

21. Lorimer, "Failure of the English Guiana Ventures," 4–5.

22. The Dutch had settled Essequibo by 1638 and some colonists had ventured up the Orinoco River by that year (Klooster, *Dutch Moment*, 59). Berbice was settled as a private Zeeland venture starting in 1627 (199). The Dutch West India Company was chartered in 1621 (34–43). For an overview of Dutch colonization in the Guianas, see Roitman, "Second Is Best."

23. Arbell, *Jewish Nation of the Caribbean*, 45.

24. Lorimer, "Failure of the English Guiana Ventures," 5.

25. Lorimer, "Failure of the English Guiana Ventures," 5. Lorimer cites "a deposition made by Sir Henry Colt after he was captured by the Spaniards at Trinidad in 1633" as evidence of early English settlement in Suriname, although the basis for her assertion of a continued presence until the 1650s is unclear (27n21).

26. [Scott], "Description of Guyana," 141. The settlers appear to have been the remnant of a previous attempt to establish a presence in Tobago, which was launched from Barbados under Warwick's patronage (Williamson, *English Colonies in Guiana*, 146). Scott's text discusses events that end in 1668. It is listed in the British Library catalog as "Guiana: History of: 1530–1668" (BL, Sloane 3662, fols. 37b–49).

27. These population figures come from Hyles, *Guiana and the Shadows of Empire*, 12. I have been unable to find figures for the indigenous mortality in the region that resulted from the Columbian Exchange. In the century and a half after 1492 the worst affected parts of the Americas saw the death of all indigenous people, while 80 percent of indigenous peoples died in areas that were least affected. The norm appears to be around 90 percent. See Nunn and Qian, "The Columbian Exchange," 165; McNeill, *Mosquito Empires*, 16.

28. Warren, *Impartial Description of Surinam*, 4–5. See also Games, "Cohabitation, Suriname-Style," 203.

29. McNeill, *Mosquito Empires*, 61–62 (on the spread of malaria and yellow fever), 64 (on yellow fever in Barbados), 195–98 (on eighteenth-century Suriname), 32–33 (on the genetic profile of yellow fever). For immunity to malaria and yellow fever among Africans, see 61 and 239, respectively. See Kars, *Blood on the River*, 123–24, for a discussion of these diseases during the 1763 Berbice slave uprising.

30. Nunn and Qian, "Columbian Exchange," 167.

31. The term "epidemic dropsy" is used for this condition (Peitzman, *Dropsy*, 20).

32. Peitzman, *Dropsy*, 1.

33. Peitzman, *Dropsy*, 5, 10.

34. McNeill, *Mosquito Empires*, 121.

35. McNeill, *Mosquito Empires*, 34n54.

36. On Barbados's transition to a sugar economy and from indentured to enslaved labor, see Beckles, *White Servitude and Black Slavery*. Barbados's 1661 slave code largely used the word *negro* rather than *slave*; see Amussen, *Caribbean Exchanges*, 134–35. On the code's adoption and modification in Jamaica, see 140–42. The 1696 Carolina slave code drew heavily on Barbados's 1688 code and was in turn copied by Georgia (Hadden, "Fragmented Laws of Slavery," 270).

37. This term is used throughout Roberts, "Surrendering Surinam."

38. See Roberts, "Surrendering Surinam," 232. Between 1640 and 1660 the island's population rose from 14,000 to 53,300 (231–32).

39. See LaCombe, "Willoughby, Francis." See also Williamson, *English Colonies in Guiana*, 155–57 (Williamson mentions Willoughby's failed patent for Suriname on 157). For the Council of State's order regarding the patent, see *Calendar of State Papers Colonial, America and West Indies*, vol. 1 (1574–1660), 16 March 1654. For a detailed discussion of Willoughby's proprietorship, see Barber, "Power in the English Caribbean." The abortive 1654 patent is discussed on 196–97. Barber also discusses Willoughby throughout *Disputatious Caribbean*. For Willoughby's time as governor of Barbados and his removal from power in the colony, see Pestana, *English Atlantic*, 96–99, 103–8.

40. See [Scott], "Description of Guyana," 142. Williamson doubts Scott's assertion that three hundred settlers accompanied Rowse in 1650 (*English Colonies in Guiana*, 153n1).

41. See *Calendar of State Papers Colonial, America and West Indies*, vol. 5 (1661–1668), 6 May 1663 (no. 451). For the unabridged text, see Jan Jacob Hartsinck, *Beschryving van Guiana*, 522–58.

42. Tanner MSS, 54, fol. 147, quoted in Williamson, *English Colonies in Guiana*, 153. Williamson cites this as evidence that colonization first occurred in 1651. However, his other evidence remains unconvincing: the 1663 grant of proprietorship gives the year as 1650, while his reference to John Oxenbridge's pamphlet *Seasonable Proposition* lacks a decisive date for English settlement (in *English Colonies in Guiana*, 153n1, citing Oxenbridge, *Seasonable Proposition*, 7).

43. Barber, "Power in the English Caribbean," 196; LaCombe, "Willoughby, Francis."

44. Williamson, *English Colonies in Guiana*, 156–58. On Rowse's relationship to Willoughby, see Barber, "Power in the English Caribbean," 194–95. Scott's account gives Rowse the credit not only for the establishment of the colony but also for its subsequent growth. It describes him as leaving "it in a flourishing condition, and in perfect peace with the Indians" in 1654 ("Description of Guyana," 143).

45. Roberts, "Surrendering Surinam," 233–34. The 1654 population number refers to male settlers.

46. Barber, "Power in the English Caribbean," 197.

47. Williamson, *English Colonies in Guiana*, 158–60.

48. Hartsinck, *Beschryving van Guiana*, 527–28.

49. Hartsinck, *Beschryving van Guiana*, 531–32.

50. Warren, *Impartial Description of Surinam*, 17.

51. Warren, *Impartial Description of Surinam*, 1.

52. *Calendar of State Papers Colonial, America and West Indies*, vol. 5 (1661–1668), 7 May 1661 (no. 83).

53. *Calendar of State Papers Colonial, America and West Indies*, vol. 5 (1661–1668), 1 November 1663 (no. 577). The figured listed in *Calendar of State Papers* is four thousand. However, as Alison Games notes, this is a mistranscription of the original manuscript ("Cohabitation, Suriname-Style" 202n10).

54. This fact is noted in Williamson, *English Colonies in Guiana*, 163–64, which also uses these sources to describe the colony's growing population.

55. See Games, "Cohabitation, Suriname-Style," 217. Her table on p. 217 provides the most comprehensive analysis of Suriname's changing population during this period.

56. See *Trans-Atlantic Slave Trade Database*. The voyage IDs for the vessels are as follows: 9,587 (*Swallow*), 9,601 (*Happy Adventure*), 9,612 (*William*), and 28,050 (*York*). I have

searched during the period of English rule using Suriname as principal, first, and second place of landing. I have been unable to find Barbados-Suriname voyages for the period in the accompanying *Intra-American Slave Trade Database*.

57. Hall, *Slavery and African Ethnicities*, 127–28; 133.

58. Hall, *Slavery and African Ethnicities*, 129–30; 133–34.

59. BL, Add. MSS, 61644C, fol. 11v.

60. Price, *Alabi's World*, xiii.

61. See Van den Berg and Aboh, "Done Already?"

62. See *Petitie Inwoners*, 11 March 1671, ZA, 2035-225.

63. BL, Sloane MSS 3662, fol. 27r. See also Williamson, *English Colonies in Guiana*, 164. A slightly different version of Byam's journal, from Bodleian Library, Ashmolean MSS 842, fols. 109–22, appears in print as Byam, "Exact Narrative," in Harlow, *Colonising Expeditions*, 199–222. This gives the number of men as "upwards of a 1000 [sic]" (199).

64. [Scott], "Description of Guyana," 144. See also BL, Sloane MSS 3662, fol. 27r.

65. Byam, "Exact Narrative," 203. Williamson, quoting from elsewhere in Byam's journal, gives a figure of five hundred men who were able to defend the colony that year (*English Colonies in Guiana*, 164).

66. Byam reported five hundred "officers and soldiers" at the time ("Exact Narrative," 221). Assuming many of them were settlers with families, it is reasonable to infer a population of triple this size. This fits with L. L. E. Rens's suggestion, based on the lists of English departing after the Dutch conquest, that the settler population by 1667 was somewhere between one thousand and two thousand ("Analysis of Annals," 31). Byam's figure of five hundred might, however, have also included Jewish settlers, who were not exempt from military service during wartime ("Grant of Privileges," 180).

67. Burnard, "European Migration to Jamaica," 777.

68. Burnard, "European Migration to Jamaica," 775.

69. NA UK, CO 278/3, 101–5.

70. Sanford, *Surinam Justice*, fol. A2v.

71. For the most comprehensive account of these disputes, see Barber, "Power in the English Caribbean," 205–11, on which I draw here. As Barber notes, it is unclear whether Behn had any firsthand experience of Suriname (207n84). See also Behn, *Oroonoko*. On Willoughby's death, see LaCombe, "Willoughby, Francis." There is some confusion about the year of Allin's attack on Willoughby. Scott's "Description of Guiana" states that it took place in 1665 (144). Although William Byam's journal confirms that Willoughby was present in Suriname in May of that year (BL, Sloane MSS 3662, fol. 27r), elsewhere Byam states that he had arrived in November 1663 and was attacked in January 1664 (*Exact Relation*, 2–8). Barber relies on Byam's *Exact Relation* for her account.

72. BL, Add. MSS, 61644B, fols. 3r–v. On Andrew Clifford's baptism, see fol. 8v. Alice Clifford's name appears on Jeronimy's own certificate of baptism, reproduced in BL, Add. MSS, 61644C, fol. 98r. For the original record see Jeronemy Cleford, Baptism, 24 May 1657, Egham, St. John, Surrey, EG/1/2, *Anglican Parish Registers*, Surrey History Centre, accessed via *Ancestry Library*. The family appears on the 1675 passenger list in NA UK, CO 278/3, 102, and *Calendar of State Paper Colonial, America and West Indies*, vol. 9 (1675–1676 and Addenda 1574–1674), 22 September 1675 (no. 675, vii). A 1675 source describes Andrew Clifford as a millwright (NA UK, CO 1/35, no. 28, fol. 223v). On

specklewood, see Games, "Cohabitation, Suriname-Style," 204. Elsewhere, Clifford gives the year the family moved to Suriname as 1665 (*Jeronimy Clifford's Answer*, 4).

73. A Scottish community had been established by 1667 (Worthington, "Sugar, Slave-Owning, Suriname," 4).

74. Hartsinck, *Beschryving van Guiana*, 550.

75. For the specific and general uses of the term *denizen*, see Coke, *The First Part of the Institutes of the Lawes of England*, fol. 129r (cited in *Oxford English Dictionary*, s.v. "denizen"). See the following paragraphs for the status achieved by becoming a denizen, which conferred some benefits while retaining a number of restrictions that applied to aliens.

76. As James Kettner notes, the "same common law principles that made subjects of the Scottish *postnati* applied equally well to persons born in America. . . . All children born under the king's protection were natural-born subjects in all the dominions" (*Development of American Citizenship*, 65). For the case itself see *Calvin v. Smith*, in *English Reports*, 77:377, and Howell, *Cobbett's Complete Collection of State Trials*, 2:559. I discuss its implications for immigrants in London in Selwood, "English-Born Reputed Strangers," and chap. 3 of Selwood, *Diversity and Difference*.

77. People who became denizens generally continued to pay aliens' taxes and customs (Selwood, *Diversity and Difference*, 39n97, 49; Kettner, *Development of American Citizenship*, 31–32).

78. Amussen, *Caribbean Exchanges*, 129–30, 134; the quotations are on 134.

79. "Report of Mr. Sergeant Baldwin re. Laws of Barbados," CO 29/3, 6, quoted in Amussen, *Caribbean Exchanges*, 133.

80. "An Act for the Governing of Negroes," 160. For the development of the Barbados slave code and its culmination in the 1688 law, see Amussen, *Caribbean Exchanges*, 129–40. The Barbados law "provided the basis for all later slave codes in the English colonies" (Amussen, *Caribbean Exchanges*, 144).

81. The fact that Suriname's patent confined its wording about birthright subjecthood to those whose parents were "natives or denizens of England" likely reflects its intended English audience and formulaic composition, rather than language directly designed to enable slavery (Hartsinck, *Beschryving van Guiana*, 550).

82. Hartsinck, *Beschryving van Guiana*, 533–34.

83. Hartsinck, *Beschryving van Guiana*, 534–36.

84. Kettner, *Development of American Citizenship*, 79; see, in particular, n. 49.

85. "Second Virginia Charter," 209.

86. Hartsinck, *Beschryving van Guiana*, 551.

87. NA UK, CO 1/27, no. 58, fol. 169v. See *Calendar of State Papers Colonial, America and West Indies*, vol. 7 (1669–1674), 17 December 1671 (no. 697).

88. *Colonial Entry Book*, no. 94, 97, in Friedenwald, "Material for the History of the Jews," 75–76. On the petition of the Port Royal Merchants, see 73–75. I discuss these sources and Lynch's letter in Selwood, "Present at the Creation," 203–4.

89. Burnard, "European Migration to Jamaica," 790.

90. O'Reilly, "Working for the Crown," 134–35.

91. O'Reilly, "Working for the Crown," 130–31, 136–37.

92. Thompson, *Contest for the Delaware Valley*, 184. This recapitulated prior Dutch treatment of Swedes and Finns in the Delaware Valley (see 152–53, 176–77). On the

articles negotiated between the English and Dutch in New Netherland, see "Articles of Agreement," 2–3.

93. Hartsinck, *Beschryving van Guiana*, 533.

94. Kettner, *Development of American Citizenship*, 79.

95. Kettner, *Development of American Citizenship*, 83.

96. Kettner, *Development of American Citizenship*, 85.

97. Page, *Letters of Denization*, i–ii. Both methods were expensive, but denization, which took place by letters patent, was also available when parliament was not in session (Ross, "Naturalisation of Jews in England," 60).

98. Hatfield, *Atlantic Virginia*, 99; "Extracts from Proceedings of the House of Burgesses," 391.

99. "Extracts from Proceedings of the House of Burgesses," 391.

100. "Historical and Genealogical Notes," 136.

101. Kettner, *Development of American Citizenship*, 74–75, 80. The Crown's rejection of the wider validity of colonial naturalization appears definitive by the 1680s (see 94).

102. Kettner, *Development of American Citizenship*, 79–80.

103. See Hirst, "English Republic."

104. See Pestana, "Lost Liberty and Laboring People in the Atlantic World," chap. 6 of *English Atlantic*.

105. Black, *British Seaborne Empire*, 73.

106. Israel, *Diasporas*, 396, 403, 407. The Jewish population of Dutch Brazil had reached around 1,450 by the 1640s (Israel, *Diasporas*, 367).

107. On the events of the readmission, see Katz, *Philo-Semitism*, 190–244. On the Atlantic context, see Israel, *Diasporas*, 407–20.

108. By 1680 seventeen of Port Royal's 507 householders were Jewish (Newman, "Sephardim of the Caribbean," 451–52). The numbers were higher in Barbados: in the same year Bridgetown's 404 householders included 54 Jews; a total of 184 Jews lived on the island, out of a white population of 20,000. For the Bridgetown population, see Samuel, "Review of the Jewish Colonists in Barbados," 8; for the total Jewish population, see Israel, *Diasporas*, 522; the total white population comes from the 1679–80 Barbados census, cited in Samuel, "Jewish Colonists," 3.

109. On anti-Jewish complaints, see NA UK, CO 1/47, no. 6; *Calendar of State Papers Colonial, America and West Indies*, vol. 11 (1681–1685), 9 June 1681 (no. 134); Israel, *Diasporas*, 397–98, 523–25.

110. Rens, "Analysis of Annals," 33–34, 36 (for the Jewish population under English rule); Israel, *Diasporas*, 527 (for 1675). One 1665 source lists fifteen hundred Englishmen who were capable of bearing arms, which was presumably an undercount of the larger English population (Games, "Cohabitation, Suriname-Style," 217).

111. For suggestions of a Jewish presence before the 1660s, see Williamson, *English Colonies in Guiana*, 154; Oppenheim, "Early Jewish Colony," 97; Wolf, "American Elements," 80; Barber, "Power in the English Caribbean," 204. For scholarship questioning this early presence, see Cohen, "Misdated Ketubah"; Cohen, "Egerton Manuscript"; Rens, "Analysis of Annals," 29–31.

112. For the petition, see NA UK, CO 1/15, fols. 59v–60r. See also *Calendar of State Papers Colonial, America and West Indies*, vol. 5 (1661–1668), 8 April 1661 (no. 65). Here "Henry Benjamin de Caseres" is transcribed as "Henry Bernard de Caseres." For the de-

cision of the Council for Foreign Plantations, which included a debate about the desirability of Jewish settlement in the colonies more generally, see NA UK, CO 1/15, no. 75, fols. 143r–v. See also *Calendar of State Papers Colonial, America and West Indies*, vol. 5 (1661–1668), 24 July 1661 (no. 140). I discuss this debate in Selwood, "Left Behind," 584–85.

113. Sanford, *Surinam Justice*, 40 ("The deposition of John Venman aged twenty-eight years or thereabouts"). The deposition of James Maxwel [sic], on 41, contains almost identical wording. Rens discusses these examples in "Analysis of Annals," 30 and 43n6. For more on Sanford, including his accusations against Byam, see Barber, "Power in the English Caribbean," 207–10.

114. Sanford, *Surinam Justice*, 36–37.

115. Rens, "Analysis of Annals," 36.

116. Israel, *Diasporas*, 401–2; Rens, "Analysis of Annals," 33–36; Williamson, *English Colonies in Guiana*, 178–79. Rens locates the arrival of Jews from Cayenne "in the second half of 1665" while also leaving open the possibility of settlement the following year, emphasizing that their arrival occurred after the authorities issued the 1665 "Grant of Privileges. ("Analysis of Annals," 34, 36).

117. "Grant of Privileges." The earliest surviving version of the grant appears to be the Dutch copy printed in David de Isaac Cohen Nassy's *Essai Historique sur la Colonie de Surinam* 2:122–25. For an English translation of Nassy's history, see *Historical Essay on the Colony of Surinam*. Here the grant appears in app. 2, 188–89. According to Williamson, "There is no record of this grant in English archives, but a Dutch copy is preserved at Paramaribo" (*English Colonies in Guiana*, 165n4.) Williamson cites J. S. Roos, rabbi of the Dutch congregation in Paramaribo, who refers to an "official Dutch translation (Col. Arch.)" without providing further details (Roos, "Additional Notes," 130). No manuscript copy survives in the National Archives of Suriname, although it is possible that one might be preserved in the archives of the Jewish community in Paramaribo, or in the National Archives of the Netherlands. I am grateful to Jonathan Israel, Natalie Zemon Davis, Laura Leibman, and the National Archives of Suriname for answering my queries about the possible existence of a manuscript.

118. "Grant of Privileges."

119. NA UK, SP 44/18, 78–79. See also Katz, *Philo-Semitism*, 243. The expansive nature of the 1665 grant led Lucien Wolf to claim that "the honor of first practicing Jewish emancipation belongs to British America" ("American Elements," 86).

120. See Henriques, "Jewish Emancipation Controversy"; Katz, "Jews of England and 1688," 236, 248; Ross, "Naturalisation of Jews in England," 60, 62; Page, *Letters of Denization*, i–ii; Kettner, *Development of American Citizenship*, 31–32. According to statute 22 Henry VIII c. 8, most denizens paid the same customs and duties as nondenizen aliens (see *Statutes of the Realm*, 3:325–26).

121. This was the case in Jamaica (*Calendar of State Papers Colonial, America and West Indies*, vol. 7 [1669–1674], 31 December 1670 [no. 367]). While Jews in Rhode Island received a statement of protection from the colony's assembly in 1684, it was offered to them in their capacity as strangers (Ellen Smith and Jonathan D. Sarna, introduction to Goodwin and Smith, eds., *Jews of Rhode Island*, 2).

122. See Cohen, "Egerton Manuscript," 339–40; Israel, *Diasporas*, 401. The Sephardic proposals were made in 1657. They reached English secretary of state John Thurloe by the following year, when he received a translation sent by John Longland,

the English agent in Livorno (Cohen, "Egerton Manuscript," 340). For Longland's translation of the proposals, see BL, Egerton MSS 2395, fol. 46. It is reproduced in Oppenheim, "Early Jewish Colony," 176–78, and Cohen, "Egerton Manuscript," 341–43. Lucien Wolf, writing in 1897, mistook Longland's translation for original "privileges . . . granted by the Commonwealth to the Brazilian Jews who settled in Surinam in 1654" ("American Elements," 85). Wolf's suggestion that rights were extended this early has been convincingly refuted (Oppenheim, "Early Jewish Colony," 161; Cohen, "Egerton Manuscript," 340).

123. Haefeli, *New Netherland*, 83; see also chap. 2.

124. War with the Dutch formally commenced in March 1665, although conflict began during the previous year. The grant was issued on 17 August 1665 (Jonathan I. Israel, *Dutch Republic*, 766; "Grant of Privileges," 180).

125. "Grant of Privileges," 179.

126. Kettner, *Development of American Citizenship*, 83–86. General naturalization did not become a reality in England until the early eighteenth century and then only briefly, although unsuccessful proposals had arisen as early as the 1660s (Selwood, *Diversity and Difference*, 122–24).

127. Hartsinck, *Beschryving van Guiana*, 533.

128. Kettner, *Development of American Citizenship*, 33, 93–96; quotation on 33. In 1682 the authorities in Nevis seized the ship of Henry Brunett, who had been naturalized in Virginia, and argued that he remained an alien according to the 1660 Navigation Acts. Chief Justice Francis North confirmed the seizure as legally valid, stating that "a colonial grant could convey local privileges only." His decision "came to be generally accepted in London" (94). The 1672 Rabba Couty case produced a ruling in the opposite direction, as the Privy Council confirmed the right of a Jewish New Yorker to trade with Jamaica after authorities challenged his status as an Englishmen and seized his goods. It is unclear whether Couty was endenized, naturalized, or born in an English colony (Snyder, "Rules, Rights and Redemption," 152).

129. "Grant of Privileges," 180. For the possible location of the site, see Ben-Ur and Frankel, *Remnant Stones*, 24–25.

2. Staying English in Dutch Suriname (1667–1687)

1. NA UK, CO 1/21, no. 21, fols. 42r–v. This chapter includes some material first published in Jacob Selwood, "Left Behind: Subjecthood, Nationality, and the Status of Jews after the Loss of English Surinam," *Journal of British Studies* 54, no. 3 (July 2015): 578–601 (© 2015 Cambridge University Press, reprinted with permission), which was initially developed in Selwood, "Present at the Creation," esp. 198–203).

2. NA UK, CO 1/21, no. 21, fol. 42v.

3. NA UK, CO 1/21, no. 21, fol. 43r.

4. Byam, "Exact Narrative," 216.

5. There is some ambiguity concerning this date. The report in NA UK, CO 1/21, no. 21, fol. 44r, lists the date of the articles as concluded on "the 16th of March stilo novo" (and thus 6 March, Old Style). However, the copy of Byam's account printed in Harlow gives the date as "6 of March stylo novo 1667" (Byam, "Exact Narrative," 219).

6. Jeronimy Clifford was born in May 1657. For his record of baptism, see Jeronemy Cleford, Baptism, 24 May 1657, Egham, St. John, Surrey, EG/1/2, *Anglican Parish Registers*, Surrey History Centre, accessed via *Ancestry Library*.

7. For the full text of the 1667 Articles of Capitulation, see "Articles Concluded." I discuss the departure of English colonists later in the chapter.

8. NA UK, CO 278/3, 148–49.

9. Games, "Cohabitation, Suriname-Style," 237.

10. On the causes and course of the war, see Israel, *Dutch Republic*, 766–74. On the Treaty of Breda and its subsidiary articles and declarations, see Chalmers, *Collection of Treaties*, 1:133–61. The treaty confirmed the territories held by both powers as of 10/20 May 1667. By this time the English had lost Suriname (Games, "Cohabitation, Suriname-Style," 213).

11. On the conquest of New Netherland and its aftermath, see chap. 10 of Haefeli, *New Netherland*.

12. Byam, "Exact Narrative," 200–201 (quotations on 201).

13. Byam, "Exact Narrative," 203.

14. Byam, "Exact Narrative," 204–5.

15. Byam, "Exact Narrative," 205–6.

16. Byam, "Exact Narrative," 206–7.

17. Byam, "Exact Narrative," 208.

18. Byam, "Exact Narrative," 209–11.

19. The assembly and the council had presented him with a draft letter to Lord Willoughby justifying the surrender of the colony. For the text, see Byam, "Exact Narrative," 212–14. The letter is addressed to Francis Willoughby despite the fact that he had disappeared at sea in July 1666, after which his brother William took over as Barbados's governor. He bequeathed his proprietorship of Suriname to Frances Brereton and Elizabeth Jones, his daughters, and to Henry Willoughby, his nephew (LaCombe, "Willoughby, Francis"; Roberts, "Surrendering Surinam," 240).

20. Byam, "Exact Narrative," 215.

21. BL, Sloane MSS 3662, fols. 33v–34v. The proposals are part of Byam's "Exact Narrative of the State of Guyana," a version of which can be found in full in BL, Sloane MSS 3662, fols. 27–37. They are omitted from the text printed in Harlow, *Colonising Expeditions*, 199–222 (see Byam, "Exact Narrative," 215, for the omission). Harlow's text draws on the version found in Bodleian Library, Ashmolean MSS, fols. 109–22, which differs slightly from the version in Sloane MSS. As Alison Games notes, the proposals relating to freedom of religion "echoed the religious liberties extended to Jews in Suriname in 1665, a possible inspiration for the articles proposed by the vanquished English" (Games, "Cohabitation, Suriname-Style," 207).

22. Byam, "Exact Narrative," 215.

23. Byam, "Exact Narrative," 216.

24. "Articles Concluded," 217.

25. "Articles Concluded," 217. For a further manuscript version of the articles, see NA UK, CO 1/21, no. 21 ("narrative of the taking of the English colony of Suriname by the Zealand fleet, together with the articles of surrender"), fols. 43r–44r. This is abstracted in *Calendar of State Papers Colonial, America and West Indies*, vol. 5 (1661–1668), 24 February/6 March 1667 (no. 1421).

26. "Articles Concluded," 218–19.

27. "Articles Concluded," 216–17.

28. "Articles Concluded," 218–19. Alison Games discusses the drafting of the articles and their relationship to the initial proposals in Games, "Cohabitation, Suriname-Style," 207–10.

29. "Articles of Agreement," 2–3.

30. Games, "Cohabitation, Suriname-Style," 208–9. Games notes the importance of the use of the word *cohabit* in article 4 of the 1667 document ("Cohabitation, Suriname-Style," 209).

31. See Games, "Cohabitation, Suriname-Style," 212–13. She mentions Banister's appointment as governor on 215. For the Treaty of Breda, see Chalmers, *Collection of Treaties*, 1:133–61. The order restoring territory that was held as of 10/20 May 1667 is on 150–51. For a Dutch account of the English recapture and occupation of the colony, see Johan Tressry, letter, 13 January 1668, ZA, 2035-007. On Henry Willoughby, see Roberts, "Surrendering Surinam," 240.

32. *Instructie Engelse Kroon aan Willoughby*, 14 February 1668, ZA, 2035-087. The date of this source, an English-language copy in the Zeeland archives, is ambiguous. While the date on the manuscript is 14 February 1668, it is listed in the archives as 4 February 1668, a reversal of correct Old Style–New Style conversion. I have been unable to find a reference to this source in the *Calendar of State Papers*.

33. Games, "Cohabitation, Suriname-Style," 213.

34. William Willoughby accused the Dutch of coercing English settlers to stay (Games, "Cohabitation, Suriname-Style," 215).

35. Rens, "Analysis of Annals," 38; Games, "Cohabitation, Suriname-Style," 215.

36. Games, "Cohabitation, Suriname-Style," 215–16; Weterings, "Should We Stay," 136; Zijlstra and Weterings, "Colonial Life," 80–81.

37. For the source of Byam's numbers, see Byam, "Exact Narrative," 221. My overall figure of one thousand to fifteen hundred is based on tripling Byam's figure of five hundred to account for family members. This fits with L. L. E. Rens's suggestion of a settler population of between one thousand and two thousand by 1667, which he bases on the number of English settlers who left after the Dutch conquest ("Analysis of Annals," 31). Byam's figure, however, may well have included Jews, who were not exempt from military service during wartime ("Grant of Privileges," 180). Rens suggests a maximum of two hundred Jews in 1667 ("Analysis of Annals," 36).

38. Games, "Cohabitation, Suriname-Style," 217. It is difficult to tell the extent to which the enslaved population had declined by this point, if indeed it had. Justin Roberts suggests that there were around 3,750 slaves in Suriname by 1663. He infers this figure as a proportion of a count of 5,000 inhabitants provided by Renatus Enys. Alison Games, conversely, suggests that Enys's number refers only to Europeans (Roberts, "Surrendering Surinam," 235n31; Games, "Cohabitation, Suriname-Style," 202, 217).

39. Games, "Cohabitation, Suriname-Style," 216. She notes the probable undercount on 216n52.

40. Julius Lichtenbergh, letter, 30 April 1670, ZA, 2035-216.

41. For a concise summary of both missions, see Rens, "Analysis of Annals," 38–40. For documents relating to the 1671 mission see NA UK, CO 278/2, 33–56. For memoranda for the second mission following the Treaty of Westminster, see NA UK, CO 278/2, 61–75.

Documents relating to the 1675 mission can be found in NA UK, CO 278/3. Tom Weterings discusses both evacuation missions in Weterings, "Should We Stay," 134–40.

42. Rens, "Analysis of Annals," 38.

43. Zijlstra and Weterings, "Colonial Life," 80–81.

44. Roberts, "Surrendering Surinam," 247–49, 256. As Roberts notes, some members of the Barbadian elite held hopes of retaking Suriname, although these aspirations went nowhere (255–56.)

45. *Calendar of State Papers Colonial, America and West Indies*, vol. 7 (1669–1674), 16 January 1672 (no. 734). Alison Games suggests that Banister "must have meant 105 English *people*, and 517 slaves (or possibly 517 people in total)" ("Cohabitation, Suriname-Style," 217, table 1, n. f; 228n69). This interpretation is borne out by the number of colonists who remained behind and left in 1675 (see the subsequent discussion). There is no evidence that Jews were present among the people evacuated in 1671 (Rens, "Analysis of Annals," 39).

46. NA UK, CO 278/2, 53. The precise date of departure is unclear from Banister's narrative, but it occurred soon after the delegation delivered a list of grievances to the governor on 6 March (NA UK, CO 278/2, 53). Banister reported his arrival in Port Royal Bay, Jamaica, on 12 March 1671 (NA UK, CO 278/2, 54).

47. NA UK, CO 278/2, 57.

48. NA UK, CO 278/2, 58–60.

49. NA UK, CO 278/2, 58–59.

50. *Petitie Inwoners*, 11 March 1671, ZA, 2035-225. One of the signatories, Marcus Brandt, served as one of the three commissioners appointed by the Crown to evacuate the English in 1675 (see, for example, NA UK, CO 278/3, 97). He also appears as "Mark Brent" in English sources and is discussed as such later in the chapter.

51. NA UK, CO 278/2, 60.

52. Rommelse, "The Role of Mercantilism," 606; Israel, *Dutch Republic*, 812–13.

53. Article 5, Treaty of Westminster, in Chalmers, *Collection of Treaties*, 1:173–74. The full text of the treaty is on 172–77. The date of the treaty (9/19 February 1674) is on 172 and 177.

54. NA UK, CO 278/3, 7–9. The full text of the letter is on 5–9.

55. NA UK, CO 278/2, 67. The inhabitants' 1671 petition to the Zeeland States had described the colony as consisting of a total of five hundred white settlers, twenty-five hundred black inhabitants and five hundred indigenous slaves, with fifty-two plantations possessing sugar mills (*Petitie Inwoners*, 11 March 1671, ZA, 2035-225).

56. Pieter Versterre, letter, 8 May 1675, ZA, 2035-257. Here Versterre uses the terms *Engelsche natie*, *Joodsche natie*, and *Duijtsche natie* to describe Suriname's English, Jewish, and Dutch populations, respectively.

57. Bodian, *Hebrews of the Portuguese Nation*, 6, 147–48. For examples of Jewish uses of the term *Hebrew nation*, see the sources quoted on 48, 62, 128, 134.

58. In 1688 Barbadian authorities forbade non-denizen Jews "in any sea-port town of [*sic*] island" from owning more than one slave (Friedenwald, "Material for the History of the Jews," 97). There is a vast literature on the emergence of racial categories and their relationship to slavery. For an example focusing on Barbados and Jamaica in the seventeenth century, see Amussen, *Caribbean Exchanges*. For the intersection of race and gender, see Hall, *Things of Darkness*.

59. See this book's introduction for further discussion of the meaning of the term *nation* and its relationship to subjecthood as well as the relationship between subjecthood and race.

60. NA UK, CO 278/3, 148–49.

61. NA UK, CO 278/3, 149–50. The Dutch also compiled their own lists, both of departing English and of the remaining Dutch and Jewish inhabitants, which Versterre included in a 4 July 1675 letter (24 June, Old Style; Pieter Versterre, letter, 4 July 1675, ZA, 2035-260). The lists of the Jewish, Dutch, and English inhabitants can be found in ZA 2035-261, 2035-262 and 2035-263, respectively.

62. The commissioners' 9 June letter was, however, addressed to "His Majesty's subjects in Suriname as well the Hebrew nation as English," suggesting that they already intended to include Jewish passengers. However, this notation appears in the same hand as the rest of Cranfield's narrative and so might not have been part of the original correspondence (NA UK, CO 278/3, 150).

63. NA UK, CO 278/3, 151.

64. NA UK, CO 278/3, 151–52. Alison Games also discusses this episode in "Cohabitation, Suriname-Style," 230–31. That subjecthood transcended nationality was an implication of *Calvin's Case* (1608), in which Scots born after the accession of James VI of Scotland to the throne of England were deemed to be subjects in England. This principle also applied in the colonies (Kettner, *Development of American Citizenship*, 16–28, 65). On Scots in Suriname, see Worthington, "Sugar, Slave-Owning, Suriname," 1–18.

65. Pieter Versterre, letter, 16 December 1675, ZA, 2035-271.

66. NA UK, CO 278/3, 155–56. It remains difficult to discern which indigenous groups the English entered into alliances with and thus who might have worked as their servants. Evidence suggests that they allied with people whom they labeled as *Caribs* and as *Arawaks*, terms that in the Guianas broadly map onto the Kalinago and Lokono people, respectively. On the English alliance with the Caribs, see Games, "Cohabitation, Suriname-Style," 202; on the alliance with the Arawaks, see Whitehead, "Caribbean Ethnic Soldiering," 365. The 1667 Articles of Capitulation stipulated that "the Charibees, our neighbors, shall be used civilly" ("Articles Concluded," 218). For the indigenous peoples to whom these terms refer, see Hyles, *Guiana and the Shadows of Empire*, 11, and Whitehead, "Carib Ethnic Soldiering," 361. Hyles notes that *Arawak* referred broadly to the Taino people, while Whitehead notes that the term applied to the Lokono people in coastal Guyana.

67. NA UK, CO 278/3, 157. In fact, none of the articles of capitulation explicitly stipulated the removal of free servants, indigenous or otherwise. Article 19 refers only to the removal of "slaves and goods etc" ("Articles Concluded," 219).

68. Pieter Versterre, letter, 16 December 1675, ZA, 2035-271. As Karwan Fatah-Black notes, in the same letter Versterre requested that the Zeeland States ask the English king to return indigenous people taken by the English and emphasized his fear of attack (*White Lies and Black Markets*, 29). The English seem ultimately to have left with three free and thirty-one enslaved indigenous people (discussed later in the chapter).

69. Games, "Cohabitation, Suriname-Style," 232–33; Buve, "Governor Johannes Heinsius," 39–47.

70. NA UK, CO 278/3, 158–59. A copy of the English protest note also exists in the Zeeland archives (*Protestnota Engelse Commissarisen*, ZA, 2035-273).

71. NA UK, CO 278/3, 160.

72. NA UK, CO 278/3, 160. As Games notes, the colonists feared that Cranfield might want them to settle in the Bahamas or another colony. Once in Jamaica, many of them ended up settling in Saint Elizabeth Parish, where they joined those who had left with James Banister in 1671 (Games, "Cohabitation, Suriname-Style" 230, 234). Justin Roberts argues that the colonists from Suriname became vital to Jamaica's success ("Surrendering Surinam").

73. NA UK, CO 278/3, 161. The full petition is on 160–61.

74. NA UK, CO 278/3, 164–65.

75. The evacuation numbers are contained in a report written on 30 May 1676 and presented to the Privy Council on 31 January 1677 (NA UK, CO 278/3, 166–68; the passenger figures appear on 167). The two Jews on board were Isaac de la Parr and Gabriell de Solis. Their names appear on the passenger list for the *Hercules* at *Calendar of State Papers Colonial, America and West Indies*, vol. 9 (1675–1676 and Addenda 1574–1674), 22 September 1675 (no. 675, vii). Rens assumes that de Solis is Jewish based on his name ("Analysis of Annals," 40–41).

76. NA UK, CO 278/3, 164.

77. Roberts, "Surrendering Surinam," 249.

78. Governor Sir William Stapleton to Lords of Trade and Plantations, Nevis, 7 February 1680, *Calendar of State Papers Colonial, America and West Indies*, vol. 10 (1677–1680), 7 February 1680 (no. 1291).

79. *Calendar of State Papers Colonial, America and West Indies*, vol. 10 (1677–1680), 23 January 1680 (no. 1281 i). Sir William Stapleton refers to this list as containing the names of the English settlers who were left behind after the 1680 evacuation to Antigua (Governor Sir William Stapleton to Lords of Trade and Plantations, Nevis, 7 February 1680, *Calendar of State Papers Colonial, America and West Indies*, vol. 10 [1677–1680], 7 February 1680 [no. 1291]).

80. Games, "Cohabitation, Suriname-Style," 237. This figure comes from counting English names in the 1684 census, which is available at NA Den Haag, Sociëteit van Suriname, 1.05.03, 213, fols. 204v–33r. Games discusses the 1680 evacuation to Antigua in "Cohabitation, Suriname-Style," 233–34.

81. NA UK, CO 278/3, 151.

82. Israel, *Diasporas*, 527. The size of the average Jewish family in the colony is unclear. Rens suggests that the community was no larger than two hundred people in 1667 ("Analysis of Annals," 36). According to the English commissioners, one Dutch source reported 130 Dutch colonists and an additional garrison of 140 troops (Hollander, "Documents," 13; Rens, "Analysis of Annals," 40). A July 1675 list of inhabitants sent by Versterre to Zeeland names 57 Jewish settlers (ZA, 2035-261), 134 Dutch settlers (ZA, 2035-262), and 76 English settlers (ZA, 2035-263). The Jewish and Dutch names are all those of men (with one possible exception). The English list includes only settlers who intended to leave the colony. It includes the names of some women as well as oblique references to wives and children.

83. Hollander, "Documents," 17. This is discussed by Rens ("Analysis of Annals," 41), who states that the document was included with Cranfield's passenger lists.

84. NA UK, PC 2/65, 120, 128. The petitioners described themselves as "his Majesty's subjects being made free denizens by letters patents under the Great Seal," an

interesting assertion given that if they were in Suriname in 1665, they would have been English subjects by virtue of the "Grant of Privileges" (NA UK, PC 2/65, 120). In 2012 Aviva Ben-Ur and Rachel Frankel suggested that the ten Jewish families who were petitioning for departure successfully left Suriname in 1677, basing this claim on Nassy's *Essai Historique* (*Remnant Stones*, 28). Rens critiques Nassy's reliability and argues that the petitioners probably remained in the colony ("Analysis of Annals," 41–43). The copy of the protest note from the English commissioners in the Zeeland archives contains an addendum by Versterre claiming that he had permitted Jews who were "free denizens of England" ("vrije dinnissen van Engelandt") to leave (*Protestnota Engelse Commissarisen*, ZA, 2035-273, fol. 2v). Given that it appears no more than two Jews departed in 1675, this may have been a post facto explanation intended for his superiors.

85. Ben-Ur and Frankl, *Remnant Stones*, 30–31; the quotation is on 31. The Jewish population of Suriname had reached 232 by 1684 (30). See also Ben-Ur, *Jewish Autonomy*. By 1791 there were 1,330 Jews in Suriname (Vink, *Creole Jews*, 26–27; here Vink also lists the numbers for 1684 and 1690). Natalie Zemon Davis discusses the Nassy family, including Samuel Nassy, in "Regaining Jerusalem."

86. By the 1680s the Scottish community in Suriname was centered around the planter Henry MacKintosh (discussed later in this chapter and the following one). MacKintosh was part of a network of Highland merchants who traded sugar from Suriname to Scotland (Worthington, "Sugar, Slave-Owning, Suriname").

87. NA Den Haag, Sociëteit van Suriname, 1.05.03, 213, fols. 204v–33r. See the analysis of the census in Games, "Cohabitation, Suriname-Style," 217–18. The overall figures appear in the table on 217 and the totals are broken down by group on 218.

88. Games, "Cohabitation, Suriname-Style," 237. For full information see 238, table 2.

89. Games, "Cohabitation, Suriname-Style," 233.

90. The Cliffords appear to be the only English people who were both in Suriname in 1680–1684 and also included on the list of passengers who were evacuated in 1675. Here I rely on the list of English settlers in the colony during those years in Games, "Cohabitation, Suriname-Style," 238, table 2, which includes names from both the 1684 census and correspondence from 1680. For the 1684 census there are only surname matches or similarities with the 1675 list: Philip Thomas appears in the census and William Thomas in the 1675 count; Andrew and Dolorosa Knight left in 1675 while William Knights was in Suriname in 1684. For the census, see NA Den Haag, Sociëteit van Suriname, 1.05.03, 213, fols. 204v–33r. For the 1675 passenger list, see *Calendar of State Papers Colonial, America and West Indies*, vol. 9 (1675–1676 and Addenda 1574–1674), 22 September 1675 (no. 675, vii).

91. See chapter 4.

92. NA UK, CO 278/3, 102. On another version of the passenger list they appear as "Andrew, Alice and Hierome Clifford." See *Calendar of State Papers Colonial, America and West Indies*, vol. 9 (1675–1676 and Addenda 1574–1674), 22 September 1675 (no. 675, vii). For Jeronimy Clifford's record of baptism, see Jeronemy Cleford, Baptism, 24 May 1657, Egham, St. John, Surrey, EG/1/2, *Anglican Parish Registers*, Surrey History Centre, accessed via *Ancestry Library*.

93. The total numbers are listed in a report written on 30 May 1676 and presented to the Privy Council on 31 January 1677. See NA UK, CO 278/3, 166–68 (the passenger

figures appear on 167). The proportion of colonists traveling with slaves comes from the passenger list (NA UK, CO 278/3, 101–5).

94. The statement about the money owed to Clifford is in NA UK, CO 1/35, no. 28, fol. 223v, and in less detail in *Calendar of State Papers Colonial, America and West Indies*, vol. 9 (1675–1676 and Addenda 1574–1674), 6 April to 29 September 1675 (no. 683).

95. *Calendar of State Papers Colonial, America and West Indies*, vol. 9 (1675–1676 and Addenda 1574–1674), 10 August 1676 ([no. 1009]). Simpson's name appears on two petitions signed by colonists, from 1669 (ZA, 2035-129) and 1671 (ZA, 2035-225).

96. *Calendar of State Papers Colonial, America and West Indies*, vol. 9 (1675–1676 and Addenda 1574–1674), 8 June 1676 (nos. 943, 943 ii.). In November 1674 Pringall and MacKintosh had made an agreement with Simpson "for the sale of two Plantations containing 1,600 acres of land for 600,000 lb. muscovado sugar" (*Calendar of State Papers Colonial, America and West Indies*, vol. 7 [1669–1674], 7 November 1674 [no. 1380]; I am grateful to David Worthington for telling me about this reference).

97. [Clifford], *The Case of Jeronimy Clifford Late Planter in Surinam*, 2 (the pamphlet can be found in BL, Add. MSS, 61644C, fols. 66r–67v).

98. BL, Add. MSS, 61644C, fols. 62r–v.

99. See *Discription of the Coleny of Surranam*.

100. "Articles Concluded," 218 (article 5).

101. Article 12 of the charter bound trade from Suriname directly to the Dutch Republic, stipulating that the colony's "fruits, wares and produce" could only be transported there (Fatah-Black, *White Lies and Black Markets*, 47). For the original Dutch text of the charter, see ZA, 2035, 3.16.507 (Octroy 1683).

102. Clifford, *Jeronimy Clifford's Answer*, 4 (the pamphlet can be found in BL, Add. MSS, 61644C, fols. 45r–46v).

103. BL, Add. MSS, 61644C, fol. 41r; NA Den Haag, SG, 1.01.02, 1953, 6 December 1700, fols. 10v–11r. The English translation uses the phrase "notoriously completed the tenor of the aforesaid Capitulation of Anno 1667" (BL, Add. MSS, 61644C, fol. 41r). The interpretation of the States General is part of a December 1700 response to a "memorial" by Alexander Stanhope, the Crown's envoy to the United Provinces, who had pressed Clifford's case for compensation. This was translated into English and can be found in BL, Add. MSS, 61644C, fols. 37r–44r. The original can be found in NA Den Haag, SG, 1.01.02, 589 (Eerste Minuten), 6 December 1700, fols. 4r–15r, and NA Den Haag, SG, 1.01.02, 1953, 6 December 1700, fols. 4r–17r (Geresumeerde Minuten). Here I quote from the English translation in Clifford's manuscript. However, I have checked all quotations against the original for accuracy and provide cross-references to the relevant folios, using the "geresumeerde minuten." I found only minor differences between the two versions and none in the passages that I quote here.

104. BL, Add. MSS, 61644C, fol. 41v; NA Den Haag, SG, 1.01.02, 1953, 6 December 1700, fol. 12r.

105. BL, Add. MSS, 61644C, fol. 62v; fols. 63v–64r.

106. BL, Add. MSS, 61644C, fols. 41r–v; NA Den Haag, SG, 1.01.02, 1953, 6 December 1700, fols. 11r–v. The explicit claim that the couple married in Zeeland is on BL, Add. MSS, 61644C, fol. 40v; NA Den Haag, SG, 1.01.02, 1953, 6 December 1700, fols. 10r–v.

107. See voyage IDs 9921, 10362, and 21209, respectively, in the *Trans-Atlantic Slave Trade Database*.

108. BL, Add. MSS, 61644C, fol. 64r.

109. Jeronimy Cliffard, Marriage, 2 August 1683, Holy Trinity Minories, City of London, P69/TRI2/A/008/MS09243, *Church of England Parish Registers, 1538–1812*, London Metropolitan Archives, accessed via *Ancestry Library*.

110. Clifford notes Baroen's 10 July 1687 acquittal of a debt owed to him, describing him as "a Dutchman . . . married to my wife's sister" (BL, Add. MSS, 61644C, fol. 32r). Charges drawn up by Suriname's provisional fiscal against Clifford in 1692 also reference Baroen as Clifford's brother-in-law (NA UK, SP 84/588, 62v). The same page also refers to a letter written *from* Matson's "brother in law to Mr. Thomas Baroen." Here the word "to" is probably an error, unless Matson had a second sibling (for which there is no other evidence). No sources refer to Jeronimy Clifford as having a sibling. Baroen's last name is spelled "Baron" throughout Clifford's papers.

111. BL, Add. MSS, 61644C, fols. 62v–63r.

112. BL, Add. MSS, 61644C, fols. 63r–v. The details of Corbitt's partnership with Versterre are somewhat confusing. Clifford states that after Corbitt's death Versterre ordered the abandonment of Corcabo and the removal of its "slaves, horses, cattle and other movables" to Mattappy, which he judged "to be the better land" (BL, Add. MSS, 61644C, fol. 63r). Presumably this was just the half of the property to which Versterre was entitled by virtue of the partnership.

113. BL, Add. MSS, 61644C, fol. 63v.

114. BL, Add. MSS, 61644C, fols. 64r–v.

115. BL, Add. MSS, 61644C, fols. 40v, 41v; NA Den Haag, SG, 1.01.02, 1953, 6 December 1700, fols. 10r, 11v. The society's record of the transaction, which took place on 31 March 1684, describes the drawing of lots, with Corcabo going to Clifford. It names Van Haagen's wife as Hendrina van Hardenbergh, identifies her as the widow of Pieter Versterre, and describes her former partnership with Matson, late widow of "Carel Maersman." It is, however, silent on the motivation for the division of the property. The record describes Clifford as now having "full ownership" over Corcabo ("in vollen eijgendom"). Mattappy is listed as "Imotapij" (NA Den Haag, Sociëteit van Suriname, 1.05.03, 227, fols. 102r–v). Further documents, also dated 31 March 1684, outline the details of the agreement. In describing the provenance of the split property, NA Den Haag, Sociëteit van Suriname, 1.05.03, 227, fols. 117r–118r, mentions Abraham Schoors as well as Meersman (fol. 117v). According to NA Den Haag, Sociëteit van Suriname, 1.05.03, 227, fols. 119r–121v, Henry MacKintosh, Clifford's future legal adversary (discussed in chapter 3), was among the witnesses to the transaction (fol. 121v).

116. BL, Add. MSS, 61644C, fol. 40v; NA Den Haag, SG, 1.01.02, 1953, 6 December 1700, fol. 10r. Pieter Versterre is explicitly referred to as the former governor on BL, Add. MSS, 61644C, fol. 41v; NA Den Haag, SG, 1.01.02, 1953, 6 December 1700, fol. 11v.

117. *Plakkaat*, 19 February 1669, ZA, 2035-114. The quotation (in my own translation) is from the third item of the *plakkaat*. I am grateful to Suze Zijlstra for pointing me to this source.

118. Van der Heijden et al., "Terugkeer van Het Patriarchaat?," 36–37 (my own translation). I am grateful to Suze Zijlstra for referring me to this article. For cover-

ture in England, and the practical and legal steps that women took to mitigate it, see Erickson, *Women and Property*.

119. BL, Add. MSS, 61644C, fol. 40v; NA Den Haag, SG, 1.01.02, 1953, 6 December 1700, fols. 10r–v.

120. Morgan, *American Slavery, American Freedom*, 164–66. The term *widowarchy* appears on 166.

121. Hamer, "Marriage and the Construction of Colonial Order," 629–30.

122. NA Den Haag, Sociëteit van Suriname, 1.05.03, 213, fols. 223v–24r. The ratio for the enslaved of African descent was much closer: 1,842 men to 1,384 women, or about 1.33 men for every woman. There were also 159 white children, 911 black children, and 38 indigenous children; the latter two groups were presumably enslaved (fols. 223v–24r).

123. In Virginia the vulnerability of widows was exacerbated by increasing legal marginalization after the 1680s (Brown, *Good Wives, Nasty Wenches*, 287).

124. On widows in colonial America who did not remarry, see Conger, *Widows' Might*.

125. Van der Meiden, *Betwist Bestuur*, 33.

126. The sale was finalized on 6 January 1683. The transfer to the West India Company took effect on 20 February 1683 (Van der Meiden, *Betwist Bestuur*, 40). For the deed of sale, see ZA, 2035-505. For the deed of transfer, see ZA, 2035-506.

127. Van der Meiden, *Betwist Bestuur*, 39–41. For Van Sommelsdijck's background, see Van der Meiden, *Betwist Bestuur*, 42–45.

128. Van der Meiden, *Betwist Bestuur*, 40 (my own translation).

129. Van der Meiden, *Betwist Bestuur*, 38–39. The quotation from the charter appears on 38. See also Fatah-Black, *White Lies and Black Markets*, 8. Membership in the Council of Polity was limited to Protestant "male heads of households with plantations," although Jews had a say in the nomination process (8). The full name of the council was the "Raad van Politie en Justitie," although in Suriname itself it became known as the "Hof van Politie" (Van der Meiden, *Betwist Bestuur*, 12, 38.) As Van der Meiden notes, *politie* is usually translated into English as "police," rather than, in this case, the more appropriate "policy" (Van der Meiden, *Betwist Bestuur*, 12). Karwan Fatah-Black uses the functionally accurate term "governing council" (*White Lies and Black Markets*, 8). I have opted to use "Council of Polity," in accordance with the terminology used by Clifford himself (see, for example, BL, Add. MSS, 61644C, fol. 21r). This sometimes appears as the "Court of Polity" (see, for example, BL, Add. MSS, 61644C, fol. 16v).

130. According to Jeronimy Clifford, Suriname's government "kept this bill of exchange in dispute at law until the latter end of the year 1684." These efforts aimed "to frustrate Andrew Clifford leaving that colony as he intended to do" (BL, Add. MSS, 61644C, fol. 62v).

131. See the 1680 list of English subjects in Suriname cited in Games, "Cohabitation, Suriname-Style," 238, table 2. The relevant maps here are *A Discription of the Coleny of Surranam* (1667), *[Surinam and Commewijne Rivers]* (1667 or later), *Caerte ofte vertooninge vande Rivieren van Suriname en commewijne* (1667 or later), and *A New Draught of Surranam upon the coast of Guianna* (c. 1675).

132. [Clifford], *The Case of Andrew Clifford and Jeronimy Clifford Late Planters in Surinam*, 1 (the pamphlet can be found in BL, Add. MSS, 61644B, fols. 58r–59v.) This

pamphlet lists 1685 as the year that Andrew Clifford left Suriname. Here the pamphlet oversimplifies the property relationship between father and son, stating simply that by that year the younger Clifford owned a third of the family plantation. In fact, that situation would not have pertained until six years later, Jeronimy Clifford having transferred a third of Corcabo to his father on two separate occasions, in 1685 and 1691 (BL, Add. MSS, 61644C, fols. 9r–9v and 11v–12v, respectively).

133. For the power of attorney, which was signed on 26 June 1684, see BL, Add. MSS, 61644C, fol. 11v. This is mentioned in a reproduction of a further transfer by Jeronimy to Andrew of another third of his plantation, in December 1691 (BL, Add. MSS, 61644C, fols. 11v–12v). The mention of Andrew Clifford's will is in BL, Add. MSS, 61644C, fol. 59r. The 1685 deed of sale is in BL, Add. MSS, 61644C, fols. 9r–v. This is followed by an inventory of the plantation in BL, Add. MSS, 61644C, fols. 10r–v. A Dutch-language copy of the deed can be found in the records of the Society of Suriname in NA Den Haag, Sociëteit van Suriname, 1.05.03, 227, fols. 104r–105v.

134. BL, Add. MSS, 61644C, fols. 9r–v.

135. BL, Add. MSS, 61644C, fols. 10r–v. A version of this deed is also included in NA UK, CO 388/75, no. 86, enclosure no. 11. It lacks an inventory of the plantation. Moreover, the total acreage listed in the deed conflicts with the number given in the December 1684 census, where Clifford's plantation was assessed at 1,560 acres with a total of fifty-three slaves (NA Den Haag, Sociëteit van Suriname, 1.05.03, 213, fols. 205v–206r). This makes it the second-largest plantation in Suriname, after Francis Bruninge's 1,800 acres (Games, "Cohabitation, Suriname-Style," 238, table 2).

136. [Clifford], *Case of Andrew Clifford and Jeronimy Clifford Late Planters in Surinam*, 1.

137. BL, Add. MSS, 61644C, fol. 31r.

138. [Clifford], *The Case of Mr. Jeronimy Clifford, Merchant and Planter of Surinam* (1720), 8. The exact date of the 1685 gift from Hampson is unclear, as the 1720 pamphlet lists it as 19 February 1685 and Clifford's 1707 manuscripts as 19 September of the same year (BL, Add. MSS, 61644C, fol. 58r). Saint Elizabeth's Parish was the destination of many emigrants from Suriname (Games, "Cohabitation, Suriname-Style," 234).

139. NA UK, CO 278/3, 103. Hampson, whose name appears here as "Hamson," is listed as leaving with his wife and thirty-three slaves; Watson is listed with his wife and twenty-six slaves.

140. Suriname's authorities would later allege that Clifford had acquired this land dishonestly (see NA UK, SP 84/588, fol. 61r, discussed in chapter 3).

141. Historians differ about the amount of de facto freedom women were able to achieve in the Netherlands during the early modern period. Van der Heijden, Meerkerk, and Schmidt suggest that women gained greater autonomy ("Terugkeer van Het Patriarchaat?," esp. 48–50). Deborah Hamer tempers this picture of growing female independence, noting "conflicting attitudes in the Dutch Republic about women's activities outside of the home." Anxiety about single women was accompanied by moralizing that sought to constrain the activities of married women beyond the household (Hamer, "Marriage and the Construction of Colonial Order," 630–32; quotation on 632).

142. The marriage took place on 2 August 1683 Old Style, 12 August New Style (BL, Add. MSS, 61644C, fol. 64r); the contract was made in Middelberg on 4 August 1683, presumably New Style (BL, Add. MSS, 61644C, fol. 7r). I am grateful to the

Zeeland Archives for attempting to find the original copy of the contract, which apparently has not survived.

143. BL, Add. MSS, 61644C, fol. 64v. See fol. 62r for the year.

144. BL, Add. MSS, 61644B, fol. 4r.

145. BL, Add. MSS, 61644C, fols. 7r–v.

146. BL, Add. MSS, 61644C, fol. 64v.

147. Van der Heijden, Meerkerk, and Schmidt, "Terugkeer van Het Patriarchaat?," 36–37 (discussed previously).

148. BL, Add. MSS, 61644C, fol. 8r.

149. NA UK, SP 84/588, fol. 54r. See below for the accusations of infidelity. The petition itself is undated. For the governor's response (discussed later in the chapter), see NA UK, SP 84/588, fol. 55v. For the original Dutch-language manuscripts, of which these are accurate translations, see NA Den Haag, Sociëteit van Suriname, 1.05.03, 227, fols. 106r–107r. The version in the UK archives is on NA UK, SP 84/588, fols. 53r–55v.

150. NA UK, SP 84/588, fol. 53r.

151. NA UK, SP 84/588, fol. 55r.

152. NA UK, SP 84/588, fols. 53r–v.

153. NA UK, SP 84/588, fol. 53v.

154. NA UK, SP 84/588, fol. 54r.

155. NA UK, SP 84/588, fols. 54r–v.

156. NA UK, SP 84/588, fol. 54v. The Dutch-language original describes the plate as *silver servies*, or "silver tableware" (NA Den Haag, 1.05.03, 227, fol. 106v).

157. NA UK, SP 84/588, fol. 55r.

158. NA UK, SP 84/588, fols. 55r–v. Here Thyssen's name appears as "Thuyssen." I am opting to use the former spelling in accordance with sources that I cite in chapter 3.

159. NA UK, SP 84/588, 61v. This reference appears in charges against Clifford by Suriname's provisional fiscal that were issued in January 1692 (discussed in chapter 3).

160. NA UK, SP 84/588, fol. 57r. Here I quote from the English-language translation of the commissioners' report, in NA UK, SP 84/588, fols. 57r–59v. For the Dutch version see NA Den Haag, Sociëteit van Suriname, 1.05.03, 227, fols. 114r–15v.

161. NA UK, SP 84/588, fol. 57r–v.

162. NA UK, SP 84/588, fols. 57v–58r. Here Hampson's name appears as "Hamson," as it does in the Dutch-language original (NA Den Haag, Sociëteit van Suriname, 1.05.03, 227, fol. 114r).

163. NA UK, SP 84/588, fol. 58v.

164. NA UK, SP 84/588, fol. 59r.

165. NA UK, SP 84/588, fols. 58r–v. This is a reference to Thomas Baroen, who is identified elsewhere as a Dutch man married to an unnamed sister of Matson (BL, Add. MSS, 61644C, fol. 32r).

166. NA UK, SP 84/588, fols. 59r–v.

167. NA UK, SP 84/588, fols. 58v, fol. 59r.

168. NA UK, SP 84/588, fols. 59r–v.

169. BL, Add. MSS, 61644C, fols. 13r–v. Van Vredenburgh is listed as a member of the council on BL, Add. MSS, 61644C, fol. 19v. For the original Dutch-language version of Matson's retraction, see NA Den Haag, Sociëteit van Suriname, 1.05.03, 227,

fols. 112r–v. Unlike the translated version, this lacks a date, although the authorities' response is also dated 10 April 1687 (NA Den Haag, Sociëteit van Suriname, 1.05.03, 227, fols. 113r).

170. BL, Add. MSS, 61644C, fols. 13v–14r. For the Dutch-language manuscript, see NA Den Haag, Sociëteit van Suriname, 1.05.03, 227, fols. 112v–13v.

171. BL, Add. MSS, 61644C, fol. 14r.

172. BL, Add. MSS, 61644C, fol. 14v. For the reference to her death, see *Conduct of the Dutch*, 37. Matson appears to have left Suriname without paying the fine of five thousand pounds of sugar: on 17 December 1688 the fiscal issued an order for its collection from Clifford's plantation (NA Den Haag, Sociëteit van Suriname, 1.05.03, 227, fol. 113v).

173. BL, Add. MSS, 61644C, fols. 15r–v. The last manuscript reference to Matson appears in a copy of another document granting Clifford power of attorney, dated 17 April 1707 (BL, Add. MSS, 61644C, fols. 94r–95r; discussed in chapter 4).

174. BL, Add. MSS, 61644C, fol. 14v.

175. BL, Add. MSS, 61644C, fol. 13r.

176. BL, Add. MSS, 61644B, fol. 12r.

177. BL, Add. MSS, 61644C, fol. 31r.

178. See NA Den Haag, Sociëteit van Suriname, 1.05.03, 213, fols. 219v–220r (for Baroen) and fols. 205v–206r (for Clifford).

179. BL, Add. MSS, 61644C, fol. 32r. His papers also list a 1 December 1683 "account current" owed to Baroen (BL, Add. MSS, 61644C, fol. 58r).

180. BL, Add. MSS, 61644C, fol. 13v.

181. BL, Add. MSS, 61644C, fol. 13v.

3. The Glorious Revolution in Suriname (1688–1695)

1. There is a voluminous historiography on the events of the Glorious Revolution and its subsequent implications. See, for example, Schwoerer, *Revolution of 1688–1689*; Israel, *Anglo-Dutch Moment*; Pincus, *1688*; Sowerby, *Making Toleration*. On Anglo-Dutch relations in the seventeenth century see, for example, Rubright, *Doppelgänger Dilemmas*; Jardine, *Going Dutch*; Games, *Inventing the English Massacre*.

2. France continued to back James after his removal from power, supporting his last stand in Ireland in 1690 and the ensuing movement for the Jacobite cause and hosting his exiled court. While Louis XIV recognized William as king in 1697, he did not disavow James II's claim to the throne (Miller, *James II*, 239). France then continued to host the court of James Edward Stuart, the Jacobite James III (see chap. 4 of Corp, with Gregg, Erskine-Hill, and Scott, *A Court in Exile*). On Jacobitism in the century after the Glorious Revolution, see Monod, *Jacobitism and the English People*.

3. Steele, "Communicating an English Revolution," 335–36.

4. Steele, "Communicating an English Revolution," 338–40.

5. Steele, "Communicating an English Revolution," 342.

6. Steele, "Communicating an English Revolution," 341, 344–45, 340.

7. Stanwood, *Empire Reformed*, 124.

8. Steele, "Communicating an English Revolution," 346.

9. Steele, "Communicating an English Revolution," 354; Johnson, "Revolution of 1688–9," 222.

NOTES TO PAGES 79-83

10. Balmer, *Perfect Babel of Confusion*, 33, 49.

11. See, for example, Stanwood, *Empire Reformed*, 105. Fear of French attack, possibly in alliance with indigenous people, pervaded the Dominion of New England (97–99).

12. "Articles of Agreement," 2–3.

13. See Stanwood, *Empire Reformed*, 103–6 (for the role of anti-Catholicism in the New York rebellion); 119–20 (for the tendency to blame Catholic agents rather than James himself).

14. Roeber, "The Origin of Whatever Is Not English among Us," 226–37. See Balmer, *Perfect Babel of Confusion*, for an analysis of colonial Dutch religious culture from the English conquest to the American revolution.

15. The position of English colonial officials during the Glorious Revolution is discussed throughout Steele, "Communicating an English Revolution."

16. For the course of the war in the Americas, see Klooster, *Dutch Moment*, 106–12. In 1677 England and the Dutch Republic agreed on a mutual defense alliance, foreshadowing their 1689 coalition (see Klooster and Oostindie, *Realm between Empires*, 27; and Haley, "Anglo-Dutch Rapprochement," 614–48).

17. Zijlstra and Weterings, "Colonial Life," 84.

18. Zijlstra and Weterings, "Colonial Life," 86–87.

19. Zijlstra and Weterings, "Colonial Life," 88–90.

20. See the discussion later in this chapter.

21. Klooster and Oostindie, *Realm between Empires*, 27–28.

22. This was despite the fact that in each province the stadholder held the position of captain-general (see Israel, *Dutch Republic*, 304–5).

23. Israel, *Dutch Republic*, 700–701.

24. Israel, *Dutch Republic*, 791–92, 794.

25. Israel, *Dutch Republic*, 798–803.

26. Israel, *Dutch Republic*, 816–17.

27. Israel, *Dutch Republic*, 826, 837, 847–49.

28. Israel, *Dutch Republic*, 854, 856.

29. The 1685 deed of sale is in BL, Add. MSS, 61644C, fols. 9r–v. This is followed by an inventory of the plantation in BL, Add. MSS, 61644C, fols. 10r–v. A Dutch-language copy of the deed can be found in the records of the Society of Suriname in NA Den Haag, Sociëteit van Suriname, 1.05.03, 227, fols. 104r–105v.

30. NA UK, SP 84/588, fols. 54r–v. For the governor's response see NA UK, SP 84/588, fol. 55v. For the original Dutch-language manuscripts, of which these are accurate translations, see NA Den Haag, Sociëteit van Suriname, 1.05.03, 227, fols. 106r–107r. The version in the UK archives is in NA UK, SP 84/588, fols. 53r–55v.

31. BL, Add. MSS, 61644C, fols. 13r–14v. For the Dutch-language manuscript of the court's response see NA Den Haag, Sociëteit van Suriname, 1.05.03, 227, fols. 112v–113v.

32. BL, Add. MSS, 61644C, fol. 31v.

33. [Clifford], *The Case of Mr. Jeronimy Clifford, Merchant and Planter of Surinam* (1720), 3. For the States General on Lodge, see BL, Add. MSS, 61644C, fols. 41r–v.

34. [Clifford], *The Case of Mr. Jeronimy Clifford, Merchant and Planter of Surinam* (1720), 3.

35. BL, Add. MSS, 61644B, fol. 11r.

36. BL, Add. MSS, 61644B, fols. 11r–v.

37. BL, Add. MSS, 61644B, fol. 11v.

38. BL, Add. MSS, 61644C, fol. 31v. Elsewhere Clifford refers to "several other prosecutions" relating to the matter (BL, Add. MSS, 61644B, fol. 158r).

39. [Clifford], *The Case of Andrew Clifford and Jeronimy Clifford Late Planters in Surinam*, 2 (the pamphlet can be found in BL, Add. MSS, 61644B, fols. 58r–59v).

40. BL, Add. MSS, 61644C, fol. 31v. Clifford had dealt with Aries in the past: in May 1685 the two signed a contract and Aries provided Clifford with a "procuration" (BL, Add. MSS, 61644C, fol. 58r).

41. See NA Den Haag, Sociëteit van Suriname, 1.05.03, 213, fols. 214v–215r and 226v–227r, respectively.

42. See NA UK, SP 84/588, fol. 61r (discussed later in the chapter). For the gift from Hampson, see [Clifford], *The Case of Mr. Jeronimy Clifford, Merchant and Planter of Surinam* (1720), 8. For Hampson's appearance on the 1675 passenger list, see NA UK, CO 278/3, 103.

43. [Clifford], *The Case of Andrew Clifford and Jeronimy Clifford Late Planters in Surinam*, 2.

44. Clifford states that he had cargo on Woodbury's ship (BL, Add. MSS, 61644C, fols. 31v–32r). An inventory of manuscripts in his papers lists a "bill of sale for the ship Bristol Merchant from Sam: Woodbury to J: Clifford" dated 25 August 1688, as well as a deposition relating to the ship's sale made a decade later "before the Court of Schepen in the Hague" (BL, Add. MSS, 61644C, fol. 58v). In 1692 Suriname's provisional fiscal would allege that Clifford was co-owner of the *Bristol Merchant* (see NA UK, SP 84/588, fols. 63r–v; discussed later in the chapter).

45. BL, Add. MSS, 61644C, fol. 32r.

46. [Clifford], *The Case of Andrew Clifford and Jeronimy Clifford Late Planters in Surinam*, 2. Elsewhere he presents this protest as including a complaint about the 10 April 1687 arrest on his estate caused by his wife's appeal to the governor (BL, Add. MSS, 61644B, fol. 12v).

47. He was imprisoned for refusing to take the oath on 20 April 1689. Imposition of the thirty thousand pound fine and his forced request for forgiveness took place on 5 August. Here I am assuming that the latter resulted in his release (BL, Add. MSS, 61644B, fol. 12v; BL, Add. MSS, 61644C, fol. 32r).

48. Clifford, *Jeronimy Clifford's Answer*, 1 (the pamphlet can be found in BL, Add. MSS 61644C, fols. 45r–46v).

49. "Articles Concluded," 217, art. 2.

50. Zijlstra and Weterings, "Colonial Life," 84.

51. Steele, "Communicating an English Revolution," 338–39; Dunn, *Sugar and Slaves*, 134.

52. BL, Add. MSS, 61644C, fols. 41r, 41v; NA Den Haag, SG, 1.01.02, 1953, 6 December 1700, fols. 10v, 12r.

53. Worthington, "Sugar, Slave-Owning, Suriname," 4–6 (quotations on 5 and 6).

54. Worthington, "Sugar, Slave-Owning, Suriname," 2.

55. MacInnes, *Union and Empire*, 162. I am grateful to David Worthington for this reference.

56. BL, Add. MSS, 61644C, fols. 16r–v. Clifford refers to his "administration of Captain Samuel Lodge['s] estate" on BL, Add. MSS, 61644C, fol. 33v.

57. BL, Add. MSS, 61644C, fol. 16v.

58. BL, Add. MSS, 61644C, fol. 17r.

59. BL, Add. MSS, 61644C, fols. 17r–v. This is a summary of Clifford's response, written by the fiscal, Peter Madrich.

60. BL, Add. MSS, 61644C, fols. 18v–19v. The date of the petition, on fol. 18r, is obscured. However, it is listed as 6 September 1691 in the index to Clifford's papers on BL, Add. MSS, 61644B, fol. 4v.

61. BL, Add. MSS, 61644C, fols. 19r–v.

62. BL, Add. MSS, 61644C, fol. 19v.

63. BL, Add. MSS, 61644C, fols. 20r–v.

64. BL, Add. MSS, 61644C, fols. 21r–v.

65. See chapter 2.

66. NA UK, SP 84/588, fol. 61r. According to the fiscal, Clifford "had permitted the procuration of Benito Aries to Oliver Hampson (who was holder of said Benito Aries goods) to be revoked, and agreed in a manner so as to possess himself of the lands, which to this present time he very unjustly holds, and thereby keeps out the right owner" (fol. 61r).

67. NA UK, SP 84/588, fol. 61v. Regland appears in this account as "Maria Tanner . . . widow of John Reglands." (NA UK, SP 84/588, fol. 61v). Although the document is undated, it contains a reference to a 3 January 1692 petition from Clifford (NA UK, SP 84/588, fol. 65v). The fiscal's name appears in his subsequent sentence against Clifford, dated 9 January 1692 (BL, Add. MSS, 61644C, fols. 22r–23r). In her 1687 complaint Matson had referred to Regland simply as Clifford's mistress and a "whore" (NA UK, SP 84/588, fols. 54r, 55r). A subsequent order for her arrest then mentions Regland by name (NA UK, SP 84/588, fols. 55r–v).

68. NA UK, SP 84/588, fols. 62r–v. Elsewhere Clifford describes him as "a Dutchman . . . married to my wife's sister" (BL, Add. MSS, 61644C, fol. 32r).

69. NA UK, SP 84/588, fols. 62v–63r. Thyssen identifies the ship's co-owner as "Mr. Bruyning" (probably referring to Francis Bruninge, an English planter for whom Clifford would later serve as executor, as discussed later in the chapter). For more on Bruninge see Games, "Cohabitation, Suriname-Style," 211, 236–37.

70. NA UK, SP 84/588, fol. 63v.

71. NA UK, SP 84/588, fol. 64r.

72. NA UK, SP 84/588, fols. 65r–v.

73. BL, Add. MSS, 61644C, fols. 22r–v.

74. BL, Add. MSS, 61644C, fols. 22v–23r.

75. BL, Add. MSS, 61644C, fols. 23r–v. The recommendation of the provisional fiscal and the sentence of the criminal court, which appear in English in BL, Add. MSS, 61644C fols. 22r–23v, are reproduced in Dutch in Hartsinck, *Beschryving Van Guiana*, 860–62. An English-language version appears in *Dutch Displayed*, 20–23, as found "in the archives of the board of trade" (20). (This may be a reference to an English-language manuscript copy in NA UK, SP 84/588, fols. 67r–69v.) The court's sentence took place on the same day as the issuance of the provisional fiscal's report, 9 January 1692 (BL, Add. MSS, 61644C, fol. 23v). The version in NA UK, SP 84/588 provides an erroneous date of 9 February 1692 (NA UK, SP 84/588, fol. 69v). The other versions mentioned here give the date as 9 January 1692.

76. [Clifford], *The Case of Andrew Clifford and Jeronimy Clifford Late Planters in Surinam*, 2.

77. See BL, Add. MSS, 61644C, fol. 12v, for the date of the transaction.

78. BL, Add. MSS, 61644C, fol. 12v (dated 18 August 1692). On Andrew Clifford's departure and the grant of power of attorney, see [Clifford], *The Case of Andrew Clifford and Jeronimy Clifford Late Planters in Surinam*, 1. The power of attorney is also mentioned in BL, Add. MSS, 61644C, fol. 11v.

79. For the original transfer, see BL, Add. MSS, 61644C, fols. 9r–v. The 1691 inventory is in BL, Add. MSS, 61644C, fols. 11r–v. Although undated, it immediately precedes the dated deed of sale (BL, Add. MSS, 61644C, fols. 11v–12v). It is also marked with the numerals *9* and *10*, corresponding to the index of Clifford's papers in BL, Add. MSS, 61644B, fol. 4v, which dates both as 10 December 1692 (this is an error, as the deed itself contains the date 10 December 1691 on BL, Add. MSS, 61644C, fol. 12v).

80. BL, Add. MSS, 61644C, fol. 11r. The 1685 acreage is listed on BL, Add. MSS, 61644C, fol. 10r. The 1684 records list Corcabo as comprising 1,560 acres (NA Den Haag, Sociëteit van Suriname, 1.05.03, 213, fols. 205v–206r, and Games, "Cohabitation, Suriname-Style," 238, table 2).

81. BL, Add. MSS, 61644C, fols. 11r–v. See BL, Add. MSS, 61644C, fols. 10r–v, for the 1685 inventory. In placing a value on enslaved black adults, the 1685 inventory did not distinguish by gender and instead listed them all at four thousand pounds each (BL, Add. MSS, 61644C, fol. 10r). Including "Angola" in a slave's name may, at least, have accurately reflected his or her origins. As Natalie Zemon Davis notes, "From the 1660s through the 1730s, West India Company records show us that the vast majority of slaves purchased in Suriname came from the Bight of Benin and the Angola Coast" ("Regaining Jerusalem," 28).

82. BL, Add. MSS, 61644C, fols. 11v–12v; the terms of the first transfer are on BL, Add. MSS, 61644C, fols. 9r–v.

83. BL, Add. MSS, 61644C, fol. 32v. The vessel's name is listed on BL, Add. MSS, 61644C, fol. 59r.

84. BL, Add. MSS, 61644C, fols. 32v–33r; BL, Add. MSS, 61644B, fol. 14r. The amount of the fine appears on BL, Add. MSS, 61644B, fol. 14r. The damages that were claimed appear on BL, Add. MSS, 61644C, fol. 33r.

85. BL, Add. MSS, 61644B, fol. 14r; BL, Add. MSS, 61644C, fol. 33r.

86. BL, Add. MSS, 61644C, fol. 60r.

87. BL, Add. MSS, 61644B, fols. 70r–v. In his charges against Clifford the fiscal had named one "Mr. Bruyning" as the person with whom Clifford co-owned the *Bristol Merchant*, which sailed under the command of Samuel Woodbury (see NA UK, SP 84/588, fol. 63r).

88. Clifford, *Jeronimy Clifford's Answer*, 3.

89. [Clifford], *The Case of Andrew Clifford and Jeronimy Clifford Late Planters in Surinam*, 2.

90. BL, Add. MSS, 61644C, fol. 30r.

91. Here I quote from a translation in *Dutch Displayed*, 17–19. The original is in NA Den Haag, SG, 1.01.02, 515, fols. 4v–5r (16 October 1694). The text printed in *The Dutch Displayed* is an accurate idiomatic translation except for a few minor details. For example, the printed version describes Clifford's imprisonment as lasting for "these four

years past" while the original lists its duration as two years ("nu twee jaaren"). The original states that Clifford requested permission to return to his birthplace with his goods while the printed version (trimmed in my quotation here) states that he asked to "return with his goods and slaves." In addition, the Barbadian governors appear as "Sir Edward Steede and Colonel Kendal" in *Dutch Displayed* and as "Sir Edwin Steed en Colonel Kendall" in the original.

92. BL, Add. MSS, 61644B, fol. 15r.

93. *Dutch Displayed*, 19. This also appears in BL, Add. MSS, 61644C, fol. 24r.

94. BL, Add. MSS, 61644B, fol. 15r. The 1763 text *The Case and Replication of the Legal Representatives of Jeronimy Clifford* dates Clifford's release to 10 May 1695 rather than 4 May. See *Case and Replication*, 18. This date is also given by Clifford in a December 1696 petition to the States General (BL, Add. MSS, 61644C, fol. 30r).

95. Clifford, *Jeronimy Clifford's Answer*, 1.

96. BL, Add. MSS, 61644C, fol. 26r.

97. BL, Add. MSS, 61644C, fol. 27r.

98. BL, Add. MSS, 61644C, fols. 27r–v.

99. BL, Add. MSS, 61644C, fol. 60r.

100. BL, Add. MSS, 61644C, fol. 27v. Here he states that "on the 13th of October I went to Barbados and from that island on the 1st March 1695/6 I departed for Europe." The English government issued him with a pass to travel to Holland on 31 July 1696 (NA UK, SP 44/346, 384). He seems to have arrived in Amsterdam by September, when he was in touch with George Clifford, one of the proprietors of the Society of Suriname and seemingly no relation (Clifford, *Jeronimy Clifford's Answer*, 3). He took his case directly to the Society of Suriname on the anniversary of his departure (BL, Add. MSS, 61644C, fol. 27v).

101. NA Den Haag, Sociëteit van Suriname, 1.05.03, 227, fols. 110r–111r. The document appointing Le Brun (who is listed as Francois Le Bruijn) is dated 1 October 1695. Clifford was clearly expecting trouble in his absence: a week later he directed a possible "execution" against him to be paid out of the plantation's cattle (see NA Den Haag, Sociëteit van Suriname, 1.05.03, 227, fol. 108r; the source is a copy from Le Brun's records).

102. NA UK, CO 388/75, no. 120iii, fol. 3r; BL, Add. MSS, 61644B, fols. 174r–76r.

103. NA UK, SP 84/588, fol. 53v. For Matson's full allegations against Clifford, see NA UK, SP 84/588, fols. 53r–55v, and NA Den Haag, Sociëteit van Suriname, 1.05.03, 227, fols. 106r–107r (discussed in chapter 2).

104. BL, Add. MSS, 61644C, fols. 14r–v.

105. [Clifford], *The Case of Andrew Clifford and Jeronimy Clifford Late Planters in Surinam*, 2–3.

106. Stanwood, *Empire Reformed*, 124.

107. See Games, "Cohabitation, Suriname-Style," 209, for the use of the term *cohabit* in the articles of capitulation and the word's English and Dutch meanings at the time.

108. NA UK, SP 84/588, fol. 64r.

109. BL, Add. MSS, 61644C, fol. 41v; NA Den Haag, SG, 1.01.02, 1953, 6 December 1700, fol. 12r.

4. Colonial Subjecthood in England and the Netherlands (1696–1737)

1. Clifford, *The Case of Jeronimy Clifford, Merchant and Planter of Surinam* (1714), 4. As Clifford noted in 1701, after leaving Suriname he had "left my father's part there" (Clifford, *Jeronimy Clifford's Answer*, 2; the pamphlet can be found in BL, Add. MSS, 61644C, fols. 45r–46v).

2. NA UK, SP 44/346, 384.

3. BL, Add. MSS, 61644C, fol. 27v. There are signs that he was in Amsterdam a month earlier, where he was engaged in dealings with George Clifford (apparently, no relation), who was one of the directors of the Society of Suriname (see Clifford, *Jeronimy Clifford's Answer*, 3).

4. For the text of these accords, see, respectively, "Articles Concluded," and Treaty of Westminster, in Chalmers, *Collection of Treaties*, 1:172–77.

5. BL, Add. MSS, 61644C, fols. 28v–29v; the quotation is on fol. 29v. Clifford's request was conveyed by a notary on 13 October 1696. Clifford states that he was in Amsterdam on this date (BL, Add. MSS, 61644C, fol. 29r).

6. BL, Add. MSS, 61644B, fols. 17r–v.

7. Clifford, *Jeronimy Clifford's Answer*, 2. Villiers was appointed envoy extraordinary to the States General in May 1695, before becoming ambassador extraordinary to France in July 1698. He became Earl of Jersey in October 1697 (Handley, "Villiers, Edward").

8. BL, Add. MSS, 61644C, fol. 31r. The "memorial" is on BL, Add. MSS, 61644C, fols. 31r–34v.

9. BL, Add. MSS, 61644C, fols. 35r–v. This is from an English translation in Clifford's papers. The original resolution (which accords with the translation) can be found in NA Den Haag, SG, 1.01.02, 1907, 16 February 1697, fols. 6r–7r (Ordinaris Resoluties, Geresumeerde Minuten). The initial draft of this response is in NA Den Haag, SG, 1.01.02, 543, 16 February 1697, pages unnumbered (Ordinaris Resoluties, Eerste Minuten).

10. Clifford, *Case of Jeronimy Clifford, Merchant and Planter of Surinam* (1714), 10. Jersey had served as envoy extraordinary to the States General since May 1695. In 1697 he was appointed envoy to the Rijswijk peace conference, as well as lord justice of Ireland. He left the Netherlands in November 1697, the same month he was made a member of the Privy Council and received his earldom (Handley, "Villiers, Edward").

11. Clifford, *Case of Jeronimy Clifford* (1714), 10.

12. Clifford, *Case of Jeronimy Clifford* (1714), 11. See BL, Add. MSS, 61644C, fol. 93r, for a similar version of these events. He tells a different story in a 1701 pamphlet, claiming that he had informed Jersey he would settle his case for 120,000 guilders. He would then give the rest of his claim to the king "or to the States General, towards the charge of the war." However, he added, he "never received any answer thereof" (Clifford, *Jeronimy Clifford's Answer*, 2–3; quotation on 3).

13. *Dutch Displayed*, 25–26. This followed Clifford's petitioning of the Crown in April 1697 (25–26). The advocates' examination is dated 30 September 1697 on BL, Add. MSS, 61644C, fol. 61r. The "treaty of commerce" refers to the 1674 Marine Treaty (see Chalmers, *Collection of Treaties*, 1:177–89).

14. NA UK, CO 323/2, no. 84, fol. 223r (date on fol. 224v). See *Calendar of State Papers Colonial, America and West Indies*, vol. 16 (1697–1698), [10 January 1698] (no. 161). Clifford had returned to the Netherlands around this time, and he penned a petition

in December 1697 from the Hague in which he complained that Henry MacKintosh and the West India Company had sent claims against him to Francis Le Brun, Corcabo's manager. The plantation, he wrote, was the property of his father, who desired that it not be molested by people with demands against his son. At the end of the petition he stated his intention to return to Suriname within eighteen or twenty months (NA Den Haag, Sociëteit van Suriname, 1.05.03, 227, fols. 100r–v).

15. *Journal of the House of Commons*, vol. 12, 1697–1699 (London: His Majesty's Stationery Office, 1803), 235 (18 April 1698). Further members were added to the committee on April 30. See *Journal of the House of Commons*, 12: 247 (30 April 1698). See also [Clifford], *The Case of Andrew Clifford and Jeronimy Clifford Late Planters in Surinam*, 3 (the pamphlet can be found in BL, Add. MSS 61644B, fols. 58r–59v).

16. The report is reproduced in [Clifford], *The Case of Andrew and Jeronimy Clifford*, 1–3. Here I quote from 2–3.

17. [Clifford], *The Case of Andrew Clifford and Jeronimy Clifford Late Planters in Surinam*, 3. The first two and a half pages of this pamphlet, prior to the mention of Jersey, are similar to a Dutch-language manuscript in a 1699 collection of documents held by the Society of Suriname (NA Den Haag, Sociëteit van Suriname, 1.05.03, 227, fols. 96r–98v). In another 1699 account Clifford states simply that the Dutch ambassador acted "by his agents," not mentioning Jersey by name but perhaps implying his collusion with the United Provinces ([Clifford], *The Case of Andrew and Jeronimy Clifford*, 1).

18. See Sir Joseph Williamson's memorial, printed in [Clifford], *The Case of Andrew and Jeronimy Clifford*, 3. Here the text refers to the "articles of peace in the year 1667," presumably a reference to the Articles of Capitulation rather than to that year's Treaty of Breda.

19. NA Den Haag, SG, 1.01.02, 1929, 30 December 1698, fols. 9v–11v. The text refers to the "tractaten van vreede in de jaar 1667" (fol. 10v). The context and the use of the plural suggest that this refers to the 1667 Articles of Capitulation rather than the 1667 Treaty of Breda (the singular *tractaat* is used to refer to the 1674 peace treaty on fol. 10r). See also NA Den Haag, SG, 1.01.02, 565, 30 December 1698, fols. 7r–8r. For the text of the charter, see ZA, 2035, 3.16.507 (Octroy 1683).

20. NA Den Haag, SG, 1.01.02, 577, 7 December 1699, fol. 3v. See also NA Den Haag, SG, 1.01.02, 1907, 16 February 1697, fol. 7r, and NA Den Haag, SG, 1.01.02, 1931, 27 February 1699, fol. 6v.

21. NA Den Haag, SG, 1.01.02, 577, 16 December 1699, fols. 3r–v.

22. Clifford, *Jeronimy Clifford's Answer*, 3. This request appears in the State's resolutions for 30 December 1699, preceded by a further appeal by Clifford for 3,750 guilders in a matter relating to the shipping of cargo. In the latter affair the States referred him "to the High Council in Holland where the matter is pending" (NA Den Haag, SG, 1.01.02, 577, 30 December 1699, fols. 3v–4r). The request for 250,000 guilders and the States' response is on fols. 4r–v. The States resolved to abide by its previous resolutions in the matter.

23. James Vernon to Lord Ambassador Williamson, NA UK, SP 32/15, fols. 338r–v. This is transcribed in *Calendar of State Papers Domestic*, William III (1699–1700), 14 March 1699. Vernon had asked Williamson for information regarding Clifford's case in the postscript to a 7 March 1699 letter (NA UK, SP 32/15, fol. 337v, in *Calendar of State Papers Domestic*, William III [1699–1700], 7 March 1699).

24. See [Clifford], *The Case of Andrew and Jeronimy Clifford* [1699]; Clifford, *Korte en Klare Aenwysingh* (1699), in NA UK, CO 388/75, No. 51(i); [Clifford], *The Case of Andrew Clifford and Jeronimy Clifford Late Planters in Surinam* (1701), in BL, Add. MSS 61644B, fols. 58r–59v; Clifford, *Jeronimy Clifford's Answer* (1701), in BL, Add. MSS, 61644C, fols. 45r–46v; [Clifford], *The Case of Jeronimy Clifford Late Planter in Surinam* (1704), in BL, Add MSS 61644C, fols. 66r–67v; Clifford, [*Untitled*] (1704), in BL, Add. MSS 61644C, fols. 68r–69v; Clifford, *The Case of Jeronimy Clifford, Merchant and Planter of Surinam. Paper, No. 160* (1711); Clifford, *The Case of Jeronimy Clifford, Merchant and Planter of Surinam* (1714); [Clifford], *The Case of Mr. Jeronimy Clifford, Merchant and Planter of Surinam* (1720). The undated pamphlet was included in papers that Clifford sent to Lord Stanhope in 1718 (Clifford, *The Case of Mr. Jeronimy Clifford, Merchant and Planter of Surinam* [c. 1718], in NA UK, T1/215, no. 9b). It is different in content than the 1720 pamphlet of the same name. The texts with archival references were missing from the *Early English Books Online* and *Eighteenth-Century Collections Online* databases at the time of this writing.

25. BL, Add. MSS, 61644C, fol. 48r.

26. BL, Add. MSS, 61644B, fol. 120v. On the same page Clifford also refers to "2 copies of the Articles of Capitulation that was made upon the surrender of Suriname by the English to the Dutch in the year 1665 translated out of English into Dutch," at a cost of four guilders. Here Clifford gives the date of the Dutch pamphlet as February 1699, which conflicts with the November 1699 date listed in the text itself. The February date is either erroneous or refers to a different pamphlet printed earlier that year. For the date of the Dutch pamphlet, see the title page of Clifford, *Korte en Klare Aenwysingh*.

27. [Clifford], *The Case of Andrew and Jeronimy Clifford*, 1. The text of the pamphlet lists no date or author. *Early English Books Online* lists the date as 1699, from publication information provided by Donald Wing's *Short-Title Catalogue of Books Printed in England, Scotland, Ireland, Wales, and British America, and of English Books Printed in Other Countries, 1641–1700*. I assume that the pamphlet was produced by Jeronimy Clifford that year. Clifford's British Library manuscripts refer to "Andrew and Jeronimy Clifford's English printed case to the House of Commons Anno 1699" (BL, Add. MSS, 61644C, fol. 48r). For the later pamphlet, discussed previously, see [Clifford], *The Case of Andrew Clifford and Jeronimy Clifford Late Planters in Surinam*, which discusses Jersey's role on 3.

28. The total of Clifford's damages is in Clifford, *Korte en Klare Aenwysingh*, 8.

29. Clifford, *Korte en Klare Aenwysingh*, 9.

30. Clifford, *Korte en Klare Aenwysingh*, 10.

31. The States General was responding to a memorial by another English envoy to the Hague, Alexander Stanhope, which is dated 20 September 1700 in Dutch archival sources. The 1766 text *Dutch Displayed* erroneously lists the date as 20 January 1700 (see 26). The original manuscript for Stanhope's memorial appears in French in NA Den Haag, SG, 1.01.02, 1950, 20 September 1700, fols. 5r–v, and NA Den Haag, SG, 1.01.02, 586, 20 September 1700, unnumbered insert. It is printed in translation in *Case and Replication*, 62–64. The response of the States General appears in NA Den Haag, SG, 1.01.02, 1953, 6 December 1700, fols. 4r–17r, and NA Den Haag, SG, 1.01.02, 589, 6 December 1700, fols. 4r–15r. This is translated in Clifford's manuscripts in BL, Add. MSS, 61644C, fols. 37r–44r. Here I quote from the translations, having confirmed their

idiomatic accuracy against the original. A small portion of the text, not quoted here, differs between the two versions (see BL, Add. MSS, 61644C, fols. 38v–39r, and NA Den Haag, SG, 1.01.02, 1953, 6 December 1700, fols. 6v–7v).

32. Alexander Stanhope to the States General (*Case and Replication*, 63–64).

33. BL, Add. MSS, 61644C, fol. 37v (NA Den Haag, SG, 1.01.02, 1953, 6 December 1700, fol. 5r). After receiving Stanhope's memorial, the States had forwarded it to the province of Holland and West Friesland and the Society of Suriname (NA Den Haag, SG, 1.01.02, 1950, 20 September 1700, fol. 5v). The States of Holland considered it on 21 October 1700 and resolved, in turn, that it be examined by the lords of Amsterdam, Rotterdam, and Hoorn along with the directors of the colony of Suriname (NA Den Haag, Staten van Holland, 3.01.04.01, 134, 444 [21 October 1700]).

34. BL, Add. MSS, 61644C, fols. 38r–v (NA Den Haag, SG, 1.01.02, 1953, 6 December 1700, fols. 6r–v).

35. BL, Add. MSS, 61644C, fol. 40v (NA Den Haag, SG, 1.01.02, 1953, 6 December 1700, fol. 9v).

36. BL, Add. MSS, 61644C, fols. 41r–v (NA Den Haag, SG, 1.01.02, 1953, 6 December 1700, fols. 11r–v). In fact, the couple had married in London. See chapter 3, which includes an extensive discussion of their marriage.

37. BL, Add. MSS, 61644C, fol. 40v (NA Den Haag, SG, 1.01.02, 1953, 6 December 1700, fol. 10r).

38. BL, Add. MSS, 61644C, fols. 43r and 41r (NA Den Haag, SG, 1.01.02, 1953, 6 December 1700, fols. 14v and 10v).

39. BL, Add. MSS, 61644C, fol. 40v (NA Den Haag, SG, 1.01.02, 1953, 6 December 1700, fol. 10v).

40. BL, Add. MSS, 61644C, fol. 41r (NA Den Haag, SG, 1.01.02, 1953, 6 December 1700, fols. 10v–11r). In the States' full wording, Clifford was "likewise notoriously in his own possession reputed for a subject of their High and Mighties from the time after his return with his wife to Suriname" (BL, Add. MSS, 61644C, fol. 41r). The Dutch original reads: "Ook notoirlij voor sijn persoon selfs voor een onderdaen van haer Ho: Mo: heeft waeren werden gerespecteert soo lang hij met sijn wedercomst in Suriname met sijn voors: huijs vrouw" (NA Den Haag, SG, 1.01.02, 1953, 6 December 1700, fol. 10v).

41. BL, Add. MSS, 61644C, fol. 41v (NA Den Haag, SG, 1.01.02, 1953, 6 December 1700, fol. 12r).

42. BL, Add. MSS, 61644C, fol. 44r (NA Den Haag, SG, 1.01.02, 1953, 6 December 1700, fols. 16v–17r).

43. BL, Add. MSS, 61644C, fols. 42r–v (NA Den Haag, SG, 1.01.02, 1953, 6 December 1700, fols. 12r–13r).

44. BL, Add. MSS, 61644C, fols. 43r–v (NA Den Haag, SG, 1.01.02, 1953, 6 December 1700, fols. 14v–15v). For the States' 1698 resolution allowing passes, see NA Den Haag, SG, 1.01.02, 1929, 30 December 1698, fols. 9v–11v, and NA Den Haag, SG, 1.01.02, 565, 30 December 1698, fols. 7r–8r.

45. BL, Add. MSS, 61644C, fol. 37v (NA Den Haag, SG, 1.01.02, 1953, 6 December 1700, fol. 5r). For the initial ruling that compensation was a matter for the ordinary courts, see NA Den Haag, SG, 1.01.02, 1907, 16 February 1697, fols. 6r–7r.

46. Clifford, *Jeronimy Clifford's Answer to the States-General's Allegations*. This was accompanied by another pamphlet printed during the same month. See [Clifford], *The*

NOTES TO PAGES 107–110

Case of Andrew Clifford and Jeronimy Clifford Late Planters in Surinam. Neither text has been digitized by *Early English Books Online* or *Eighteenth-Century Collections Online*. Both list 6 March 1701 as the date of printing on their final page. BL, Add. MSS, 61644B, fol. 6r, includes a reference to *Jeronimy Clifford's Answer* that provides its date of printing as "6 March 1700/1," indicating that the year printed in both pamphlets is 1701 New Style.

47. Clifford, *Jeronimy Clifford's Answer*, 1.

48. Clifford, *Jeronimy Clifford's Answer*, 4.

49. Clifford, *Jeronimy Clifford's Answer*, 1. The pamphlet included a claim that in 1695 the Society had "displaced their governor, and sent him for home" because of his treatment (3). In fact, Clifford's case appears to have played no role in the dismissal of the then-governor Johan van Scharphuizen, whom the Society recalled due to a dispute over financial matters and the provision of slaves. Its choice of successor, Paul van der Veen, signaled a desire for governors who lacked substantial interests in the colony (see Van der Meiden, *Betwist Bestuur*, 64–67).

50. Clifford, *Jeronimy Clifford's Answer*, 2. The States General's resolution cited the twelfth article of the Society of Suriname's charter as requiring ships to sail from the United Provinces, the fourth article for the payment of "last money or tonnage," and the eleventh article in regard to infringing on the West India Company (BL, Add. MSS, 61644C, fol. 43v, and NA Den Haag, SG, 1.01.02, 1953, 6 December 1700, fols. 15r–v).

51. Clifford, *Jeronimy Clifford's Answer*, 2.

52. Clifford, *Jeronimy Clifford's Answer*, 2. For context for the persistence of interimperial trade after the Navigation Acts, see Koot, *Empire at the Periphery*.

53. Translated and quoted in Fatah-Black, *White Lies and Black Markets*, 47 (parentheses in the original). For the original Dutch text, see ZA, 2035, 3.16.507 (Octroy 1683). The charter is dated 1682 on the title page and the date of printing is listed as 1683. Article 12 is on page 9.

54. Fatah-Black, *White Lies*, 47. See 41–46 for a discussion of trade before the formation of the Society of Suriname.

55. Clifford, *Jeronimy Clifford's Answer*, 4.

56. Clifford, *Jeronimy Clifford's Answer*, 2.

57. BL, Add. MSS, 61644C, fols. 41r, 41v (NA Den Haag, SG, 1.01.02, 1953, 6 December 1700, fols. 10v, 12r).

58. For the referral of Clifford's petition to committee, see *Journal of the House of Commons*, 13: 479 (9 April 1701). The quotation is from *Case and Replication*, 70–71.

59. The king's message to the Commons is reproduced in *Case and Replication*, 70–71. The text is also included in the journal of the Commons, followed by a letter from the States General to the king regarding relations with France and a letter from Stanhope to Secretary Hedges (*Journal of the House of Commons*, 13: 518–20 [8 May 1701]).

60. *Journal of the House of Commons*, 13: 523 (9 May 1701). *The Case of Andrew Clifford and Jeronimy Clifford Late Planters in Surinam* was published that March and is written as an address to parliament, although its first two and a half pages resemble an earlier manuscript in Dutch from no later than 1699 (see [Clifford], *The Case of Andrew Clifford and Jeronimy Clifford Late Planters in Surinam* and NA Den Haag, Sociëteit van Suriname, 1.05.03, 227, fols. 96r–98v). Andrew Clifford seems to disappear from the records after spring 1701.

61. NA UK, CO 388/75, no. 50, fol. 1r. This was received and read on 28 October 1701 (fol. 2v). Clifford had first made a more general request for "leave to inspect the books in the office relating to Surinam, and to take copies of such papers as he may find serviceable to him." The committee read the request on 23 October 1701 and responded by asking him to be more specific (NA UK, CO 391/14, 186).

62. NA UK, CO 391/14, 190 (see *Calendar of State Papers Colonial, America and West Indies*, vol. 19 [1701], 28 October 1701 [no. 973]).

63. See NA UK, CO 278/3, 102.

64. NA UK, CO 278/3, 157–59; quotation on 158. See chapter 2.

65. NA UK, CO 388/75, no. 51ii, fol. 1r. This was one of three petitions read by the Crown in April 1702 (NA UK, CO 388/75, no. 51, enclosures ii, iii, iv). They were read by the Queen-in-Council on 21 April 1702. See NA UK, CO 388/75, no. 51, fol. 1r. The numbered order of enclosures for the Calendar of State Papers entry for NA UK, CO 388/75, no. 51 differs from those marked on the manuscripts. Here I refer to the latter. See *Calendar of State Papers Colonial, America and West Indies*, vol. 20 (1702), 21 April 1702 (no. 360).

66. NA UK, CO 388/75, no. 52, fols. 1r–2r.

67. *Calendar of State Papers Colonial, America and West Indies*, vol. 20 (1702), 29 May 1702 (no. 542). The Queen-in-Council issued orders for this to be done on 31 May 1702 (CO 388/75, no. 59, fol. 1r). The enclosure marks this order as received on 11 September 1702 and read on the 15th (fol. 2v).

68. See the 10 February 1718 letter from Clifford to Lord Stanhope in NA UK, T1/215, fol. 58v (discussed later in the chapter).

69. The petition is printed in Clifford, [*Untitled*], 1–2.

70. Clifford, [*Untitled*], 1–2. The procuration to Stanhope is also referenced in BL, Add. MSS, 61644B, fol. 6r, and BL, Add. MSS, 61644C, fols. 56r–v.

71. Clifford, [*Untitled*], 3. Clifford had sent an earlier petition to Hedges on 27 April 1703 (2–3).

72. Clifford, [*Untitled*], 4. Clifford wrote that he "could get no answer thereof" (3).

73. Quoted in *Dutch Displayed*, 38. The date is on 37. I have been unable to find this memorial in the resolutions of the States General.

74. *Dutch Displayed*, 38.

75. In November 1703 he penned another point-by-point reply to the States General's resolution of 6 December 1700. This survives in manuscript only and its audience and distribution are unclear (BL, Add. MSS, 61644C, fols. 62r–65r). He published two pamphlets the following February. See [Clifford], *The Case of Jeronimy Clifford Late Planter in Surinam* ("Anno 1704" is written in manuscript on the first page) and Clifford, [*Untitled*]. The pamphlets themselves are included in BL, Add. MSS, 61644C, fols. 66r–69v. Clifford's index to these papers (in BL, Add. MSS, 61644B) lists them as "My printed case which I delivered over to her Maty and both houses of parliament" and "My printed letter which I delivered over to her Maty and both houses of parliament" and both are dated 10 February 1703/4 (BL, Add. MSS, 61644B, fol. 6v).

76. BL, Add. MSS, 61644C, fols. 70v–71r (the petition begins on fol. 70r). For the original manuscript, see NA UK, CO 388/75, no. 86, enclosure 2. This was part of a large collection of papers that Clifford sent to the Crown (see NA UK, CO 388/75, no. 86, and its voluminous enclosures).

NOTES TO PAGES 113-117

77. BL, Add. MSS, 61644C, fol. 72r. This is an apparently accurate transcription of the partially legible manuscript in NA UK, CO 388/75, no. 86, fol. 1r.

78. NA UK, CO 388/75, no. 87, fol. 1r.

79. NA UK, CO 389/36, 178.

80. In the 1720 *Case of Mr. Jeronimy Clifford, Merchant and Planter of Surinam*, Clifford refers to "being imprisoned in the Rules of the Fleet and King's-Bench Prisons, ever since April, 1704" and stated that he had been imprisoned for "fifteen years" ([Clifford], *The Case of Mr. Jeronimy Clifford, Merchant and Planter of Surinam* [1720], 9).

81. NA UK, CO 388/75, no. 89, fol. 1v. The board received Clifford's letter on 12 May 1704 (see fol. 2v). As late as 1704 Clifford employed an intermediary in Suriname named Thomas Caruthers (see, for example, BL, Add. MSS, 61644B, fols. 177r–v, and the discussion later in this chapter). It is unclear whether Robert Caruthers was any relation.

82. NA UK, CO 388/75, no. 89, fols. 2r–v.

83. Brown, *A History of the Fleet Prison*, xvii, 4, 2. The prison had existed since at least 1197. Clifford would have lived in the building erected in 1670 to replace the structure destroyed in the Great Fire of London (1). This was destroyed by the Gordon riots in 1780 (Condon, "Fleet Prison," 457).

84. Brown, *A History of the Fleet Prison*, xvi, xvii; Condon, "Fleet Prison," 457.

85. Brown, *A History of the Fleet Prison*, 323–24.

86. Brown, *A History of the Fleet Prison*, 318, 324.

87. Brown, *A History of the Fleet Prison*, 262–63.

88. Brown, *A History of the Fleet Prison*, 267. See 268 for a map of the area in 1798.

89. Brown, *A History of the Fleet Prison*, 154.

90. Brown, *A History of the Fleet Prison*, 269–72. The 1729 figure is based on the prison's profits and initial fees (271).

91. NA UK, CO 137/10, [no. 2], fol. 2r.

92. NA UK, CO 388/75, no. 106, fol. 1r (20 November 1704). See also NA UK, CO 388/75, no. 96, fol. 1r (28 July 1704); NA UK, CO 388/75, no. 105, fol. 1r (13 November 1704).

93. NA UK, CO 388/75, no. 110i (on the verso of no. 110).

94. NA UK, CO 388/75, no. 115, fol. 1r.

95. NA UK, CO 388/75, no. 120, fol. 1r.

96. NA UK, CO 388/75, no. 121, fols. 1r–v. For an analysis of the meanings ascribed to the Amboyna massacre see Games, *Inventing the English Massacre*. On Banister, see Weterings, "Should We Stay," 136–37; Games, "Cohabitation, Suriname-Style," 215; Zijlstra and Weterings, "Colonial Life," 80–81.

97. NA UK, CO 388/75, no. 121, fol. 2r.

98. NA UK, T1/94, no. 42, fol. 157r. This copy of Clifford's petition, although undated, is included with a copy of the Privy Council's decision dated 3 May 1705 (NA UK, T1/94, no. 42, fols. 155r–v). There is an identical version of its decision in NA UK, CO 388/75, no. 123, fols. 1r–v.

99. NA UK, CO 388/75, no. 123, fols. 1r–v.

100. NA UK, CO 388/75, no. 124, fol. 1r.

101. NA UK, CO 388/75, no. 124, fols. 2v–3r.

102. NA UK, CO 388/75, no. 124, fol. 5r.

103. NA UK, CO 388/75, no. 124, fols. 3v–4r.
104. NA UK, CO 388/75, no. 124, fols. 4v–5r.
105. NA UK, CO 388/75, no. 125, fol. 1r.
106. NA UK, CO 388/75, no. 125i, as described on NA UK, CO 388/75, no. 125, fol. 2v.
107. NA UK, CO 388/75, no. 125, fol. 1v.
108. NA UK, CO 388/75, no. 126. See also CO 389/36, 294.
109. NA UK, CO 389/36, 296.
110. NA UK, CO 388/75, no. 129, fols. 1r–v; the quotation is on fol. 1v. This was received and read by the board of trade on 20 July. See fol. 2v and *Journals of the Board of Trade and Plantations,* vol. 1 (April 1704–January 1709), Journal Book K, July 1705.
111. For Clifford's letter, see NA UK, CO 388/75, no. 127, fol. 1r. For Popple's reply, see NA UK, CO 389/36, 298–99.
112. *Dutch Displayed,* 39. Further English intervention on behalf of Clifford's case did, however, take place after his death (see chapter 5).
113. Clifford, *The Case of Jeronimy Clifford, Merchant and Planter of Surinam* (1714), 4.
114. NA UK, CO 388/75, no. 120iii, fol. 3r. See chapters 2 and 3 for more on Clifford's history with Samuel Lodge.
115. For Clifford's cover letter, sent from the Fleet, see NA UK, CO 388/75, no. 120, fol. 1r. It is unclear whether Thomas Caruthers was related to Robert Caruthers, on whose instigation Clifford was arrested for debt in April 1704. See the previous discussion and CO 388/75, no. 89, fol. 1v.
116. NA UK, CO 388/75, no. 120i, fol. 1r.
117. NA UK, CO 388/75, no. 120i, fol. 1r.
118. BL, Add. MSS, 61644B, fols. 175r–v.
119. BL, Add. MSS, 61644B, fol. 176r.
120. BL, Add. MSS, 61644B, fols. 177r–v.
121. BL, Add. MSS, 61644B, fols. 180v–81r. The date of the petition is on fol. 180r.
122. NA UK, CO 388/75, no. 120ii, fols. 1r–2r. The date is listed as New Style.
123. NA UK, CO 388/75, no. 120ii, fol. 1r. ("Master" appears as "mr" in the text.)
124. NA UK, CO 388/75, no. 120ii, fol. 1v.
125. NA UK, CO 388/75, no. 120ii, fol. 2r.
126. NA UK, CO 388/75, no. 120ii, fol. 2r.
127. NA UK, CO 388/75, no. 120ii, fol. 2v.
128. NA UK, CO 388/75, no. 120iii, fols. 3v–4v. This letter is translated in BL, Add. MSS, 61644B, fols. 183r–84r. Here I paraphrase the translation. Clifford describes De Bourse as "of late agent at Suriname to the West India Company of Holland" (fol. 184r). De Bourse also served as an interpreter to Thomas Caruthers (see BL, Add. MSS, 61644B, fol. 181r).
129. See NA UK, CO 388/75, no. 120, fol. 1r, for Clifford's request that the board include the letters and other supporting documents with its report to the queen. For his claim against Lodge, see the accompanying memorandum at NA UK, CO 388/75, no. 120iii, fol. 3r.
130. See Cooke's suggestion in NA UK, CO 388/75, no. 52, fol. 2r (discussed previously).

131. NA UK, CO 388/75, no. 130, fols. 1r–v. Apparently this was not read until October. See the envelope information on NA UK, CO 388/75, no. 130i, fol. 1v ("read 12 October 1705"), and *Journals of the Board of Trade and Plantations*, vol. 1 (April 1704–January 1709), Journal Book K, October 1705.

132. NA UK, SP 84/574, fol. 171r.

133. BL, Add. MSS, 61644C, fol. 91r.

134. BL, Add. MSS, 61644C, fol. 92r.

135. BL, Add. MSS, 61644C, fol. 93v.

136. BL, Add. MSS, 61644C, fols. 96r–v. The collection of papers that Clifford sent to Sunderland constitute the manuscripts relating to his case now held by the British Library as Add. MS 61644 B–C, "Papers submitted to Sunderland on 18 July 1707 by Jeronimy Clifford, planter of Surinam, concerning his claims against the Governor and Council of Surinam and the West India Company of the United Provinces, for damage to his estate there."

137. BL, Add. MSS, 61644C, fols. 94r–95r. Unlike other sources, which list her last name as Matson, she is named in this document as "Dorathea Clifford." She had previously given her husband power of attorney in Suriname on 6 June 1687, shortly before leaving the colony (BL, Add. MSS, 61644C, fols. 15r–v). On the life of Sir Thomas Rawlinson, see Welch and Gauci, "Rawlinson, Sir Thomas."

138. NA UK, CO 388/76, no. 114, fol. 3v. The date is on fol. 1r. The council received and read his request on 4 June 1711, although its response is unclear (NA UK, CO 388/76, no. 114, fol. 4v).

139. NA UK, SP 34/17, fols. 166r–v. I am grateful to Alison Games for referring me to this source.

140. NA UK, CO 137/10, [no. 2], fol. 2r. In his February 1712 letter to Dartmouth Clifford named his location simply as "Fleet prison," suggesting that he had not yet moved to lodgings within its larger rules (NA UK, SP 34/17, fol. 166r). The William Popple addressed by Clifford in his June 1713 letter had succeeded his father of the same name as secretary of the Board of Trade in 1707 (Seccombe and Rogers, "Popple, William").

141. NA UK, CO 388/76, no. 164, fol. 1r.

142. NA UK, CO 388/76, no. 164i, fol. 1r. The privileges offered by Queen's Bench closely resembled those of the Fleet (see Brown, *A History of the Fleet Prison*, xvii).

143. NA UK, CO 388/76, no. 164, fol. 1r.

144. He wrote on 11 January 1714 (NA UK, CO 388/76, no. 165), 12 March 1714 (NA UK, CO 388/76, no. 166), and 14 April 1714 (NA UK, CO 388/76, no. 167). All three letters were written within the confines of Queen's Bench rules.

145. NA UK, CO 389/37, 74–75.

146. Clifford, *The Case of Jeronimy Clifford, Merchant and Planter of Surinam* (1714), 1. See Clifford, *The Case of Jeronimy Clifford, Merchant and Planter of Surinam. Paper, No. 160.* (1711).

147. Clifford, *The Case of Jeronimy Clifford, Merchant and Planter of Surinam* (1714), 12. It is unclear whether this references the delivery of his 1711 text to the Lords and Commons in 1713 (he lists both Houses as the 1711 pamphlet's recipient on the first page of the 1714 text) or if Clifford addressed parliament again in 1714. I have found no references to his case for either 1713 or 1714 in the Lords and Commons journals.

148. See NA UK, T1/215, fol. 54r (No. 9), which states that he delivered the petitions "to His Majesty's own hand." The petitions are enclosed as attachments (NA UK, T1/215, fols. 55r–58r [No. 9a]).

149. NA UK, T1/215, fol. 58v.

150. NA UK, T1/215, fol. 59r.

151. NA UK, T1/215, fol. 54r. An archivist's note on the manuscript in pencil suggests 13 August as the date of the petition.

152. NA UK, T4/21, 14.

153. [Clifford], *The Case of Mr. Jeronimy Clifford, Merchant and Planter of Surinam* (1720). The quotation is from page 1. The pamphlet is dated 10 May 1720 on page 12.

154. [Clifford], *The Case of Mr. Jeronimy Clifford, Merchant and Planter of Surinam* (1720), 9. The pamphlet dates the seizure of Dutch ships to 1712 rather than 1710 (11).

155. NA UK, T1/233, no. 5, fols. 19r–v. The document is undated but an archivist's hand in pencil suggests a date of "after 1720." Here Clifford states that the seized ships arrived in the Isle of Wight in late 1712.

156. NA UK, T1/233, no. 5, fols. 19r–v.

157. See Treaty of Breda, in Chalmers, *Collection of Treaties*, 1:143–44. The treaty concluded the Second Anglo-Dutch War.

158. NA UK, T1/233, no. 5, fols. 19r–v.

159. See NA UK, CO 388/75, no. 129, fols. 1r–v.

160. NA UK, T1/259, no. 35, fols. 153r–v. The Lords of the Treasury are named as the letter's recipients in *Calendar of Treasury Papers*, vol. 6, 1720–1728, volume 259, 6 April–23 August 1727, 27 July 1727 (no. 35).

161. The recipients, which include the Archbishop of Canterbury and the Lord Chancellor, are listed on NA UK, T1/259, no. 35, fols. 154r–v. The other papers include a notarized list of his 106 heirs, an extract from the 1674 treaty of peace between England and Holland, earlier correspondence relating to his case, and accounts of the damages due him. These papers, including the list of his relatives, can be found in NA UK, T1/259, no. 35, from fol. 154r to fol. 162v.

162. NA UK, CO 278/1. Unpaginated single leaf. Stamped folio pagination begins on the next leaf.

163. NA UK, CO 278/1, fol. 1v; date on fol. 1r.

164. NA UK, CO 278/1, fols. 1v–2r.

165. NA UK, CO 278/1, fol. 2r.

166. NA UK, CO 278/1, fol. 2v.

167. NA UK, CO 278/1, fol. 7v.

168. NA UK, CO 278/1, fols. 7v–8r. There is evidence that Clifford was attempting to manage Corcabo at an even later date, although this is not verified by manuscript sources. The 1760 book *Conduct of the Dutch* reprints a letter from Clifford to Suriname's governor and Council of Polity, supposedly written in 1733. It refers to a director Abraham Gillebert employed by Clifford in 1729 (*Conduct of the Dutch*, 179–81). The letter begins in note "e" on 179. It mentions Gillebert on 180.

169. NA UK, CO 278/1, fol. 1v.

170. NA UK, CO 278/1, fols. 5r–v.

171. *Case and Replication*, 96.

172. See Lavaux, *Kaart van Suriname* (1737). I am grateful to Natalie Zemon Davis for pointing me to this map and identifying the location and ownership of Corcabo. An inventory of 1744 documents describes Godefroy (spelled "Godeffroy" on the map) as a member of the council (*raadsheer*) and "stepfather-in-law of the present owner of Corcabo" (NA Den Haag, Sociëteit van Suriname, 1.05.03, 273, fol. 267).

173. *Case and Replication*, 96.

174. They did this in the full title of their anonymous work, *The Case and Replication of the Legal Representatives of Jeronimy Clifford.*

175. NA UK, PC 1/7/33, 48. See also *Case and Replication*, 136.

5. The Many Afterlives of Jeronimy Clifford (1737–1780)

1. See documents in NA UK, SP 84/588, fols. 1r–151v, and NA UK, PC 1/7/33, 1–87 (discussed in detail later in the chapter).

2. NA UK, T1/259, no. 35, fols. 155v–56v. For Yorke's memorial, see *Case and Replication*, 219–21, and NA Den Haag, SG, 1.01.02, 1328, 13 July 1762, unpaginated insertion after fol. 2v. For the 1703 intervention see *Dutch Displayed*, 37–38, and chapter 4.

3. For the group's denial of a connection to Mandel's will, see NA UK, CO 278/1, fol. 34r. The society's response and the various printed texts are discussed at length later in the chapter. For the 1770s claim, see NA UK, CO 278/1, fol. 48r.

4. Dickens, *Bleak House*. For the Clifford of the Enlightenment, see *Case and Replication*, 266, discussed later in the chapter.

5. On the Seven Years' War, see Carter, "Dutch as Neutrals." On the Fourth Anglo-Dutch War see Scott, "Sir Joseph Yorke."

6. Alison Games provides a comprehensive exploration of the relationship between the Amboyna massacre and stereotypes of Dutch cruelty, including in the eighteenth century (*Inventing the English Massacre*).

7. Bijlsma, "Alexander de Lavaux," 397, 402. See 400 for Lavaux's background.

8. The size of Corcabo on Lavaux's map is substantially less than the 1,500 acres described in Clifford's 1691 deed of sale to his father, which in turn was less than the 2,388 acres listed in its 1685 predecessor (BL, Add. MSS, 61644C, fol. 11r, and BL, Add. MSS, 61644C, fol. 10r, respectively, which are discussed in chapter 3). For a copy of the map, see Lavaux, *Kaart van Suriname*. For a later, color version, see Lavaux, *Algemeene kaart van de Colonie of Provintie van Suriname*. I am grateful to Natalie Zemon Davis for pointing me to Lavaux's work.

9. Bijlsma, "Alexander de Lavaux," 403–6. The reduction of Lavaux's sentence was made in June 1743, though he seems not to have been informed until the following year (406). Clifford was imprisoned in Fort Zeelandia in September 1691 following his dispute with Henry MacKintosh, although he served the resulting sentence in Fort Sommelsdijck (BL, Add. MSS, 61644C, fols. 18r–19v; BL, Add. MSS, 61644B, fol. 15r).

10. Mandel's letter, which was dated 27 October Old Style (7 November New Style), referred to a "Mr. Delavaux" who was traveling to Suriname by way of Boston (NA UK, SP 84/588, fol. 121r). A 1762 report into the case from the Society of Suriname describes Mandel's encounter as with "La Vaux one of the Society's engineers" and states that his journey to Suriname took place "by way of the English islands" (NA UK, PC 1/7/33, 47). For the society's report (discussed later in the chapter), see NA UK, PC 1/7/33, 1–87. The

correspondence used here consists of English translations of documents provided by the society in support of its report (NA UK, SP 84/588, fols. 1r–151v; a copy of the report is included in fols. 6r–48v). The note from the translator, Joseph Cortissos, appears on fol. 1r. An inventory of the documents can be found on fols. 149r–51v.

11. NA UK, SP 84/588, fols. 121r–v.

12. NA UK, SP 84/588, fols. 121v–22r.

13. NA UK, PC 1/7/33, 49–50. The report dates from 1762 and is discussed later in the chapter.

14. The letter was dated 14/25 November 1738 (SP 84/588, fol. 123r).

15. NA UK, SP 84/588, fol. 123v.

16. NA UK, SP 84/588, fols. 124r–v.

17. NA UK, SP 84/588, fol. 125r. In a July 1727 petition to the Lords of the Treasury Clifford had stated that he lived "at a bakers next door to the Ship Tavern at Charing Cross" (NA UK, T1/259, no. 35, fol. 153v). On the Dutch state lottery, see Huisman and Koppenol, *Daer compt de Lotery met trommels en trompetten!*, 114.

18. The letter itself only contains the Old Style date of 17 November 1738 (NA UK, SP 84/588, fol. 127r). However, subsequent correspondence refers to its date as 17/28 November (NA UK, SP 84/588, fol. 129r).

19. NA UK, SP 84/588, fols. 127r–v.

20. NA UK, SP 84/588, fols. 127v–28r.

21. NA UK, SP 84/588, fol. 135v. The date appears on fol. 135r. The text of the will is on NA UK, SP 84/588, fols. 135r–39v. The document lists four witnesses: Charles Payne, Margaret Blackbird, William Yates, and James Wright (fol. 139v). It is preceded by a letter purporting to be from Clifford (NA UK, SP 84/588, fols. 131r–33r). Both the will and Clifford's letter are English translations of Dutch texts that in turn were originally translated from the initial English version (fols. 131r and 135r). I have been unable to find the will itself in the will registers of the Prerogative Court of Canterbury (NA UK, PROB 11, searchable at https://discovery.nationalarchives.gov.uk/details/r/C12122). The Society of Suriname's 1762 report summarizes the will in NA UK, PC 1/7/33, 65–70. This document aside, the closest Clifford appears to have come to naming heirs was in a 1727 petition to the Lords of the Treasury, in which he stated that he had 106 "poor relations" in Kent who might benefit from his claim (NA UK, T1/259, no. 35, fols. 153r–v; discussed in chapter 4). Their names are listed in NA UK, T1/259, no. 35, fols. 155v–56v.

22. See chapter 3.

23. NA UK, SP 84/588, fol. 136v.

24. NA UK, SP 84/588, fols. 136v–37r. Clifford may have been buried in Bermondsey, Southwark, rather than in Stepney. The parish records for St. Mary Magdalen include a 1737 burial record for one Ironimus Clifford (Ironimus Clifford, Burial, 14 September 1737, St. Mary Magdalen, Bermondsey, Southwark, Surrey, P71/MMG/007, *Church of England Parish Registers, 1538–1812*, London Metropolitan Archives, accessed via Ancestry Library). I am grateful to Karina Salih for searching St. Mary Magdalen churchyard for Clifford's grave and the interior of the church for a memorial (both, alas, in vain).

25. NA UK, SP 84/588, fol. 137r.

26. NA UK, SP 84/588, fols. 138r–v.

27. NA UK, SP 84/588, fol. 139r.

28. NA UK, SP 84/588, fol. 139v.

29. NA UK, SP 84/588, fol. 129r. The letter is dated 8/19 December 1738.
30. NA UK, SP 84/588, fols. 129r–v.
31. NA UK, SP 84/588, fols. 141r–v. Hop's letter is dated 17 April 1739 and refers to a 26 March letter from the society (NA UK, SP 84/588, fol. 141r). These dates are presumably New Style.
32. NA UK, SP 84/588, fols. 143r–v (28 April 1739).
33. NA UK, SP 84/588, fols. 143v–44r.
34. NA UK, SP 84/588, fols. 145r–v (12 May 1739).
35. NA UK, SP 84/588, fol. 146r. Clifford had, in fact, corresponded with one John Bout in 1727, who appeared to act as his agent in Suriname. In a letter to Bout he had offered to sell Corcabo for "ten thousand pounds sterling" to "the widow of the late Mr. William Ped[d]y" or other related parties (NA UK, CO 278/1, fol. 7v, which is discussed in chapter 4).
36. NA UK, PC 1/7/33, 63–64. This is according to the society's 1762 report.
37. NA UK, SP 84/588, fol. 147r.
38. NA UK, PC 1/7/33, 64–65.
39. It is possible that their names appear in the Fleet prison commitment books held by the UK National Archives (NA UK, PRIS 1). I was unable to consult these records as planned due to the 2020 novel coronavirus pandemic.
40. *Journals of the Board of Trade and Plantations*, vol. 8 (January 1742–December 1749), vol. 56, June 1748. The 1705 report request was, presumably, the one produced that year by Samuel Shepherd and John Gardner (discussed in chapter 4).
41. In August 1768 George Lookup, the spokesperson for the group, denied connection to the "sham will" sent by Mandel (NA UK, CO 278/1, fol. 34r, discussed later in the chapter).
42. The 1750 memorial was mentioned in the group's 1759 petition to the Crown, which in turn was reproduced in a 1761 report by attorney general Charles Pratt to the Earl of Bute (NA UK, SP 44/139, 141–57; the petition appears on 141–50 and the reference to the 1750 memorial to the Prince of Orange is on 148). I am grateful to Alison Games for pointing me to this source and to a related 1762 letter by Bute (138–40), which dates the petition to 27 June 1759 (138). The party's 1750 efforts are also mentioned in a 1762 memorial to the Society of Suriname by Sir Joseph Yorke (discussed later in the chapter; see *Case and Replication*, 220).
43. NA UK, SP 44/139, 141. Lookup's name was accompanied by those of Richard Perrott, Richard Kilsha, John Kerrat, William Hewitt, Thomas Browne, Richard Earnshaw, and Richard Moreland. None of their surnames appear in Clifford's 1727 list of Kent relatives (NA UK, T1/259, no. 35, fols. 155v–56v). For Lookup's correspondence with the society, which took place in 1768 and 1769, see NA UK, CO 278/1, fols. 30r–46v (discussed later in the chapter).
44. NA UK, SP 44/139, 148.
45. NA UK, SP 44/139, 149.
46. NA UK, SP 44/139, 149–50.
47. NA UK, SP 44/139, 150.
48. NA UK, SP 44/139, 151. Pratt's name appears on 157. The Earl of Bute is listed as the recipient on 141.
49. NA UK, SP 44/139, 157.

50. *Dutch Displayed*, 41. The Privy Council report is quoted on this page, which also describes the lord president's endorsement of the case and its referral to committee. The Earl of Bute had informed the petitioners that he had sent the matter to the lord president of the council in February 1762 (NA UK, SP 44/139, 157). The letter also appears in NA UK, CO 278/1, fols. 22r–v. For Bute's letter to the lord president, see NA UK, CO 278/1, fols. 24r–25v.

51. Quoted in *Case and Replication*, 220–21. This is an accurate idiomatic translation of the original document, which is in French. It can be found in NA Den Haag, SG, 1.01.02, 1328, 13 July 1762, in an unpaginated insertion after fol. 2v.

52. NA Den Haag, SG, 1.01.02, 1328, 13 July 1762, fol. 3r.

53. The report appears in English translation in both NA UK, PC 1/7/33, 1–87, and NA UK, SP 84/588, fols. 6r–48v (this version is then followed by supporting documentation relating to the report). A version of the report is also printed in *Case and Replication*, 132–210. Because this version contains some light editing, here I quote from the manuscript version in NA UK, PC 1/7/33.

54. NA UK, PC 1/7/33, 7–8.

55. NA UK, PC 1/7/33, 8–10. The couple had in fact married in London. See chapter 3.

56. NA UK, PC 1/7/33, 10–11.

57. NA UK, PC 1/7/33, 29. See chapter 4 for the States General's response to earlier English attempts to advocate Clifford's case.

58. NA UK, PC 1/7/33, 19.

59. NA UK, PC 1/7/33, 21.

60. NA UK, PC 1/7/33, 21–22. The States General had, however, responded to Willamson's memorial (NA Den Haag, SG, 1.01.02, 1929, 30 December 1698, fols. 9v–11v; discussed in chapter 4).

61. NA UK, PC 1/7/33, 44.

62. NA UK, PC 1/7/33, 45–46.

63. NA UK, PC 1/7/33, 71. For Hop's 1739 assessment, see NA UK, SP 84/588, fols. 141r–v. The society's report closely paraphrases the correspondence between Mandel and Van Meel as well as Hop's letters to the society. The correspondence itself is included with the version of the report in NA UK, SP 84/588, fols. 1r–151v (the report itself is on fols. 6r–48v).

64. NA UK, PC 1/7/33, 86.

65. NA UK, SP 84/588, fols. 3r–v. Here I quote from an English translation of the States General's resolution. The original, which accords with the translation, can be found in NA Den Haag, SG, 1.01.02, 1335, 22 February 1763, fols. 7r–8v. The States had first sent the report to the West India Company for further examination (NA Den Haag, SG, 1.01.02, 2694, 8 October 1762, fols. 6r–v).

66. NA UK, SP 84/588, fol. 3v.

67. NA UK, SP 84/588, fol. 4r.

68. *Conduct of the Dutch*; *Case and Replication*.

69. *Conduct of the Dutch*, title page. For an example of a relation of the "state of public affairs," see 127 (the phrase does not appear on the title page).

70. The society's report makes up the third section of *Case and Replication*, on 131–215.

71. For example, "The Dutch neglected to perform the capitulation for Suriname" (*Case and Replication*, 6) repeats part of a sentence on the top of page 15 of *Conduct of the Dutch*. The text dates the 1759 petition to 3 June, contradicting the 27 June date provided by the Earl of Bute (see, respectively, *Case and Replication*, 102, and NA UK, SP 44/139, 38).

72. *Case and Replication*, 401–2.

73. *Conduct of the Dutch*, 205. It is unclear whether this is a reference to the 1674 Treaty of Westminster or to the Marine Treaty of the same year (for these treaties, see, respectively, Chalmers, *Collection of Treaties*, 1:172–77 and 1:177–89).

74. *Conduct of the Dutch*, 175.

75. *Conduct of the Dutch*, 181.

76. *Conduct of the Dutch*, 205–6.

77. *Case and Replication*, 240–41. This is presumably a reference to the fifth article of the 1674 Treaty of Westminster (see article 5, "Treaty of Westminster," in Chalmers, *Collection of Treaties*, 1:173–74).

78. *Case and Replication*, 241.

79. *Case and Replication*, 99.

80. *Case and Replication*, 100–101.

81. *Case and Replication*, 101–2.

82. NA UK, CO 278/1, fol. 29r. This was conveyed in a letter from one Mr. Wood to the "executors of Clifford at the Somerset Coffee House," which stated that Count Welderen had passed on a message to Lord Weymouth. Welderen is referred to as the Dutch envoy in NA UK, CO 278/1, fol. 38v.

83. For Lookup's full exchange with the society, which lasted from to June 1768 to March 1769, see NA UK, CO 278/1, fols. 30r–46v.

84. NA UK, CO 278/1, fol. 30r.

85. NA UK, CO 278/1, fol. 31v.

86. NA UK, CO 278/1, fol. 32r.

87. NA UK, CO 278/1, fol. 32v.

88. NA UK, CO 278/1, fol. 34r.

89. NA UK, CO 278/1, fol. 35r (8 September 1768).

90. For Lookup's letter see NA UK, CO 278/1, fol. 35v (27 September 1768). The documentation is not included with the surviving letter. The society's response is on NA UK, CO 278/1, fol. 36v.

91. NA UK, CO 278/1, fol. 37v. None of the enclosures are included with the letter.

92. NA UK, CO 278/1, fol. 41r. The date is missing from the letter itself due to a torn page. However, an enclosing page on fol. 42v lists 7 March 1769 as the date of the correspondence. Lookup himself refers to a 7 March letter from the directors (fol. 45r).

93. NA UK, CO 278/1, fol. 45r (17 March 1769).

94. *Dutch Displayed*, 47–48.

95. NA UK, SP 84/589, fol. 90r.

96. NA UK, SP 84/589, fol. 92v.

97. NA UK, SP 84/589, fol. 92r.

98. NA UK, SP 84/589, fols. 92r–v.

99. NA UK, SP 84/589, fol. 93r.

100. *Journals of the Board of Trade and Plantations*, vol. 13 (January 1768–December 1775), vol. 77, November 1770. The collection of papers in NA UK, SP 84/588 begins with an affirmation from Cortissos that he had accurately translated them from French and Dutch, which is dated 16 May 1763 (SP 84/588, fol. 1r). A copy of the society's 1762 report is included in fols. 6r–48v.

101. *Conduct of the Dutch*, 219–20.

102. *Case and Replication*, 266, quoting the society's report.

103. *Case and Replication*, 266.

104. NA UK, PC 1/7/33, 10–11.

105. *Case and Replication*, 265.

106. *Case and Replication*, 280.

107. *Case and Replication*, 301.

108. *Case and Replication*, 326.

109. *Case and Replication*, 266.

110. See Carter, "Dutch as Neutrals." On Dutch activity in West Africa in the eighteenth century, see chap. 3 of Klooster and Oostindie, *Realm between Empires*. On conflict with the British in India, see Menezes, "Bengal and the Dutch."

111. The two texts associated with George Lookup's party, *The Conduct of the Dutch* and *The Case and Replication*, had set the terms of the discussion early in the decade, appearing in 1760 and 1763 respectively. They were followed in 1766 by *The Dutch Displayed*, which outlined a litany of past and present Dutch offenses, Clifford's treatment included. This was answered the same year by *A Short and Modest Reply*, a pro-Dutch work purportedly of English authorship. *Dutch Modesty Exposed to English View* in turn attacked *A Short and Modest Reply* in 1767 and was joined that year by a series of anti-Dutch letters to the *Public Advertiser*. See *Conduct of the Dutch* (1760); *Case and Replication* (1763); *Dutch Displayed* (1766); *A Short and Modest Reply* (1766); *Dutch Modesty* ([1767]). (A typographical error on the title page of *Dutch Modesty Exposed to English View* lists the date of printing in Roman numerals as "MCCCLXVII.") See the following discussion for references to the letters in the *Public Advertiser*.

112. Games, *Inventing the English Massacre*, 149. Along with the employees of the English East India Company, the Dutch also executed either nine or ten Japanese soldiers and a Bengali man, all of whom worked for the Dutch East India Company (1).

113. Games, *Inventing the English Massacre*, 163.

114. Games, *Inventing the English Massacre*, 169.

115. *Conduct of the Dutch*, 190. In fact the Dutch East India Company had paid £85,000 to its English equivalent and £3,615 to the victims' estates (Games, *Inventing the English Massacre*, 147). The text of *The Conduct of the Dutch* is silent on which entity made the payment, referring simply to "the Dutch" (190).

116. *Conduct of the Dutch*, 205. See Menezes, "Bengal and the Dutch."

117. *Dutch Displayed*, title page.

118. *Dutch Displayed*, frontispiece. The picture is identical to one that appears in John Harris's *Navigantium atque bibliotheca* (1744–1748), vol. 1, between pages 878 and 879. I am grateful to Alison Games for identifying this source, which is reproduced in *Inventing the English Massacre*, 173. The first version appeared in the frontispiece of the East India Company's 1624 *True Relation of the unjust, cruel, and barbarous proceedings against the*

English at Amboyna In the East-Indies (reproduced in Games, *Inventing the English Massacre*, 94; see also Skinner, *True Relation*). Games's book discusses various versions of this image into the nineteenth century. See app. 2 for a list of the many manifestations of the *True Relation*.

119. *Dutch Displayed*, 2, 1.

120. *Dutch Displayed*, 2–7; the quotation is on 2.

121. *Dutch Displayed*, 8–16, 16–48, 48–68.

122. *Dutch Displayed*, 49.

123. *Dutch Displayed*, 49.

124. *Dutch Displayed*, 51; the date appears on 50. On the events at Dixcove, see Klooster and Oostindie, *Realm between Empires*, 101.

125. *Dutch Displayed*, 52.

126. *Dutch Displayed*, 50, 52.

127. *Dutch Displayed*, 52.

128. *Dutch Displayed*, 54. See Menezes, "Bengal and the Dutch"; Games, *Inventing the English Massacre*, 174. In his account of the events in Bengal, Robert Clive had compared Dutch actions to Amboyna (174).

129. *Dutch Displayed*, 56.

130. *Dutch Displayed*, 60.

131. *Dutch Displayed*, 61.

132. *Dutch Displayed*, 66–67. The 1674 treaty mentioned there is either the Treaty of Westminster or the Marine Treaty.

133. *Dutch Displayed*, 68.

134. *Public Advertiser*, 29 April 1767 (letter 17). I am grateful to Alison Games for providing copies of the letters, which she discusses in *Inventing the English Massacre*, 175–77. As she notes, Touverson was responding to another text, *The Short and Modest Reply* (discussed later in the chapter), which was an answer to *The Dutch Displayed* (*Inventing the English Massacre*, 176). Games discusses the original Gabriel Towerson, who was in charge of the English post in Amboyna, throughout the book's early chapters.

135. Games, *Inventing the English Massacre*, 176. For the originals see *A True Declaration of the Newes that came out of the East-Indies* (London, 1624) and *An Answer unto the Dutch Pamphlet* (London, 1624). Full references to these documents appear in Games, *Inventing the English Massacre*, 252n47 and 235n116, respectively. They are listed in the *English Short Title Catalog* only as variant titles to John Skinner's 1624 *True Relation*.

136. *Public Advertiser*, 6 February 1767, issue 10068. Touverson frames this first letter as a response to *A Short and Modest Reply* (discussed later in the chapter).

137. *Public Advertiser*, 15 June 1767, issue 10177 (letter 21).

138. *Public Advertiser*, 20 July 1767, issue 10199 (letter 26).

139. *Public Advertiser*, 13 July 1767, issue 10198 (letter 25).

140. *Public Advertiser*, 6 April 1767, issue 10093 (letter 15); italics in the original.

141. *Public Advertiser*, 27 July 1767, issue 10214 (letter 28).

142. *Public Advertiser*, 19 May 1767, issue 11504 (letter [19]).

143. At the time of the Glorious Revolution there was no consensus that the removal of James II was justified on contractarian grounds (Pincus, *1688*, 294). The implications of Locke's *Second Treatise* were contested during the eighteenth century, when they were "retrojected" onto Whig thought while also used by Jacobites against the Hanovarians

(Stanton, "Locke and His Influence," 36). Locke wrote his *Second Treatise* before the events of the Glorious Revolution, probably in 1680 or 1681 (Milton, "Dating Locke's 'Second Treatise'"). For the original text, see Locke, *Two Treatises of Government* [. . .]. For a recent scholarly edition, see Locke, *Two Treatises of Government and a Letter Concerning Toleration*.

144. *Conduct of the Dutch*, 70.

145. *Conduct of the Dutch*, 88. For the ill-fated attempt to establish a Scottish colony in Darien, Panama, in the late 1690s, see McPhail, "Through a Glass, Darkly."

146. *Conduct of the Dutch*, 89.

147. *Conduct of the Dutch*, 177.

148. *Conduct of the Dutch*, 128.

149. *Conduct of the Dutch*, 179.

150. *Dutch Displayed*, 54. The 1759 Axim attack is mentioned on 53.

151. *Dutch Displayed*, 54.

152. *Dutch Displayed*, 65.

153. *Dutch Displayed*, 62.

154. *Dutch Displayed*, 63, 64.

155. *Dutch Displayed*, 62.

156. *Dutch Displayed*, 66.

157. *Short and Modest Reply*, 6.

158. *Short and Modest Reply*, 15–16.

159. *Short and Modest Reply*, 60.

160. *Short and Modest Reply*, 64. The work discusses Clifford in the appendix, which runs from 64–72.

161. *Dutch Modesty*, 19–20.

162. *Dutch Modesty*, 17.

163. *Dutch Modesty*, 15.

164. *Dutch Modesty*, 6.

165. *Dutch Modesty*, 6, 9.

166. *Dutch Modesty*, 9.

167. *Dutch Modesty*, 29. Here the text refers to the fifth article of the Treaty of Westminster. While not mentioning passports by name, this states that at the king's request the States General should provide "full and sufficient letters and instructions" to Suriname's governor for the removal of the English (see Treaty of Westminster, in Chalmers, *Collection of Treaties*, 1:174).

168. *Dutch Modesty*, 30.

169. *Dutch Modesty*, 31.

170. *Dutch Modesty*, 31–32.

171. See "An Act for the further Limitation of the Crown and better securing the Rights and Liberties of the Subject," 1701, 12 & 13 Will. 3, c. 2, in *Statutes of the Realm*, 7:636–638.

172. This had been noted at the time of the Hanoverian succession. Writing in 1713, Daniel Defoe mocked the anti-Dutch views of those who opposed the accession of the future George I, while the periodical *Britain* identified hostility to the Dutch with Jacobitism. The *Examiner*, however, attacked the Dutch Republic for its toleration of Catholicism (Coombs, *Conduct of the Dutch: British Opinion and the Dutch Alliance during the War of the Spanish Succession*, 376–77).

173. As Paul Monod has noted, while remaining hostile to William III, Jacobite satire around the time of the Hanoverian succession tended to ridicule George I and dismiss the idea that Hanover posed a threat to British interests (Monod, *Jacobitism and the English People*, 58–59).

174. For a discussion of the war, see Scott, "Sir Joseph Yorke." On the last action associated with Lookup's group (discussed previously), see *Journals of the Board of Trade and Plantations*, vol. 13 (January 1768–December 1775), vol. 77, November 1770.

175. NA UK, CO 278/1, fol. 47r. The document itself is undated. An archivist's note in pencil on fol. 48v lists the date in parentheses as 1770. This must be incorrect, as the document refers to the year 1774 on fol. 47v and also contains circumstantial references to the Fourth Anglo-Dutch War on fol. 48r.

176. NA UK, CO 278/1, fols. 47r–v.

177. NA UK, CO 278/1, fols. 47v–48r.

178. NA UK, CO 278/1, fol. 48r.

179. This is supported by the letter's addressee. The Earl of Hillsborough, Wills Hill, succeeded Weymouth as secretary of state for the southern department in 1779 and served until 1782 (Marshall, "Hill, Wills").

180. Klooster and Oostindie, *Realm between Empires*, 235.

181. Klooster and Oostindie, *Realm between Empires*, 235; Hyles, *Guiana and the Shadows of Empire*, 45, 7.

Conclusion

1. Emphasis on the salience of the moment of birth came from Sir Edward Coke (*Calvin v. Smith*, in *English Reports*, 77:377–411, esp. 391 and 394).

2. See Muller, *Subjects and Sovereign*, for a discussion of this process in the Mediterranean, Grenada, Quebec, and Calcutta during the eighteenth century.

3. The *Trans-Atlantic Slave Trade Database* lists 2,226,870 people who were transported on British ships between 1551 and 1775.

4. See *Somerset v. Stewart*, in *English Reports*, 98:499, and Howell, *Cobbett's Complete Collection of State Trials*, 20:1–82 (case no. 548).

5. Rabin, "In a Country of Liberty," 5–6, 19; Shyllon, *Black People in Britain*, 24–25.

6. Paley, "After Somerset," 178–79.

7. As Dana Rabin notes, in his ruling Chief Justice Mansfield defined Somerset "as a foreigner from Virginia" (Rabin, "In a Country of Liberty," 19).

8. Rabin, "In a Country of Liberty," 22.

9. Rabin, "In a Country of Liberty," 20.

10. Muller notes "familiar ideas that English subjects were distinguished from enslaved persons" during the eighteenth century (Muller, *Subjects and Sovereign*, 155). She discusses the perceived benefits of subjecthood in chapter 2, esp. 46–47. For the inheritance of property, which by the 1630s was affirmed as a subject's right, see Kettner, *Development of American Citizenship*, 38–39.

11. See Shyllon, *Black People in Britain*, 17 (all quotations appear here). See also Amussen, *Caribbean Exchanges*, 219.

12. Noting the difficulty in determining accurate figures, Ruth Paley suggests that by the late eighteenth century there were between three thousand and fifteen thou-

sand people of African descent in England, including both the free and the enslaved (Paley, "After *Somerset*," 184). Dana Rabin suggests that during the eighteenth century there were between ten thousand and fifteen thousand black people in London and five thousand elsewhere in England, mainly in Bristol and Liverpool ("In a Country of Liberty," 7). For the sixteenth and seventeenth centuries see Habib, *Black Lives in the English Archives*; Amussen, *Caribbean Exchanges*, chap. 6.

13. Enslaved people formed a majority of the population of Barbados by 1661 (Amussen, *Caribbean Exchanges*, 130). South Carolina had an enslaved black majority population by 1710 (Wood, *Black Majority*, 116).

14. NA UK, SP 44/346, 384.

15. *Calvin v. Smith*, in *English Reports*, 77:383.

Bibliography

Manuscript Sources

British Library, London (cited as BL)

Additional MSS, 61644 B-C: Papers submitted to Sunderland on 18 July 1707 by Jeronimy Clifford, planter of Surinam, concerning his claims against the Governor and Council of Surinam and the West India Company of the United Provinces.

Additional MSS, 30218: Opinions of the law-officers of the Crown and others, chiefly upon matters connected with the revenue, 1673–1707.

Egerton MSS, 2395: Miscellaneous official papers relating to the English settlements in America and the West Indies.

Sloane MSS, 3662.

Folger Shakespeare Library, Washington, DC

"Legal case regarding inheritance of David Salter's heirs ca. 1650–1660s?," call. no. X.d.564.

Nationaal Archief, Den Haag, Netherlands (cited as NA Den Haag)

1.01.02: Archief van de Staten-Generaal, (1431) 1576–1796: 258–1733, Eerste Minuten; 1734–3094, Geresumeerde Minuten.

1.05.03: Archief van de Sociëteit van Suriname, (1650) 1682–1795 (1796): 212–403, Ingekomen brieven en papieren van de Gouverneur en andere overheidspersonen, 1683–1794.

3.01.04.01: Staten van Holland, 1572–1795: 1–173, 175–280, Gedrukte resoluties van de Staten van Holland over de jaren 1524–1795.

National Archives, United Kingdom (cited as NA UK)

CO 1/15: America and West Indies, Colonial Papers, 1661.
CO 1/21: America and West Indies, Colonial Papers, 1667.
CO 1/27: America and West Indies, Colonial Papers, July–December 1671.
CO 1/35: America and West Indies, Colonial Papers, August–December 1675.
CO 1/47: America and West Indies, Colonial Papers, June–December 1681.
CO 137/10: Board of Trade, Original Correspondence, 1713–1715.
CO 278/1: Secretary of State, Original Correspondence, 1728–1800.
CO 278/2: Colonial Office and Predecessors, Surinam Original Correspondence, Entry Book of Copies of Agreements, etc., 1667–1674.

CO 278/3: Colonial Office and Predecessors, Surinam Original Correspondence, Entry Book of Commissions, etc., 1668–1677.
CO 323/2: Board of Trade: Original Correspondence, 1696–1698.
CO 388/75: Board of Trade: Accounts and Establishments, 1696–1705.
CO 388/76: Board of Trade: Accounts and Establishments, 1705–1715.
CO 389/36: Board of Trade: Petitions, Orders in Council, Accounts, 1696–1710.
CO 389/37: Board of Trade: Petitions, Orders in Council, Accounts, 1711–1750.
CO 391/14: Board of Trade: Minutes, 1701–1702.
PC 1/7/33: Records of the Privy Council: Answer Given by the Director of the Surinam Society to the States General of the United Provinces Concerning the Claim of Andrew and Jeronimy Clifford to one of the Principal Plantations in Surinam, 7 October 1762.
PC 2/65: Privy Council Registers, Charles II, October 1675–April 1677.
PROB 11: Records of the Prerogative Court of Canterbury, Wills and Letters of Administration.
SP 32/15: Secretaries of State: State Papers, Domestic, William and Mary, A Series of Newsletters in Manuscript Addressed to Sir Joseph Williamson as Ambassador in Holland by Vernon, and by Ellis and Ward, Under Secretaries, 1698–1699.
SP 34/17: Secretaries of State: State Papers, Domestic, Anne, 1710–1712.
SP 44/18: Secretaries of State: State Papers, Entry Books, Petitions, 1664–1668.
SP 44/139: Secretaries of State: State Papers, Entry Books, Domestic, Secretary's Letter Books, 1760–1771.
SP 44/346: Warrants and Passes, 1694–1697.
SP 84/574: Secretaries of State: State Papers, Foreign, Holland, Supplementary, 1700–1708.
SP 84/588: Secretaries of State: State Papers, Foreign, Holland, Supplementary, the Case of Andrew Clifford and his son Jeronimy Clifford, Merchants and Sugar Planters in Surinam, Guinea, and their Claim against the Dutch Governor and Council of Surinam, 1763.
T1/94: Treasury Board Papers and In-Letters, April–June 1705.
T1/215: Treasury Board Papers and In-Letters, August–November 1718.
T1/233: Treasury Board Papers and In-Letters, January–March 1721.
T1/259: Treasury Board Papers and In-Letters, April–August 1727.
T4/21: Treasury: Reference Books of Applications, Registers of Papers Read at the Board, July 1718–February 1721.

Zeeuws Archief (Zeeland Archives), Middelburg, Netherlands (cited as ZA)
2035: Staten van Zeeland en hunne Gecommitteerde Raden (1574) 1578–1795 (1799), 2035.1, 2035.2.
    Accessible remotely at: GIDS102: Gids *Staten van Zeeland en Suriname*, 1667–1684 (1692), Gids 3: Ingekomen stukken betreffende Suriname en omliggende kwartieren, 1667–1683. https://www.zeeuwsarchief.nl/onderzoek-het-zelf/archief/?mizig=210&miadt=239&micode=GIDS102&miview=inv2#inv3t3.
    Partially transcribed at: https://files.archieven.nl/239/f/GIDS102/2035-transcripties.pdf.

BIBLIOGRAPHY

Electronic Databases

Ancestry Library, https://www.ancestrylibrary.com.
British History Online, https://www.british-history.ac.uk.
Early English Books Online, https://proquest.libguides.com/eebopqp/content.
Eighteenth-Century Collections Online, https://www.gale.com/intl/primary-sources/eighteenth-century-collections-online.
Intra-American Slave Trade Database, https://www.slavevoyages.org/voyage/database.
Trans-Atlantic Slave Trade Database, https://www.slavevoyages.org/voyage/database.

Printed Primary Sources

"An Act for the Governing of Negroes." In *The Laws of Barbados Collected in One Volume*, ed. William Rawlin, 156–64. London, 1699.
An Answer unto the Dutch Pamphlet [. . .]. London, 1624.
"Articles Concluded between Commander Abraham Crynsens . . . & Colonel William Byam." In *Colonising Expeditions to the West Indies and Guiana, 1623–1667*, ed. Vincent T. Harlow, 216–19. London: Hakluyt Society, 1925.
"Articles of Agreement between the Honourable Sir Robert Carr Knight on the Behalf of His Majesty of Great Britain, and the Burgomasters [. . .]." In *Delaware Papers (English Period)*, ed. Charles Gerhring, 20:2–3. New York Historical Manuscripts: Dutch. Baltimore: Genealogical Publishing Co., 1977.
Behn, Aphra. *Oroonoko*. Edited by Joanna Lipking. Norton Critical Editions. New York: W. W. Norton, 1997.
———. *Oroonoko, or, The Royal Slave: A True History*. London, England, 1688.
Byam, William. "An Exact Narrative of the State of Guyana." In *Colonising Expeditions to the West Indies and Guiana, 1623–1667*, ed. Vincent T. Harlow, 199–222. London: Hakluyt Society, 1925.
———. *An Exact Relation of the Most Execrable Attempts of John Allin Committed on the Person of His Excellency Francis Lord Willoughby of Parham [. . .]*. London, 1665.
Caerte ofte vertooninge vande Rivieren van Suriname en commenwijne [. . .]. [Amsterdam?], [1667 or later]. Map. https://jcb.lunaimaging.com/luna/servlet/detail/JCBMAPS~1~1~1613~102060003:Caerte-ofte-vertooninge-vande-Rivie.
Calendar of State Papers Colonial, America and West Indies. 46 vols. Edited by W. Noel Sainsbury et al. London: Her Majesty's Stationery Office, 1860–1969. https://www.british-history.ac.uk/search/series/cal-state-papers--colonial--america-west-indies.
Calendar of State Papers Domestic, William and Mary. 11 vols. Edited by William John Hardy and Edward Bateson. London: Her Majesty's Stationary Office, 1895–1937. https://www.british-history.ac.uk/search/series/cal-state-papers--domestic--will-mary.
Calendar of Treasury Papers. 6 vols. Edited by Joseph Redington. London: Her Majesty's Stationery Office, 1868–1889. https://www.british-history.ac.uk/search/series/cal-treasury-papers.
The Case and Replication of the Legal Representatives of Jeronimy Clifford [. . .]. London, 1763.
Chalmers, George. *A Collection of Treaties between Great Britain and Other Powers*. London, 1790.

BIBLIOGRAPHY

[Clifford, Jeronimy]. *The Case of Andrew and Jeronimy Clifford.* [London], [1699].
———. *The Case of Andrew Clifford and Jeronimy Clifford Late Planters in Surinam.* London, 1701.
———. *The Case of Jeronimy Clifford Late Planter in Surinam.* London, 1704.
Clifford, Jeronimy. *The Case of Jeronimy Clifford, Merchant and Planter of Surinam.* Paper, No. 160. London, 1711.
———. *The Case of Jeronimy Clifford, Merchant and Planter of Surinam [. . .].* London, 1714.
———. *The Case of Mr. Jeronimy Clifford, Merchant and Planter of Surinam.* [London?], [1718].
[Clifford, Jeronimy]. *The Case of Mr. Jeronimy Clifford, Merchant and Planter of Surinam.* London, 1720.
Clifford, Jeronimy. *Jeronimy Clifford's Answer to the States-General's Allegations.* London, 1701.
———. *Korte en klare aenwysingh van de saecke in questie tusschen de geoctriyeerde Society van Suriname ende Andries en Jeronimo Cliffort [. . .].* N.p., 1699.
———. [Untitled]. London, 1704.
Coke, Edward. *The First Part of the Institutes of the Lawes of England. Or, A Commentarie vpon Littleton, Not the Name of a Lawyer Onely, But of the Law It Selfe.* London, 1628.
———. *The Conduct of the Dutch, Relating to Their Breach of Treaties with England [. . .].* London, 1760.
A Discription of the Coleny of Surranam Drawne in the Yeare 1667. [London?], 1667. Map. https://jcb.lunaimaging.com/luna/servlet/detail/JCBMAPS~1~1~1616~102100004:A-Discription-of-the-Coleny-of-Surr.
Dickens, Charles. *Bleak House.* 1853. Oxford World's Classics. Oxford: Oxford University Press, 2008.
The Dutch Displayed; Or, A Succinct Account of the Barbarities, Rapines and Injustices, Committed by the Subjects of Holland upon Those of England [. . .]. London, 1766.
Dutch Modesty Exposed to English View [. . .]. London, 1767.
"Extracts from Proceedings of the House of Burgesses of Virginia, 1652–1661." *Virginia Magazine of History and Biography* 8, no. 4 (1901): 386–97. https://www.jstor.org/stable/4242377.
Friedenwald, Herbert. "Material for the History of the Jews in the British West Indies." *Publications of the American Jewish Historical Society* 5 (1897): 45–101.
"Grant of Privileges by the Governor, Council, and Assembly of Surinam, to the Jews [. . .]." Pp. 179–80 in Samuel Oppenheim, "An Early Jewish Colony in Western Guiana." *Publications of the American Jewish Historical Society* 16 (1907): 95–186.
Harlow, Vincent T., ed. *Colonising Expeditions to the West Indies and Guiana, 1623–1667.* London: Hakluyt Society, 1925.
Harris, John. *Navigantium Atque Bibliotheca [. . .].* London, 1744–48.
Hartsinck, Jan Jacob. *Beschryving van Guiana, of de Wilde Kust, in Zuid-America [. . .].* Amsterdam, 1770.
"Historical and Genealogical Notes." *William and Mary Quarterly* 27, no. 2 (1918): 132–43. https://www.jstor.org/stable/1915249.

Hollander, J. H. "Documents Related to the Attempted Departure of the Jews from Surinam in 1675." *Publications of the American Jewish Historical Society* 6 (1897): 9–29.

Howell, Thomas Bayly et al., eds.. *A Complete Collection of State Trials and Proceedings for High Treason and Other Crimes and Misdemeanors from the Earliest Period to the Year 1783 [. . .]*. 34 vols. London: Longmans, 1809–1828.

Journal of the House of Commons. Vol. 13, *1699–1702*. London: His Majesty's Stationery Office, 1803.

Journals of the Board of Trade and Plantations. 14 vols. Edited by K. H. Ledward. London: His Majesty's Stationery Office, 1920–1938. https://www.british-history.ac.uk/search/series/jrnl-trade-plantations.

Lavaux, Alexander de. *Algemeene kaart van de Colonie of Provintie van Suriname*. Amsterdam, 1737–1757. Map.

———. *Kaart van Suriname*. Suriname; Netherlands, 1737. Map. https://www.rijksmuseum.nl/en/collection/NG-539.

Locke, John. *Two Treatises of Government [. . .]*. London, 1690.

———. *Two Treatises of Government and a Letter Concerning Toleration*. Edited by Ian Shapiro. Rethinking the Western Tradition. New Haven, CT: Yale University Press, 2003.

Nassy, David. *Historical Essay on the Colony of Surinam, 1788*. Edited by Jacob R. Marcus and Stanley F. Chyet. Translated by Simon Cohen. Publications of the American Jewish Archives No. 8. Cincinnati, Ohio: American Jewish Archives, 1974.

Nassy, David de Isaac Cohen. *Essai historique sur la Colonie de Surinam [. . .]*. Paramaribo, 1788.

Oxenbridge, John. *A Seasonable Proposition of Propagating the Gospel by Christian Colonies in the Continent of Guaiana [. . .]*. [London?], 1670.

Page, William, ed. *Letters of Denization and Acts of Naturalization for Aliens in England, 1509–1603*. Huguenot Society of London, Quarto Series. Lymington, UK: Huguenot Society Publications, 1893.

Public Advertiser. London, 1767.

Quinn, David B., ed. *New American World: A Documentary History of North America to 1612*. 5 vols. New York: Arno Press, 1979.

Sanford, Robert. *Surinam Justice in the Case of Several Persons Proscribed by Certain Usurpers of Power in That Colony [. . .]*. London, 1662.

[Scott], [John]. "The Description of Guyana." In *Colonising Expeditions to the West Indies and Guiana, 1623–1667*, ed. Vincent T. Harlow, 132–48. London: Hakluyt Society, 1925.

"The Second Virginia Charter." In *New American World: A Documentary History of North America to 1612*, ed. David B. Quinn, 5:205–12. New York: Arno Press, 1979.

A Short and Modest Reply, to a Book Intituled, The Dutch Displayed. London, 1766.

Skinner, John. *A True Relation of the Vniust, Cruell, and Barbarous Proceedings against the English at Amboyna in the East-Indies [. . .]*. London, 1624.

Southerne, Thomas. *Oroonoko a Tragedy, as It Is Acted at the Theatre-Royal by His Majesty's Servants*. London, 1696.

The Statutes of the Realm. 11 vols. London: Dawsons of Pall Mall, 1963.

[*Surinam and Commewijne Rivers*]. [Amsterdam?], [1667 or later]. Map. https://jcb.lunaimaging.com/luna/servlet/detail/JCBMAPS~1~1~1614~102110002:-Surinam-and-Commewijne-rivers.

Thornton, John. *A New Draught of Surranam upon the Coast of Guianna*. London, [c. 1675]. Map. https://jcb.lunaimaging.com/luna/servlet/detail/JCBMAPS~1~1~2107~108720001:A-New-Draught-of-Surranam-upon-the.

A True Declaration of the Newes That Came out of the East-Indies [. . .]. London, 1624.

Warren, George. *An Impartial Description of Surinam upon the Continent of Guiana in America [. . .]*. London, 1667.

Wood, Alexander Renton, et al., eds. *English Reports*. 176 vols. Edinburgh: W. Green, 1900–1932.

Secondary Sources

Amussen, Susan Dwyer. *Caribbean Exchanges: Slavery and the Transformation of English Society, 1640–1700*. Chapel Hill: University of North Carolina Press, 2007.

Anderson, Benedict. *Imagined Communities: Reflections on the Origin and Spread of Nationalism*. Rev. ed. London: Verso, 2006.

Arbell, Mordehay. *The Jewish Nation of the Caribbean: The Spanish-Portuguese Jewish Settlements in the Caribbean and the Guianas*. Jerusalem: Gefen Publishing House, 2002.

Arena, Carolyn. "Aphra Behn's *Oroonoko*, Indian Slavery, and the Anglo-Dutch Wars." In *The Torrid Zone: Caribbean Colonization and Cultural Interaction in the Long Seventeenth Century*, ed. L. H. Roper, 31–45. Carolina Lowcountry and the Atlantic World. Columbia: University of South Carolina Press, 2018.

Balmer, Randall Herbert. *A Perfect Babel of Confusion: Dutch Religion and English Culture in the Middle Colonies*. Religion in America Series. Oxford: Oxford University Press, 1989.

Barber, Sarah. *The Disputatious Caribbean: The West Indies in the Seventeenth Century*. New York: Palgrave Macmillan, 2014.

———. "Power in the English Caribbean: The Proprietorship of Lord Willoughby of Parham." In *Constructing Early Modern Empires: Proprietary Ventures in the Atlantic World, 1500–1750*, ed. Bertrand Van Ruymbeke and Louis H. Roper, 189–212. The Atlantic World 11. Leiden: Brill, 2007.

Beckles, Hilary McD. *White Servitude and Black Slavery in Barbados, 1627–1715*. Knoxville: University of Tennessee Press, 1989.

Benton, Lauren A. *A Search for Sovereignty: Law and Geography in European Empires, 1400–1900*. Cambridge: Cambridge University Press, 2010.

Ben-Ur, Aviva. *Jewish Autonomy in a Slave Society: Suriname in the Atlantic World, 1651–1825*. Philadelphia: University of Pennsylvania Press, 2020.

Ben-Ur, Aviva, and Rachel Frankel. *Remnant Stones: The Jewish Cemeteries and Synagogues of Suriname: Essays*. Cincinnati, OH: Hebrew Union College Press, 2012.

Bijlsma, R. "Alexander de Lavaux en Zijne Generale Kaart van Suriname 1737." *New West Indian Guide / Nieuwe West-Indische Gids* 2, no. 1 (1921): 397–406. https://doi.org/10.1163/22134360-90001837.

Black, Jeremy. *The British Seaborne Empire*. New Haven, CT: Yale University Press, 2004.
Bodian, Miriam. *Hebrews of the Portuguese Nation: Conversos and Community in Early Modern Amsterdam*. The Modern Jewish Experience. Bloomington: Indiana University Press, 1997.
Brown, Kathleen M. *Good Wives, Nasty Wenches, and Anxious Patriarchs: Gender, Race, and Power in Colonial Virginia*. Published for the Institute of Early American History and Culture. Chapel Hill: University of North Carolina Press, 1996.
Brown, Roger Lee. *A History of the Fleet Prison, London: The Anatomy of the Fleet*. Lewiston, NY: Mellen, 1996.
Burnard, Trevor. "European Migration to Jamaica, 1655–1780." *William and Mary Quarterly* 53, no. 4 (October 1, 1996): 769–96. https://doi.org/10.2307/2947143.
Buve, Raymond T. J. "Governor Johannes Heinsius: The Role of van Aerssen's Predecessor in the Surinam Indian War, 1678–1680." In *Current Anthropology in the Netherlands*, ed. Peter Kloos and Henri J. M Claessen, 39–47. Rotterdam: Nederlandse Sociologische en Anthropologische Vereniging, 1975.
Carter, Alice Clare. "The Dutch as Neutrals in the Seven Years' War." *International and Comparative Law Quarterly* 12, no. 3 (1963): 818–34. http://www.jstor.org/stable/756291.
Cohen, Robert. "The Egerton Manuscript." *American Jewish Historical Quarterly* 62, no. 4 (June 1973): 333–47.
———. "The Misdated Ketubah: A Note on the Beginnings of the Surinam Jewish Community." *American Jewish Archives* 36, no. 1 (January 1984): 12–15.
Colley, Linda. *Britons: Forging the Nation, 1707–1837*. New Haven, CT: Yale University Press, 1992.
Condon, Richard H. "The Fleet Prison." *History Today* 14, no. 7 (July 1964): 453–60.
Conger, Vivian Bruce. *The Widows' Might: Widowhood and Gender in Early British America*. New York: New York University Press, 2009.
Coombs, Douglas. *The Conduct of the Dutch: British Opinion and the Dutch Alliance during the War of the Spanish Succession*. The Hague: Martinus Nijhoff, for the University College of Ghana Publications Board, 1958.
Corp, Edward T., with Edward Gregg, Howard Erskine-Hill, and Geoffrey Scott. *A Court in Exile: The Stuarts in France, 1689–1718*. Cambridge: Cambridge University Press, 2004.
Davis, Natalie Zemon. "Regaining Jerusalem: Eschatology and Slavery in Jewish Colonization in Seventeeth-Century Suriname." *Cambridge Journal of Postcolonial Literary Inquiry* 3, no. 1 (January 2016): 11–38. https://doi.org/10.1017/pli.2015.29.
Dunn, Richard S. *Sugar and Slaves: The Rise of the Planter Class in the English West Indies, 1624–1713*. Chapel Hill: University of North Carolina Press, 1972.
Erickson, Amy Louise. *Women and Property in Early Modern England*. London: Routledge, 1993.
Fatah-Black, Karwan. *White Lies and Black Markets: Evading Metropolitan Authority in Colonial Suriname, 1650–1800*. Atlantic World 31. Leiden: Brill, 2015.
Games, Alison. "Cohabitation, Suriname-Style: English Inhabitants in Dutch Suriname after 1667." *William and Mary Quarterly* 72, no. 2 (April 1, 2015): 195–242. https://doi.org/10.5309/willmaryquar.72.2.0195.

———. *Inventing the English Massacre: Amboyna in History and Memory.* New York: Oxford University Press, 2020.

———. "Violence on the Fringes: The Virginia (1622) and Amboyna (1623) Massacres." *History* 99, no. 336 (July 2014): 505–29. https://doi.org/10.1111/1468-229X.12064.

Goodwin, George M., and Ellen Smith, eds. *The Jews of Rhode Island.* Waltham, MA: Brandeis University Press and University Press of New England, 2004.

Habib, Imtiaz H. *Black Lives in the English Archives, 1500–1677: Imprints of the Invisible.* Aldershot, UK: Ashgate, 2008.

Hadden, Sally. "The Fragmented Laws of Slavery in the Colonial and Revolutionary Eras." In *The Cambridge History of Law in America,* ed. Michael Grossberg and Christopher L. Tomlins. Vol. 1, *Early America (1580–1815),* 253–87. Cambridge: Cambridge University Press, 2008.

Haefeli, Evan. *New Netherland and the Dutch Origins of American Religious Liberty.* Philadelphia: University of Pennsylvania Press, 2012.

Haley, K. H. D. "The Anglo-Dutch Rapprochement of 1677." *English Historical Review* 73, no. 289 (1958): 614–48. https://www.jstor.org/stable/557267.

Hall, Gwendolyn Midlo. *Slavery and African Ethnicities in the Americas: Restoring the Links.* Chapel Hill: University of North Carolina Press, 2005.

Hall, Kim. *Things of Darkness: Economies of Race and Gender in Early Modern England.* Ithaca, NY: Cornell University Press, 1995.

Hamer, Deborah. "Marriage and the Construction of Colonial Order: Jurisdiction, Gender and Class in Seventeenth-Century Dutch Batavia." *Gender & History* 29, no. 3 (November 2017): 622–40. https://doi.org/10.1111/1468-0424.12316.

Handley, Stuart. "Villiers, Edward, First Earl of Jersey (1655?–1711)." In *Oxford Dictionary of National Biography.* Oxford: Oxford University Press, 2004. https://doi.org/10.1093/ref:odnb/28289.

Hatfield, April Lee. *Atlantic Virginia: Intercolonial Relations in the Seventeenth Century.* Philadelphia: University of Pennsylvania Press, 2004.

Henriques, U. R. Q. "The Jewish Emancipation Controversy in Nineteenth-Century Britain." *Past & Present,* no. 40 (1968): 126–46. http://www.jstor.org/stable/650071.

Hirst, Derek. "The English Republic and the Meaning of Britain." *Journal of Modern History* 66 (1994): 451–86. https://doi.org/10.1086/244882.

Huisman, Anneke, and Johan Koppenol. *Daer compt de lotery met trommels en trompetten!: Loterijen in de Nederlanden tot 1726.* Hilversum, Netherlands: Uitgeverij Verloren, 1991.

Hyles, Joshua R. *Guiana and the Shadows of Empire: Colonial and Cultural Negotiations at the Edge of the World.* Lanham, MD: Lexington Books, 2014.

Israel, Jonathan I., ed. *The Anglo-Dutch Moment: Essays on the Glorious Revolution and Its World Impact.* Cambridge: Cambridge University Press, 1991.

———. *Diasporas within a Diaspora: Jews, Crypto-Jews, and the World of Maritime Empires (1540–1740).* Brill's Series in Jewish Studies 30. Boston: Brill, 2002.

———. *The Dutch Republic: Its Rise, Greatness, and Fall, 1477–1806.* Oxford: Oxford University Press, 1995.

Jardine, Lisa. *Going Dutch: How England Plundered Holland's Glory.* New York: Harper, 2008.

Johnson, Richard R. "The Revolution of 1688–9 in the American Colonies." In *The Anglo-Dutch Moment: Essays on the Glorious Revolution and Its World Impact*, ed. Jonathan I. Israel, 215–40. Cambridge: Cambridge University Press, 1991.

Kars, Marjoleine. *Blood on the River: A Chronicle of Mutiny and Freedom on the Wild Coast*. New York; London: New Press, 2020.

Katz, David S. "The Jews of England and 1688." In *From Persecution to Toleration: The Glorious Revolution and Religion in England*, ed. Peter Grell, Jonathan Irvine Israel, and Nicholas Tyacke, 217–49. Oxford: Oxford University Press, 1991.

———. *Philo-Semitism and the Readmission of the Jews to England, 1603–1655*. Oxford Historical Monographs. Oxford: Clarendon Press, 1982.

Kettner, James H. *The Development of American Citizenship, 1608–1870*. Chapel Hill: University of North Carolina Press, 1978.

Klooster, Wim. *The Dutch Moment: War, Trade, and Settlement in the Seventeenth-Century Atlantic World*. Ithaca, NY: Cornell University Press, 2016.

Klooster, Wim, and Gert Oostindie. *Realm between Empires: The Second Dutch Atlantic, 1680–1815*. Ithaca, NY: Cornell University Press, 2018.

Koot, Christian. *Empire at the Periphery: British Colonists, Anglo-Dutch Trade, and the Development of the British Atlantic, 1621–1713*. New York: New York University Press, 2011.

Kupperman, Karen Ordahl. "English Perceptions of Treachery, 1583–1640: The Case of the American 'Savages.'" *Historical Journal* 20, no. 2 (June 1977): 263–87. https://doi.org/10.1017/S0018246X00011079.

LaCombe, Michael. "Willoughby, Francis, Fifth Baron Willoughby of Parham (Bap. 1614, d. 1666), Colonial Governor." In *Oxford Dictionary of National Biography*. Oxford: Oxford University Press, 2004. https://doi.org/10.1093/ref:odnb/29597.

Lorimer, Joyce. "The Failure of the English Guiana Ventures 1595–1667 and James I's Foreign Policy." *Journal of Imperial and Commonwealth History* 21, no. 1 (January 1993): 1–30.

MacInnes, Allan I. *Union and Empire: The Making of the United Kingdom in 1707*. Cambridge Studies in Early Modern British History. Cambridge: Cambridge University Press, 2007.

Marshall, Peter. "Hill, Wills, First Marquess of Downshire (1718–1793), Politician." In *Oxford Dictionary of National Biography*. Oxford: Oxford University Press, 2004. https://doi.org/10.1093/ref:odnb/13317.

McNeill, John Robert. *Mosquito Empires: Ecology and War in the Greater Caribbean, 1620–1914*. New Approaches to the Americas. New York: Cambridge University Press, 2010.

McPhail, Bridget. "Through a Glass, Darkly: Scots and Indians Converge at Darien." *Eighteenth-Century Life* 18, no. 3 (1994): 129–47.

Menezes, S. L. "Bengal and the Dutch." *USI Journal* 113, no. 474 (October 1983): 358–68.

Miller, John. *James II*. 3rd ed. Yale English Monarchs. New Haven, CT: Yale University Press, 2000.

Milton, J. R. "Dating Locke's 'Second Treatise.'" *History of Political Thought* 16, no. 3 (1995): 356–90. https://www.jstor.org/stable/26215876.

Monod, Paul Kléber. *Jacobitism and the English People, 1688–1788*. Cambridge: Cambridge University Press, 1989.
Morgan, Edmund Sears. *American Slavery, American Freedom: The Ordeal of Colonial Virginia*. New York: W. W. Norton, 1975.
Muller, Hannah Weiss. *Subjects and Sovereign: Bonds of Belonging in the Eighteenth-Century British Empire*. New York: Oxford University Press, 2017.
Newman, Aubrey. "The Sephardim of the Caribbean." In *The Sephardi Heritage*. Vol. 2, *The Western Sephardim*, ed. W. M. Schwab and R. D. Barnett, 445–73. Grendon, UK: Gibraltar Books, 1989.
Nunn, Nathan, and Nancy Qian. "The Columbian Exchange: A History of Disease, Food, and Ideas." *Journal of Economic Perspectives* 24, no. 2 (2010): 163–88. https://doi.org/10.1257/jep.24.2.163.
Oppenheim, Samuel. "An Early Jewish Colony in Western Guiana." *Publications of the American Jewish Historical Society* 16 (1907): 95–186.
O'Reilly, William. "Working for the Crown: German Migrants and Britain's Commercial Success in the Early Eighteenth-Century American Colonies." *Journal of Modern European History* 15, no. 1 (February 2017): 130–56. https://doi.org/10.17104/1611-8944-2017-1-130.
Ouboter, Paul E., and Rawien Jairam. *Fauna of Suriname: Amphibians of Suriname*. Leiden: Brill, 2012.
Oxford English Dictionary. 2nd ed. 20 vols. Oxford: Oxford University Press, 1989. Continually updated at http://www.oed.com/.
Paley, Ruth. "After Somerset: Mansfield, Slavery and the Law in England, 1772–1830." In *Law, Crime, and English Society, 1660–1830*, ed. Norma Landau, 165–84. Cambridge: Cambridge University Press, 2002.
Peitzman, Steven J. *Dropsy, Dialysis, Transplant: A Short History of Failing Kidneys*. Baltimore: Johns Hopkins University Press, 2007.
Pestana, Carla Gardina. *The English Atlantic in an Age of Revolution, 1640–1661*. Cambridge, MA: Harvard University Press, 2004.
Pincus, Steven C. A. *1688: The First Modern Revolution*. New Haven: Yale University Press, 2009.
Price, Richard. *Alabi's World*. Baltimore: Johns Hopkins University Press, 1990.
Pulsipher, Jenny Hale. *Subjects unto the Same King: Indians, English, and the Contest for Authority in Colonial New England*. Philadelphia: University of Pennsylvania Press, 2005.
Rabin, Dana. *Britain and Its Internal Others, 1750–1800: Under Rule of Law*. Studies in Imperialism. Manchester, UK: Manchester University Press, 2017.
———. "'In a Country of Liberty?': Slavery, Villeinage and the Making of Whiteness in the Somerset Case (1772)." *History Workshop Journal* 72, no. 1 (October 2011): 5–29. https://doi.org/10.1093/hwj/dbq050.
Rens, L. L. E. "Analysis of Annals Relating to Early Jewish Settlement in Surinam." In *The Jewish Nation in Surinam: Historical Essays*, ed. Robert Cohen, 29–46. Amsterdam: S. Emmering, 1982.
Rich, Julia, A. "Heroic Tragedy in Southerne's Oroonoko (1695): An Approach to a Split-Plot Tragicomedy." *Philological Quarterly* 2 (1983): 187–200.

Roberts, Justin. "Surrendering Surinam: The Barbadian Diaspora and the Expansion of the English Sugar Frontier, 1650–75." *William and Mary Quarterly* 73, no. 2 (2016): 225–56. https://doi.org/10.5309/willmaryquar.73.2.0225.

Roeber, A. G. "'The Origin of Whatever Is Not English among Us': The Dutch-Speaking and German-Speaking Peoples of Colonial British America." In *Strangers within the Realm : Cultural Margins of the First British Empire*, ed. Bernard Bailyn and Philip D. Morgan, 221–83. Published for the Institute of Early American History and Culture. Chapel Hill: University of North Carolina Press, 1991.

Roitman, Jessica Vance. "Second Is Best: Dutch Colonization on the 'Wild Coast.'" In *The Torrid Zone: Caribbean Colonization and Cultural Interaction in the Long Seventeenth Century*, ed. L. H. Roper, 61–75. Carolina Lowcountry and the Atlantic World. Columbia: University of South Carolina Press, 2018.

Rommelse, Gijs. "The Role of Mercantilism in Anglo-Dutch Political Relations, 1650–74: Anglo-Dutch Mercantilism." *Economic History Review* 63, no. 3 (September 7, 2009): 591–611. https://doi.org/10.1111/j.1468-0289.2009.00491.x.

Roos, J. S. "Additional Notes on the History of the Jews in Surinam." *American Jewish Historical Quarterly* 13 (1905): 127–38.

Ross, J. M. "Naturalisation of Jews in England." *Transactions of the Jewish Historical Society of England* 24 (1975): 59–72.

Rubright, Marjorie. *Doppelgänger Dilemmas: Anglo-Dutch Relations in Early Modern English Literature and Culture*. Philadelphia: University of Pennsylvania Press, 2014.

Ruediger, Dylan. "'Neither Utterly to Reject Them, Nor Yet to Drawe Them to Come In': Tributary Subordination and Settler Colonialism in Virginia." *Early American Studies, An Interdisciplinary Journal* 18, no. 1 (Winter 2020): 1–31. https://doi.org/10.1353/eam.2020.0002.

Ruediger, Russell Dylan. "Tributary Subjects: Affective Colonialism, Power, and the Process of Subjugation in Colonial Virginia, c. 1600–c. 1740." PhD diss., Georgia State University, 2017.

Samuel, Wilfred S. "Review of the Jewish Colonists in Barbados, 1680." *Transactions of the Jewish Historical Society of England* 13 (1936): 1–47.

Schwoerer, Lois G., ed. *The Revolution of 1688–1689: Changing Perspectives*. Cambridge: Cambridge University Press, 1992.

Scott, H. M. "Sir Joseph Yorke, Dutch Politics and the Origins of the Fourth Anglo-Dutch War." *Historical Journal* 31, no. 3 (September 1988): 571–89. https://doi.org/10.1017/S0018246X00023499.

Seccombe, Thomas, and C. S. Rogers. "Popple, William (1700/01–1764), Government Official and Writer." In *Oxford Dictionary of National Biography*. Oxford: Oxford University Press, 2004. https://doi.org/10.1093/ref:odnb/22545.

Selwood, Jacob. *Diversity and Difference in Early Modern London*. Farnham, UK: Ashgate, 2010.

———. "'English-Born Reputed Strangers': Birth and Descent in Seventeenth-Century London." *Journal of British Studies* 44, no. 4 (2005): 728–53. https://doi.org/10.1086/431939.

———. "Left Behind: Subjecthood, Nationality, and the Status of Jews after the Loss of English Surinam." *Journal of British Studies* 54, no. 3 (July 2015): 578–601. https://doi.org/10.1017/jbr.2015.59.

———. "Present at the Creation: Diaspora, Hybridity and the Place of Jews in the History of English Toleration." In *Religious Tolerance in the Atlantic World: Early Modern and Contemporary Perspectives*, ed. Eliane Glaser, 193–213. Basingstoke, UK: Palgrave Macmillan, 2014.

Shyllon, F. O. *Black People in Britain, 1555–1833*. London: Published for the Institute of Race Relations, London, by Oxford University Press, 1977.

Snyder, Holly. "Rules, Rights and Redemption: The Negotiation of Jewish Status in British Atlantic Port Towns, 1740–1831." *Jewish History* 20, no. 2 (June 2006): 147–70. https://doi.org/10.1007/s10835-005-9002-z.

Sowerby, Scott. *Making Toleration: The Repealers and the Glorious Revolution*. Cambridge, MA: Harvard University Press, 2013.

Stanton, Timothy. "Locke and His Influence." In *The Oxford Handbook of British Philosophy in the Eighteenth Century*, ed. James A. Harris, 21–40. Oxford: Oxford University Press, 2013.

Stanwood, Owen. *The Empire Reformed: English America in the Age of the Glorious Revolution*. Early American Studies. Philadelphia: University of Pennsylvania Press, 2011.

Steele, Ian K. "Communicating an English Revolution to the Colonies, 1688–1689." *Journal of British Studies* 24 (1985): 333–57. https://www.jstor.org/stable/175523.

Suranyi, Anna. *The Genius of the English Nation: Travel Writing and National Identity in Early Modern England*. Newark: University of Delware Press, 2008.

Thompson, Mark L. *The Contest for the Delaware Valley: Allegiance, Identity, and Empire in the Seventeenth Century*. Baton Rouge: Louisiana State University Press, 2013.

Van der Heijden, Manon, Elise van Nederveen Meerkerk, and Ariadne Schmidt. "Terugkeer van Het Patriarchaat? Vrije Vrouwen in de Republiek." *Tijdschrift Voor Sociale En Economische Geschiedenis* 6, no. 3 (October 2009): 26–52. https://doi.org/10.18352/tseg.453.

Van der Meiden, G. W. *Betwist bestuur: de eerste bestuurlijke ruzies in Suriname 1651–1753*. 2nd rev. ed. Amsterdam: Bataafsche Leeuw, 2008.

Ven den Berg, Margot C., and Enoch O. Aboh. "Done Already? A Comparison of Completive Markers in the Gbe Languages and Sranan Tongo." *Lingua: International Review of General Linguistics* 129 (May 5, 2013): 150–72. https://doi.org/10.1016/j.lingua.2013.02.010.

Vink, Wieke. *Creole Jews: Negotiating Community in Colonial Suriname*. Leiden: KITLV Press, 2010.

Walsham, Alexandra. *Charitable Hatred: Tolerance and Intolerance in England, 1500–1700*. Politics, Culture, and Society in Early Modern Britain. Manchester, UK: Manchester University Press, 2006.

Welch, Charles, and Perry Gauci. "Rawlinson, Sir Thomas (Bap. 1647, d. 1708)." In *Oxford Dictionary of National Biography*. Oxford: Oxford University Press, 2004. https://doi.org/10.1093/ref:odnb/23194.

Weterings, Tom. "Should We Stay or Should We Go? Being on Opposing Sides after a Colonial Takeover." *Journal of Early American History* 4 (2014): 130–48. https://doi.org/10.1163/18770703-00402004.

Whitehead, Neil Lancelot. "Carib Ethnic Soldiering in Venezuela, the Guianas, and the Antilles, 1492–1820." *Ethnohistory* 37, no. 4 (Fall 1990): 357–85. https://doi.org/10.2307/482860.

Williamson, James Alexander. *English Colonies in Guiana and on the Amazon, 1604–1668*. Oxford: Clarendon Press, 1923.

Wilson, Kathleen. "The Performance of Freedom: Maroons and the Colonial Order in Eighteenth-Century Jamaica and the Atlantic Sound." *William and Mary Quarterly* 66, no. 1 (2009): 45–86. https://doi.org/10.2307/40212041.

Wing, Donald. *Short-Title Catalogue of Books Printed in England, Scotland, Ireland, Wales, and British America and of English Books Printed in Other Countries, 1641–1700*. 2nd rev. ed. 4 vols. New York: Modern Language Association of America, 1972–1998.

Wolf, Lucien. "American Elements in the Resettlement." *Transactions of the Jewish Historical Society of England* 3 (1896–1898): 76–100.

Wood, Peter H. *Black Majority: Negroes in Colonial South Carolina from 1670 through the Stono Rebellion*. New York: Knopf, 1974.

Worthington, David. "Sugar, Slave-Owning, Suriname and the Dutch Imperial Entanglement of the Scottish Highlands before 1707." *Dutch Crossing* 44, no. 1 (May 10, 2019): 3–20. https://doi.org/10.1080/03096564.2019.1616141.

Zijlstra, Suze. "Anglo-Dutch Suriname: Ethnic Interaction and Colonial Transition in the Caribbean, 1651–1682." PhD diss., Universiteit van Amsterdam, 2015.

———. "Een Fragmentarisch Verleden: De Zeventiende-Eeuwse Kolonisatie van Suriname in Historiografisch Perspectief." In *Verkenningen in de Historiografie van Suriname: Van Koloniale Geschiedenis Tot Geschiedenis van Het Volk*, ed. Maurits Hassankhan, Jerome Egger, and Eric Jagdew, 297–324. Paramaribo: Anton de Kom Universiteit van Suriname, 2013.

Zijlstra, Suze, and Tom Weterings. "Colonial Life in Times of War: The Impact of European Wars on Suriname." In *The Torrid Zone: Caribbean Colonization and Cultural Interaction in the Long Seventeenth Century*, ed. L. H. Roper, 76–91. Carolina Lowcountry and the Atlantic World. Columbia: University of South Carolina Press, 2018.

Index

Acadia, 10
Act of Settlement, 158
Act of Union, 160–62, 166
Aliens, 6, 9, 32, 33, 35, 38, 39, 52. *See also* denization; naturalization; subjecthood, definitions and scope of
Allin, John, 4, 31
Aluku people, 30
Amapá, 20
Amazon Company, 22
Amazon River, 20, 22
Amboyna, 9, 116, 130, 132, 150–51, 153–54, 160, 166
America (ship), 52, 55
American Revolution, 3, 16, 129, 158, 161, 164
Amussen, Susan, 7, 33
Andros, Edmund, 35
Anne, Queen, 99, 110–11, 124, 141, 157
Answer unto the Dutch Pamphlet, An, 153
antenati, 6
Antigua, 43, 48, 55–56, 61, 76
Antigua Merchant (ship), 61
Arawak people, 21
Aries, Benito, 83, 88
Aries, Isaac, 83
Articles of Agreement (New Netherland), 11, 34
Articles of Capitulation (Suriname), 2, 9, 11, 43–48, 50–60, 66, 74–78, 83–84, 95, 98–100, 104–7, 128, 139, 144, 147, 160, 164–65
Axim, 156
Ayscue, George, 25

Banda Islands, 45
Banister, James, 48–50, 68, 110, 116
Barbados, 4, 7–8, 18, 20, 23–27, 30, 33–36, 43, 52, 79, 84, 92–97, 108, 136, 162
Baroen, Thomas, 61, 74–75, 89
Behn, Aphra, 3, 31

Bengal, 10, 131, 151–54, 160
Benton, Lauren, 11
Berbice, 22, 80, 161
Bight of Benin, 61
Bight of Biafra, 27, 29
Board of Trade and Plantations. *See* Council of Trade and Plantations
Bout, John, 127, 138
Brandt, Marcus, 51, 68
Brazil, 22, 24, 36, 38, 48
Brent, Mark. *See* Brandt, Marcus
Bridgeman, Sir Orlando, 9
Bristol Merchant (ship), 84, 89
Broen, Marcus, 67
Brown, Roger Lee, 115
Brunett, Henry, 8, 180n128
Bruninge, Francis, 92
Bruyn Fish (ship), 91
Buckingham, Duke of. *See* Mulgrave, Earl of
Bute, Earl of, 141
Butler, Peter, 27–28
Butts v. Penny, 164
Byam, William, 3–4, 11, 26, 30–31, 42, 45–48

Caesar (enslaved man), 86–88, 91, 166–7
Calabar, 27–29, 61
Calvin v. Smith (*Calvin's Case*), 6–7, 11, 32–33, 40, 162–64, 167
Calvinism, 79, 95
Carib people, 21
Carlisle, Earl of, 24
Carolina colony, 24, 34, 49, 79, 108
Carr, Sir Robert, 11
Caruthers, Robert, 114, 121
Caruthers, Thomas, 119–21, 125
Case and Replication of the Legal Representatives of Jeronimy Clifford, The, 143–44, 149–50
Case of Andrew and Jeronimy Clifford, 103
Case of Jeronimy Clifford, Merchant and Planter of Surinam, The, 124

233

Catholicism, 77, 79, 95
Cayenne, 22, 80
Charles II, 24, 31, 38, 48–49, 51, 53, 116
Christians, 33, 38–39, 43, 47–49, 52, 57, 64, 70, 75, 83, 110
Clarendon, Earl of, 26
Clark, Manus, 62–63
Clifford, Alice, 18, 31, 58
Clifford, Andrew, 14, 18, 31, 43, 58–60, 66–67, 74–75, 82, 90–91, 94, 107, 126, 142
Clifford, George, 101
Clifford, Jeronimy
   1707 manuscript, 12–13, 122–23
   Articles of Capitulation, reliance upon, 2, 9, 11, 44, 58–60, 75–76, 78, 95, 100–102, 104–7, 128, 160
   Barbados, residence in, 15, 18, 94, 97
   Corcabo estate, 14, 16, 43–44, 60, 62–75, 82–83, 90–91, 94, 106, 119–21, 127–28, 165–66
   death, 2, 13, 16, 59, 96, 98, 128–29, 132, 153
   domestic abuse allegations, 66, 68, 70–75, 82, 89, 149, 165
   fundraising efforts, 82–83
   George Lookup petition, 140–49, 155, 158, 160
   Henry MacKintosh dispute, 58, 85–88, 90, 117, 166–67
   imprisonment, 2, 74, 78, 80, 83–92, 98–99, 113–18, 122–26, 138–39, 149, 153, 165–67
   Jamaica land purchase, 66–68, 70–76, 82–83, 93
   landowner benefits, 14, 58–60, 66–67, 75
   Mandel extortion efforts, 130–39, 142, 144, 146–47, 158–60
   marriage, 9, 14, 43, 60–65, 68–74, 76, 89, 108–9, 149–50
   pamphlet publications, 66, 92, 94, 97, 103–5, 107, 116, 124–25, 139
   prenuptial agreement, 62–64, 66–70, 72
   purported will, 16, 128–31, 134–39, 142, 144, 158
   slaveholdings, 30, 40, 58, 67, 73–74, 82–87, 91, 96–97, 117, 119, 165–67
   subjecthood status, 2, 6, 9, 43–44, 57–60, 75–76, 83–85, 95–101, 104–9, 128–29, 132, 139, 149–50, 164
   Suriname arrival, 1, 4, 18, 31, 131, 164
   Suriname departure, 2, 9, 43, 57–59, 82, 85, 93–98, 131, 142, 165
   Suriname return, 43, 57–59, 66, 88, 95, 107, 164–65
Coke, Sir Edward, 6, 167
Commewijne River, 28, 69, 133
Committee for Foreign Plantations. *See* Council of Trade and Plantations
Committee for Trade and Plantations. *See* Council of Trade and Plantations
Conduct of the Dutch, Relating to Their Breach of Treaties with England, The, 143–44, 148–51, 155–56
Cooke, Sir John, 111, 122, 145
Cooke, Edward Ephraim, 148
Coppename River, 20, 26
Corbitt, Roland, 62–63
Corcabo estate, 14, 16, 43–44, 60, 62–75, 82–83, 90–91, 94, 106, 119–21, 123, 127–28, 133, 142, 165–66
Cormantine, 45
Cortissos, Joseph, 147
Council for Foreign Plantations. *See* Council of Trade and Plantations
Council of Justice (Suriname), 71–72, 121. *See also* Council of Polity (Suriname)
Council of Polity (Suriname), 65, 86, 88, 71–72, 119–21, 127
Council of State (England), 25, 81
Council of Trade and Plantations (England/Britain), 26, 50, 51, 101, 110, 111, 114, 118, 119, 123, 124, 140, 147
Court of Polity (Suriname). *See* Council of Polity (Suriname)
Couty, Rabba, 180n128
Cowell, William, 50
Cranfield, Edward, 51–58, 84, 110
Cranwell, Elizabeth, 97
Crijnssen, Abraham, 11, 42–46, 48–49, 60, 77, 154
Cromwell, Oliver, 31, 151
Cross River, 29
Curaçao, 108
Custis, John, 35

Da Silva, Aron, 56
Darien, 23, 155
De Belgioso, Count, 159
De Bourse, Gideon, 121
De Bruyn, Gorert, 71
De Caseres, Henry Benjamin, 36
De Witt, Jan, 155–56
Delasalie, Gabriel, 119–21, 127
Demerara, 161
denization, 6–7, 32–35, 38, 48

INDEX

Dickenson, Richard, 51
Dixcove, 152
Djuka people, 30
Duke, Thomas, 36–37
Dutch Displayed, The, 112, 118, 151–54, 156–57
Dutch Modesty Exposed to English View, 156–57

East India Company (English/British), 9, 150, 154
East India Company (Dutch), 152–54
Efik people, 29, 167
Egham, 18
El Dorado, 22
Engelsman, Samuel, 61
Enys, Renatus, 26
Essequibo, 22, 37–38, 40, 161

Fort Sommelsdijck, 90, 93
Fort Zeelandia, 80, 87, 133
Fourth Anglo-Dutch War, 158–59
Franco-Dutch War (1672–78), 80
Fraso, Jacob, 36
French Guiana, 20, 22
Frost, Johan, 51
Fundamental Constitutions (Carolina), 34

Games, Alison, 49, 150
Gardner, John, 113–14, 116–18
Gelly v. Cleve, 164
George I, 124
George III, 141, 158, 162
Glorious Revolution, 3, 11–15, 76–85, 94–96, 99, 110, 131–32, 150, 155, 157–58, 161, 165
Godefroy, Charles, 128, 133
"Grant of Privileges," 4–5, 8, 13–14, 19, 25, 36–39, 43, 49–52, 56, 75–76, 179n117
Grenada, 10
Grooten, Lambert, 35
Guyana, 20, 22, 37–38, 161

Haefeli, Evan, 38
Hampson, Elizabeth, 68
Hampson, Oliver, 68, 71, 83, 88
Happy Adventure (ship), 27
Harley, Robert, 122
Hay, George, 159
Hedges, Charles, 112
Henry and Sarah (ship), 51, 55
Hercules (ship), 55
Hillsborough, Earl of, 158

Holdip, Richard, 25
Holt, Sir John, 164
Hop, Mr., 137–38, 140, 142
House of Orange, 131, 155–58
Hyde, Lawrence, 26

Igbo people, 29–30, 167
Impartial Description of Surinam, 4, 21–22, 26
India, 10, 16, 131, 150, 151–54, 162
Intra-American Slave Trade Database, 27
Isle of Wight, 124

Jacobitism, 85, 158, 161
Jamaica, 1, 5, 8, 11, 24, 30, 34–36, 43, 49–52, 55, 58, 66–68, 70–76, 84, 93, 96, 136, 163
James VI and I, 6, 162
James II, 12, 77, 79–81, 155
Jamestown, 162
Jersey, Earl of, 100–103, 105, 111–12, 122, 142
Jews, 3–5, 8, 13, 14, 19, 32, 34, 36–40, 43, 52–3, 55–6, 75–6, 83
Jodensavanne, 56
Johnson, Nathaniel, 85
Judaism. *See* Jews

Kalabari people, 29, 167
Kalinago people, 54, 184n66
Kendall, James, 93
Kilsha, Richard, 146
Korte en klare aenwysingh, 200
Kwinti people, 30

Laman, James, 158–59
Laveaux, Alexander de, 128, 132–34, 136
Le Brun, Francis, 94, 97, 119
Leeward Islands, 85
Leisler, Jacob, 79
Lichtenberg, Philip Julius, 49
Limbrey, John, 58–59
Lodge, Samuel, 60–61, 82–83, 86–87, 94, 119
Lodge, Sarah, 94, 119–20
Lokono people, 54, 184n66
Lookup, George, 140–49, 155, 158, 160
Lorimer, Joyce, 22
Lynch, Thomas, 34

MacInnes, Allan, 86
MacKintosh, Henry, 58, 85–90, 117, 166–67
Mandel, 130–39, 142, 144, 146–47, 158–60
Mansfield, Lord Chief Justice, 163–64
Marowijne River, 20, 26

INDEX

Marriage, property rights and, 44, 60, 63–4, 68–70, 76, 165
Mary, Queen, 77, 79
Maryland colony, 34, 79
Matawai people, 30
Matson, Dorothy, 9, 14, 43, 60–66, 68–76, 82, 88–89, 94, 106, 123, 126, 165
Mattappy estate, 62–63
McNeill, John, 23
Meersman, Charles, 61–64
Mendes, Abraham, 8–9
Mills, William, 119–21
Mississippi Company, 129–30, 134, 136, 138, 158–59
Monmouth Rebellion, 35
Morgan, Edmund, 64
Mulgrave, Earl of, 58

Napoleonic Wars, 159
Nassy, Samuel, 56
Naturalization
    England, 6, 38–9
    Colonial, 6–7, 34–5, 38
    Jews and, 19, 38–9
Navigation Acts, 33, 36, 39
Nawab people, 152
Nevis, 8
New Netherland, 10–12, 34, 45, 47–48, 79, 94
New York colony, 10, 78–79, 81, 92, 94–5, 108
Niger River, 29
Nine Years' War, 79
North, Francis, 8
Nova Scotia, 10

Oosterland, Jacob, 113–14, 116–17
Orinoco River, 20, 22
Oroonoko, 3, 31
Oyapock River, 20, 22

Paramaka people, 30
Paramaribo, 20, 45, 52, 56, 78, 99, 133
Penn, William, 34
Pennsylvania colony, 34, 79
Perera, Isaac, 56
Plantation Act (1740), 7–8, 35
Pomeroon, 37
Popple, William, 118, 123
postnati, 6
Pratt, Charles, 141
Pringall, William, 58
Privy Council, 33, 56, 79, 109, 118, 124–25, 141, 146

Protestantism, 12, 31, 80, 131, 158, 160–62
Public Advertiser, 153–54

Rabin, Dana, 163
Raleigh, Sir Walter, 22
Rampjaar, 81
Rawlinson, Sir Thomas, 123
Regland, Mary, 71–72, 89
Reglens, John, 71, 195n67
Restoration, 22, 25–26, 35–36
Roberts, Justin, 24, 55
Rowse, Anthony, 25
Royal Africa Company, 61

Saba, 45
Salter, David, 9
Salter, Elizabeth, 9
Sanford, Robert, 31, 36
Saramaka people, 30
Schoors, Abraham, 62–63
Scott, Major John, 22, 25
Second Anglo-Dutch War, 1, 11, 38, 44–45
Sephardim. *See* Jews
Servant, Bertram, 35
Seven Years' War, 131, 150
Shepherd, Samuel, 113–14, 116–18
Short and Modest Reply to a Book Intituled the Dutch Displayed, A, 156–57
Simpson, Roland, 58–59, 66
slavery
    Antigua Merchant (slave ship), 61
    English slave codes, 7, 24, 32–33, 52
    Happy Adventure (slave ship), 27
    indigenous people, 54–55, 67
    Intra-American Slave Trade Database, 27
    Jeronimy Clifford as slaveholder, 30, 40, 58, 67, 73–74, 82–87, 91, 96–97, 117, 119, 165–67
    malaria immunity, 23
    maroon communities, 4–5, 8, 23, 30
    mortality rate, 28, 61
    resistance efforts, 3, 8, 30, 91, 163
    Somerset v. Stewart impact, 163–64
    subjecthood negation, 7–8, 33, 40, 98, 163–64, 167
    sugar production, 3, 23, 26
    Suriname evacuation, 58
    Swallow (slave ship), 27
    Trans-Atlantic Slave Trade Database, 26–27, 61
    Wellcome (slave ship), 61
    Welvaren (slave ship), 61
    William (slave ship), 27–28
    York (slave ship), 28

INDEX

Somerset, James, 163–64
Somerset v. Stewart, 163–64
Southerne, Thomas, 3
St. Christopher, 9, 133
St. Eustatius, 45, 133
Stadholder, role of, 12, 80–1, 95, 155, 165
Stanhope, Alexander, 105, 111–12, 142
Stede, Edwyn, 93
Stewart, Charles, 163
Strangers. *See* aliens
Subjecthood, definitions and scope of, 6–11. See also slavery, subjecthood negation; Suriname, subjecthood development in
Sunderland, Earl of, 12, 122–23
Surinam Justice, 31, 36–37
Suriname
    demographic patterns, 4–6, 25–26, 30, 36, 48–49, 55–58, 64
    disease environment, 3–4, 8, 18–19, 23–24, 30, 32, 40, 45–46, 64
    Dutch conquest, 3, 5, 18–19, 28, 30, 42–50, 75, 77, 98, 110, 154
    English colonization, 18–21, 24–35, 39–41
    enslaved workforce, 3–5, 26–30, 32, 49, 54–55, 57–58, 67, 82, 86, 164
    geographic environment, 3–4, 18, 20–24, 26, 32, 133
    gold mining, 22, 26, 45, 125
    "Grant of Privileges" offer, 4–5, 8, 13–14, 19, 25, 36–39, 43, 49–52, 56, 75–76
    indigenous people, 3–5, 21–23, 25, 30, 47, 52, 54–55, 57, 67, 91
    invasion vulnerability, 45–49
    maroon settlements, 4–5, 23, 30
    mortality rates, 14, 19, 23–24, 30, 40, 64, 82
    river passageways, 28–29
    slave ship arrivals, 26–30
    Society of Suriname, 3, 5, 65, 81, 90, 92, 97, 100–108, 130–38, 141–47
    Sranan Tongo language, 30
    subjecthood development in, 5–11, 18–19, 32–41, 43, 51–57, 77, 94–95
    sugar production, 3–4, 24, 26, 37, 45, 67, 82–83
    timber exports, 25
    West India Company sale, 65
    William Byam leadership, 3–4, 11, 26, 30–31, 42, 45–48
Suriname River, 20–21, 28, 55–56, 67
Swallow (ship), 27

Tanner, Mary. *See* Regland, Mary
Texel, 61
Third Anglo-Dutch War, 50, 80, 98
Thompson, Mark, 10
Thornton, John, 29
Thyssen, Bastian, 71, 88–90
Tobago, 5, 51
Torarica, 4, 20, 26, 39, 46, 56
Touverson, Gabriel, 153–54
Towerson, Gabriel, 153
Townshend, Lord Viscount, 1, 126
Trans-Atlantic Slave Trade Database, 26–27, 61
Treaty of Breda, 11, 45, 48–49, 125
Treaty of Westminster, 50–51, 53, 98, 128, 139, 147, 160
Trevor, Thomas, 8–9
Trinidad, 22
True Declaration of the Newes that came out of the East-Indies, A, 153
Van der Meiden, G. W., 65
Van Haagen, Harman, 63, 149
Van Hardenbergh, Hendrina, 63–65
Van Meel, Secretary, 133–39, 145
Van Schandell, Hendrick, 69
Van Scharphuizen, Johan, 90, 93
Van Sommelsdijck, Cornelis van Aerssen, 5, 65, 70
Van Vredenburgh, Abraham, 72
Venezuela, 20
Venman, John, 50
Vereul, Abraham, 127
Vernon, James, 103
Versterre, Pieter, 51–55, 57, 62–63
Villiers, Edward. *See* Jersey, Earl of
Virginia colony, 8, 33–34, 64, 108, 162–63

Walloon Protestants, 80
Walpole, Sir Robert, 126
War of the Spanish Succession, 99, 109–10
Warren, George, 4, 21–23, 26
Watson, Francis, 68
Wellcome (ship), 61
Welvaren (ship), 61
West India Company (Dutch), 5, 22, 38, 40, 65, 79, 97, 102–8, 117
Weyman, Reneyer, 82
William (ship), 27–28
William III, 12, 14–15, 77–79, 84–86, 88, 90, 92, 95–96, 99, 101, 110–11, 141, 154–58, 161
Williamson, Sir Joseph, 102–4, 142
Willoughby, Francis, 4, 24–26, 30–31, 45, 48

Willoughby, Henry, 48
Willoughby, William, 48
Wood, John, 27
Woodbury, Captain, 83–85, 89, 92
Worthington, David, 86

York (ship), 28
Yorke, Sir Joseph, 130, 139, 141, 143, 145–46

Zealand (ship), 42

CPSIA information can be obtained
at www.ICGtesting.com
Printed in the USA
LVHW110818071222
734662LV00021B/735/J